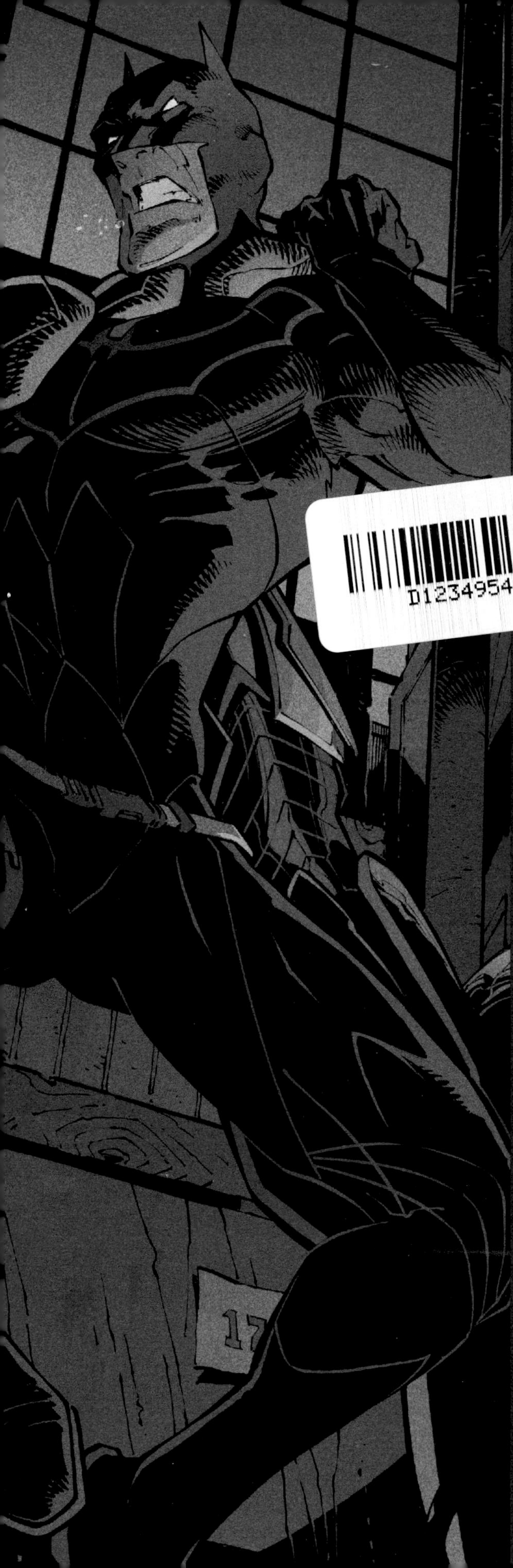

VOLUME 9

# BLOOM

# BATMAN

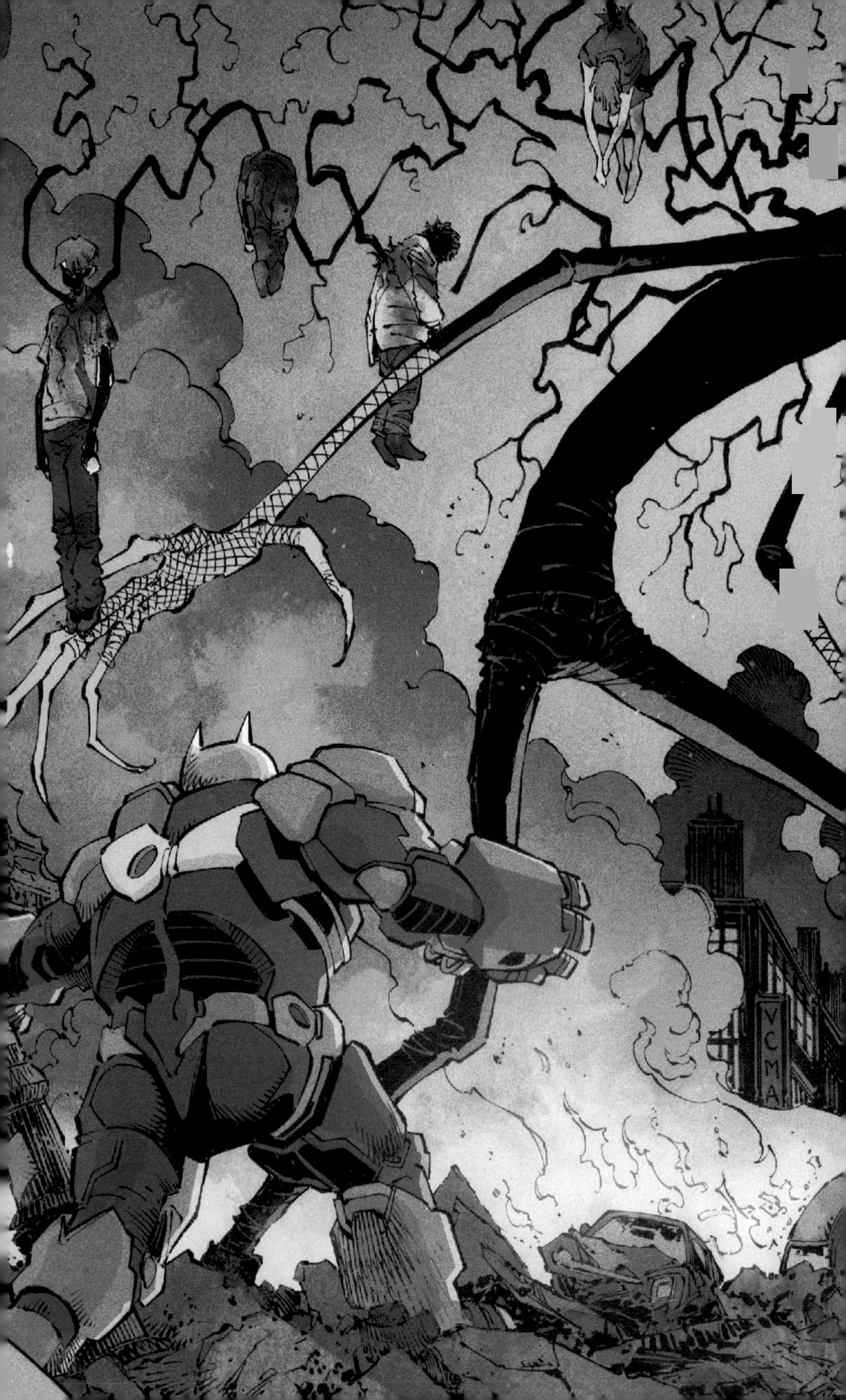
VCMA

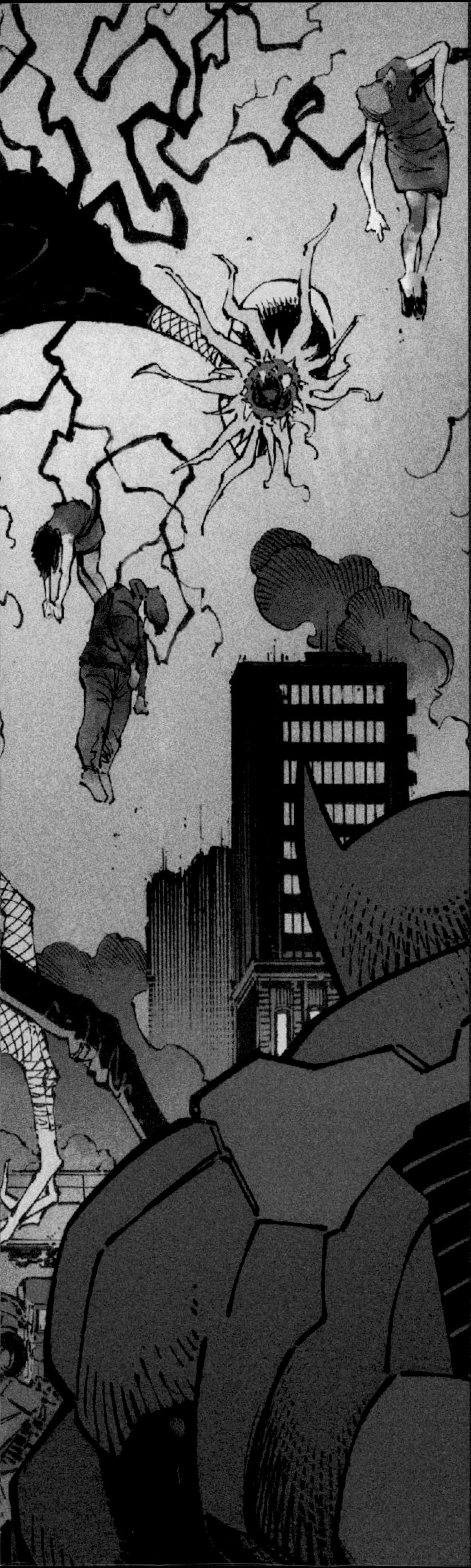

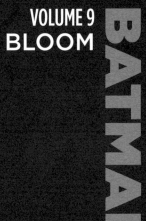

# BATMAN

## VOLUME 9
## BLOOM

WRITTEN BY
**SCOTT SNYDER**
JAMES TYNION IV

ART BY
**GREG CAPULLO**
**DANNY MIKI**
YANICK PAQUETTE
SEAN MURPHY

COLOR BY
**FCO PLASCENCIA**
NATHAN FAIRBAIRN
MATT HOLLINGSWORTH

LETTERS BY
**STEVE WANDS**

COLLECTION COVER ART BY
**GREG CAPULLO, DANNY MIKI & FCO PLASCENCIA**

BATMAN CREATED BY
**BOB KANE with BILL FINGER**

BATMAN VOLUME 9: BLOOM

Published by DC Comics. Compilation and all new material Copyright © 2016 DC Comics. All Rights Reserved. Originally published in single magazine form in BATMAN 46-50, DETECTIVE COMICS 27 Copyright © 2014, 2016 DC Comics. All Rights Reserved. All characters, their distinctive likenesses and related elements featured in this publication are trademarks of DC Comics. The stories, characters and incidents featured in this publication are entirely fictional. DC Comics does not read or accept unsolicited submissions of ideas, stories or artwork.

DC Comics, 2900 West Alameda Ave., Burbank, CA 91505
Printed by LSC Communications, Salem, VA, USA. 11/11/16. First Printing.
ISBN: 978-1-4012-6922-7

Library of Congress Cataloging-in-Publication Data is available.

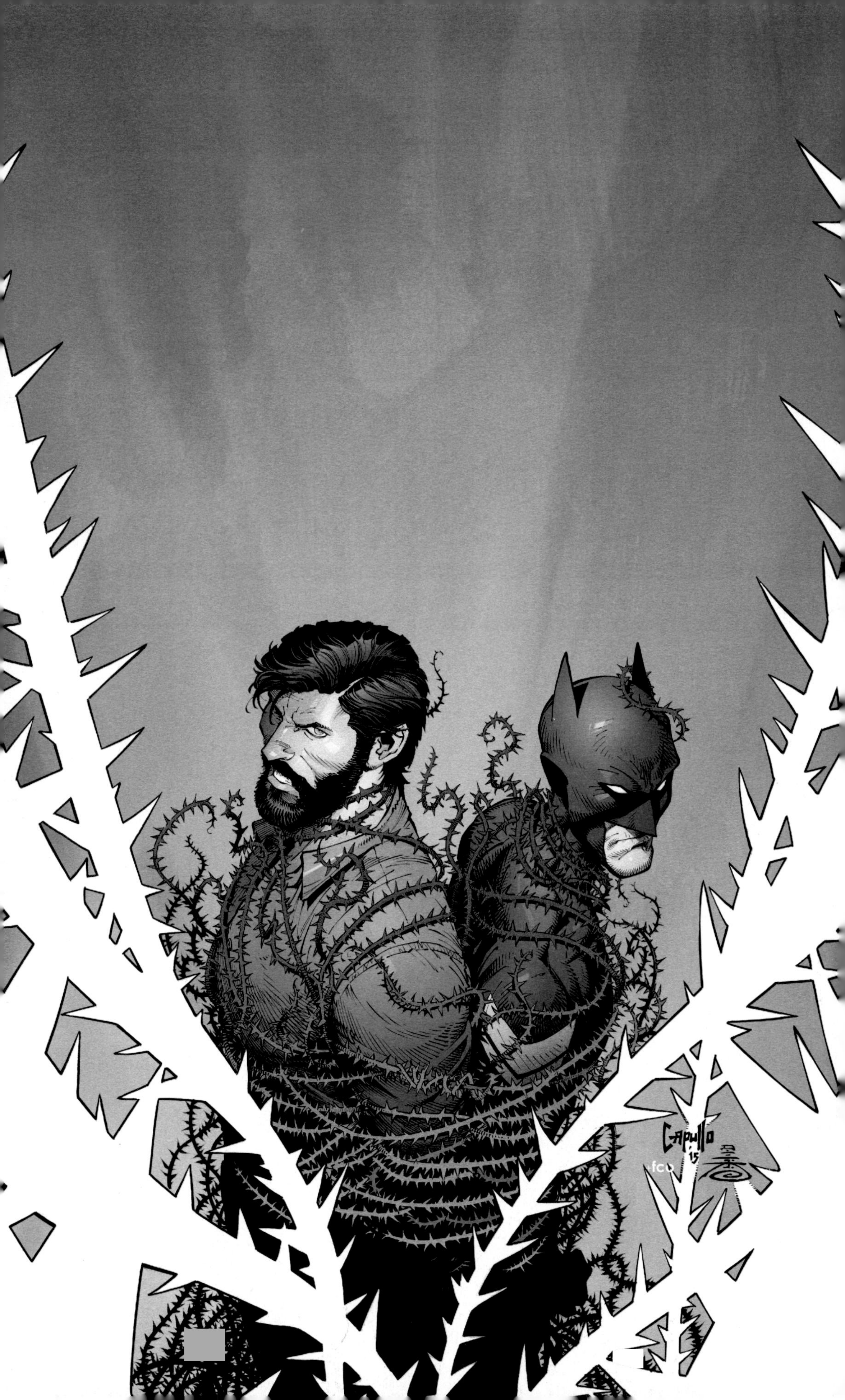
CAPULLO 15
fco

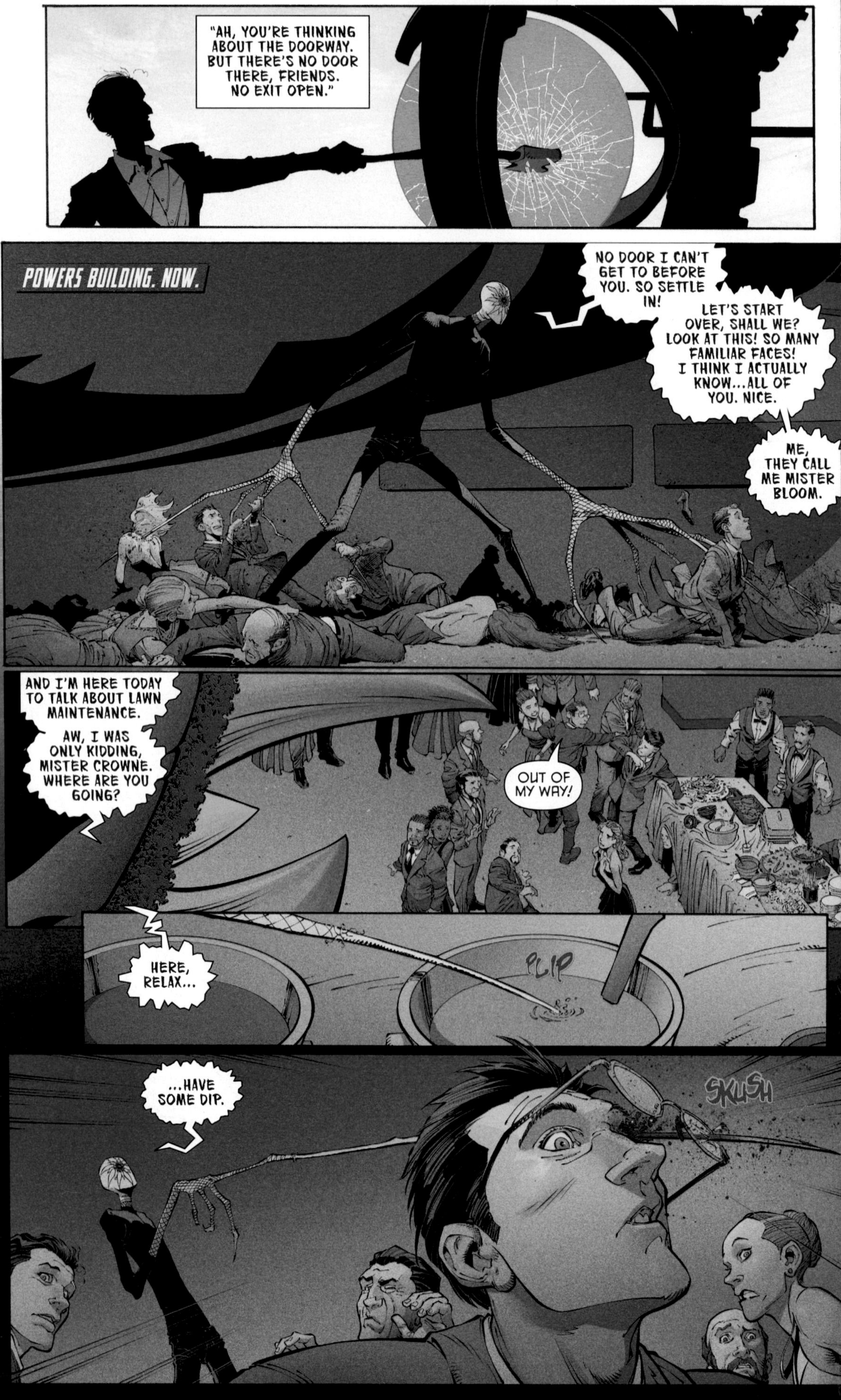
"AH, YOU'RE THINKING ABOUT THE DOORWAY. BUT THERE'S NO DOOR THERE, FRIENDS. NO EXIT OPEN."
POWERS BUILDING. NOW.
NO DOOR I CAN'T GET TO BEFORE YOU. SO SETTLE IN!
LET'S START OVER, SHALL WE? LOOK AT THIS! SO MANY FAMILIAR FACES! I THINK I ACTUALLY KNOW...ALL OF YOU. NICE.
ME, THEY CALL ME MISTER BLOOM.
AND I'M HERE TODAY TO TALK ABOUT LAWN MAINTENANCE.
AW, I WAS ONLY KIDDING, MISTER CROWNE. WHERE ARE YOU GOING?
OUT OF MY WAY!
HERE, RELAX...
PLIP
...HAVE SOME DIP.
SKUSH

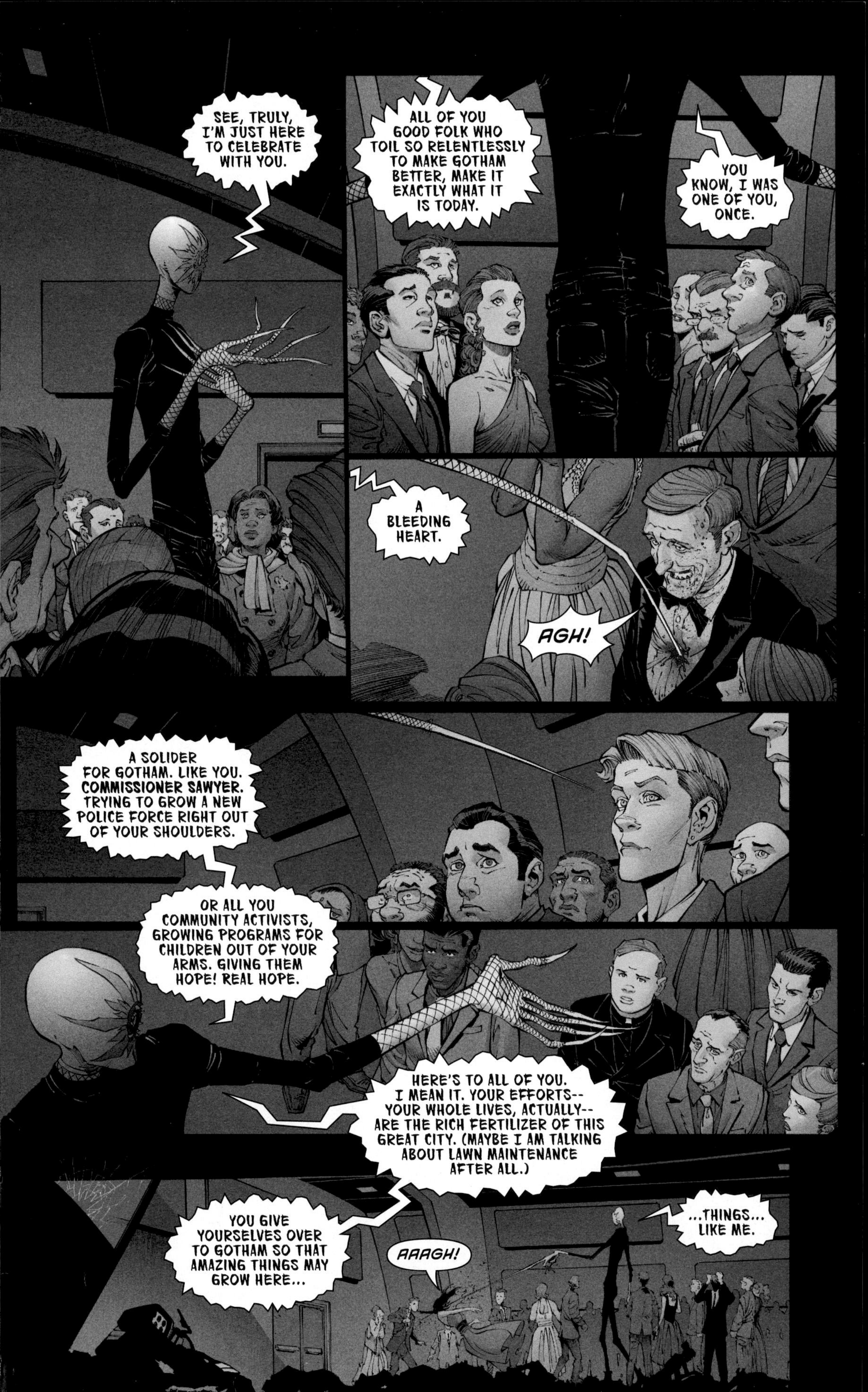
SEE, TRULY, I'M JUST HERE TO CELEBRATE WITH YOU.
ALL OF YOU GOOD FOLK WHO TOIL SO RELENTLESSLY TO MAKE GOTHAM BETTER, MAKE IT EXACTLY WHAT IT IS TODAY.
YOU KNOW, I WAS ONE OF YOU, ONCE.
A BLEEDING HEART.
AGH!
A SOLIDER FOR GOTHAM. LIKE YOU. COMMISSIONER SAWYER. TRYING TO GROW A NEW POLICE FORCE RIGHT OUT OF YOUR SHOULDERS.
OR ALL YOU COMMUNITY ACTIVISTS, GROWING PROGRAMS FOR CHILDREN OUT OF YOUR ARMS. GIVING THEM HOPE! REAL HOPE.
HERE'S TO ALL OF YOU. I MEAN IT. YOUR EFFORTS-- YOUR WHOLE LIVES, ACTUALLY-- ARE THE RICH FERTILIZER OF THIS GREAT CITY. (MAYBE I AM TALKING ABOUT LAWN MAINTENANCE AFTER ALL.)
YOU GIVE YOURSELVES OVER TO GOTHAM SO THAT AMAZING THINGS MAY GROW HERE...
AAAGH!
...THINGS... LIKE ME.

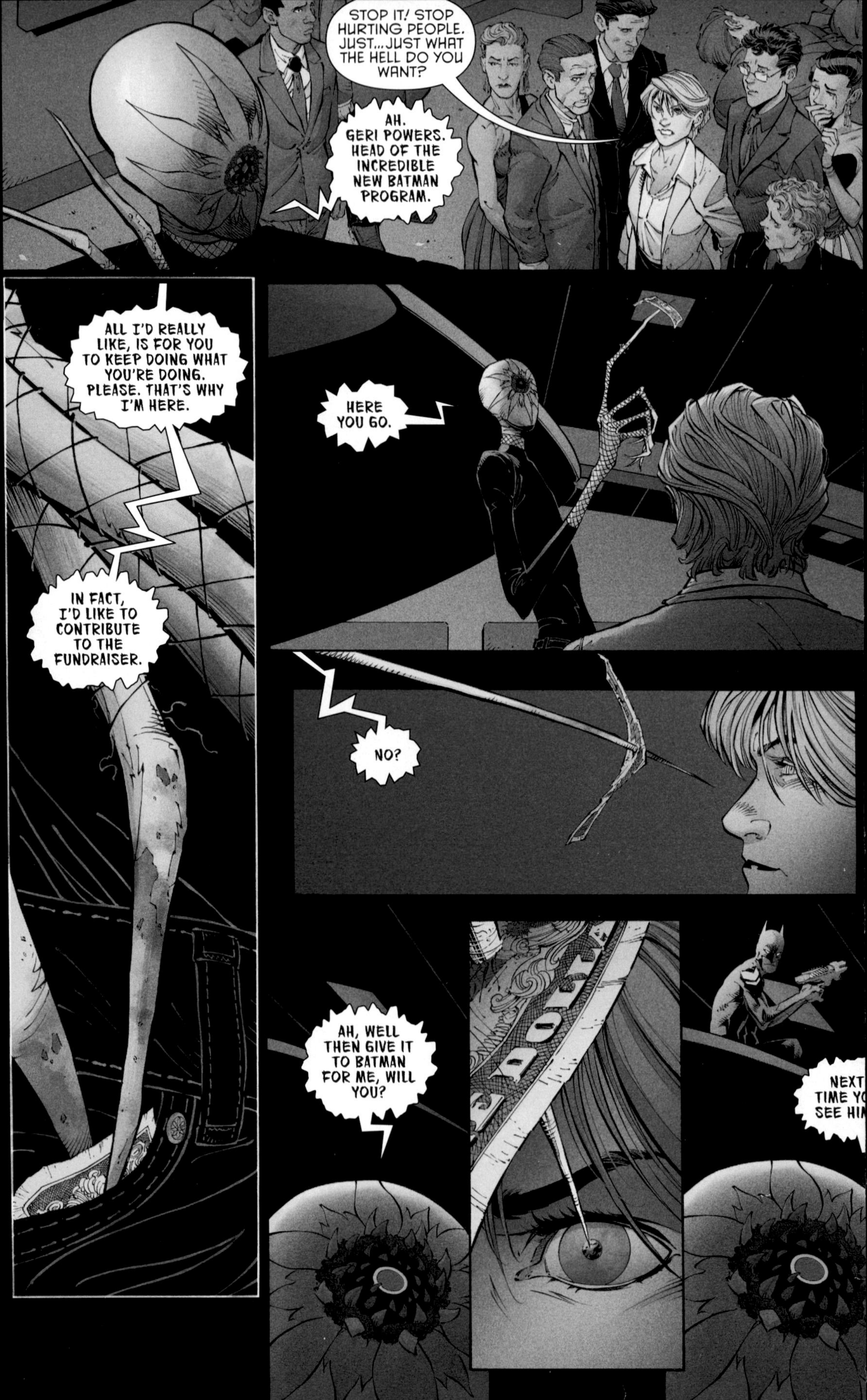
STOP IT! STOP HURTING PEOPLE. JUST...JUST WHAT THE HELL DO YOU WANT?
AH. GERI POWERS. HEAD OF THE INCREDIBLE NEW BATMAN PROGRAM.
ALL I'D REALLY LIKE, IS FOR YOU TO KEEP DOING WHAT YOU'RE DOING. PLEASE. THAT'S WHY I'M HERE.
IN FACT, I'D LIKE TO CONTRIBUTE TO THE FUNDRAISER.
HERE YOU GO.
NO?
AH, WELL THEN GIVE IT TO BATMAN FOR ME, WILL YOU?
NEXT TIME YO SEE HIM

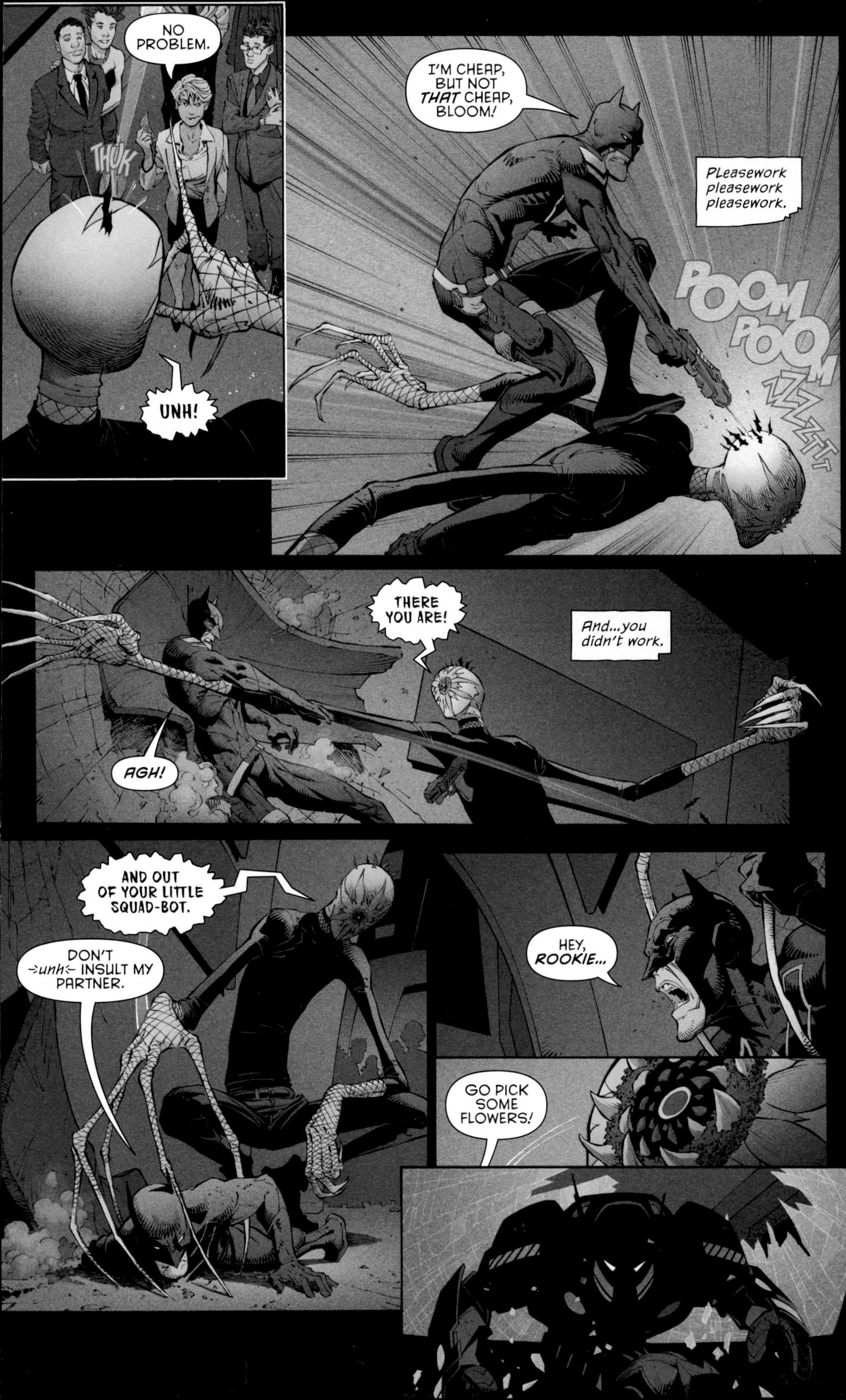
NO PROBLEM.
THUK
UNH!
I'M CHEAP, BUT NOT THAT CHEAP, BLOOM!
PLeasework pleasework pleasework.
POOM POOM
ZZZZTT
THERE YOU ARE!
And...you didn't work.
AGH!
AND OUT OF YOUR LITTLE SQUAD-BOT.
DON'T -unh- INSULT MY PARTNER.
HEY, ROOKIE...
GO PICK SOME FLOWERS!

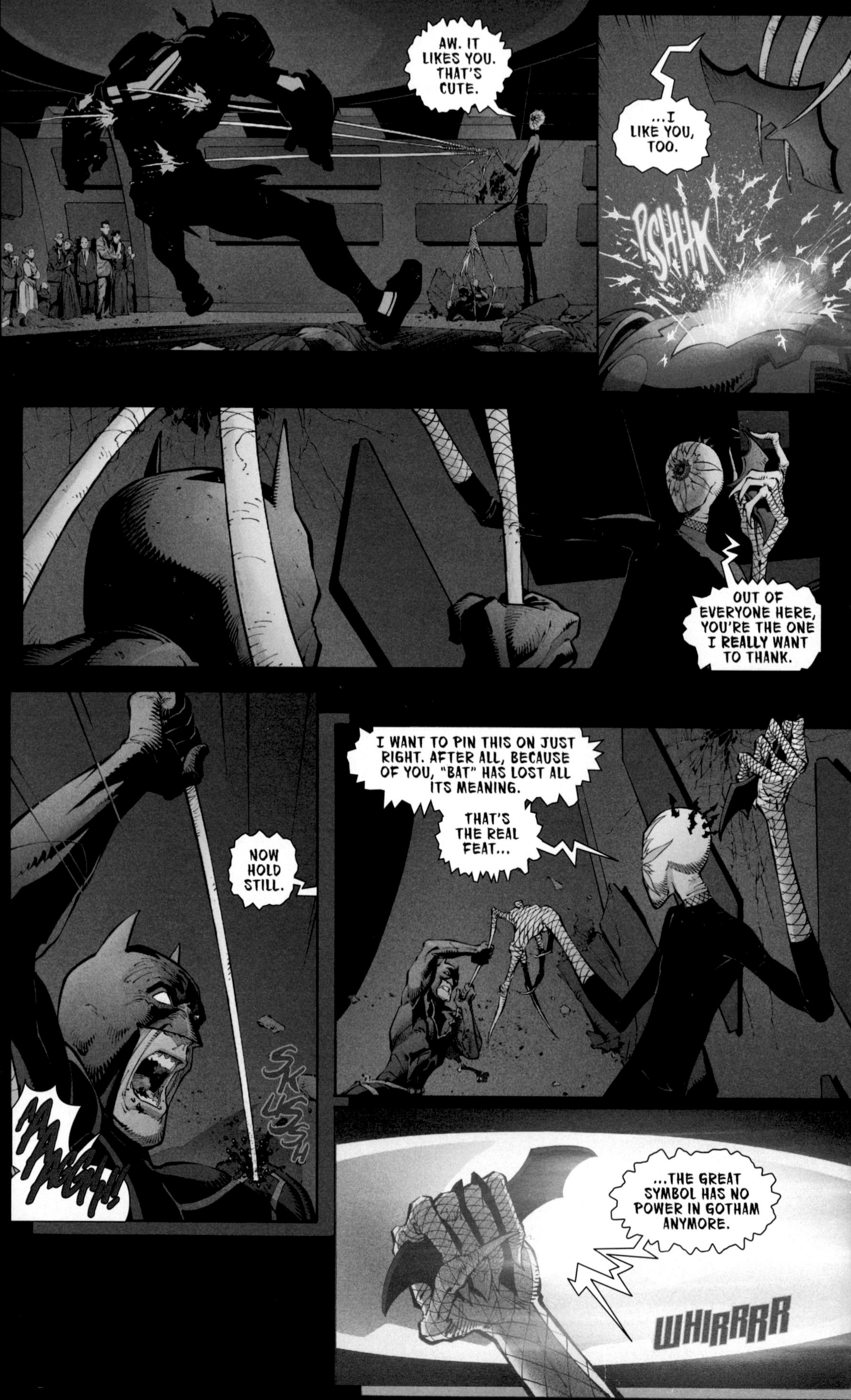
AW. IT LIKES YOU. THAT'S CUTE.
...I LIKE YOU, TOO.
PSHHK
OUT OF EVERYONE HERE, YOU'RE THE ONE I REALLY WANT TO THANK.
NOW HOLD STILL.
SKLUSSH
I WANT TO PIN THIS ON JUST RIGHT. AFTER ALL, BECAUSE OF YOU, "BAT" HAS LOST ALL ITS MEANING.
THAT'S THE REAL FEAT...
...THE GREAT SYMBOL HAS NO POWER IN GOTHAM ANYMORE.
WHIRRRR

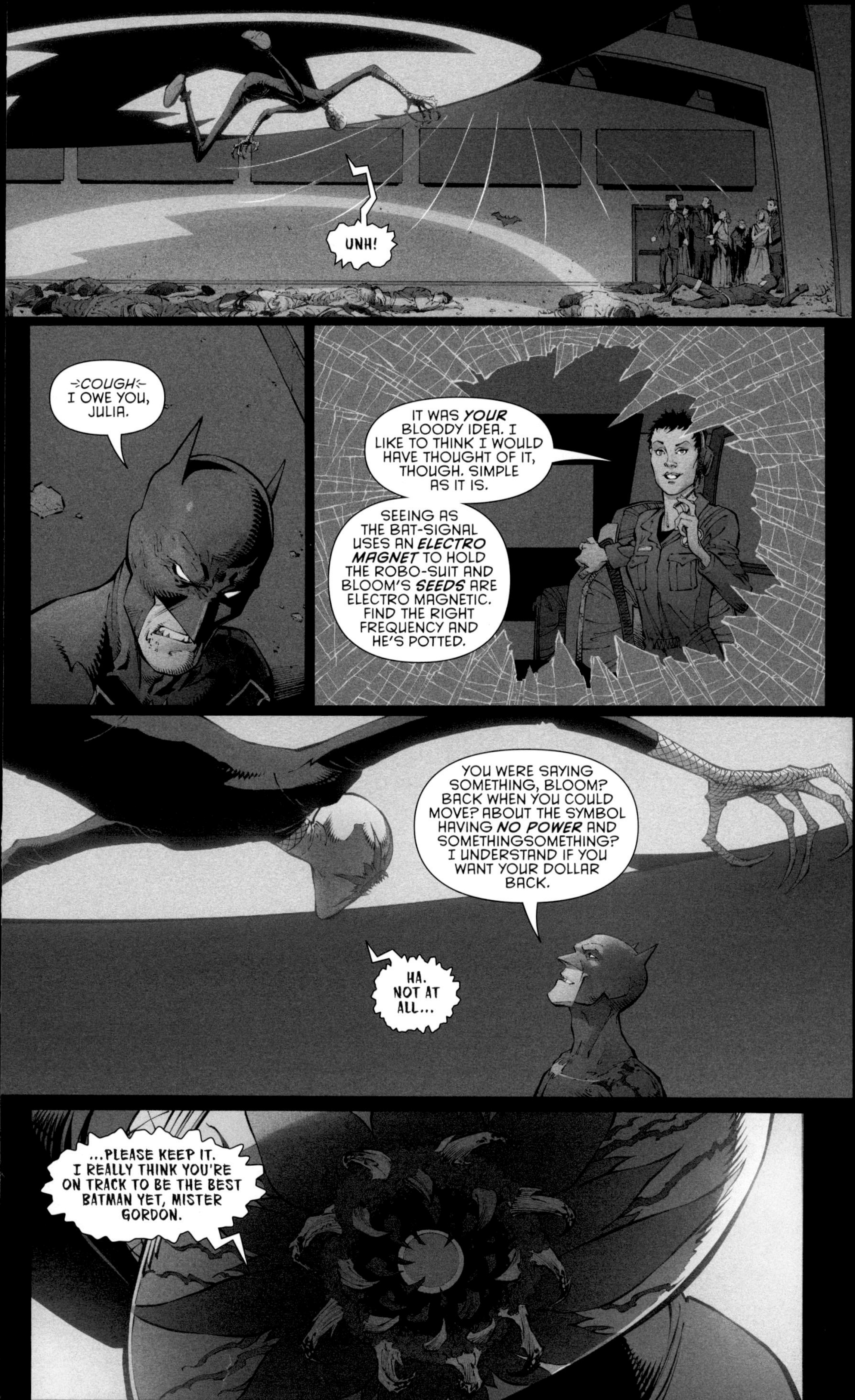
UNH!
-COUGH- I OWE YOU, JULIA.
IT WAS YOUR BLOODY IDEA. I LIKE TO THINK I WOULD HAVE THOUGHT OF IT, THOUGH. SIMPLE AS IT IS.
SEEING AS THE BAT-SIGNAL USES AN ELECTRO MAGNET TO HOLD THE ROBO-SUIT AND BLOOM'S SEEDS ARE ELECTRO MAGNETIC. FIND THE RIGHT FREQUENCY AND HE'S POTTED.
YOU WERE SAYING SOMETHING, BLOOM? BACK WHEN YOU COULD MOVE? ABOUT THE SYMBOL HAVING NO POWER AND SOMETHINGSOMETHING? I UNDERSTAND IF YOU WANT YOUR DOLLAR BACK.
HA. NOT AT ALL...
...PLEASE KEEP IT. I REALLY THINK YOU'RE ON TRACK TO BE THE BEST BATMAN YET, MISTER GORDON.

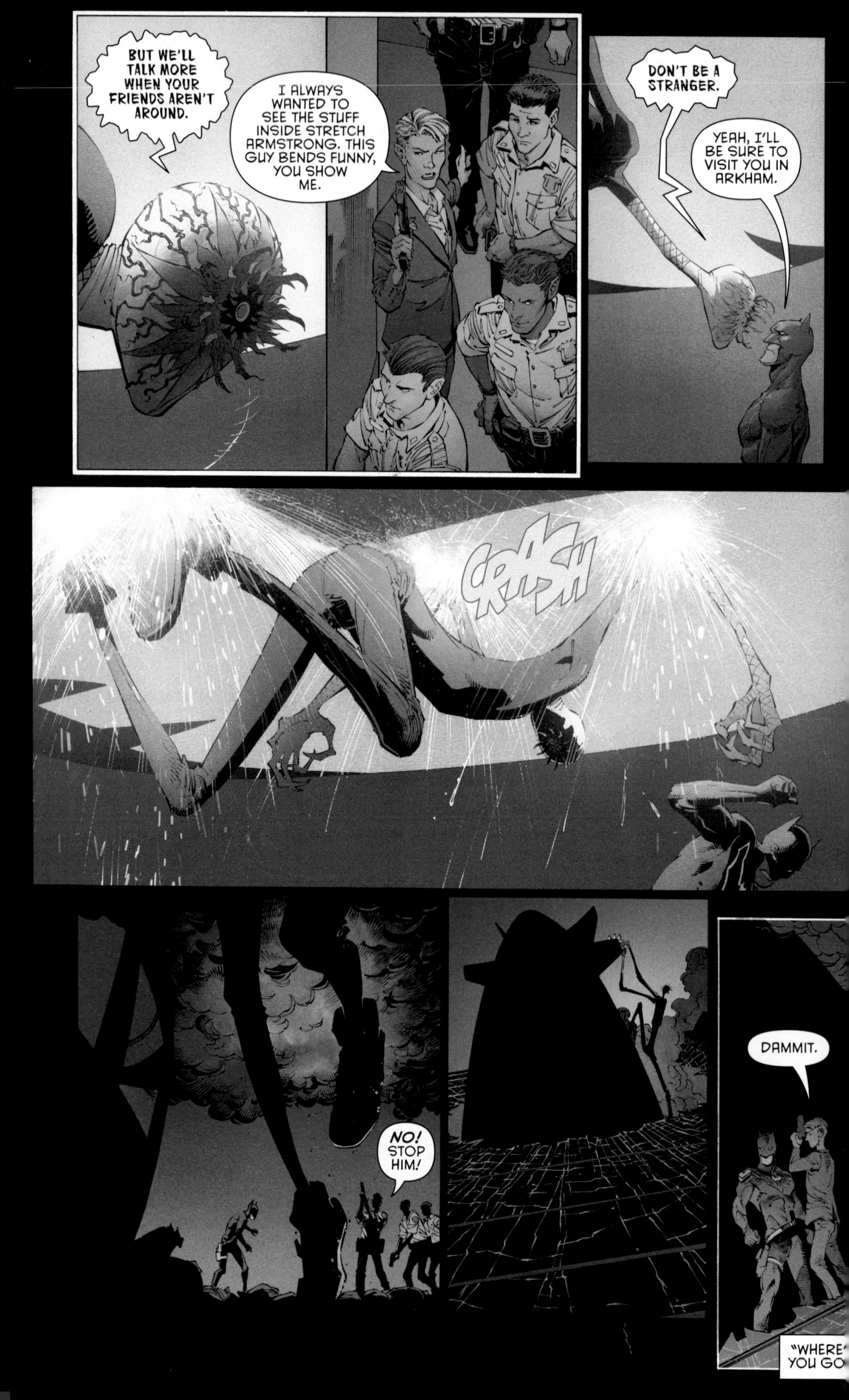
BUT WE'LL TALK MORE WHEN YOUR FRIENDS AREN'T AROUND.
I ALWAYS WANTED TO SEE THE STUFF INSIDE STRETCH ARMSTRONG. THIS GUY BENDS FUNNY, YOU SHOW ME.
DON'T BE A STRANGER.
YEAH, I'LL BE SURE TO VISIT YOU IN ARKHAM.
CRASH
NO! STOP HIM!
DAMMIT.
"WHERE' YOU GO

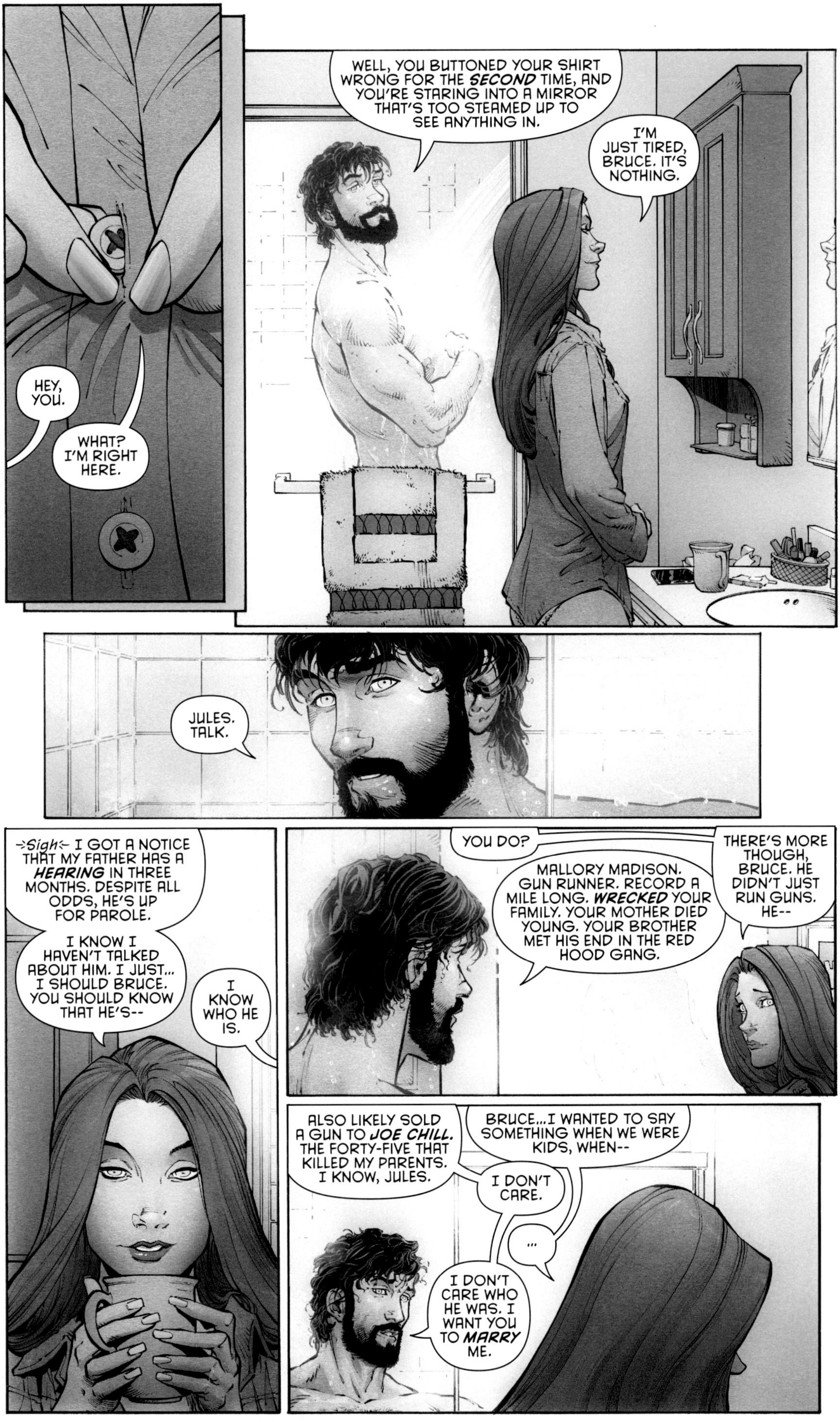
HEY, YOU.
WHAT? I'M RIGHT HERE.
WELL, YOU BUTTONED YOUR SHIRT WRONG FOR THE *SECOND* TIME, AND YOU'RE STARING INTO A MIRROR THAT'S TOO STEAMED UP TO SEE ANYTHING IN.
I'M JUST TIRED, BRUCE. IT'S NOTHING.
JULES. TALK.
-Sigh- I GOT A NOTICE THAT MY FATHER HAS A *HEARING* IN THREE MONTHS. DESPITE ALL ODDS, HE'S UP FOR PAROLE.
I KNOW I HAVEN'T TALKED ABOUT HIM. I JUST... I SHOULD BRUCE. YOU SHOULD KNOW THAT HE'S--
I KNOW WHO HE IS.
YOU DO?
MALLORY MADISON. GUN RUNNER. RECORD A MILE LONG. *WRECKED* YOUR FAMILY. YOUR MOTHER DIED YOUNG. YOUR BROTHER MET HIS END IN THE RED HOOD GANG.
THERE'S MORE THOUGH, BRUCE. HE DIDN'T JUST RUN GUNS. HE--
ALSO LIKELY SOLD A GUN TO *JOE CHILL.* THE FORTY-FIVE THAT KILLED MY PARENTS. I KNOW, JULES.
BRUCE...I WANTED TO SAY SOMETHING WHEN WE WERE KIDS, WHEN--
I DON'T CARE.
...
I DON'T CARE WHO HE WAS. I WANT YOU TO *MARRY* ME.

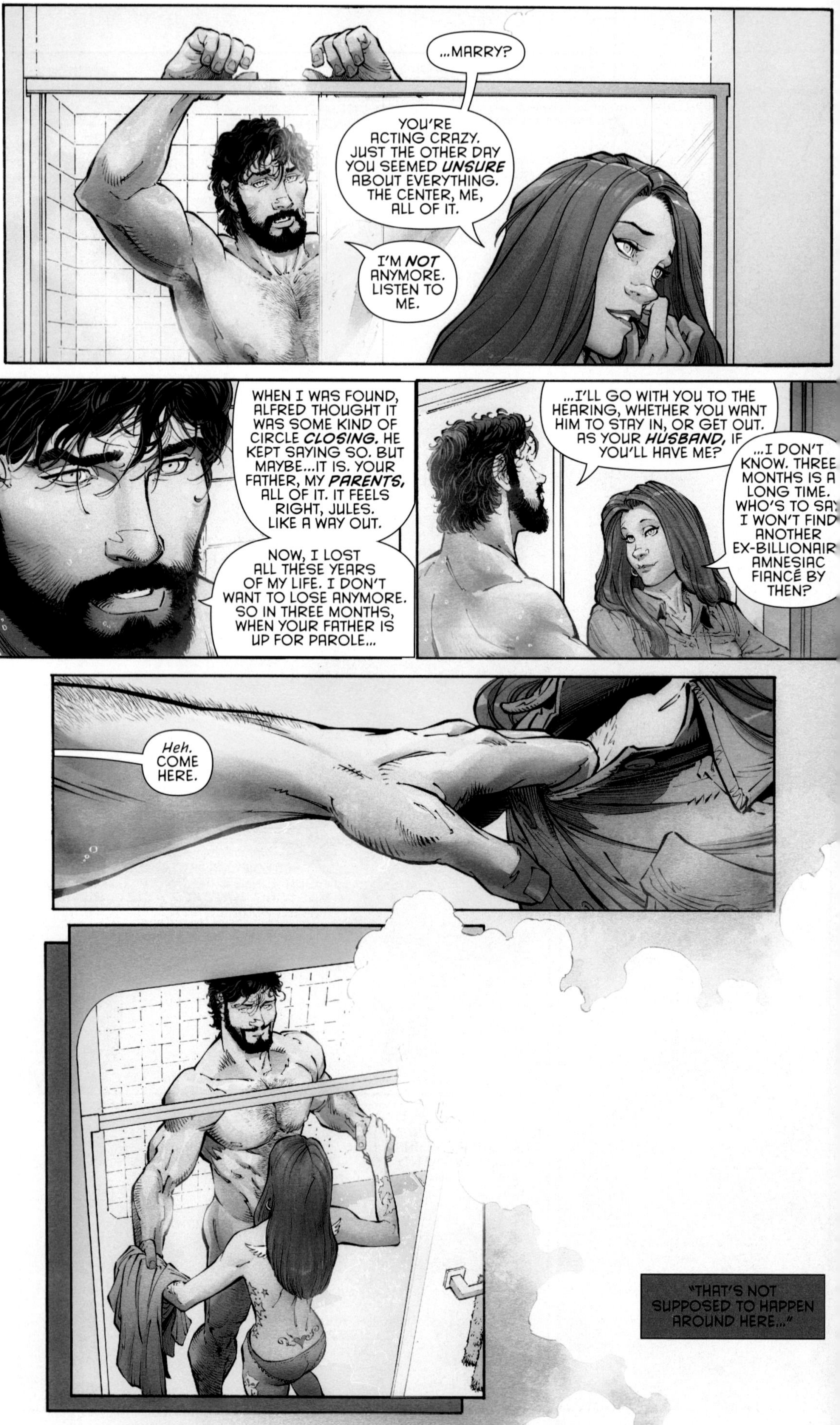
...MARRY?
YOU'RE ACTING CRAZY. JUST THE OTHER DAY YOU SEEMED *UNSURE* ABOUT EVERYTHING. THE CENTER, ME, ALL OF IT.
I'M *NOT* ANYMORE. LISTEN TO ME.
WHEN I WAS FOUND, ALFRED THOUGHT IT WAS SOME KIND OF CIRCLE *CLOSING.* HE KEPT SAYING SO. BUT MAYBE...IT IS. YOUR FATHER, MY *PARENTS,* ALL OF IT. IT FEELS RIGHT, JULES. LIKE A WAY OUT.
NOW, I LOST ALL THESE YEARS OF MY LIFE. I DON'T WANT TO LOSE ANYMORE. SO IN THREE MONTHS, WHEN YOUR FATHER IS UP FOR PAROLE...
...I'LL GO WITH YOU TO THE HEARING, WHETHER YOU WANT HIM TO STAY IN, OR GET OUT. AS YOUR *HUSBAND,* IF YOU'LL HAVE ME?
...I DON'T KNOW. THREE MONTHS IS A LONG TIME. WHO'S TO SAY I WON'T FIND ANOTHER EX-BILLIONAIR AMNESIAC FIANCÉ BY THEN?
*Heh.* COME HERE.
"THAT'S NOT SUPPOSED TO HAPPEN AROUND HERE..."

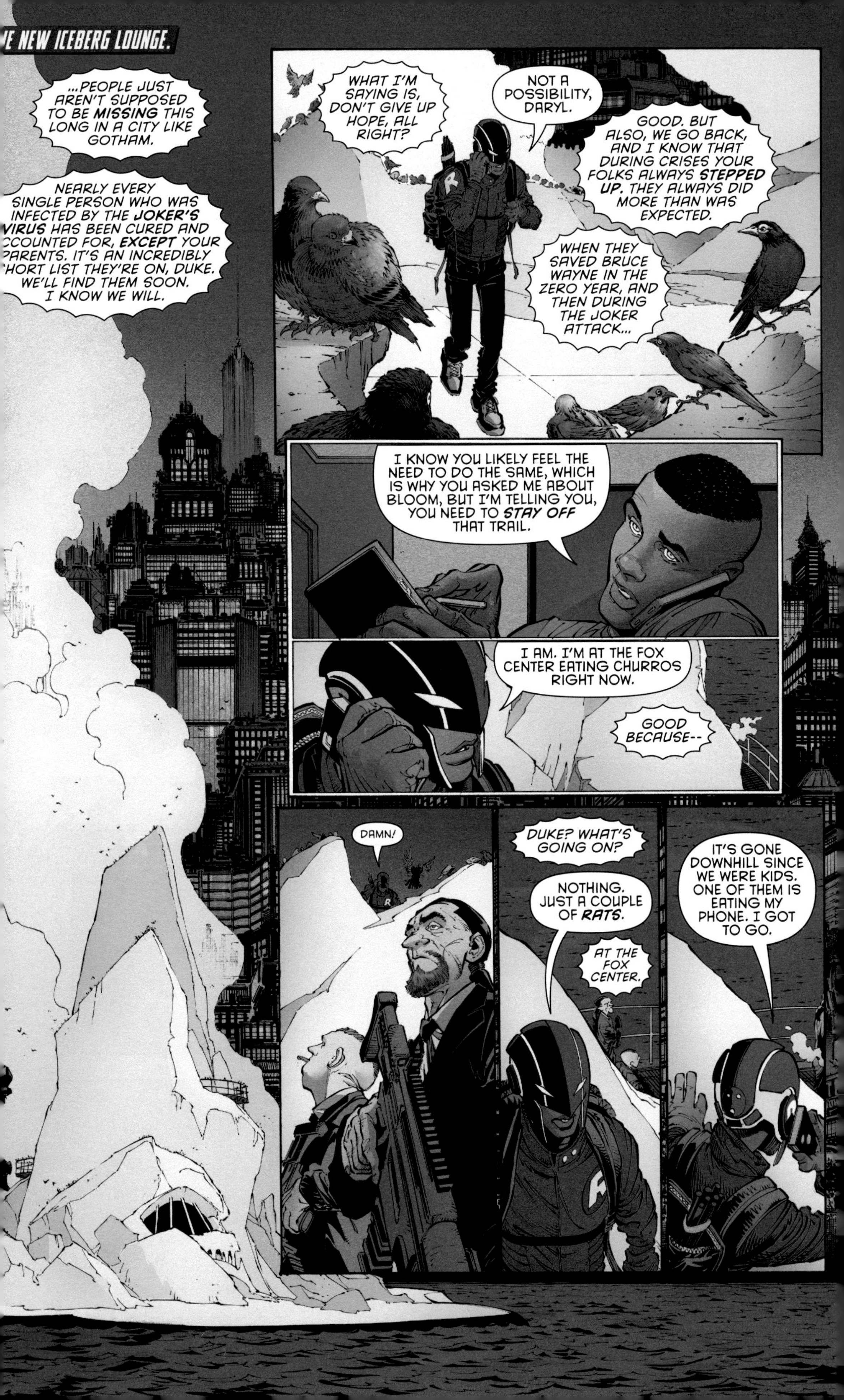
...E NEW ICEBERG LOUNGE.
...PEOPLE JUST AREN'T SUPPOSED TO BE MISSING THIS LONG IN A CITY LIKE GOTHAM.
NEARLY EVERY SINGLE PERSON WHO WAS INFECTED BY THE JOKER'S VIRUS HAS BEEN CURED AND ACCOUNTED FOR, EXCEPT YOUR PARENTS. IT'S AN INCREDIBLY SHORT LIST THEY'RE ON, DUKE. WE'LL FIND THEM SOON. I KNOW WE WILL.
WHAT I'M SAYING IS, DON'T GIVE UP HOPE, ALL RIGHT?
NOT A POSSIBILITY, DARYL.
GOOD. BUT ALSO, WE GO BACK, AND I KNOW THAT DURING CRISES YOUR FOLKS ALWAYS STEPPED UP. THEY ALWAYS DID MORE THAN WAS EXPECTED.
WHEN THEY SAVED BRUCE WAYNE IN THE ZERO YEAR, AND THEN DURING THE JOKER ATTACK...
I KNOW YOU LIKELY FEEL THE NEED TO DO THE SAME, WHICH IS WHY YOU ASKED ME ABOUT BLOOM, BUT I'M TELLING YOU, YOU NEED TO STAY OFF THAT TRAIL.
I AM. I'M AT THE FOX CENTER EATING CHURROS RIGHT NOW.
GOOD BECAUSE--
DAMN!
DUKE? WHAT'S GOING ON?
NOTHING. JUST A COUPLE OF RATS.
AT THE FOX CENTER.
IT'S GONE DOWNHILL SINCE WE WERE KIDS. ONE OF THEM IS EATING MY PHONE. I GOT TO GO.

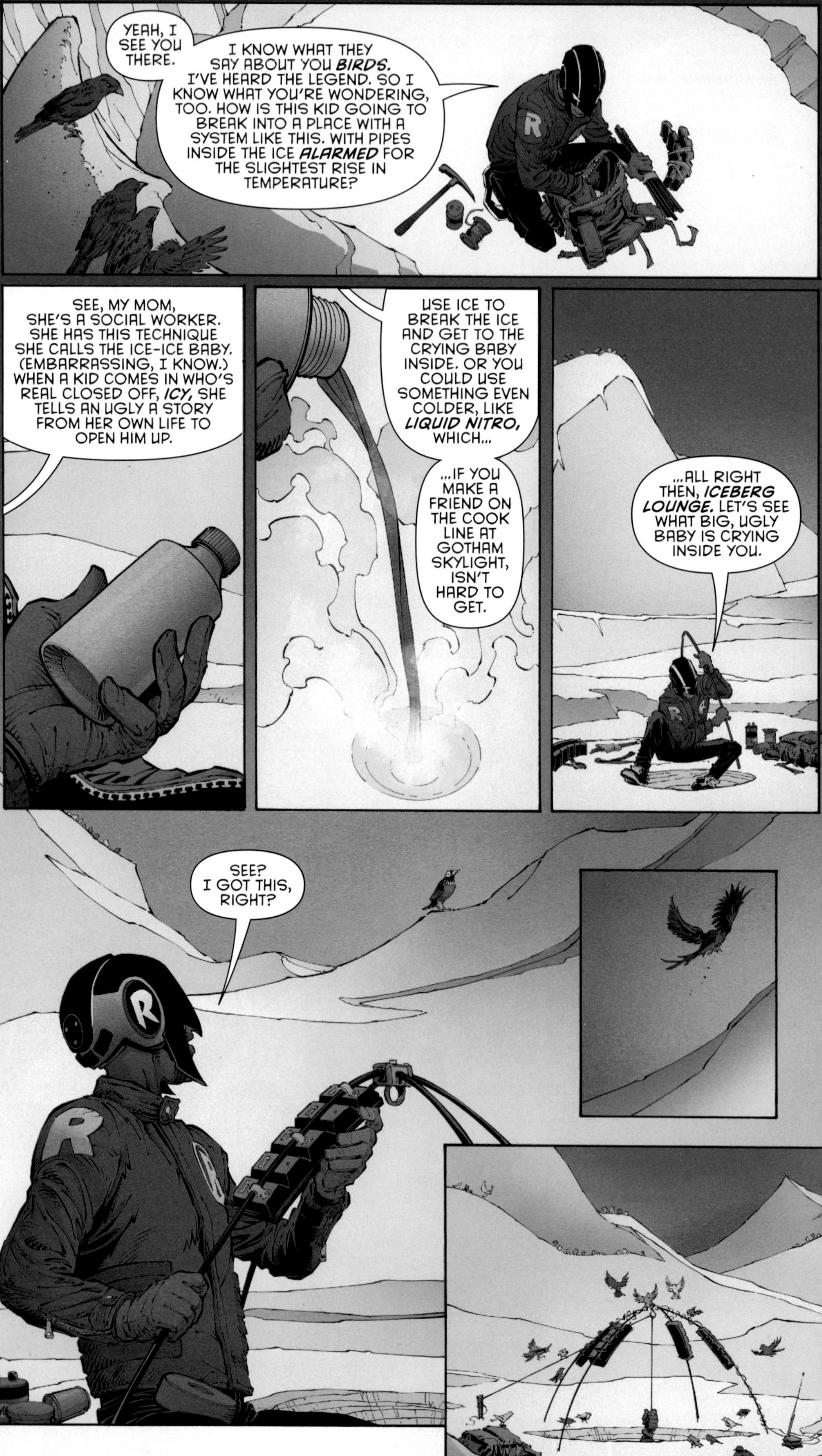
YEAH, I SEE YOU THERE.
I KNOW WHAT THEY SAY ABOUT YOU BIRDS. I'VE HEARD THE LEGEND. SO I KNOW WHAT YOU'RE WONDERING, TOO. HOW IS THIS KID GOING TO BREAK INTO A PLACE WITH A SYSTEM LIKE THIS. WITH PIPES INSIDE THE ICE ALARMED FOR THE SLIGHTEST RISE IN TEMPERATURE?
SEE, MY MOM, SHE'S A SOCIAL WORKER. SHE HAS THIS TECHNIQUE SHE CALLS THE ICE-ICE BABY. (EMBARRASSING, I KNOW.) WHEN A KID COMES IN WHO'S REAL CLOSED OFF, ICY, SHE TELLS AN UGLY A STORY FROM HER OWN LIFE TO OPEN HIM UP.
USE ICE TO BREAK THE ICE AND GET TO THE CRYING BABY INSIDE. OR YOU COULD USE SOMETHING EVEN COLDER, LIKE LIQUID NITRO, WHICH...
...IF YOU MAKE A FRIEND ON THE COOK LINE AT GOTHAM SKYLIGHT, ISN'T HARD TO GET.
...ALL RIGHT THEN, ICEBERG LOUNGE. LET'S SEE WHAT BIG, UGLY BABY IS CRYING INSIDE YOU.
SEE? I GOT THIS, RIGHT?

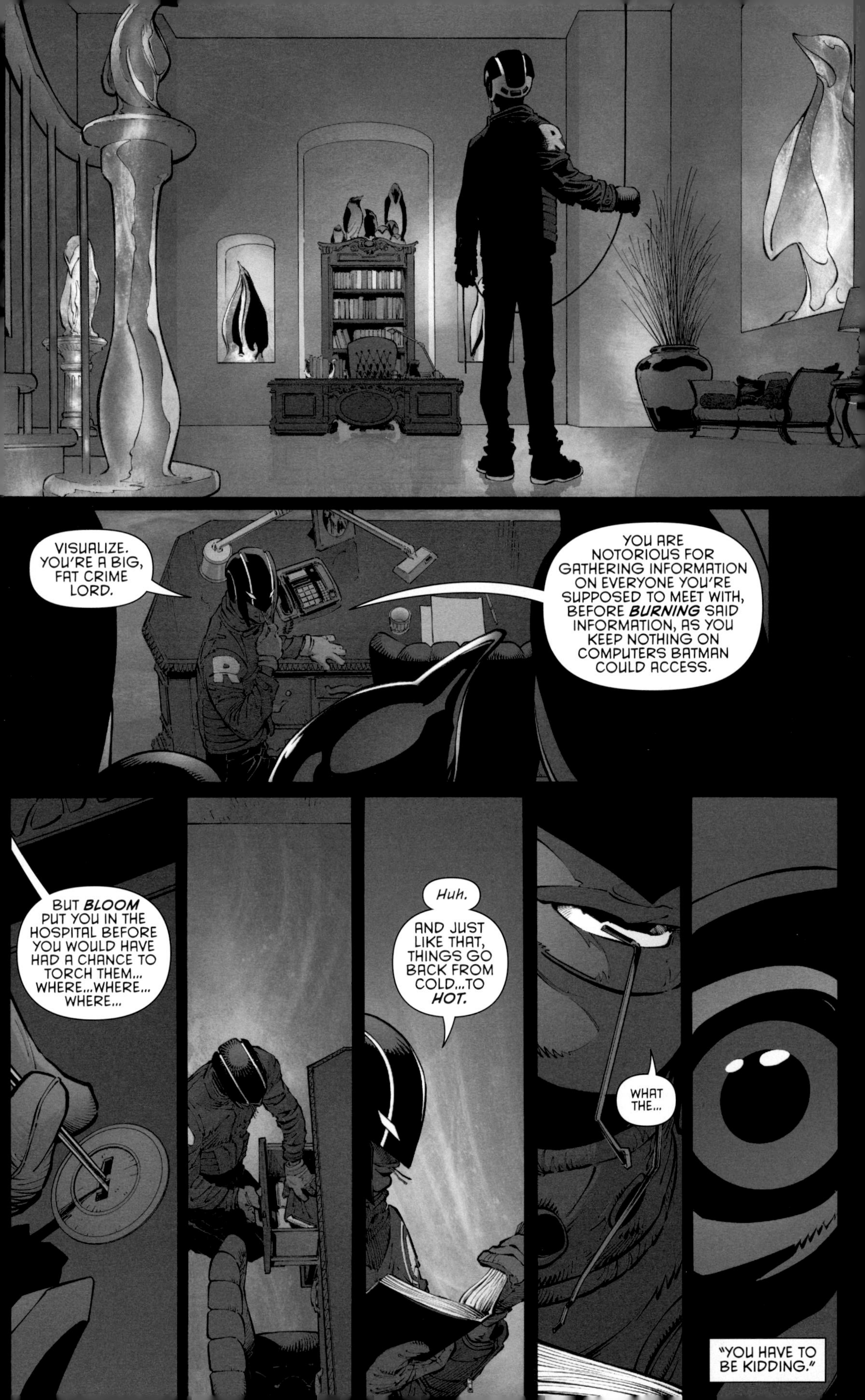

VISUALIZE. YOU'RE A BIG, FAT CRIME LORD.
YOU ARE NOTORIOUS FOR GATHERING INFORMATION ON EVERYONE YOU'RE SUPPOSED TO MEET WITH, BEFORE *BURNING* SAID INFORMATION, AS YOU KEEP NOTHING ON COMPUTERS BATMAN COULD ACCESS.
BUT *BLOOM* PUT YOU IN THE HOSPITAL BEFORE YOU WOULD HAVE HAD A CHANCE TO TORCH THEM... WHERE...WHERE... WHERE...
*Huh.*
AND JUST LIKE THAT, THINGS GO BACK FROM COLD...TO *HOT.*
WHAT THE...
"YOU HAVE TO BE KIDDING."

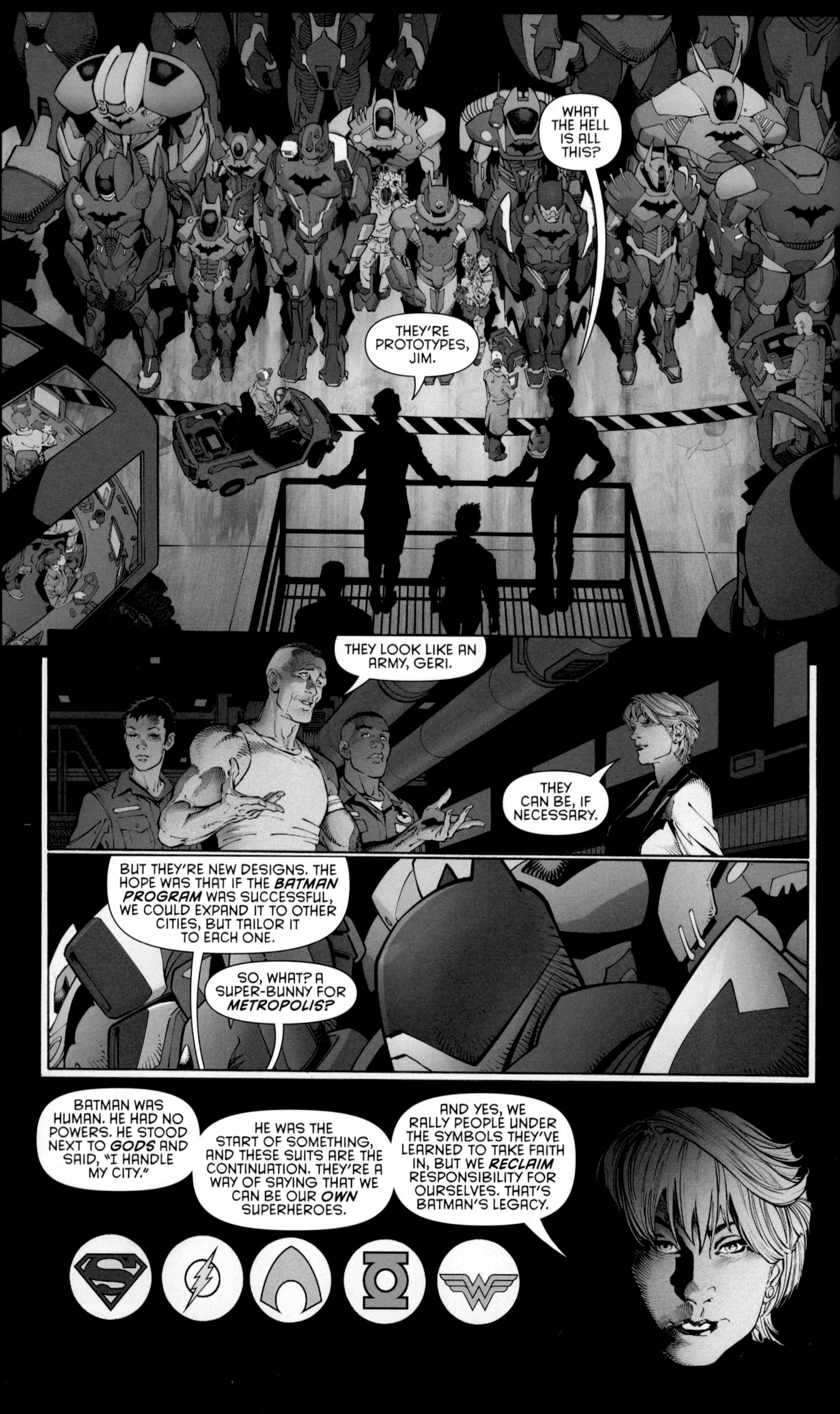
WHAT THE HELL IS ALL THIS?
THEY'RE PROTOTYPES, JIM.
THEY LOOK LIKE AN ARMY, GERI.
THEY CAN BE, IF NECESSARY.
BUT THEY'RE NEW DESIGNS. THE HOPE WAS THAT IF THE *BATMAN PROGRAM* WAS SUCCESSFUL, WE COULD EXPAND IT TO OTHER CITIES, BUT TAILOR IT TO EACH ONE.
SO, WHAT? A SUPER-BUNNY FOR *METROPOLIS?*
BATMAN WAS HUMAN. HE HAD NO POWERS. HE STOOD NEXT TO *GODS* AND SAID, "I HANDLE MY CITY."
HE WAS THE START OF SOMETHING, AND THESE SUITS ARE THE CONTINUATION. THEY'RE A WAY OF SAYING THAT WE CAN BE OUR *OWN* SUPERHEROES.
AND YES, WE RALLY PEOPLE UNDER THE SYMBOLS THEY'VE LEARNED TO TAKE FAITH IN, BUT WE *RECLAIM* RESPONSIBILITY FOR OURSELVES. THAT'S BATMAN'S LEGACY.

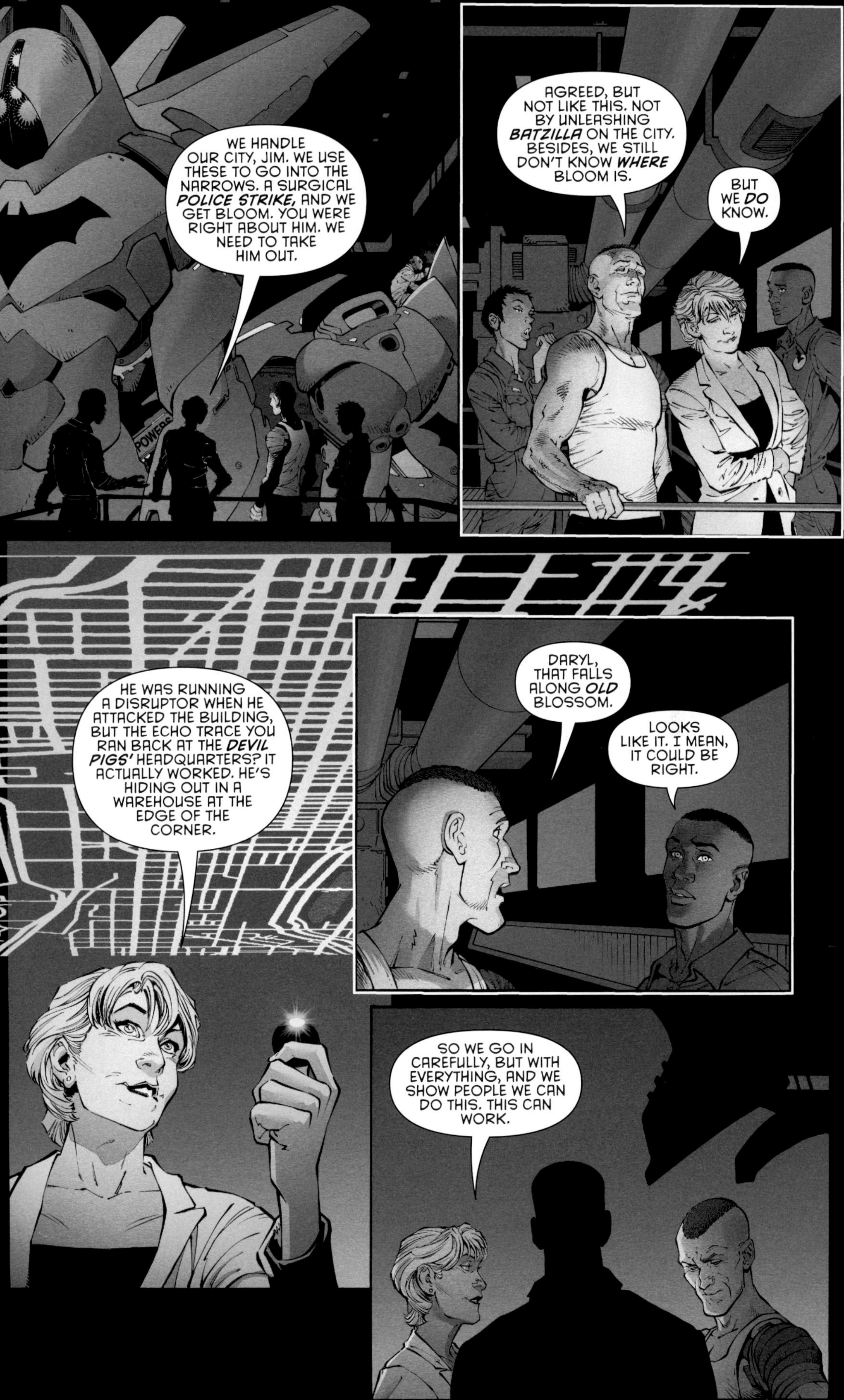

WE HANDLE OUR CITY, JIM. WE USE THESE TO GO INTO THE NARROWS. A SURGICAL POLICE STRIKE, AND WE GET BLOOM. YOU WERE RIGHT ABOUT HIM. WE NEED TO TAKE HIM OUT.
POWERS
AGREED, BUT NOT LIKE THIS. NOT BY UNLEASHING BATZILLA ON THE CITY. BESIDES, WE STILL DON'T KNOW WHERE BLOOM IS.
BUT WE DO KNOW.
HE WAS RUNNING A DISRUPTOR WHEN HE ATTACKED THE BUILDING, BUT THE ECHO TRACE YOU RAN BACK AT THE DEVIL PIGS' HEADQUARTERS? IT ACTUALLY WORKED. HE'S HIDING OUT IN A WAREHOUSE AT THE EDGE OF THE CORNER.
DARYL, THAT FALLS ALONG OLD BLOSSOM.
LOOKS LIKE IT. I MEAN, IT COULD BE RIGHT.
SO WE GO IN CAREFULLY, BUT WITH EVERYTHING, AND WE SHOW PEOPLE WE CAN DO THIS. THIS CAN WORK.

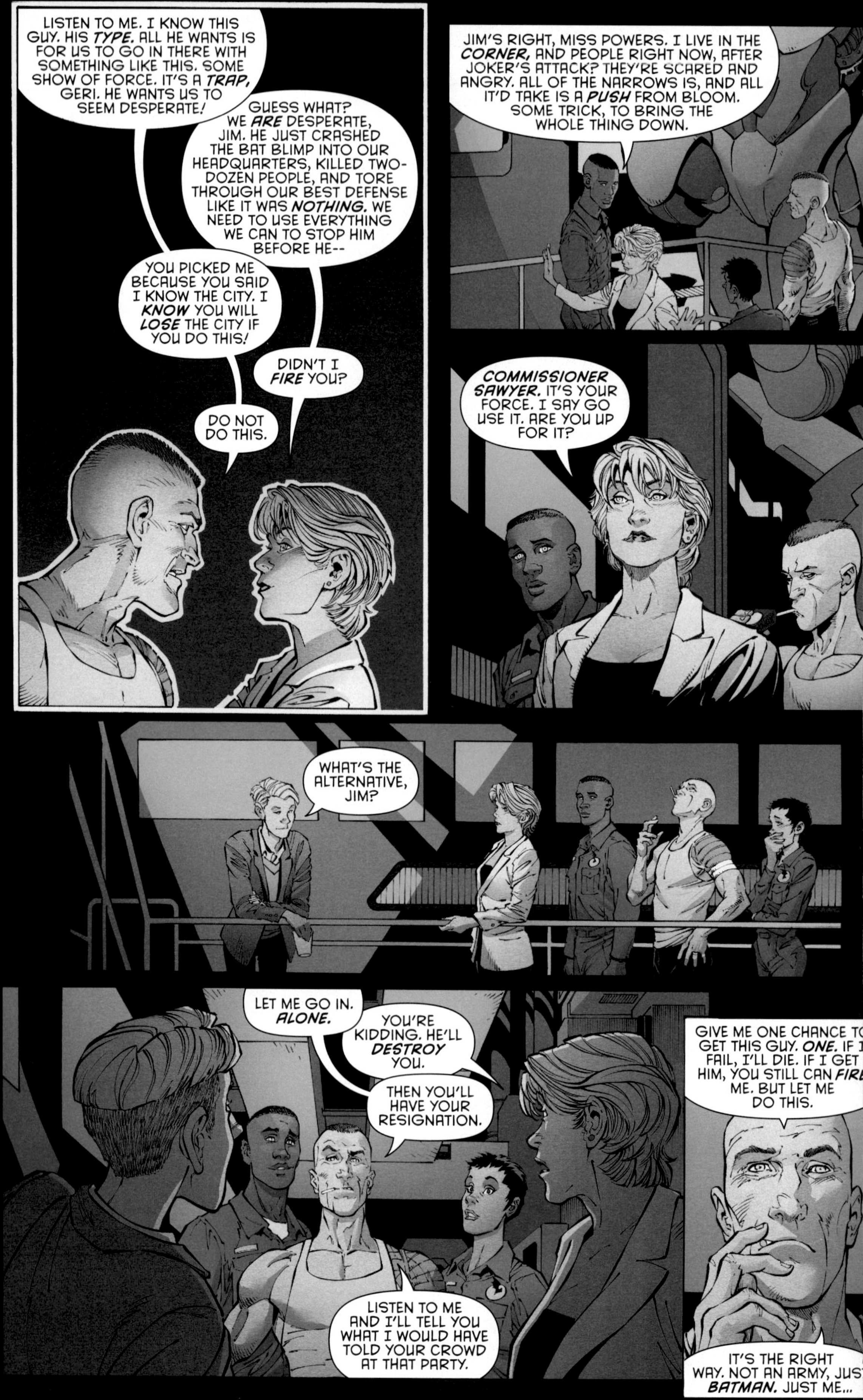

LISTEN TO ME. I KNOW THIS GUY. HIS *TYPE.* ALL HE WANTS IS FOR US TO GO IN THERE WITH SOMETHING LIKE THIS. SOME SHOW OF FORCE. IT'S A *TRAP,* GERI. HE WANTS US TO SEEM DESPERATE!
GUESS WHAT? WE *ARE* DESPERATE, JIM. HE JUST CRASHED THE BAT BLIMP INTO OUR HEADQUARTERS, KILLED TWO-DOZEN PEOPLE, AND TORE THROUGH OUR BEST DEFENSE LIKE IT WAS *NOTHING.* WE NEED TO USE EVERYTHING WE CAN TO STOP HIM BEFORE HE--
YOU PICKED ME BECAUSE YOU SAID I KNOW THE CITY. I *KNOW* YOU WILL *LOSE* THE CITY IF YOU DO THIS!
DIDN'T I *FIRE* YOU?
DO NOT DO THIS.
JIM'S RIGHT, MISS POWERS. I LIVE IN THE *CORNER,* AND PEOPLE RIGHT NOW, AFTER JOKER'S ATTACK? THEY'RE SCARED AND ANGRY. ALL OF THE NARROWS IS, AND ALL IT'D TAKE IS A *PUSH* FROM BLOOM. SOME TRICK, TO BRING THE WHOLE THING DOWN.
*COMMISSIONER SAWYER.* IT'S YOUR FORCE. I SAY GO USE IT. ARE YOU UP FOR IT?
WHAT'S THE ALTERNATIVE, JIM?
LET ME GO IN. *ALONE.*
YOU'RE KIDDING. HE'LL *DESTROY* YOU.
THEN YOU'LL HAVE YOUR RESIGNATION.
LISTEN TO ME AND I'LL TELL YOU WHAT I WOULD HAVE TOLD YOUR CROWD AT THAT PARTY.
GIVE ME ONE CHANCE TO GET THIS GUY. *ONE.* IF I FAIL, I'LL DIE. IF I GET HIM, YOU STILL CAN *FIRE* ME. BUT LET ME DO THIS.
IT'S THE RIGHT WAY. NOT AN ARMY, JUST *BATMAN.* JUST ME...

"...AND *HIM.*"

IT'S...REALLY GOOD, LIV. BUT WHAT MADE YOU DRAW THIS?

BECAUSE HE KILLED PEOPLE.

*KILLED* PEOPLE? KILLED WHO?

OLIVIA.

HE CAN'T GET YOU HERE. NOW GO BACK TO ART ROOM, OKAY HONEY?

YOU DIDN'T HEAR?

I JUST WALKED IN.

THIS *BLOOM.* HE ATTACKED THE POWERS BUILDING. TORE UP BATMAN. THEY SAY HE'S HIDING SOMEWHERE NEARBY. THE KIDS ARE ALL RILED.

LIKE SOMETHING FROM A *NIGHTMARE.*

LORD.

THE SEED...

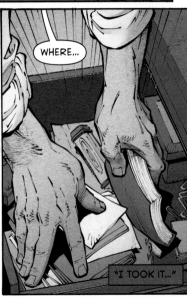

WHERE...

"I TOOK IT..."

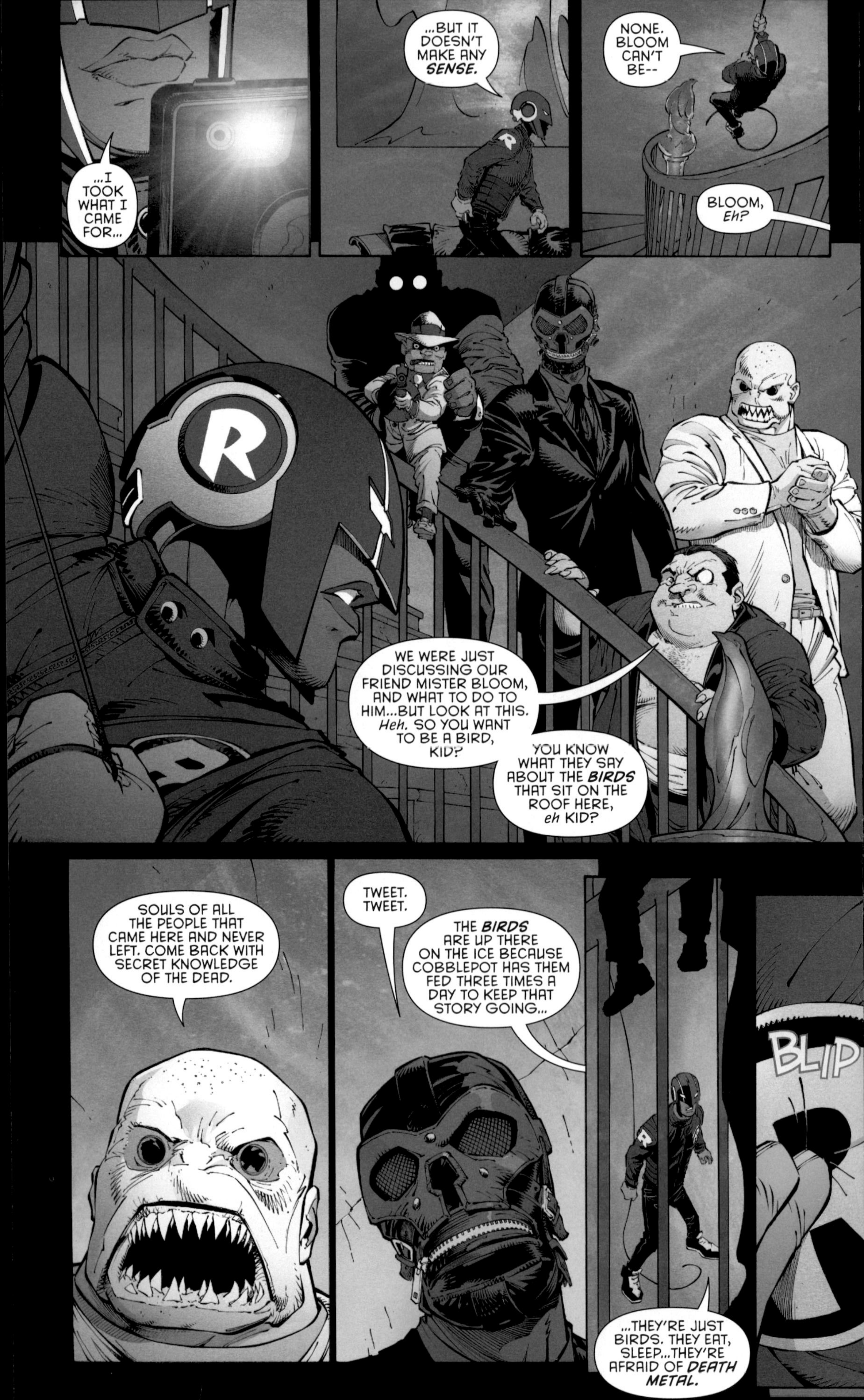
...I TOOK WHAT I CAME FOR...
...BUT IT DOESN'T MAKE ANY *SENSE.*
NONE. BLOOM CAN'T BE--
BLOOM, *Eh?*
WE WERE JUST DISCUSSING OUR FRIEND MISTER BLOOM, AND WHAT TO DO TO HIM...BUT LOOK AT THIS. *Heh.* SO YOU WANT TO BE A BIRD, KID?
YOU KNOW WHAT THEY SAY ABOUT THE *BIRDS* THAT SIT ON THE ROOF HERE, *eh* KID?
SOULS OF ALL THE PEOPLE THAT CAME HERE AND NEVER LEFT. COME BACK WITH SECRET KNOWLEDGE OF THE DEAD.
TWEET. TWEET.
THE *BIRDS* ARE UP THERE ON THE ICE BECAUSE COBBLEPOT HAS THEM FED THREE TIMES A DAY TO KEEP THAT STORY GOING...
BLIP
...THEY'RE JUST BIRDS. THEY EAT, SLEEP...THEY'RE AFRAID OF *DEATH METAL.*

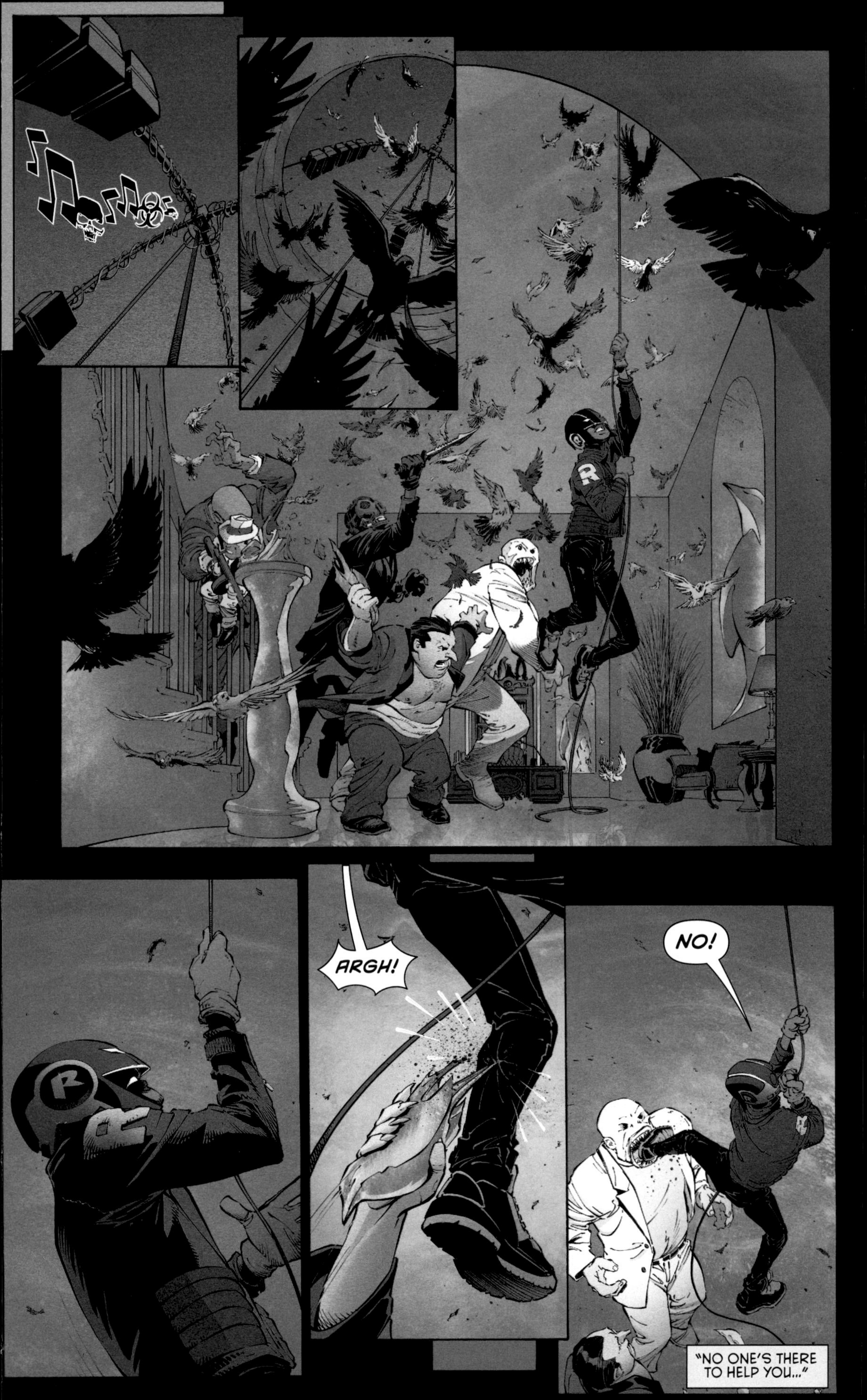
ARGH!
NO!
"NO ONE'S THERE TO HELP YOU..."

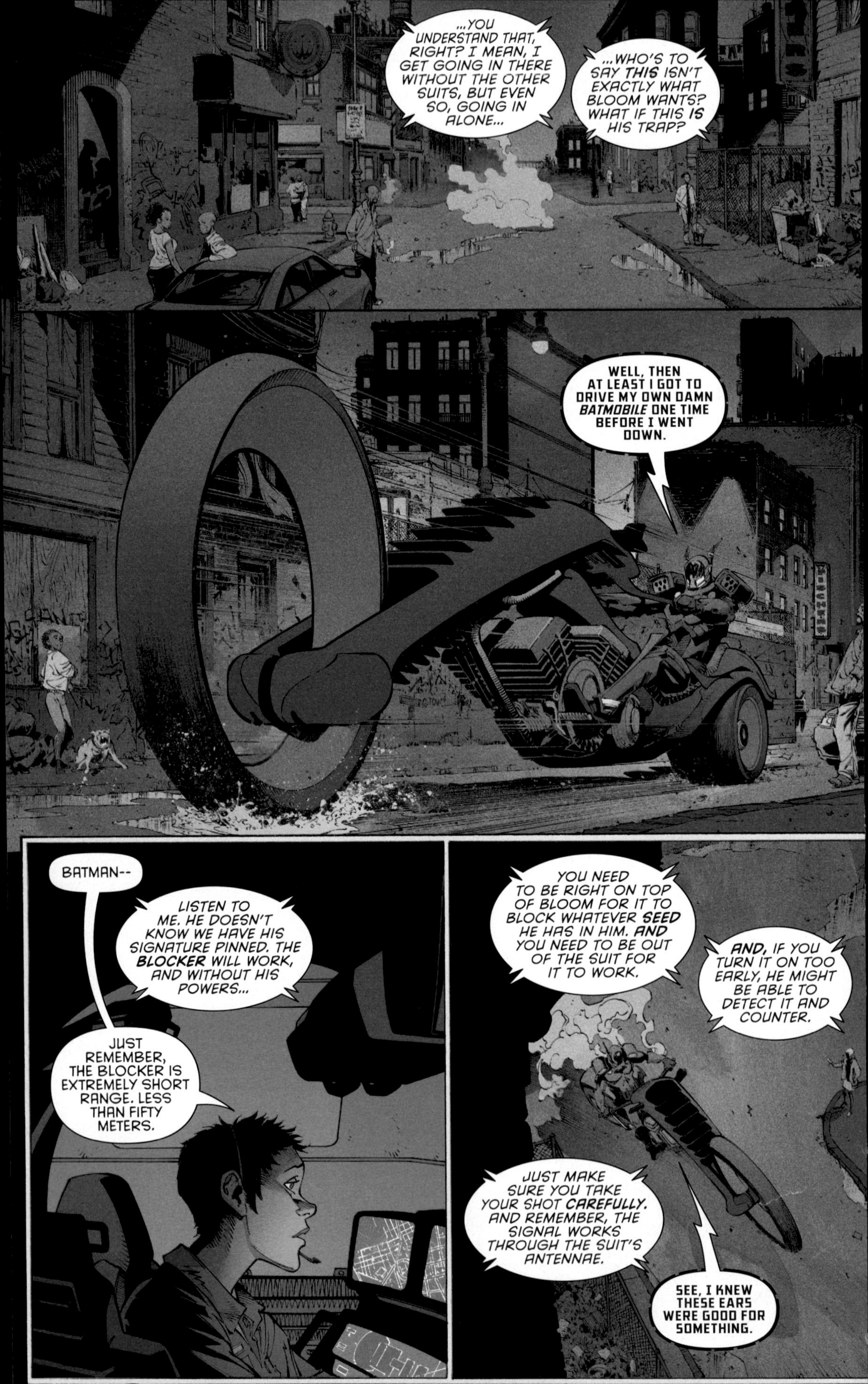
...YOU UNDERSTAND THAT, RIGHT? I MEAN, I GET GOING IN THERE WITHOUT THE OTHER SUITS, BUT EVEN SO, GOING IN ALONE...
...WHO'S TO SAY THIS ISN'T EXACTLY WHAT BLOOM WANTS? WHAT IF THIS IS HIS TRAP?
WELL, THEN AT LEAST I GOT TO DRIVE MY OWN DAMN BATMOBILE ONE TIME BEFORE I WENT DOWN.
BATMAN--
LISTEN TO ME. HE DOESN'T KNOW WE HAVE HIS SIGNATURE PINNED. THE BLOCKER WILL WORK, AND WITHOUT HIS POWERS...
JUST REMEMBER, THE BLOCKER IS EXTREMELY SHORT RANGE. LESS THAN FIFTY METERS.
YOU NEED TO BE RIGHT ON TOP OF BLOOM FOR IT TO BLOCK WHATEVER SEED HE HAS IN HIM. AND YOU NEED TO BE OUT OF THE SUIT FOR IT TO WORK.
AND, IF YOU TURN IT ON TOO EARLY, HE MIGHT BE ABLE TO DETECT IT AND COUNTER.
JUST MAKE SURE YOU TAKE YOUR SHOT CAREFULLY. AND REMEMBER, THE SIGNAL WORKS THROUGH THE SUIT'S ANTENNAE.
SEE, I KNEW THESE EARS WERE GOOD FOR SOMETHING.

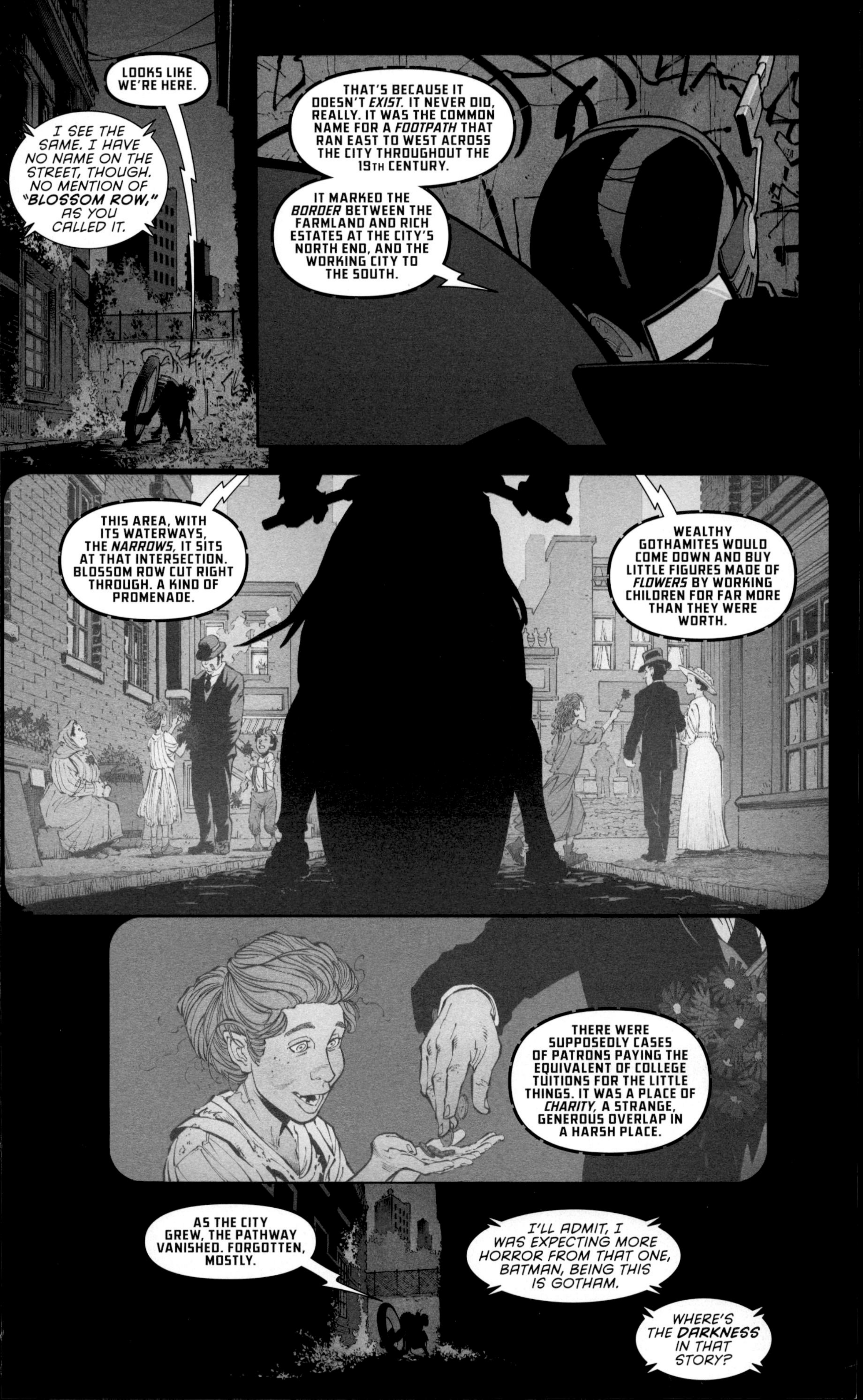
LOOKS LIKE WE'RE HERE.
I SEE THE SAME. I HAVE NO NAME ON THE STREET, THOUGH. NO MENTION OF "BLOSSOM ROW," AS YOU CALLED IT.
THAT'S BECAUSE IT DOESN'T EXIST. IT NEVER DID, REALLY. IT WAS THE COMMON NAME FOR A FOOTPATH THAT RAN EAST TO WEST ACROSS THE CITY THROUGHOUT THE 19TH CENTURY.
IT MARKED THE BORDER BETWEEN THE FARMLAND AND RICH ESTATES AT THE CITY'S NORTH END, AND THE WORKING CITY TO THE SOUTH.
THIS AREA, WITH ITS WATERWAYS, THE NARROWS, IT SITS AT THAT INTERSECTION. BLOSSOM ROW CUT RIGHT THROUGH. A KIND OF PROMENADE.
WEALTHY GOTHAMITES WOULD COME DOWN AND BUY LITTLE FIGURES MADE OF FLOWERS BY WORKING CHILDREN FOR FAR MORE THAN THEY WERE WORTH.
THERE WERE SUPPOSEDLY CASES OF PATRONS PAYING THE EQUIVALENT OF COLLEGE TUITIONS FOR THE LITTLE THINGS. IT WAS A PLACE OF CHARITY, A STRANGE, GENEROUS OVERLAP IN A HARSH PLACE.
AS THE CITY GREW, THE PATHWAY VANISHED. FORGOTTEN, MOSTLY.
I'LL ADMIT, I WAS EXPECTING MORE HORROR FROM THAT ONE, BATMAN, BEING THIS IS GOTHAM.
WHERE'S THE DARKNESS IN THAT STORY?

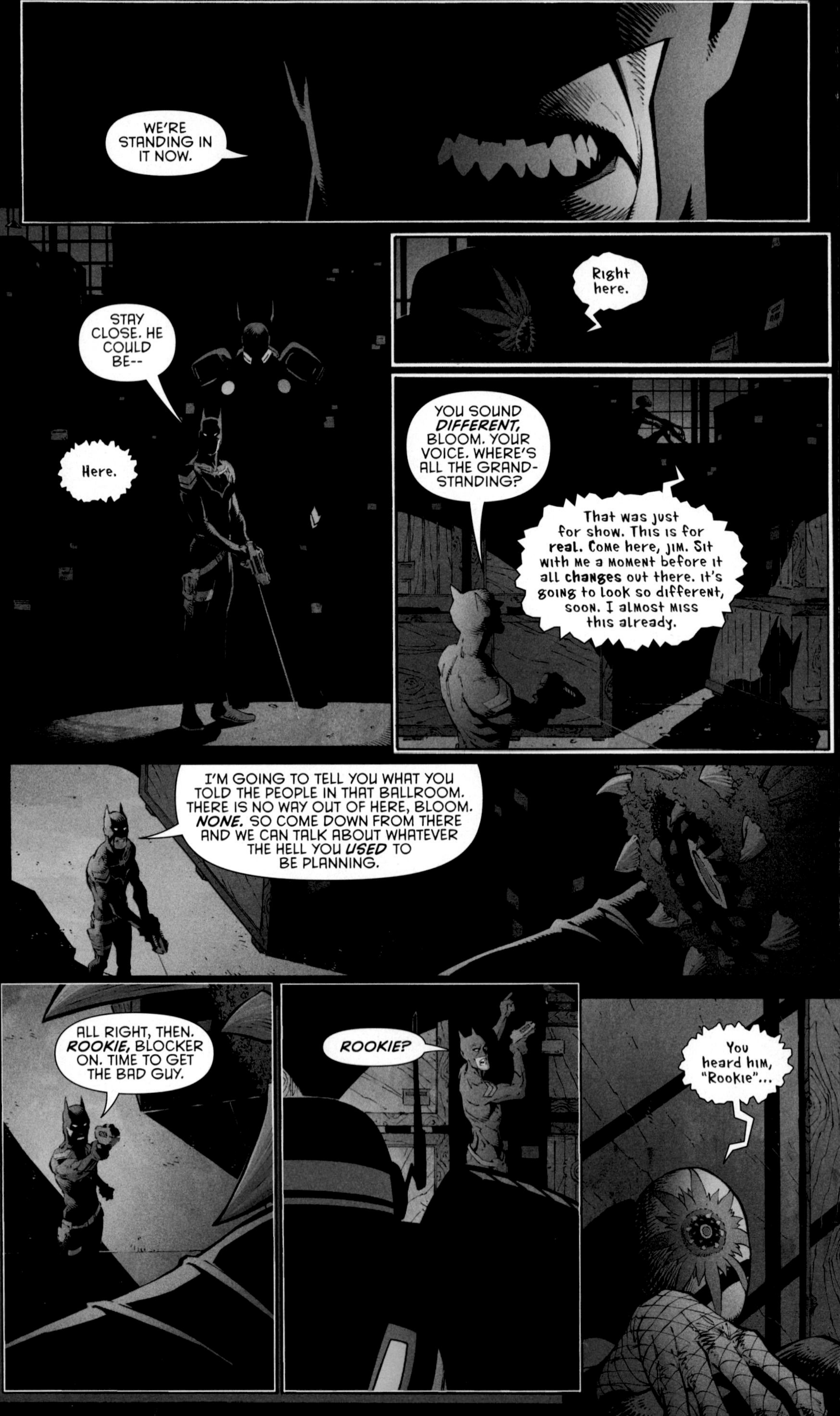
WE'RE STANDING IN IT NOW.
STAY CLOSE. HE COULD BE--
Here.
Right here.
YOU SOUND *DIFFERENT*, BLOOM. YOUR VOICE. WHERE'S ALL THE GRAND-STANDING?
That was just for show. This is for **real.** Come here, JIM. Sit with me a moment before it all **changes** out there. It's going to look so different, soon. I almost miss this already.
I'M GOING TO TELL YOU WHAT YOU TOLD THE PEOPLE IN THAT BALLROOM. THERE IS NO WAY OUT OF HERE, BLOOM. *NONE.* SO COME DOWN FROM THERE AND WE CAN TALK ABOUT WHATEVER THE HELL YOU *USED* TO BE PLANNING.
ALL RIGHT, THEN. *ROOKIE,* BLOCKER ON. TIME TO GET THE BAD GUY.
*ROOKIE?*
You heard him, "Rookie"...

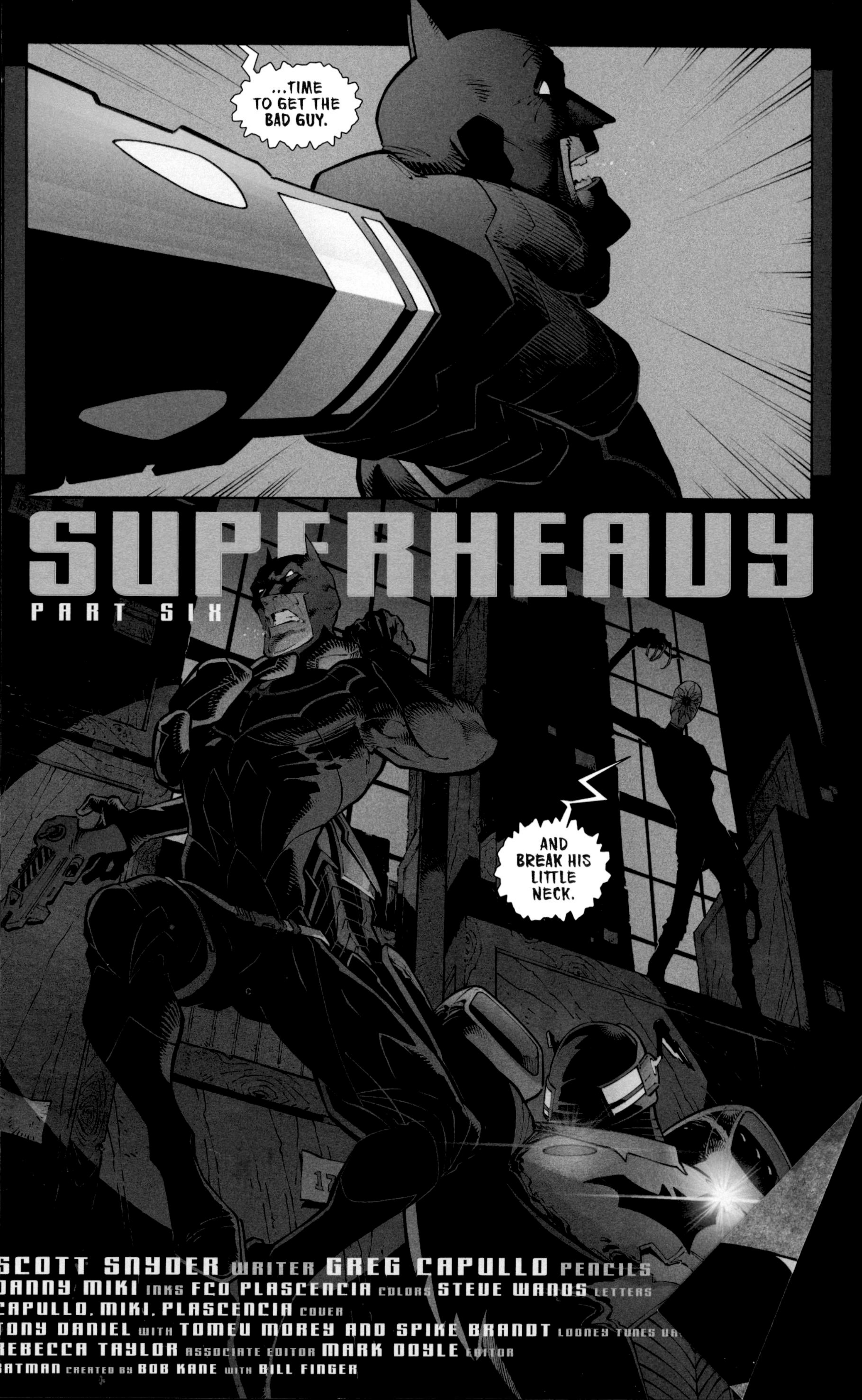
...TIME TO GET THE BAD GUY.
SUPERHEAVY
PART SIX
AND BREAK HIS LITTLE NECK.
17
SCOTT SNYDER WRITER GREG CAPULLO PENCILS
DANNY MIKI INKS FCO PLASCENCIA COLORS STEVE WANDS LETTERS
CAPULLO, MIKI, PLASCENCIA COVER
TONY DANIEL WITH TOMEU MOREY AND SPIKE BRANDT LOONEY TUNES VA
REBECCA TAYLOR ASSOCIATE EDITOR MARK DOYLE EDITOR
BATMAN CREATED BY BOB KANE WITH BILL FINGER

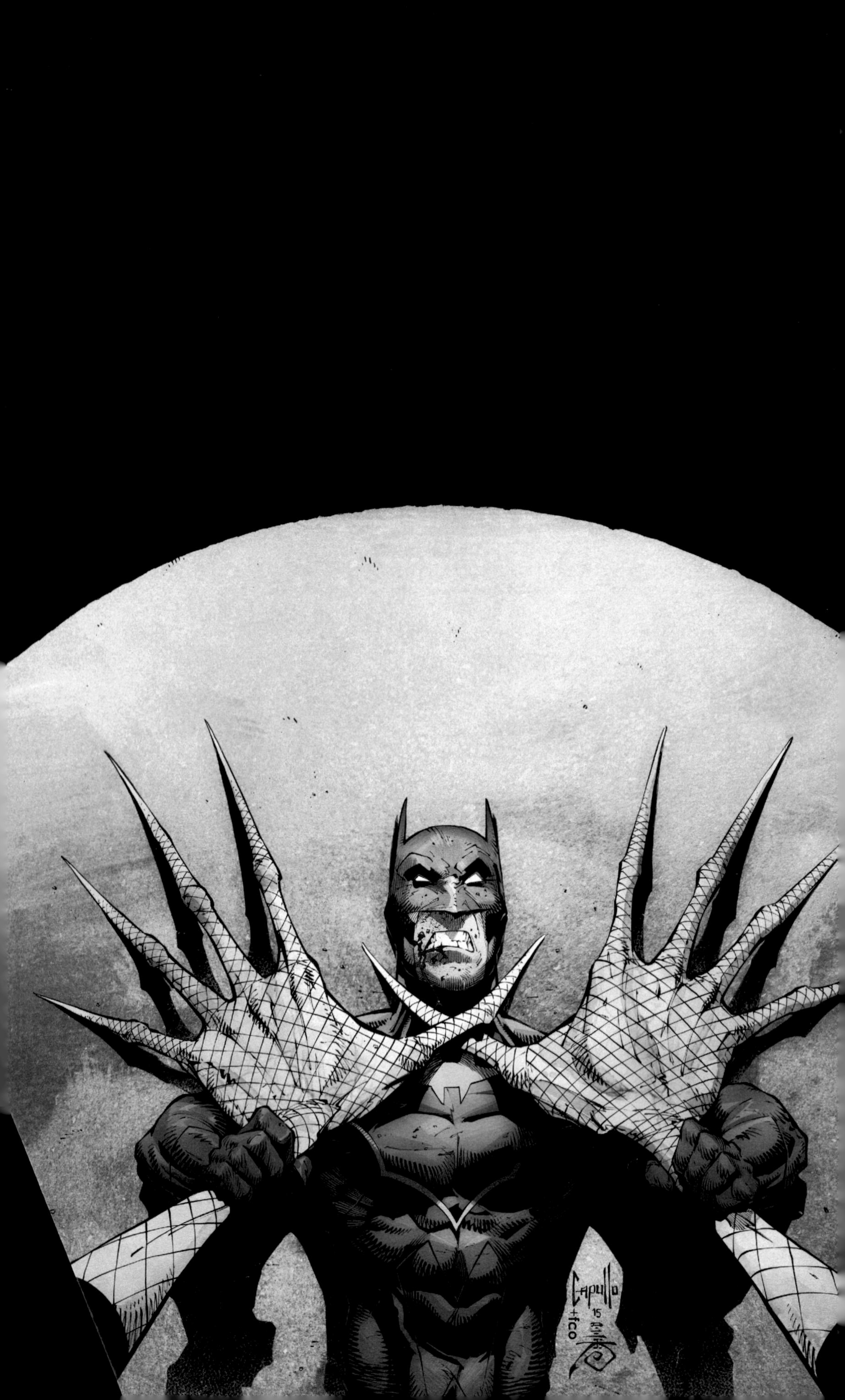

**SCOTT SNYDER** WRITER **GREG CAPULLO** PENCILS
**DANNY MIKI** INKS **FCO PLASCENCIA** COLORS **STEVE WANDS** LETTERS
**CAPULLO, MIKI, PLASCENCIA** COVER **ALEX ROSS** HARLEY'S LITTLE BLACK BOOK VARIANT COVER
**REBECCA TAYLOR** ASSOCIATE EDITOR **MARK DOYLE** EDITOR
BATMAN CREATED BY BOB KANE WITH BILL FINGER

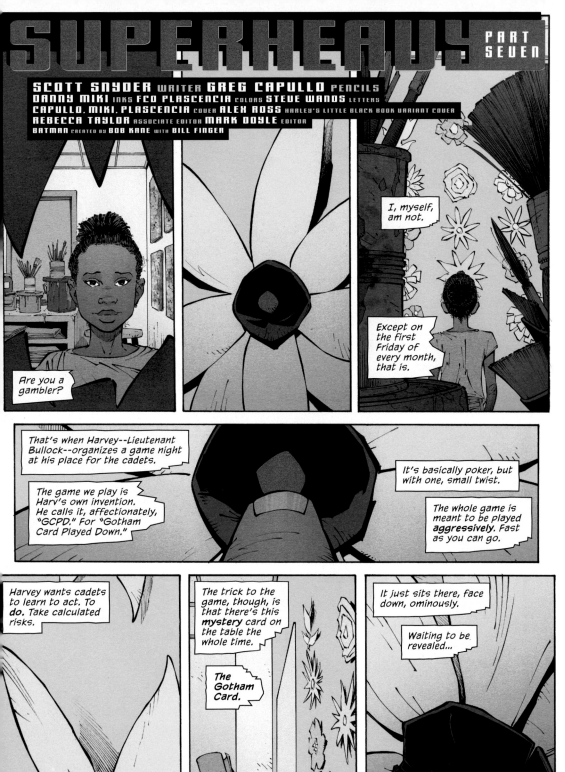

*I, myself, am not.*

*Except on the first Friday of every month, that is.*

*Are you a gambler?*

That's when Harvey--Lieutenant Bullock--organizes a game night at his place for the cadets.

The game we play is Harv's own invention. He calls it, affectionately, "GCPD." For "Gotham Card Played Down."

It's basically poker, but with one, small twist.

The whole game is meant to be played **aggressively**. Fast as you can go.

Harvey wants cadets to learn to act. To **do**. Take calculated risks.

The trick to the game, though, is that there's this **mystery** card on the table the whole time.

**The Gotham Card.**

It just sits there, face down, ominously.

Waiting to be revealed...

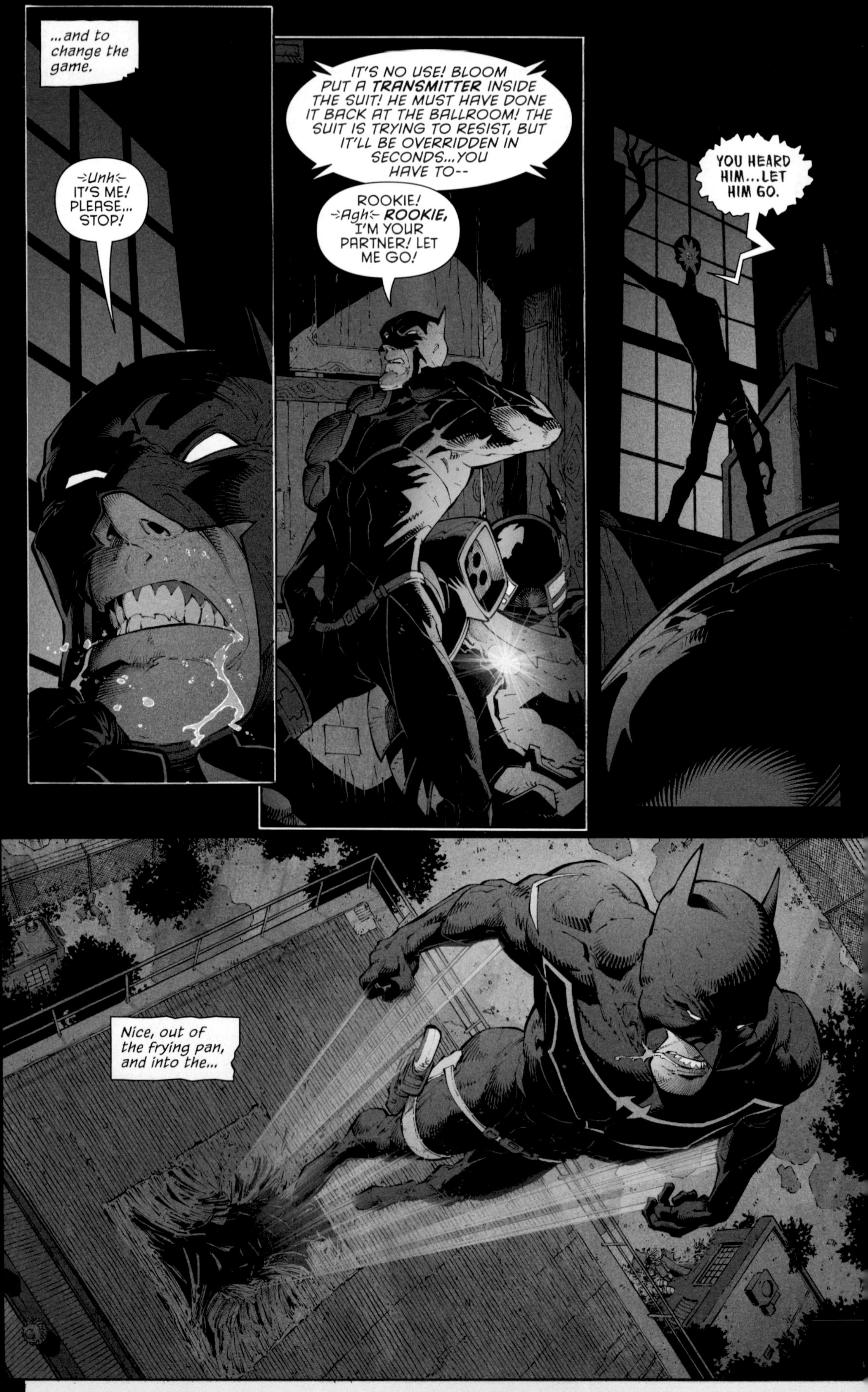
...and to change the game.
→Unh← IT'S ME! PLEASE... STOP!
IT'S NO USE! BLOOM PUT A TRANSMITTER INSIDE THE SUIT! HE MUST HAVE DONE IT BACK AT THE BALLROOM! THE SUIT IS TRYING TO RESIST, BUT IT'LL BE OVERRIDDEN IN SECONDS...YOU HAVE TO--
ROOKIE! →Agh← ROOKIE, I'M YOUR PARTNER! LET ME GO!
YOU HEARD HIM...LET HIM GO.
Nice, out of the frying pan, and into the...

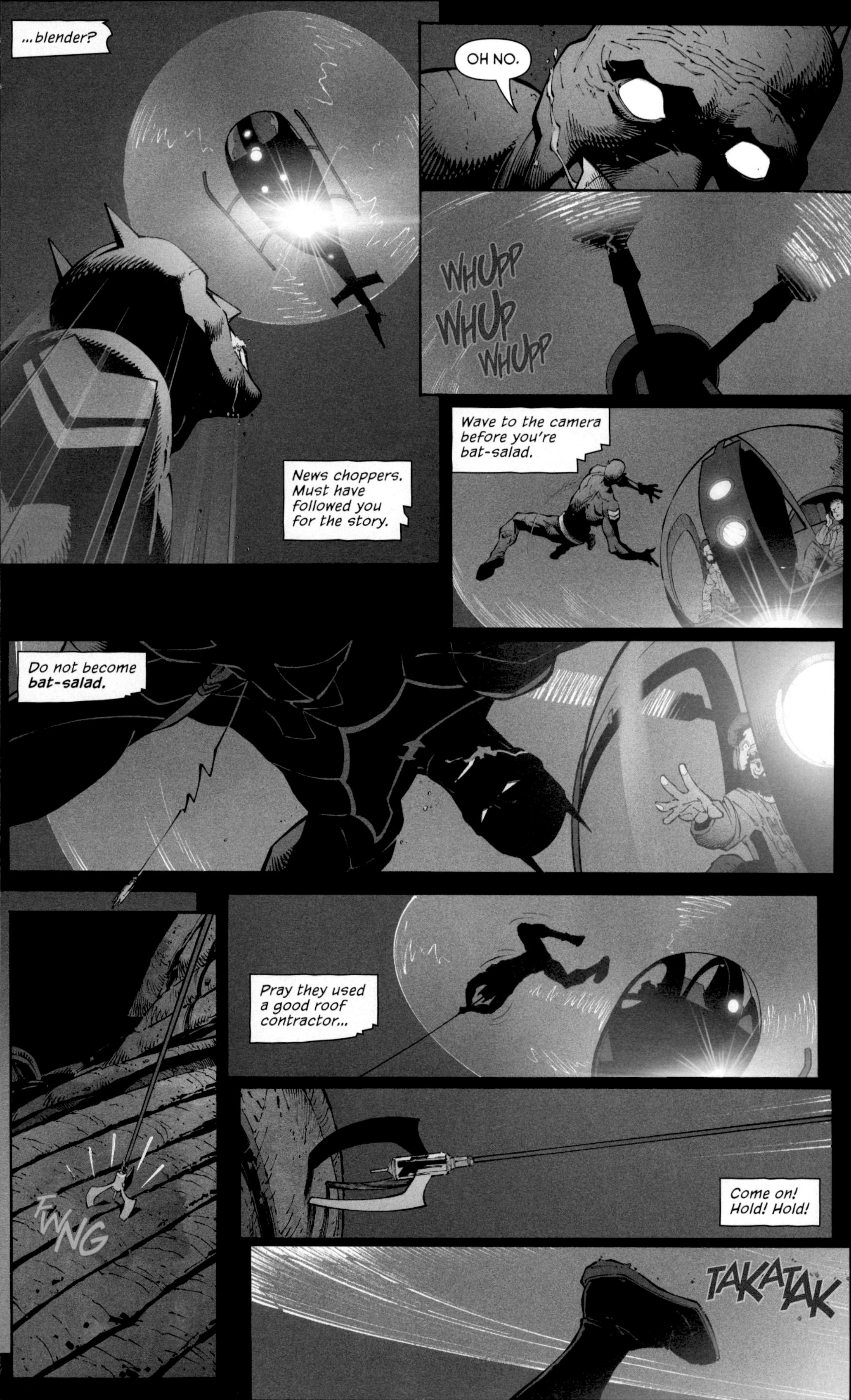

...blender?
OH NO.
WHUPP
WHUP
WHUPP
News choppers. Must have followed you for the story.
Wave to the camera before you're bat-salad.
Do not become **bat-salad.**
FWNG
Pray they used a good roof contractor...
Come on! Hold! Hold!
TAKATAK

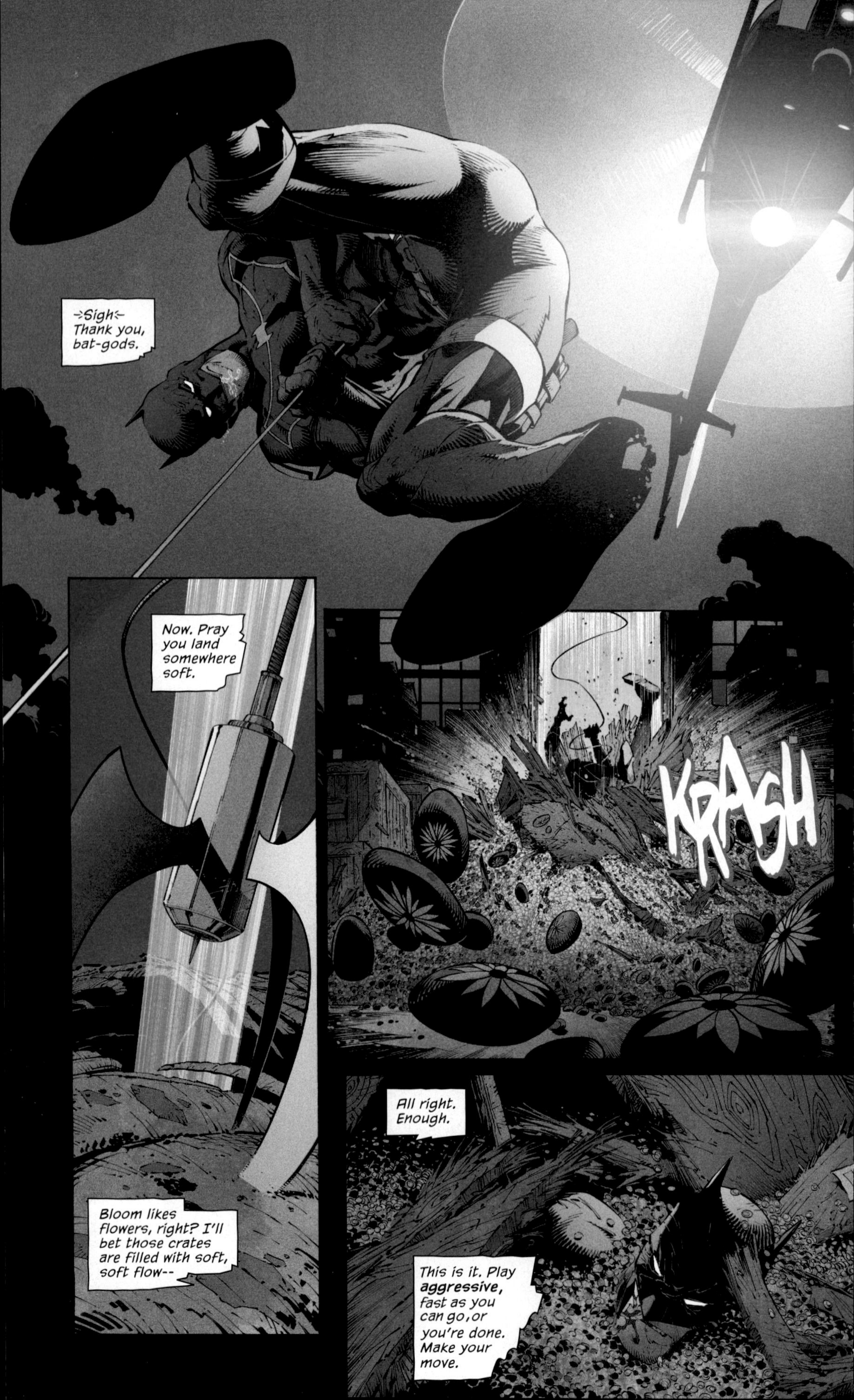

-Sigh-
Thank you, bat-gods.
Now. Pray you land somewhere soft.
Bloom likes flowers, right? I'll bet those crates are filled with soft, soft flow--
KRASH
All right. Enough.
This is it. Play **aggressive,** fast as you can go, or you're done. Make your move.

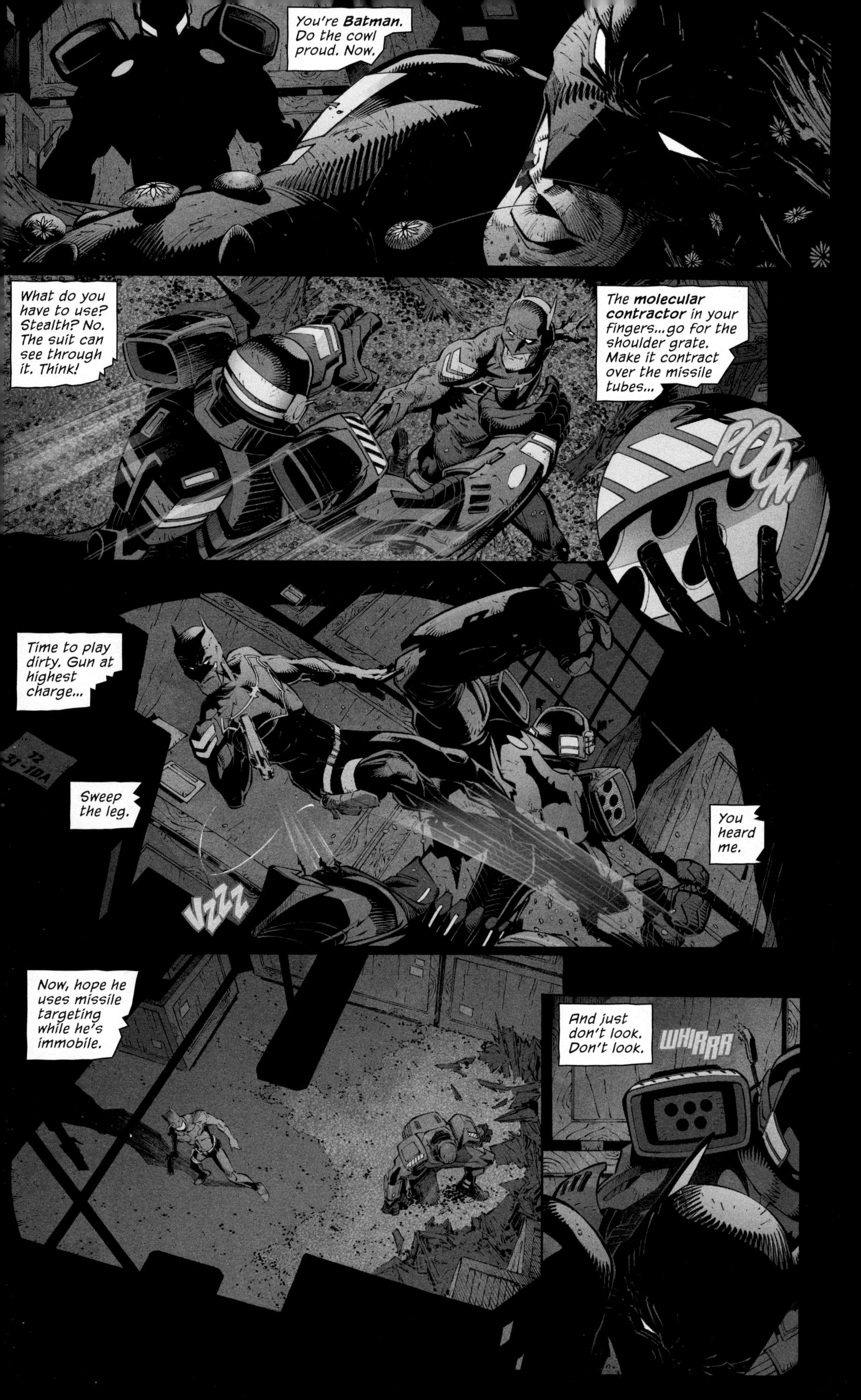
You're **Batman.** Do the cowl proud. Now.
What do you have to use? Stealth? No. The suit can see through it. Think!
The **molecular contractor** in your fingers...go for the shoulder grate. Make it contract over the missile tubes...
POOM
Time to play dirty. Gun at highest charge...
Sweep the leg.
You heard me.
VZZZ
Now, hope he uses missile targeting while he's immobile.
And just don't look. Don't look.
WHIRRR

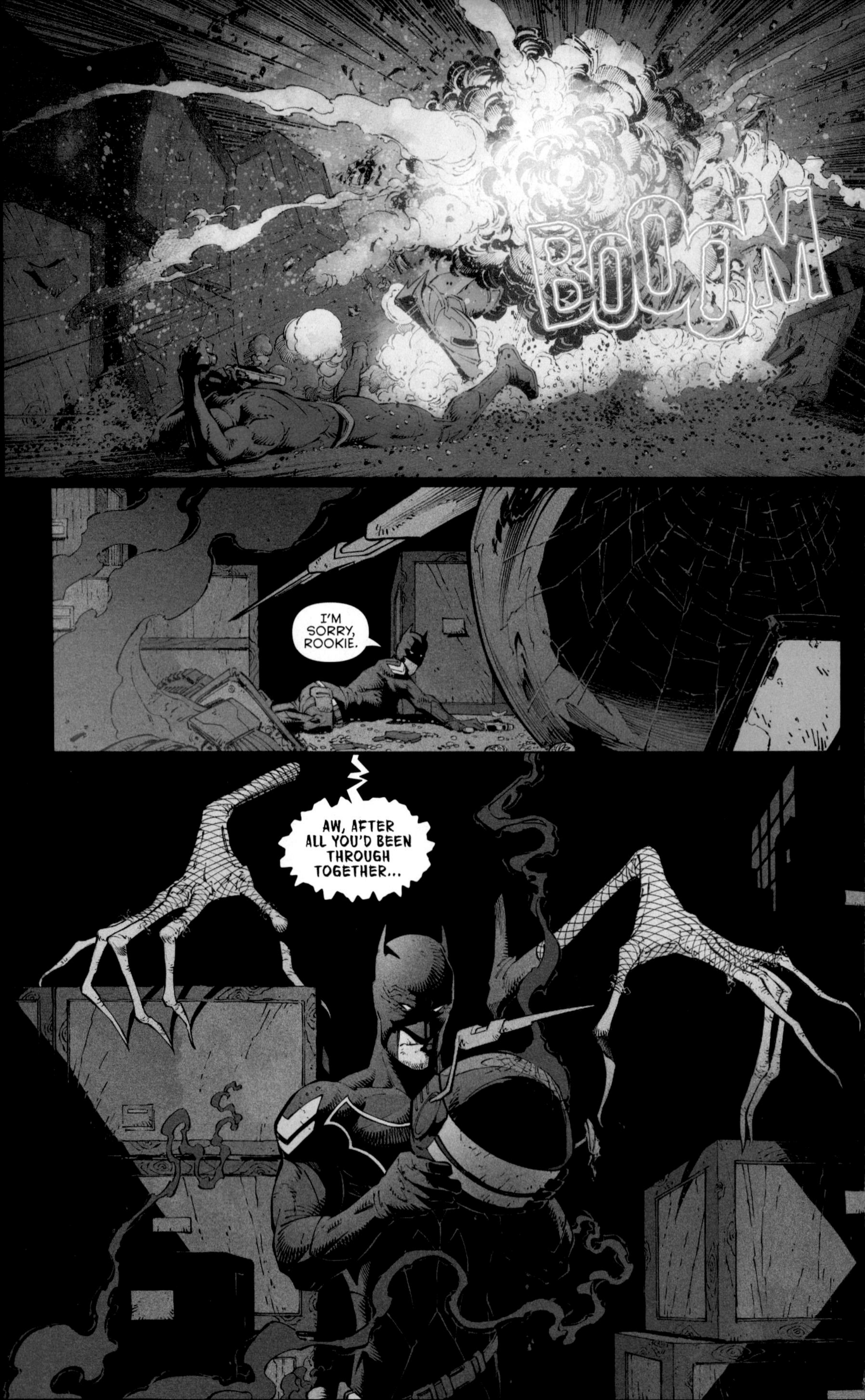
BOOOM
I'M SORRY, ROOKIE.
AW, AFTER ALL YOU'D BEEN THROUGH TOGETHER...

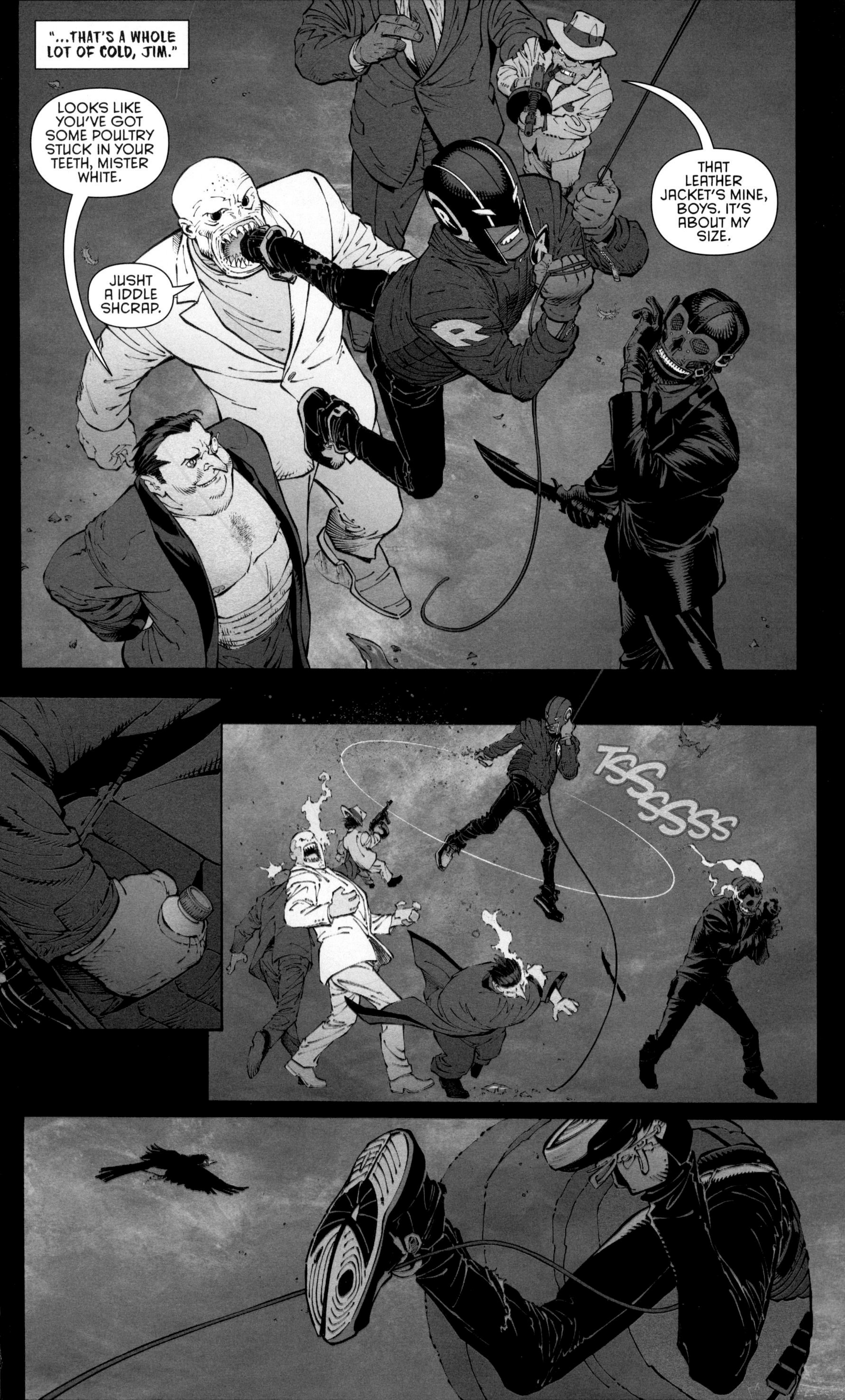
"...THAT'S A WHOLE LOT OF COLD, JIM."
LOOKS LIKE YOU'VE GOT SOME POULTRY STUCK IN YOUR TEETH, MISTER WHITE.
JUSHT A IDDLE SHCRAP.
THAT LEATHER JACKET'S MINE, BOYS. IT'S ABOUT MY SIZE.
TSSSSSS

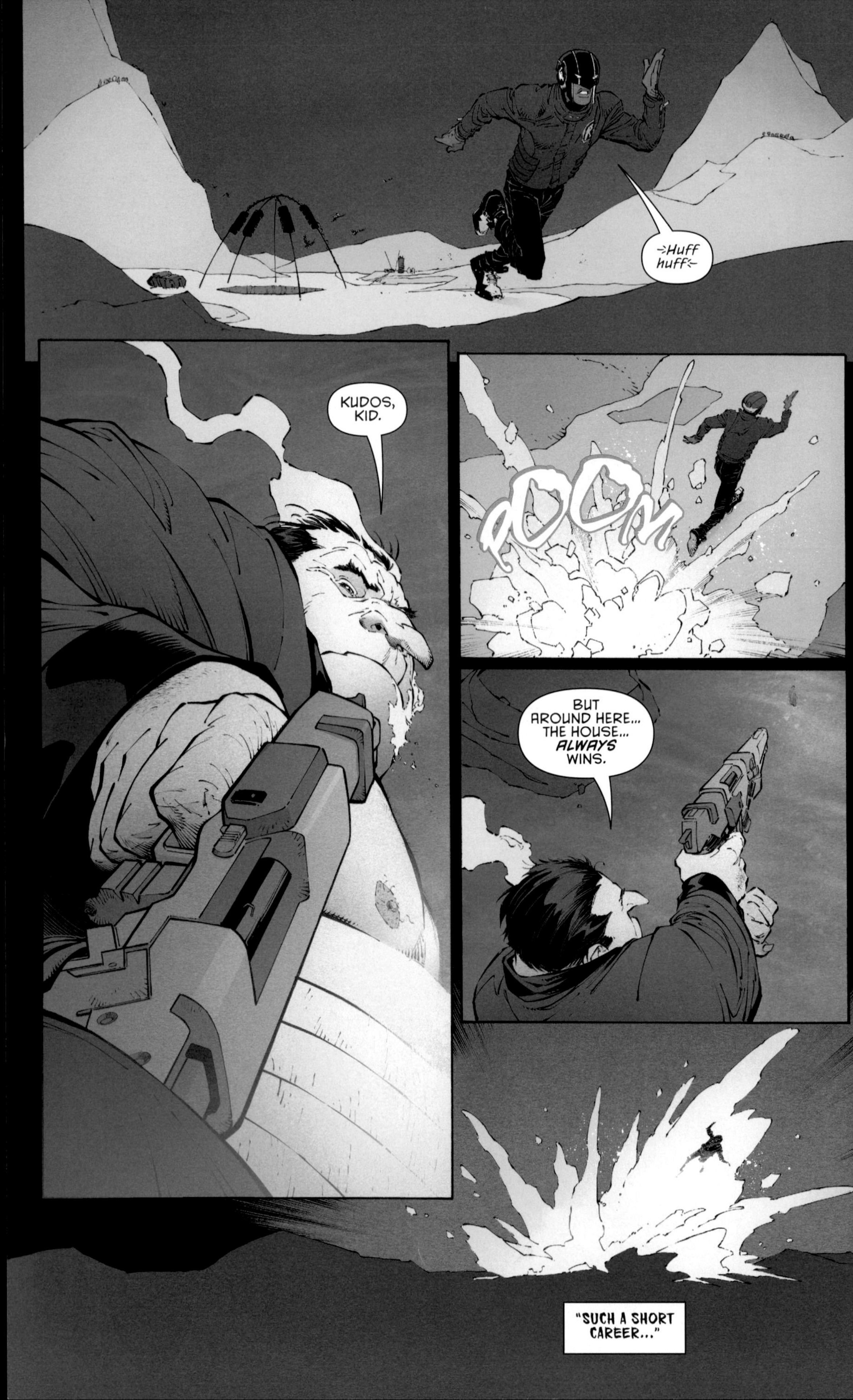

Huff huff
KUDOS, KID.
BOOM
BUT AROUND HERE... THE HOUSE... ALWAYS WINS.
"SUCH A SHORT CAREER..."

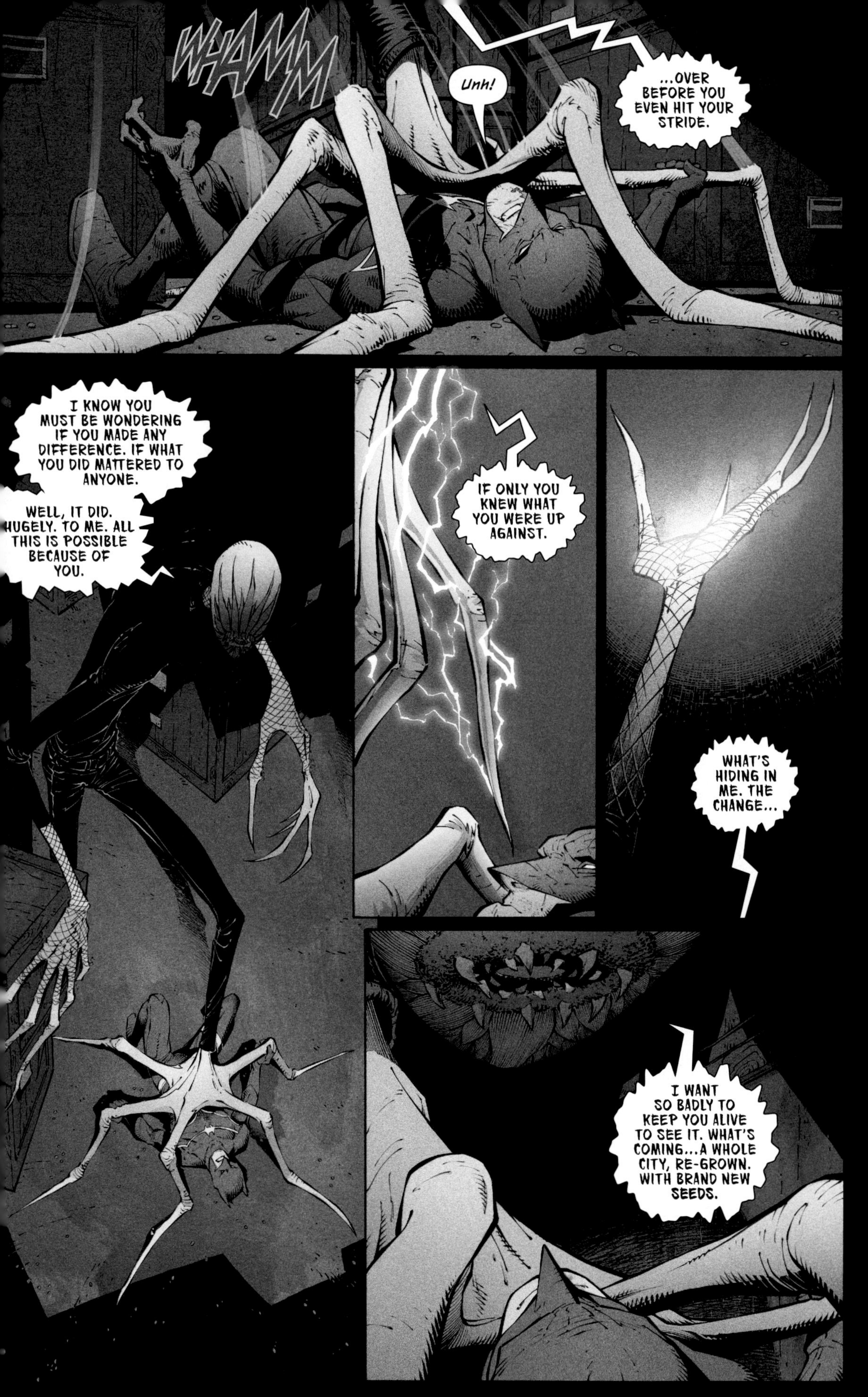
WHAMM
Unh!
...OVER BEFORE YOU EVEN HIT YOUR STRIDE.
I KNOW YOU MUST BE WONDERING IF YOU MADE ANY DIFFERENCE. IF WHAT YOU DID MATTERED TO ANYONE.
WELL, IT DID. HUGELY. TO ME. ALL THIS IS POSSIBLE BECAUSE OF YOU.
IF ONLY YOU KNEW WHAT YOU WERE UP AGAINST.
WHAT'S HIDING IN ME. THE CHANGE...
I WANT SO BADLY TO KEEP YOU ALIVE TO SEE IT. WHAT'S COMING...A WHOLE CITY, RE-GROWN. WITH BRAND NEW SEEDS.

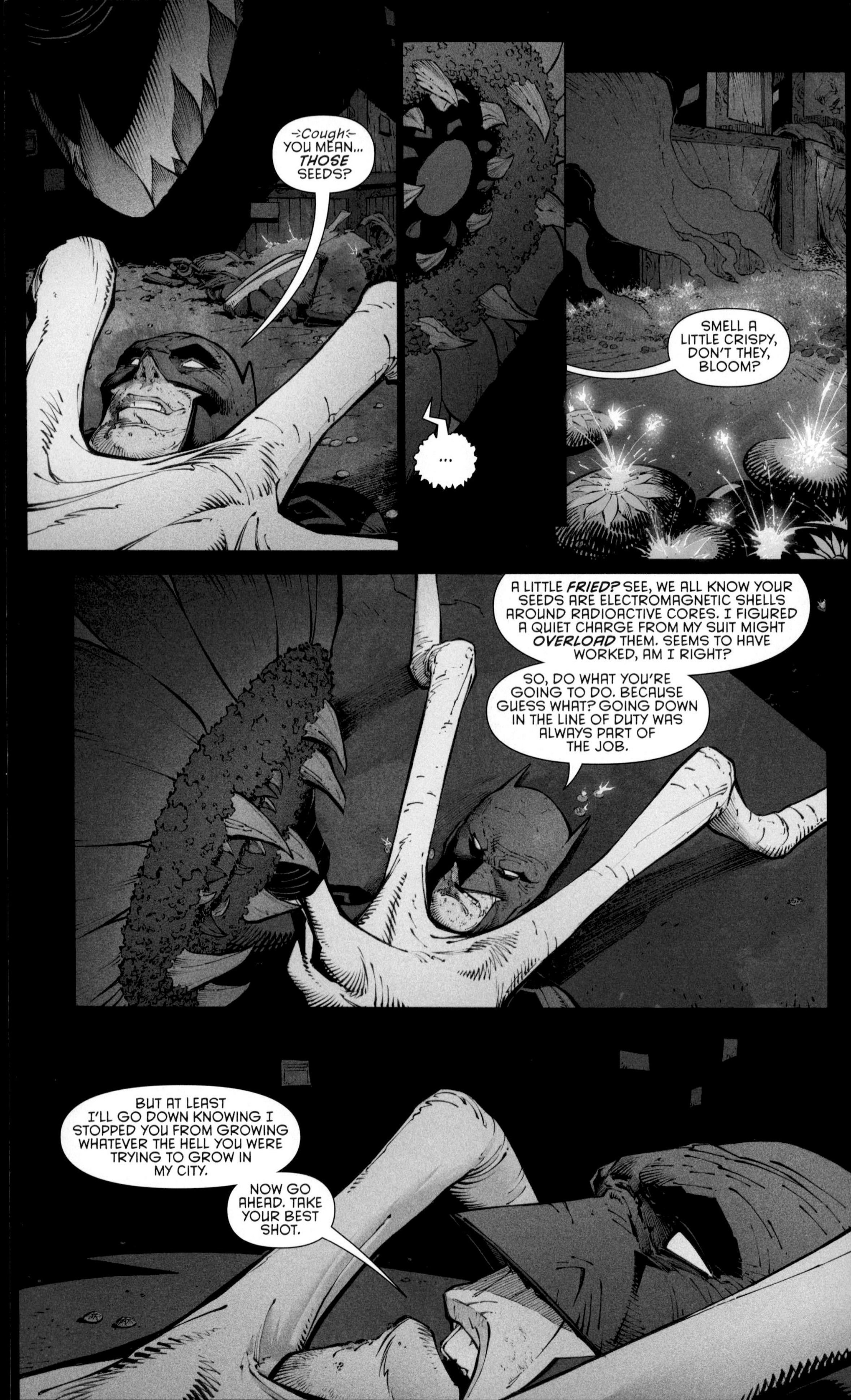

*Cough* YOU MEAN... THOSE SEEDS?
...
SMELL A LITTLE CRISPY, DON'T THEY, BLOOM?
A LITTLE FRIED? SEE, WE ALL KNOW YOUR SEEDS ARE ELECTROMAGNETIC SHELLS AROUND RADIOACTIVE CORES. I FIGURED A QUIET CHARGE FROM MY SUIT MIGHT OVERLOAD THEM. SEEMS TO HAVE WORKED, AM I RIGHT?
SO, DO WHAT YOU'RE GOING TO DO. BECAUSE GUESS WHAT? GOING DOWN IN THE LINE OF DUTY WAS ALWAYS PART OF THE JOB.
BUT AT LEAST I'LL GO DOWN KNOWING I STOPPED YOU FROM GROWING WHATEVER THE HELL YOU WERE TRYING TO GROW IN MY CITY.
NOW GO AHEAD. TAKE YOUR BEST SHOT.

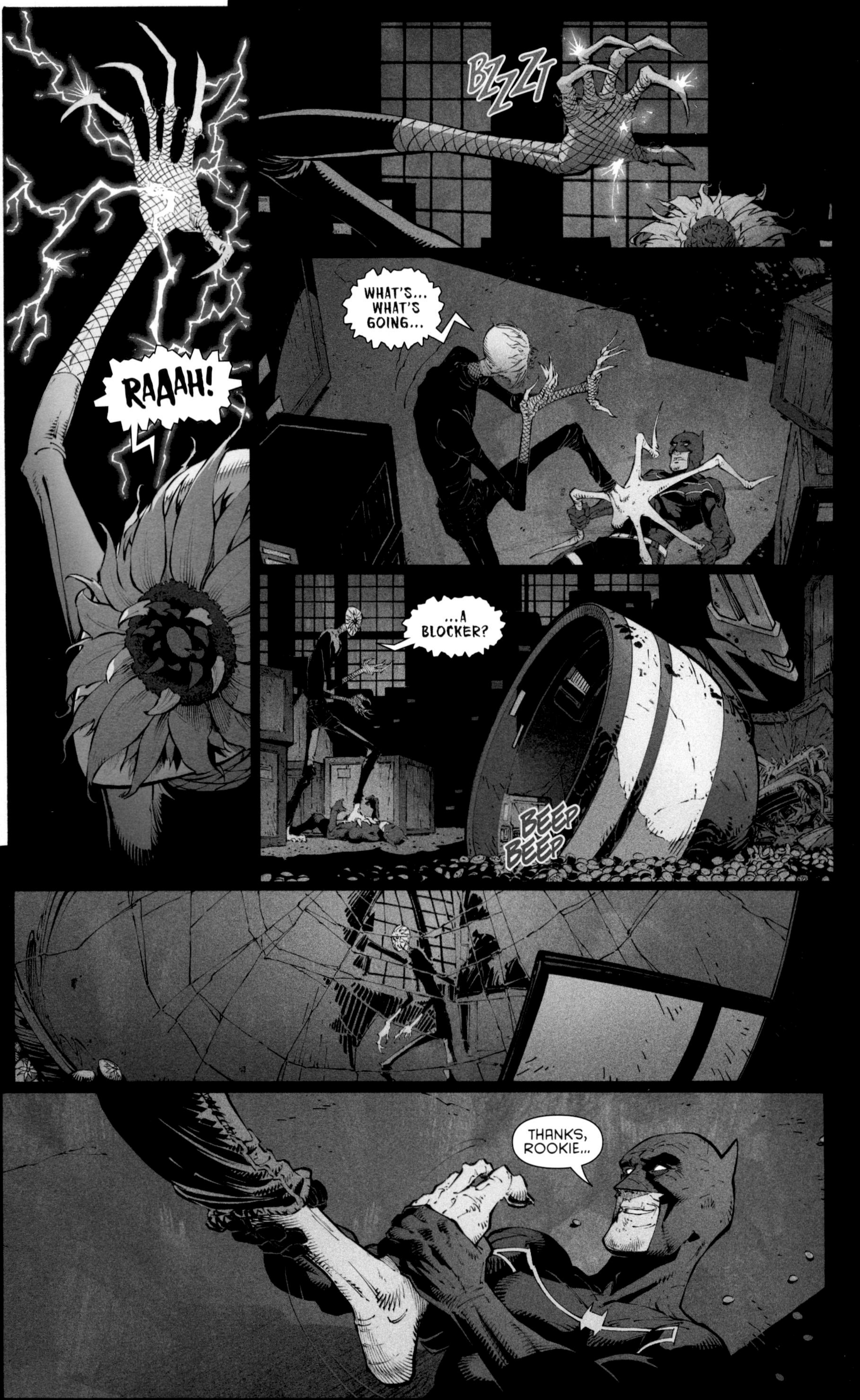
RAAAH!
BZZZT
WHAT'S... WHAT'S GOING...
...A BLOCKER?
BEEP BEEP
THANKS, ROOKIE...

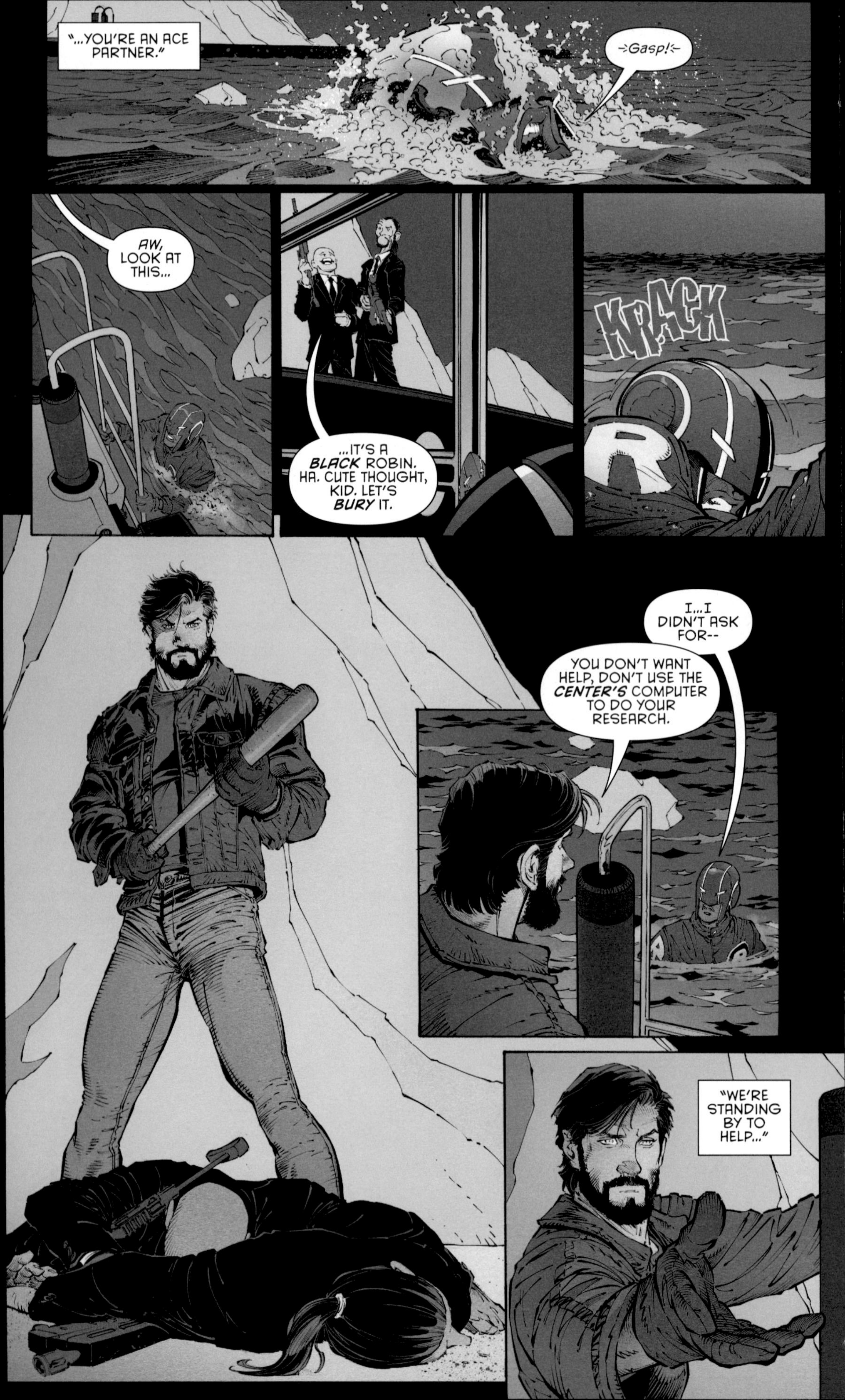
"...YOU'RE AN ACE PARTNER."
-Gasp!-
AW, LOOK AT THIS...
...IT'S A BLACK ROBIN. HA. CUTE THOUGHT, KID. LET'S BURY IT.
KRACK
I...I DIDN'T ASK FOR--
YOU DON'T WANT HELP, DON'T USE THE CENTER'S COMPUTER TO DO YOUR RESEARCH.
"WE'RE STANDING BY TO HELP..."

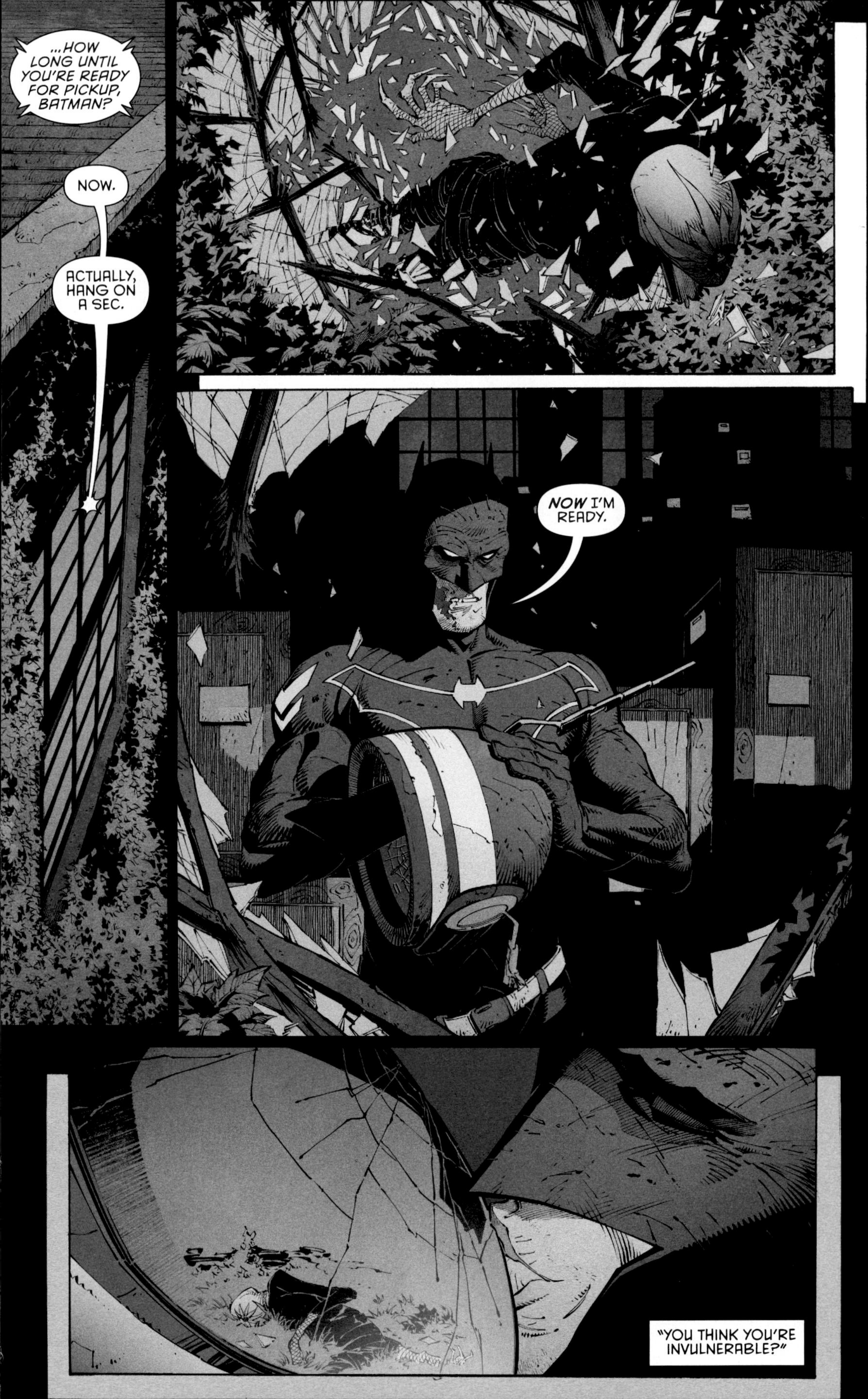
...HOW LONG UNTIL YOU'RE READY FOR PICKUP, BATMAN?
NOW.
ACTUALLY, HANG ON A SEC.
NOW I'M READY.
"YOU THINK YOU'RE INVULNERABLE?"

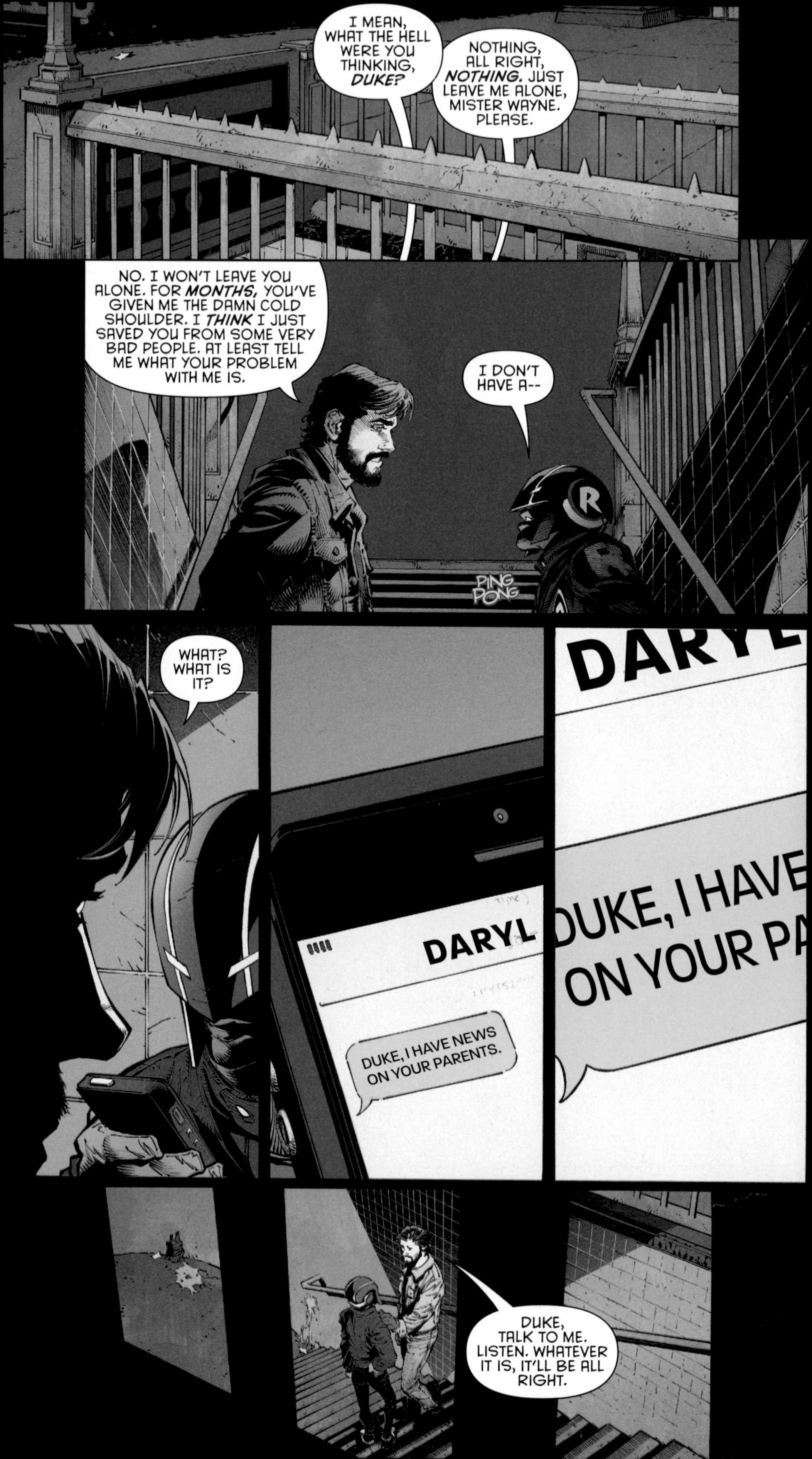
I MEAN, WHAT THE HELL WERE YOU THINKING, DUKE?
NOTHING, ALL RIGHT, NOTHING. JUST LEAVE ME ALONE, MISTER WAYNE. PLEASE.
NO. I WON'T LEAVE YOU ALONE. FOR MONTHS, YOU'VE GIVEN ME THE DAMN COLD SHOULDER. I THINK I JUST SAVED YOU FROM SOME VERY BAD PEOPLE. AT LEAST TELL ME WHAT YOUR PROBLEM WITH ME IS.
I DON'T HAVE A--
PING PONG
WHAT? WHAT IS IT?
DARYL
DUKE, I HAVE NEWS ON YOUR PARENTS.
DARYL
DUKE, I HAVE
ON YOUR PA
DUKE, TALK TO ME. LISTEN. WHATEVER IT IS, IT'LL BE ALL RIGHT.

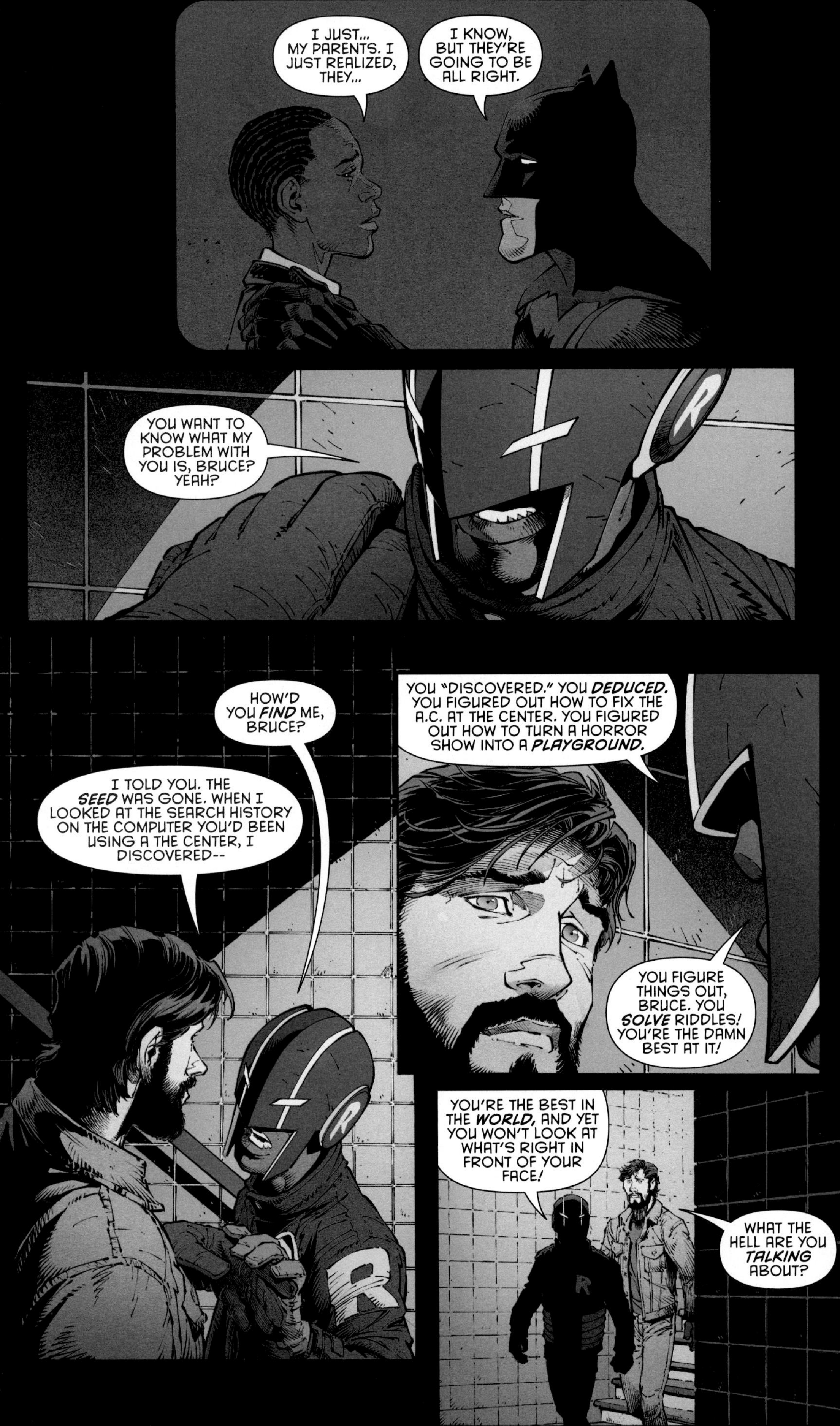

I JUST... MY PARENTS. I JUST REALIZED, THEY...
I KNOW, BUT THEY'RE GOING TO BE ALL RIGHT.
YOU WANT TO KNOW WHAT MY PROBLEM WITH YOU IS, BRUCE? YEAH?
HOW'D YOU FIND ME, BRUCE?
I TOLD YOU. THE SEED WAS GONE. WHEN I LOOKED AT THE SEARCH HISTORY ON THE COMPUTER YOU'D BEEN USING A THE CENTER, I DISCOVERED--
YOU "DISCOVERED." YOU DEDUCED. YOU FIGURED OUT HOW TO FIX THE A.C. AT THE CENTER. YOU FIGURED OUT HOW TO TURN A HORROR SHOW INTO A PLAYGROUND.
YOU FIGURE THINGS OUT, BRUCE. YOU SOLVE RIDDLES! YOU'RE THE DAMN BEST AT IT!
YOU'RE THE BEST IN THE WORLD, AND YET YOU WON'T LOOK AT WHAT'S RIGHT IN FRONT OF YOUR FACE!
WHAT THE HELL ARE YOU TALKING ABOUT?

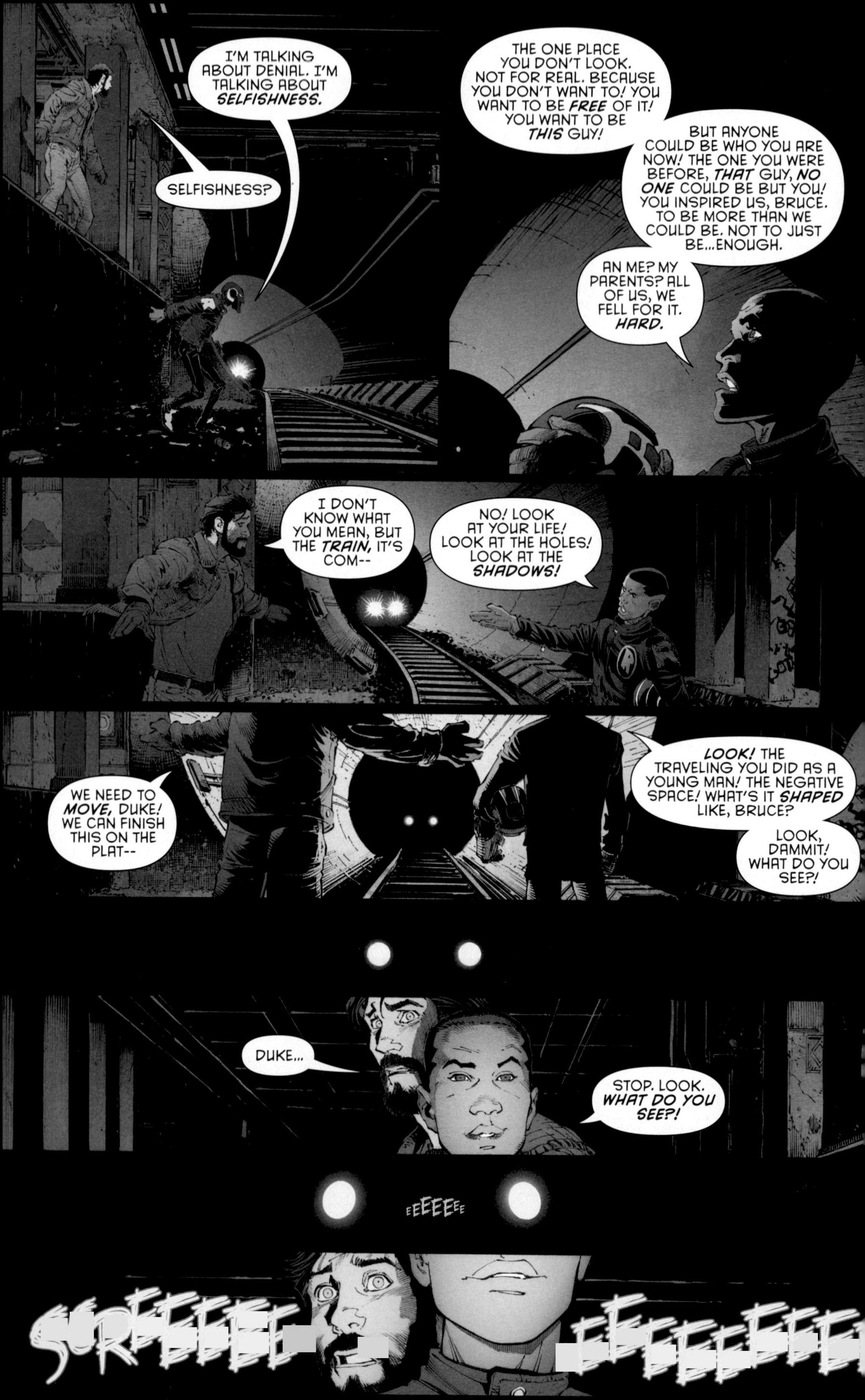
I'M TALKING ABOUT DENIAL. I'M TALKING ABOUT SELFISHNESS.
SELFISHNESS?
THE ONE PLACE YOU DON'T LOOK. NOT FOR REAL. BECAUSE YOU DON'T WANT TO! YOU WANT TO BE FREE OF IT! YOU WANT TO BE THIS GUY!
BUT ANYONE COULD BE WHO YOU ARE NOW! THE ONE YOU WERE BEFORE, THAT GUY, NO ONE COULD BE BUT YOU! YOU INSPIRED US, BRUCE. TO BE MORE THAN WE COULD BE. NOT TO JUST BE...ENOUGH.
AN ME? MY PARENTS? ALL OF US, WE FELL FOR IT. HARD.
I DON'T KNOW WHAT YOU MEAN, BUT THE TRAIN, IT'S COM--
NO! LOOK AT YOUR LIFE! LOOK AT THE HOLES! LOOK AT THE SHADOWS!
WE NEED TO MOVE, DUKE! WE CAN FINISH THIS ON THE PLAT--
LOOK! THE TRAVELING YOU DID AS A YOUNG MAN! THE NEGATIVE SPACE! WHAT'S IT SHAPED LIKE, BRUCE?
LOOK, DAMMIT! WHAT DO YOU SEE?!
DUKE...
STOP. LOOK. WHAT DO YOU SEE?!
eEEEEEe

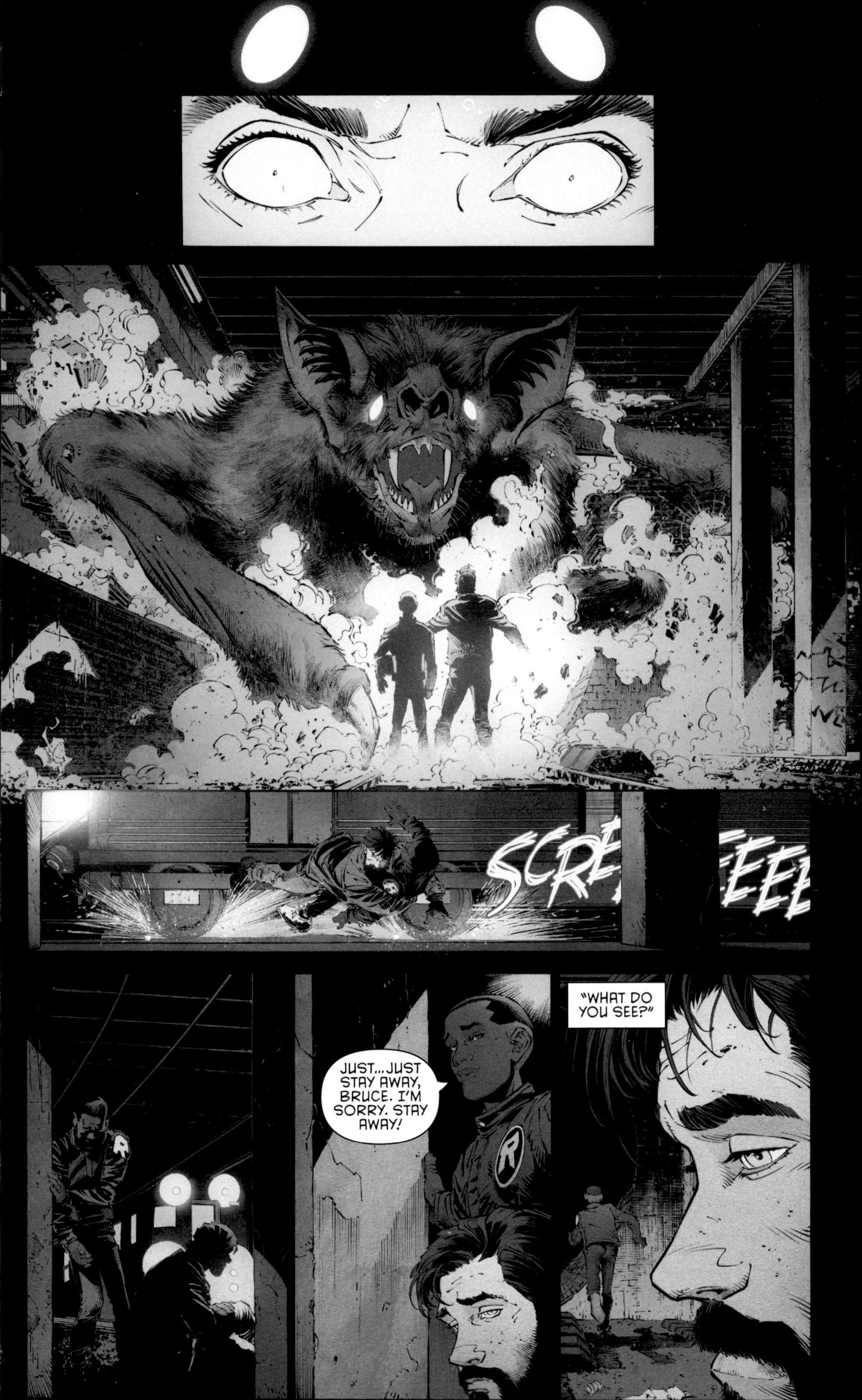
SCREEEEE
"WHAT DO YOU SEE?"
JUST...JUST STAY AWAY, BRUCE. I'M SORRY. STAY AWAY!

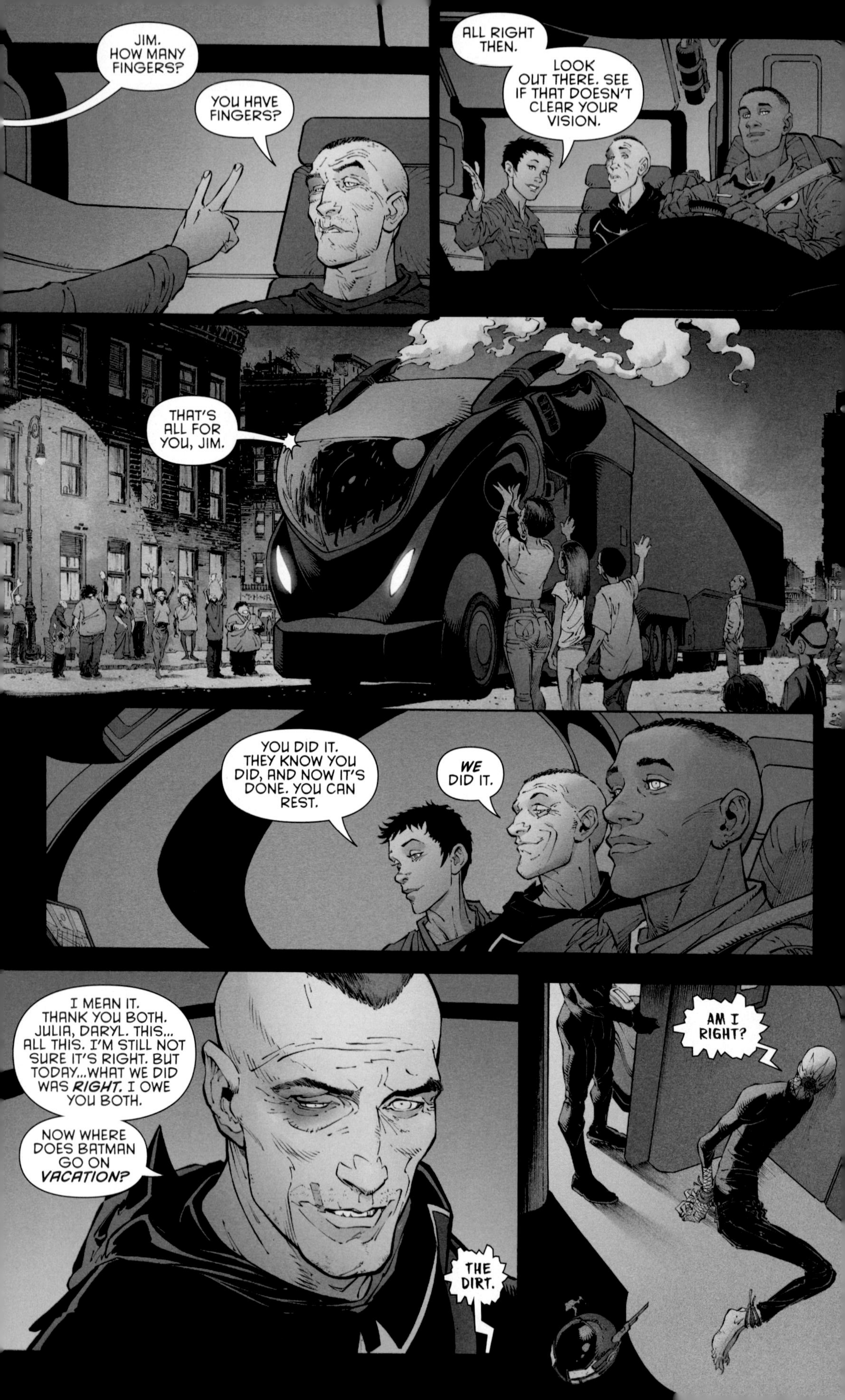
JIM. HOW MANY FINGERS?
YOU HAVE FINGERS?
ALL RIGHT THEN.
LOOK OUT THERE. SEE IF THAT DOESN'T CLEAR YOUR VISION.
THAT'S ALL FOR YOU, JIM.
YOU DID IT. THEY KNOW YOU DID, AND NOW IT'S DONE. YOU CAN REST.
WE DID IT.
I MEAN IT. THANK YOU BOTH. JULIA, DARYL. THIS... ALL THIS. I'M STILL NOT SURE IT'S RIGHT. BUT TODAY...WHAT WE DID WAS RIGHT. I OWE YOU BOTH.
NOW WHERE DOES BATMAN GO ON VACATION?
THE DIRT.
AM I RIGHT?

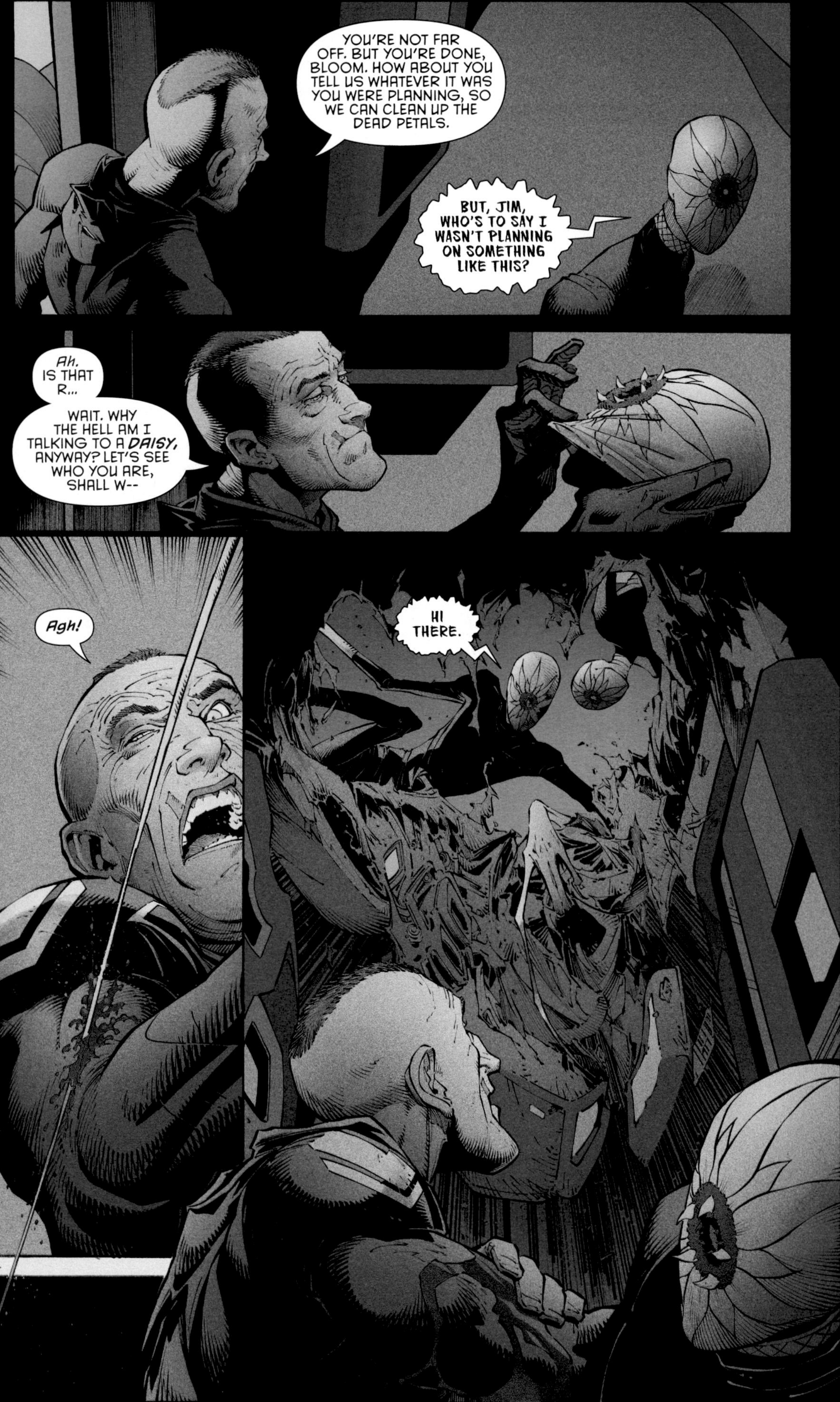
YOU'RE NOT FAR OFF. BUT YOU'RE DONE, BLOOM. HOW ABOUT YOU TELL US WHATEVER IT WAS YOU WERE PLANNING, SO WE CAN CLEAN UP THE DEAD PETALS.
BUT, JIM, WHO'S TO SAY I WASN'T PLANNING ON SOMETHING LIKE THIS?
Ah. IS THAT R...
WAIT. WHY THE HELL AM I TALKING TO A DAISY, ANYWAY? LET'S SEE WHO YOU ARE, SHALL W--
Agh!
HI THERE.

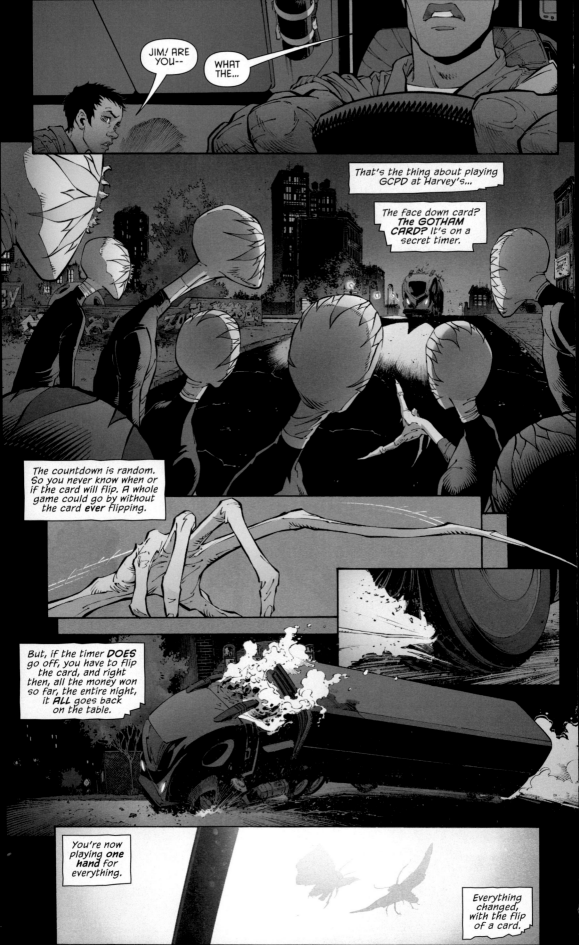

JIM! ARE YOU--

WHAT THE...

That's the thing about playing GCPD at Harvey's...

The face down card? *The GOTHAM CARD?* It's on a secret timer.

The countdown is random. So you never know when or if the card will flip. A whole game could go by without the card *ever* flipping.

But, if the timer *DOES* go off, you have to flip the card, and right then, all the money won so far, the entire night, it *ALL* goes back on the table.

You're now playing *one hand* for everything.

Everything changed, with the flip of a card.

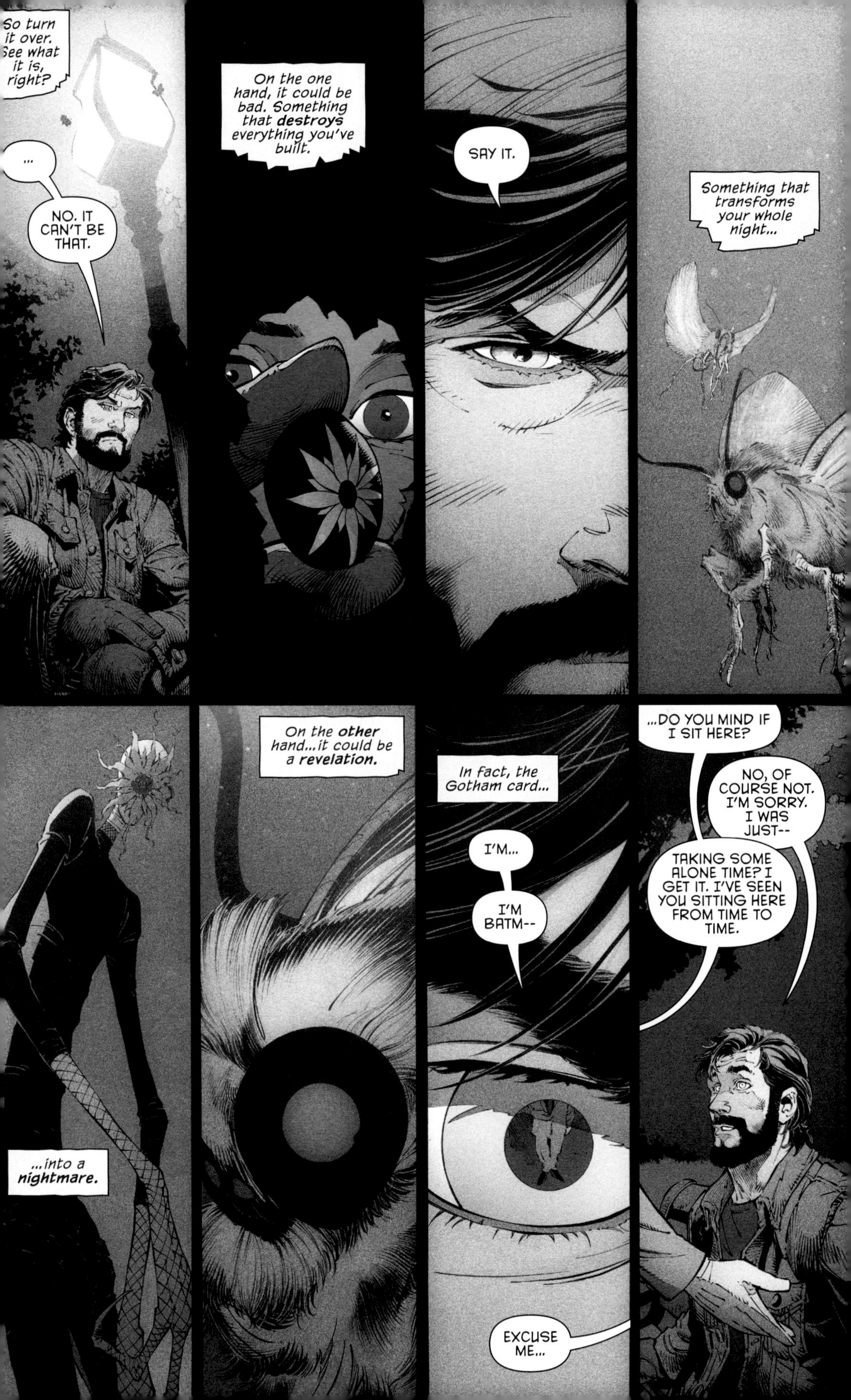
So turn it over. See what it is, right?
...
NO. IT CAN'T BE THAT.
On the one hand, it could be bad. Something that destroys everything you've built.
SAY IT.
Something that transforms your whole night...
...into a nightmare.
On the other hand...it could be a revelation.
In fact, the Gotham card...
I'M...
I'M BATM--
EXCUSE ME...
...DO YOU MIND IF I SIT HERE?
NO, OF COURSE NOT. I'M SORRY. I WAS JUST--
TAKING SOME ALONE TIME? I GET IT. I'VE SEEN YOU SITTING HERE FROM TIME TO TIME.

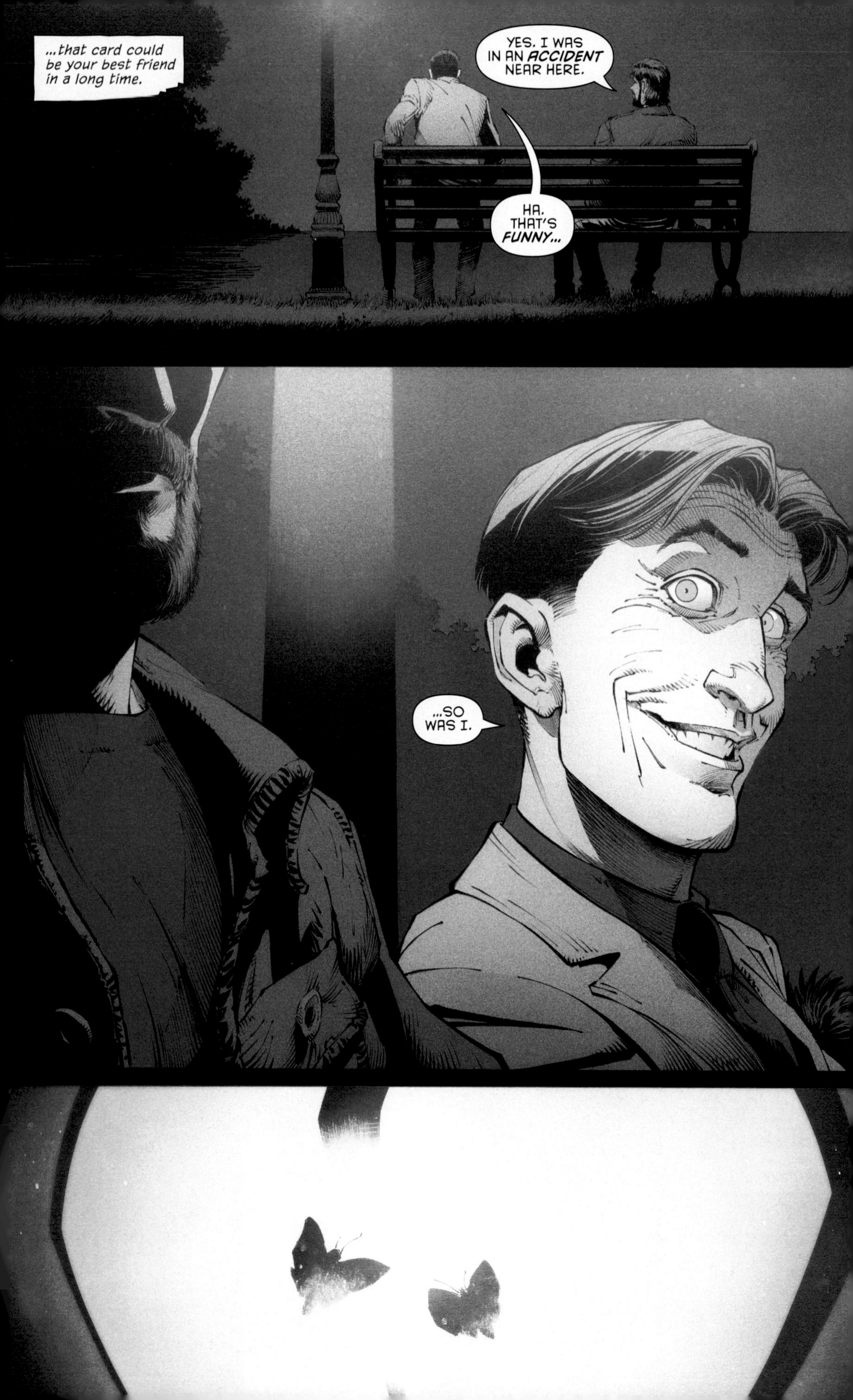
...that card could be your best friend in a long time.
YES. I WAS IN AN ACCIDENT NEAR HERE.
HA. THAT'S FUNNY...
...SO WAS I.

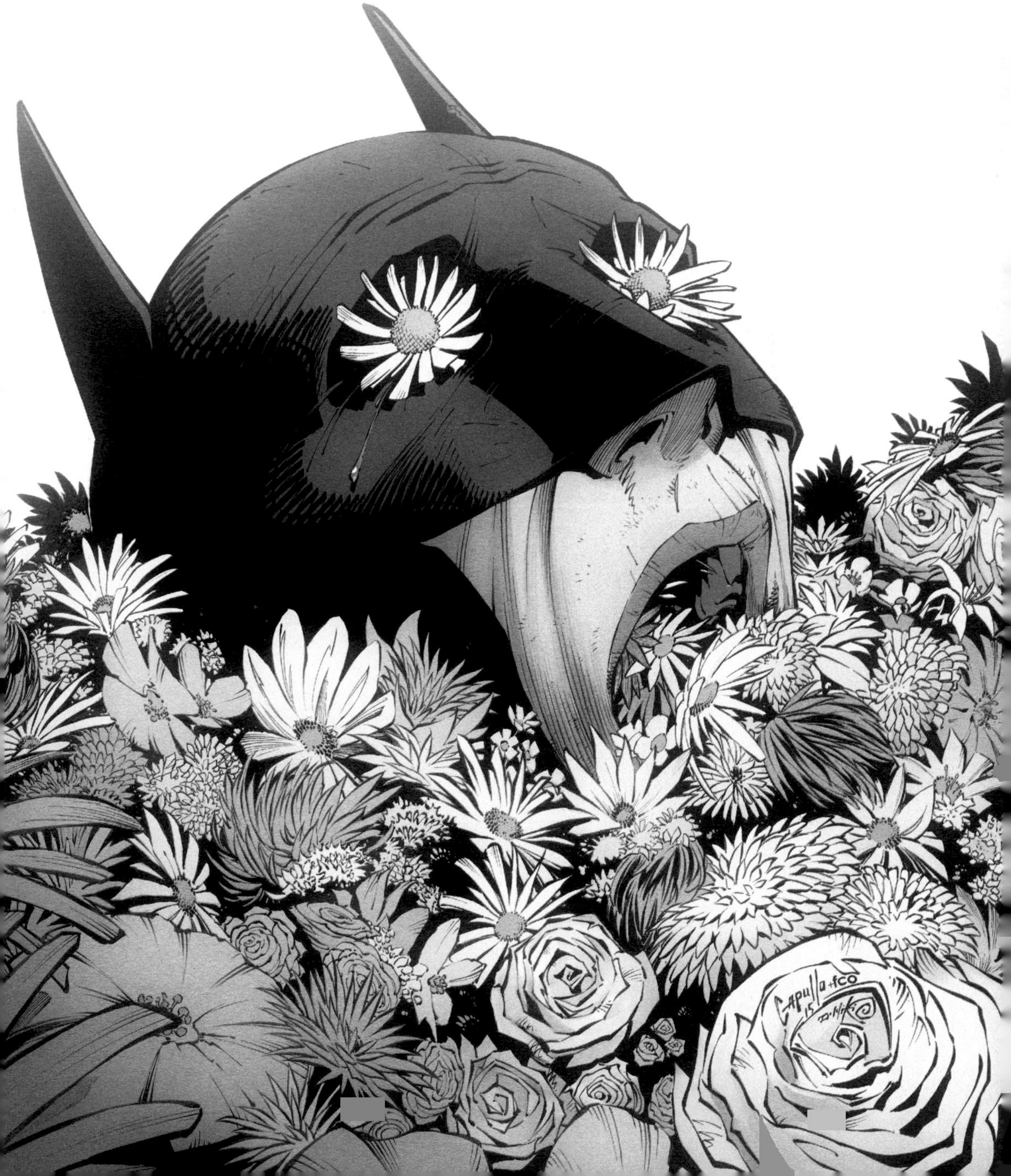

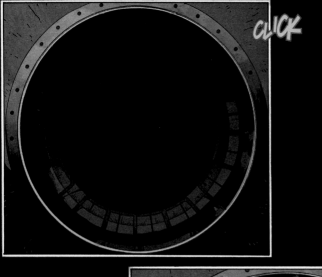

CLICK

CLICK CLICK

"FLOOR TWO, ARE YOU SEEING THIS? IT'S LOADING UP, BUT WITH TOO MUCH PIN--"

"I'M LOOKING RIGHT NOW! IT'S RUNNING TOO HOT. LIKE SOMETHING IS *FEEDING* IT... THE READINGS SUGGEST A STRANEGELT, OR EVEN A QUARK STAR, BUT THAT'S COMPLETELY OUT OF--"

CLICK

"GET IT OFFLINE!"

"BUT--"

"*RIGHT NOW...*"

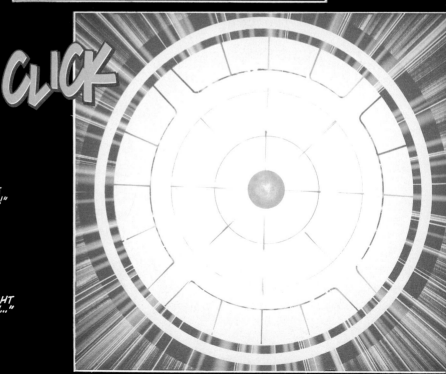

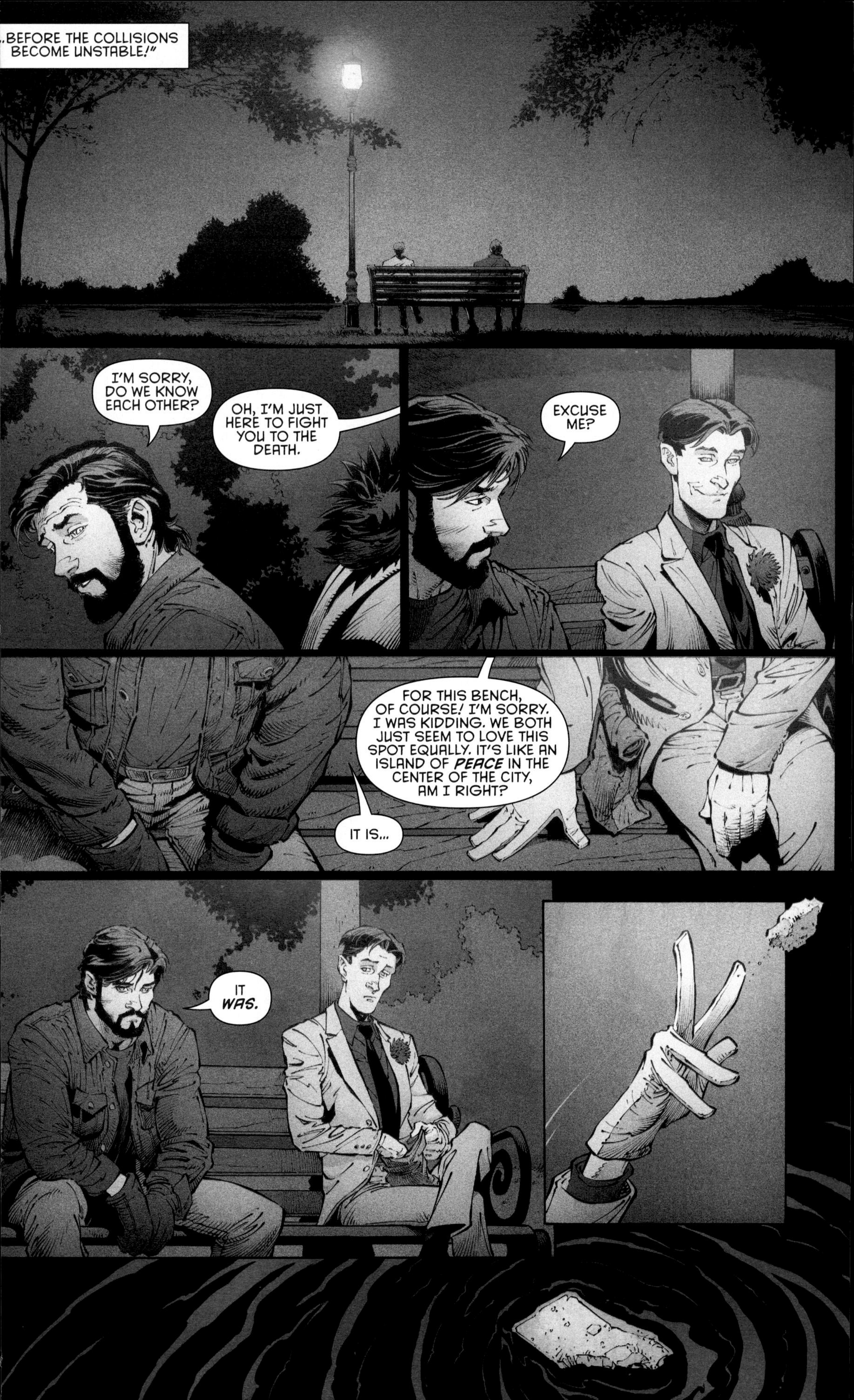

...BEFORE THE COLLISIONS BECOME UNSTABLE!"
I'M SORRY, DO WE KNOW EACH OTHER?
OH, I'M JUST HERE TO FIGHT YOU TO THE DEATH.
EXCUSE ME?
FOR THIS BENCH, OF COURSE! I'M SORRY. I WAS KIDDING. WE BOTH JUST SEEM TO LOVE THIS SPOT EQUALLY. IT'S LIKE AN ISLAND OF *PEACE* IN THE CENTER OF THE CITY, AM I RIGHT?
IT IS...
IT *WAS.*

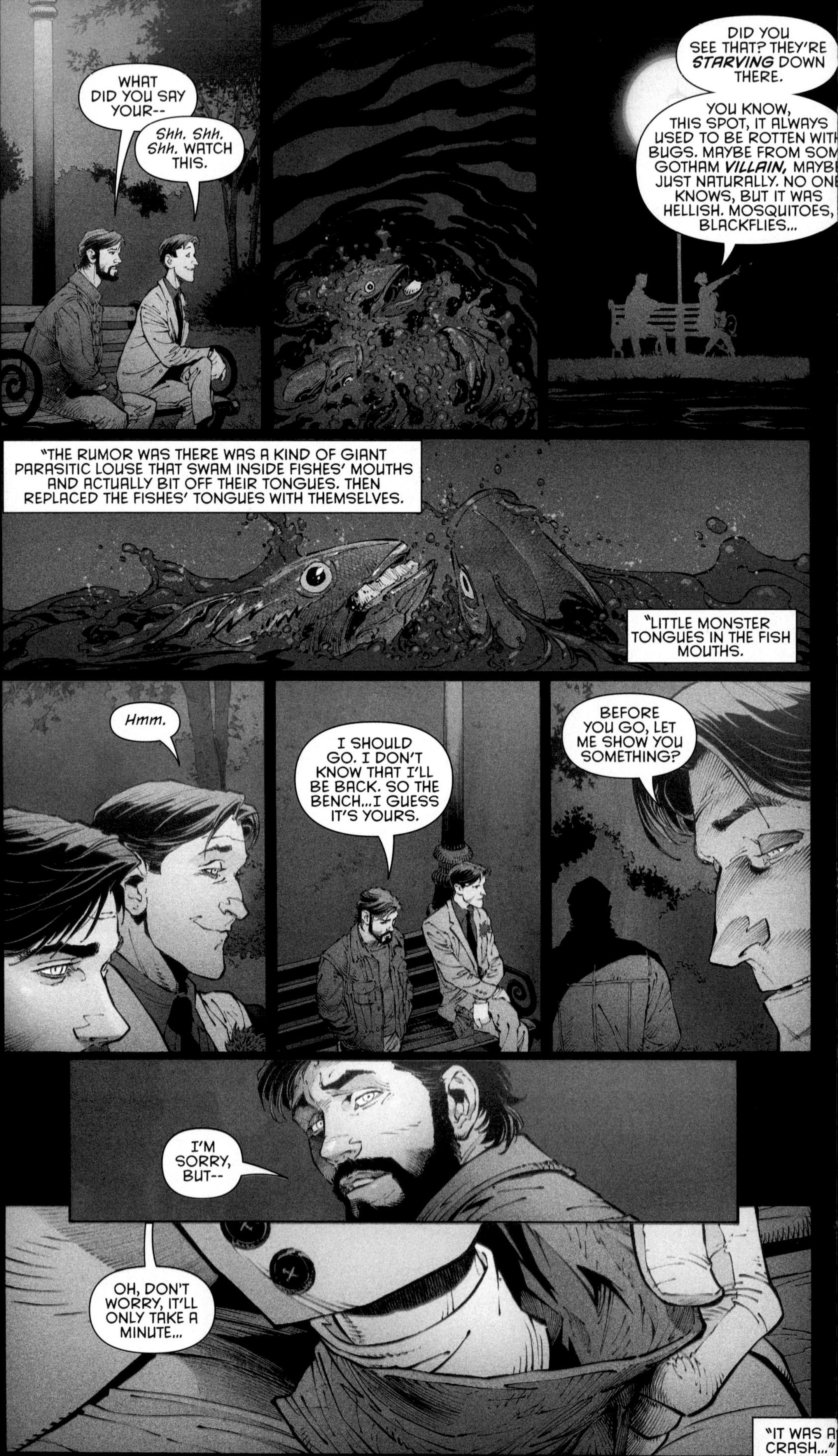
WHAT DID YOU SAY YOUR--
Shh. Shh. Shh. WATCH THIS.
DID YOU SEE THAT? THEY'RE STARVING DOWN THERE.
YOU KNOW, THIS SPOT, IT ALWAYS USED TO BE ROTTEN WITH BUGS. MAYBE FROM SOME GOTHAM VILLAIN, MAYBE JUST NATURALLY. NO ONE KNOWS, BUT IT WAS HELLISH. MOSQUITOES, BLACKFLIES...
"THE RUMOR WAS THERE WAS A KIND OF GIANT PARASITIC LOUSE THAT SWAM INSIDE FISHES' MOUTHS AND ACTUALLY BIT OFF THEIR TONGUES. THEN REPLACED THE FISHES' TONGUES WITH THEMSELVES.
"LITTLE MONSTER TONGUES IN THE FISH MOUTHS.
Hmm.
I SHOULD GO. I DON'T KNOW THAT I'LL BE BACK. SO THE BENCH...I GUESS IT'S YOURS.
BEFORE YOU GO, LET ME SHOW YOU SOMETHING?
I'M SORRY, BUT--
OH, DON'T WORRY, IT'LL ONLY TAKE A MINUTE...
"IT WAS A CRASH..."

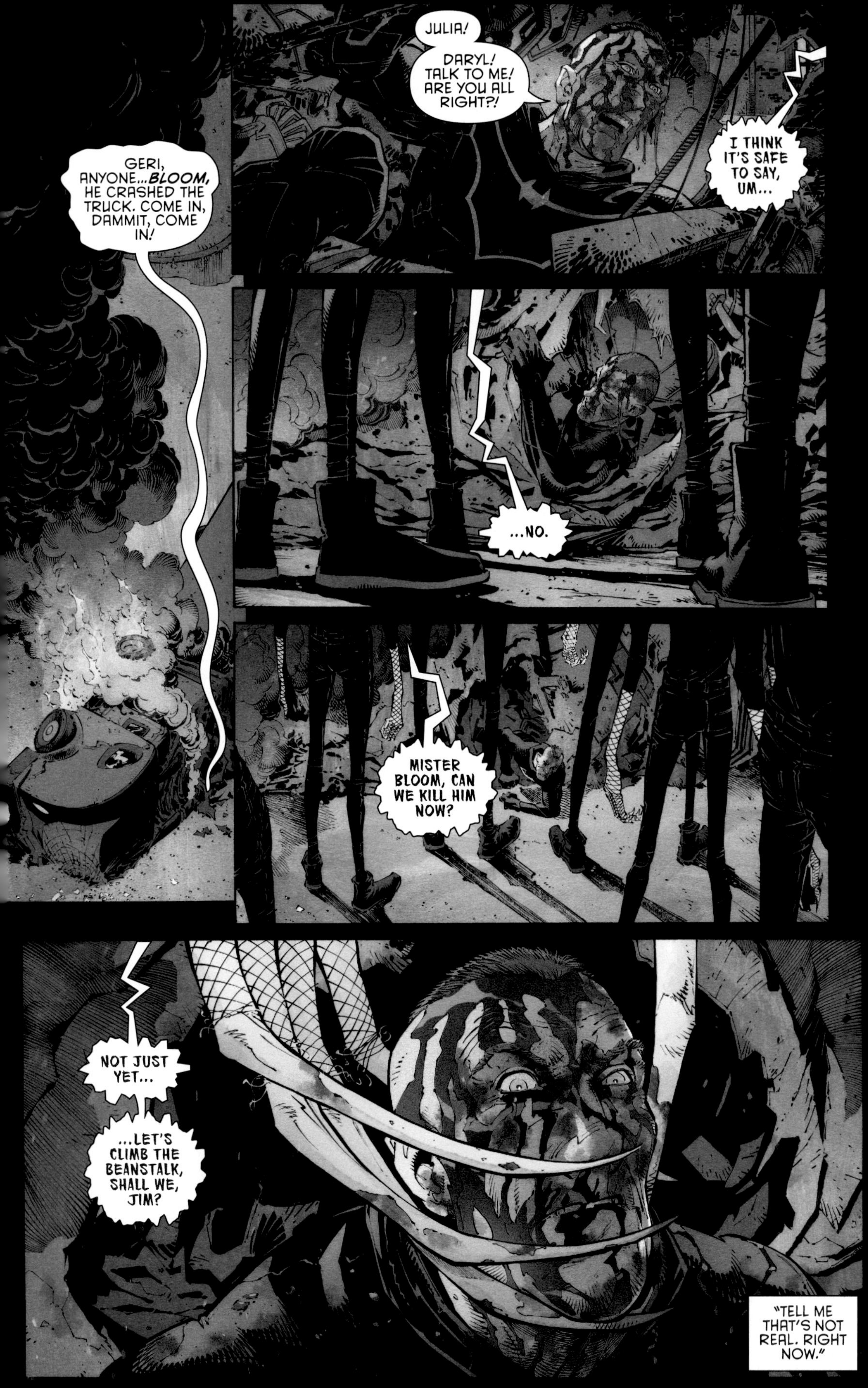
JULIA!
DARYL! TALK TO ME! ARE YOU ALL RIGHT?!
I THINK IT'S SAFE TO SAY, UM...
GERI, ANYONE...BLOOM, HE CRASHED THE TRUCK. COME IN, DAMMIT, COME IN!
...NO.
MISTER BLOOM, CAN WE KILL HIM NOW?
NOT JUST YET...
...LET'S CLIMB THE BEANSTALK, SHALL WE, JIM?
"TELL ME THAT'S NOT REAL. RIGHT NOW."

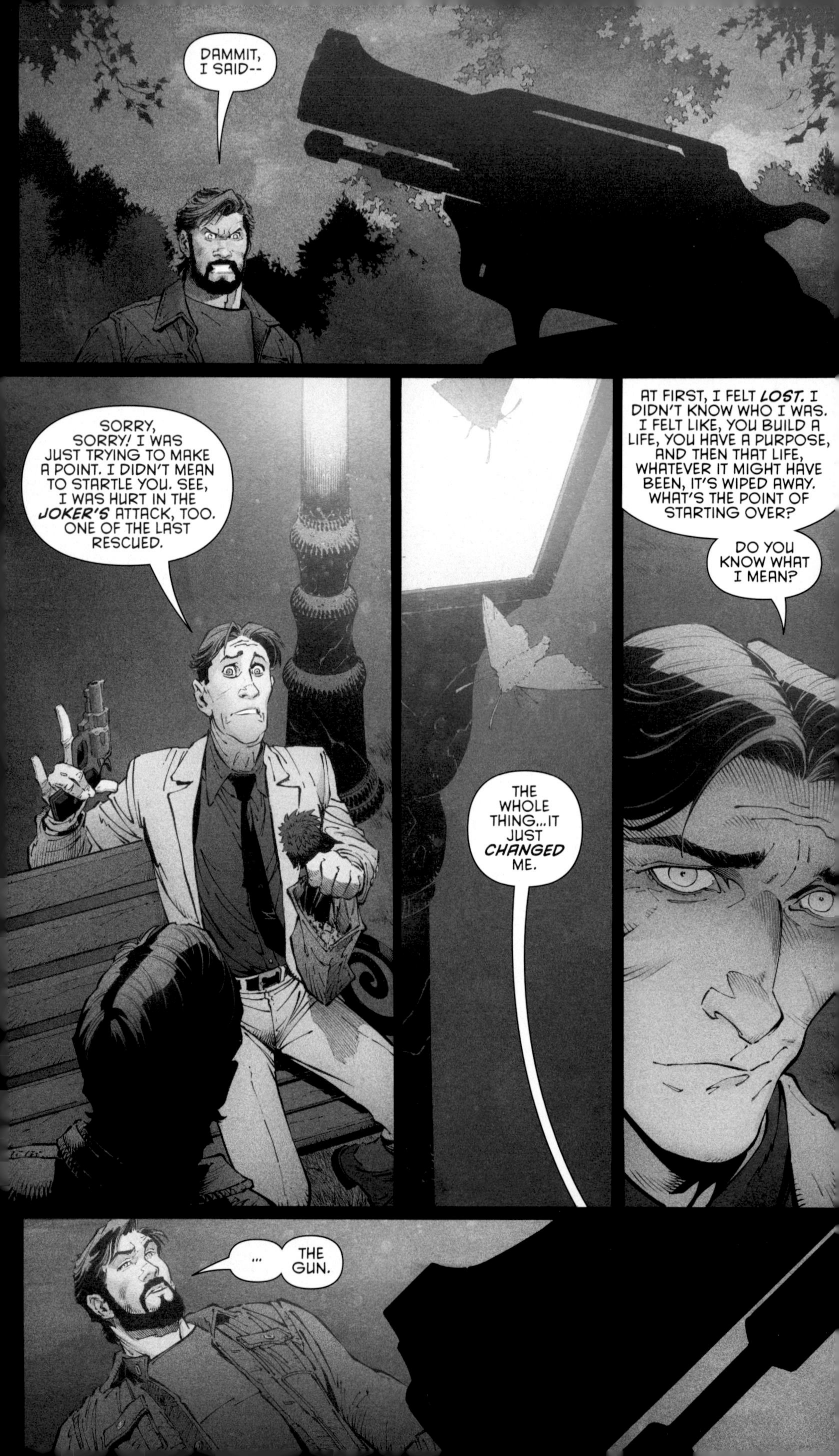
DAMMIT, I SAID--
SORRY, SORRY! I WAS JUST TRYING TO MAKE A POINT. I DIDN'T MEAN TO STARTLE YOU. SEE, I WAS HURT IN THE **JOKER'S** ATTACK, TOO. ONE OF THE LAST RESCUED.
THE WHOLE THING...IT JUST **CHANGED** ME.
AT FIRST, I FELT **LOST.** I DIDN'T KNOW WHO I WAS. I FELT LIKE, YOU BUILD A LIFE, YOU HAVE A PURPOSE, AND THEN THAT LIFE, WHATEVER IT MIGHT HAVE BEEN, IT'S WIPED AWAY. WHAT'S THE POINT OF STARTING OVER?
DO YOU KNOW WHAT I MEAN?
...
THE GUN.

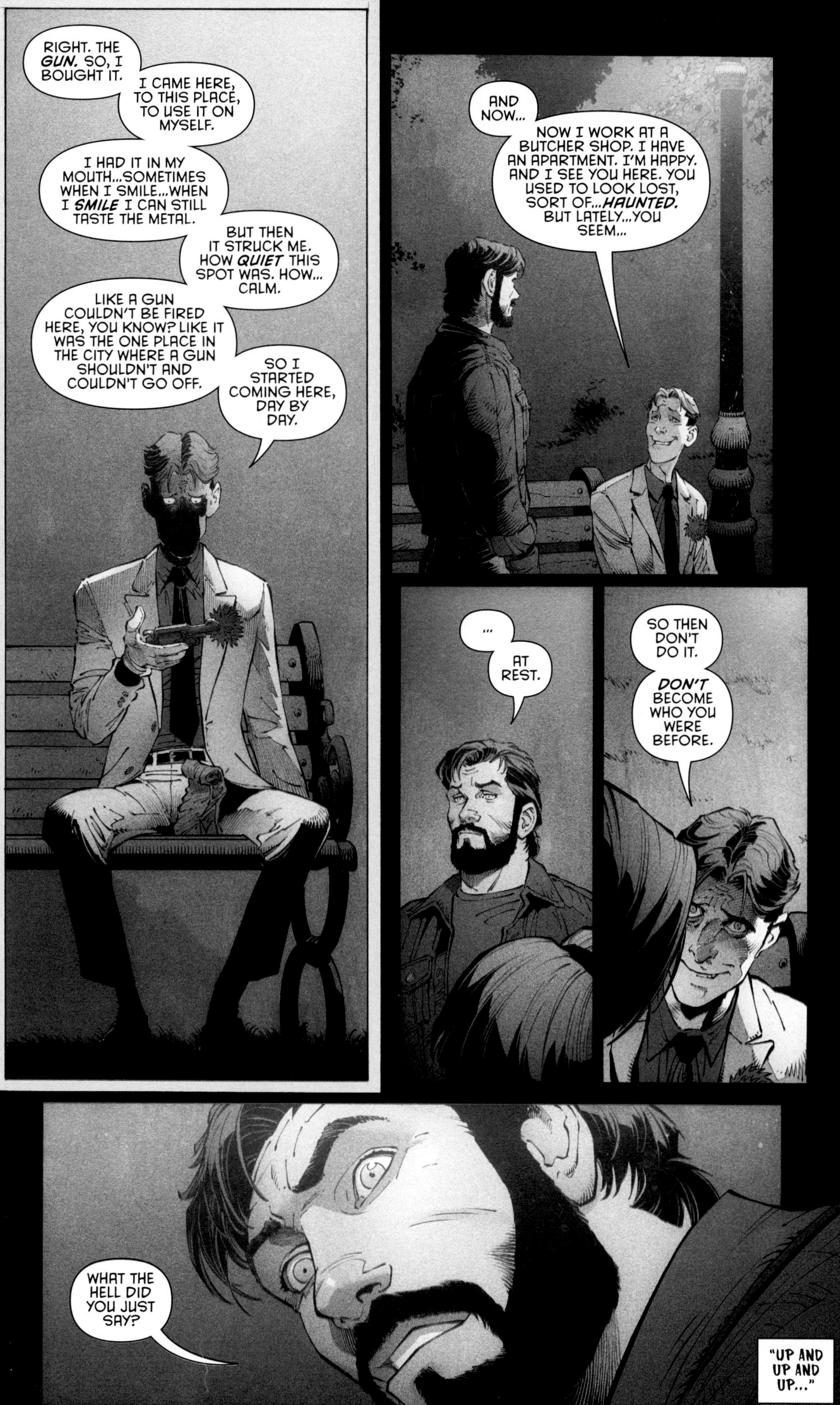
RIGHT. THE GUN. SO, I BOUGHT IT.
I CAME HERE, TO THIS PLACE, TO USE IT ON MYSELF.
I HAD IT IN MY MOUTH...SOMETIMES WHEN I SMILE...WHEN I SMILE I CAN STILL TASTE THE METAL.
BUT THEN IT STRUCK ME. HOW QUIET THIS SPOT WAS. HOW... CALM.
LIKE A GUN COULDN'T BE FIRED HERE, YOU KNOW? LIKE IT WAS THE ONE PLACE IN THE CITY WHERE A GUN SHOULDN'T AND COULDN'T GO OFF.
SO I STARTED COMING HERE, DAY BY DAY.
AND NOW...
NOW I WORK AT A BUTCHER SHOP. I HAVE AN APARTMENT. I'M HAPPY. AND I SEE YOU HERE. YOU USED TO LOOK LOST, SORT OF...HAUNTED. BUT LATELY...YOU SEEM...
...
AT REST.
SO THEN DON'T DO IT.
DON'T BECOME WHO YOU WERE BEFORE.
WHAT THE HELL DID YOU JUST SAY?
"UP AND UP AND UP..."

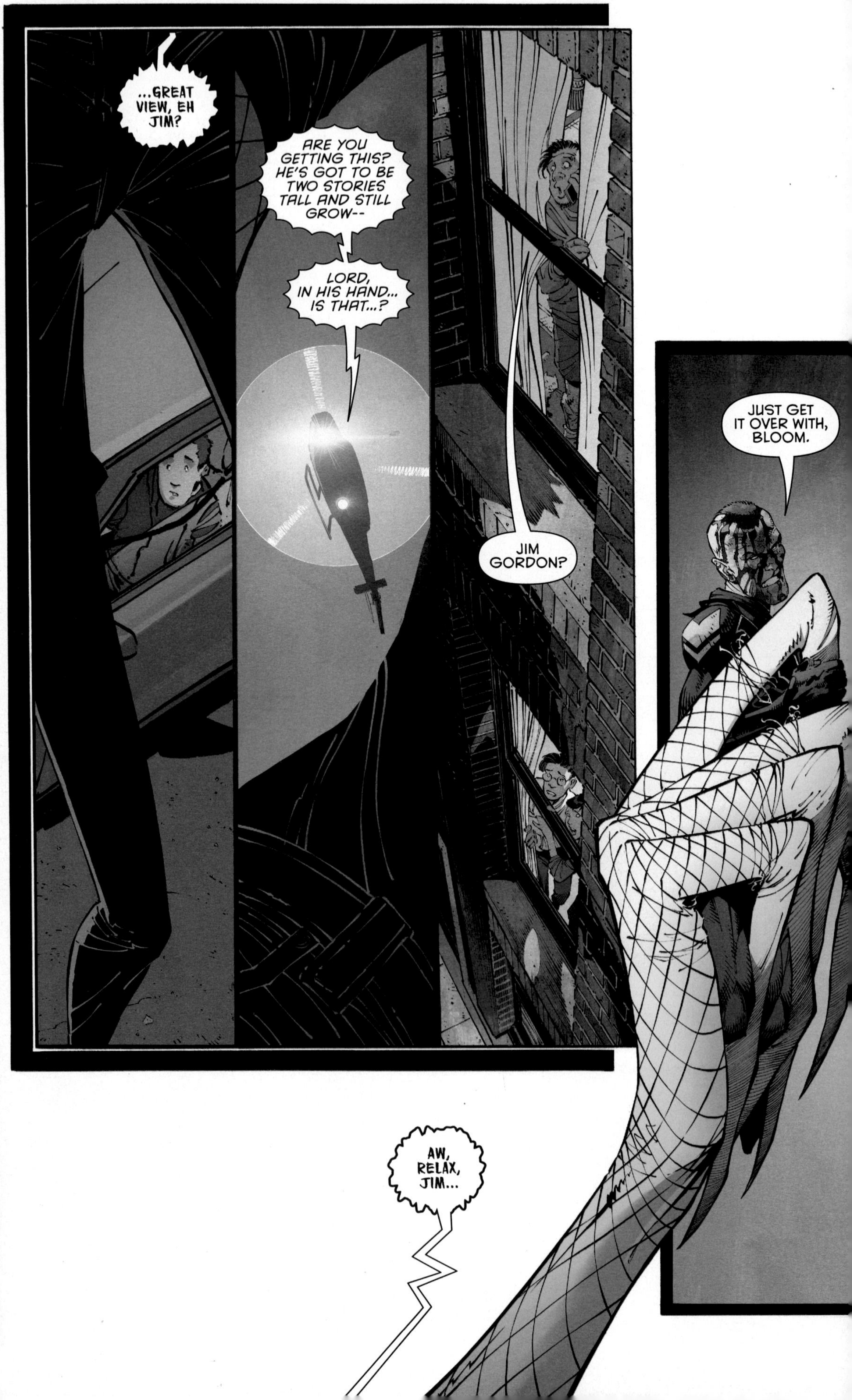
...GREAT VIEW, EH JIM?
ARE YOU GETTING THIS? HE'S GOT TO BE TWO STORIES TALL AND STILL GROW--
LORD, IN HIS HAND... IS THAT...?
JIM GORDON?
JUST GET IT OVER WITH, BLOOM.
AW, RELAX, JIM...

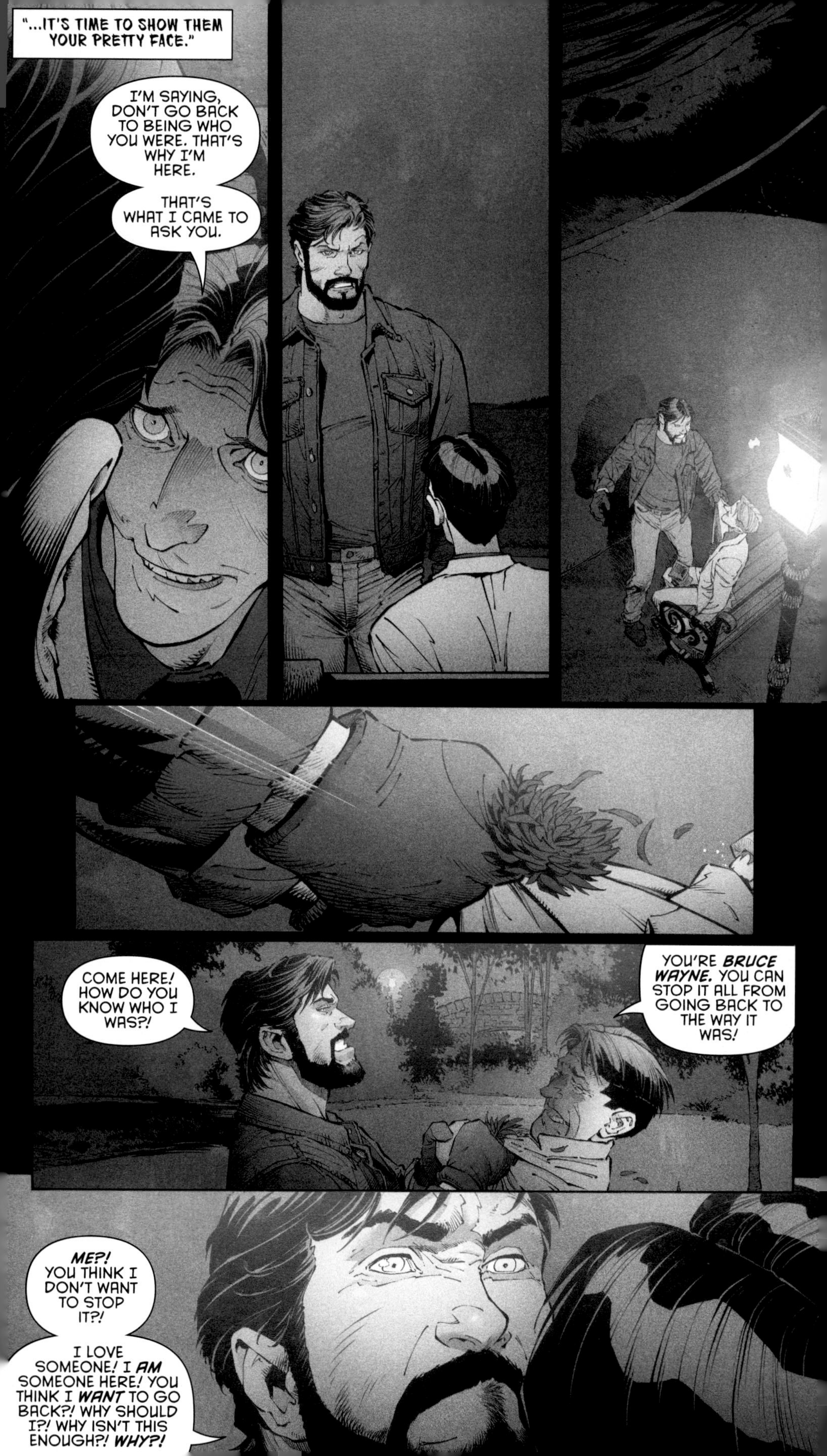

"...IT'S TIME TO SHOW THEM YOUR PRETTY FACE."
I'M SAYING, DON'T GO BACK TO BEING WHO YOU WERE. THAT'S WHY I'M HERE.
THAT'S WHAT I CAME TO ASK YOU.
COME HERE! HOW DO YOU KNOW WHO I WAS?!
YOU'RE *BRUCE WAYNE.* YOU CAN STOP IT ALL FROM GOING BACK TO THE WAY IT WAS!
*ME?!* YOU THINK I DON'T WANT TO STOP IT?!
I LOVE SOMEONE! I *AM* SOMEONE HERE! YOU THINK I *WANT* TO GO BACK?! WHY SHOULD I?! WHY ISN'T THIS ENOUGH?! *WHY?!*

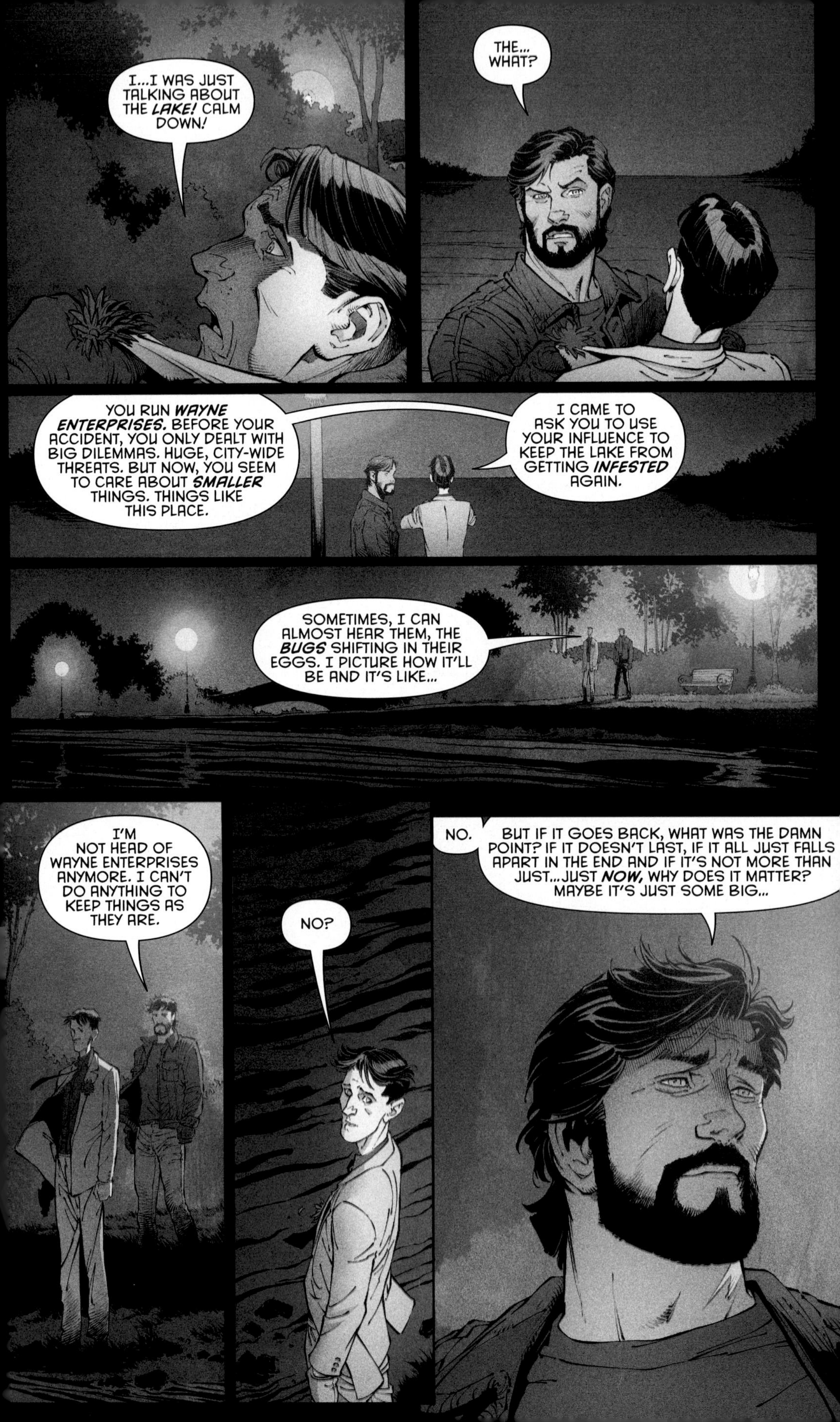
I...I WAS JUST TALKING ABOUT THE LAKE! CALM DOWN!
THE... WHAT?
YOU RUN WAYNE ENTERPRISES. BEFORE YOUR ACCIDENT, YOU ONLY DEALT WITH BIG DILEMMAS. HUGE, CITY-WIDE THREATS. BUT NOW, YOU SEEM TO CARE ABOUT SMALLER THINGS. THINGS LIKE THIS PLACE.
I CAME TO ASK YOU TO USE YOUR INFLUENCE TO KEEP THE LAKE FROM GETTING INFESTED AGAIN.
SOMETIMES, I CAN ALMOST HEAR THEM, THE BUGS SHIFTING IN THEIR EGGS. I PICTURE HOW IT'LL BE AND IT'S LIKE...
I'M NOT HEAD OF WAYNE ENTERPRISES ANYMORE. I CAN'T DO ANYTHING TO KEEP THINGS AS THEY ARE.
NO?
NO.
BUT IF IT GOES BACK, WHAT WAS THE DAMN POINT? IF IT DOESN'T LAST, IF IT ALL JUST FALLS APART IN THE END AND IF IT'S NOT MORE THAN JUST...JUST NOW, WHY DOES IT MATTER? MAYBE IT'S JUST SOME BIG...

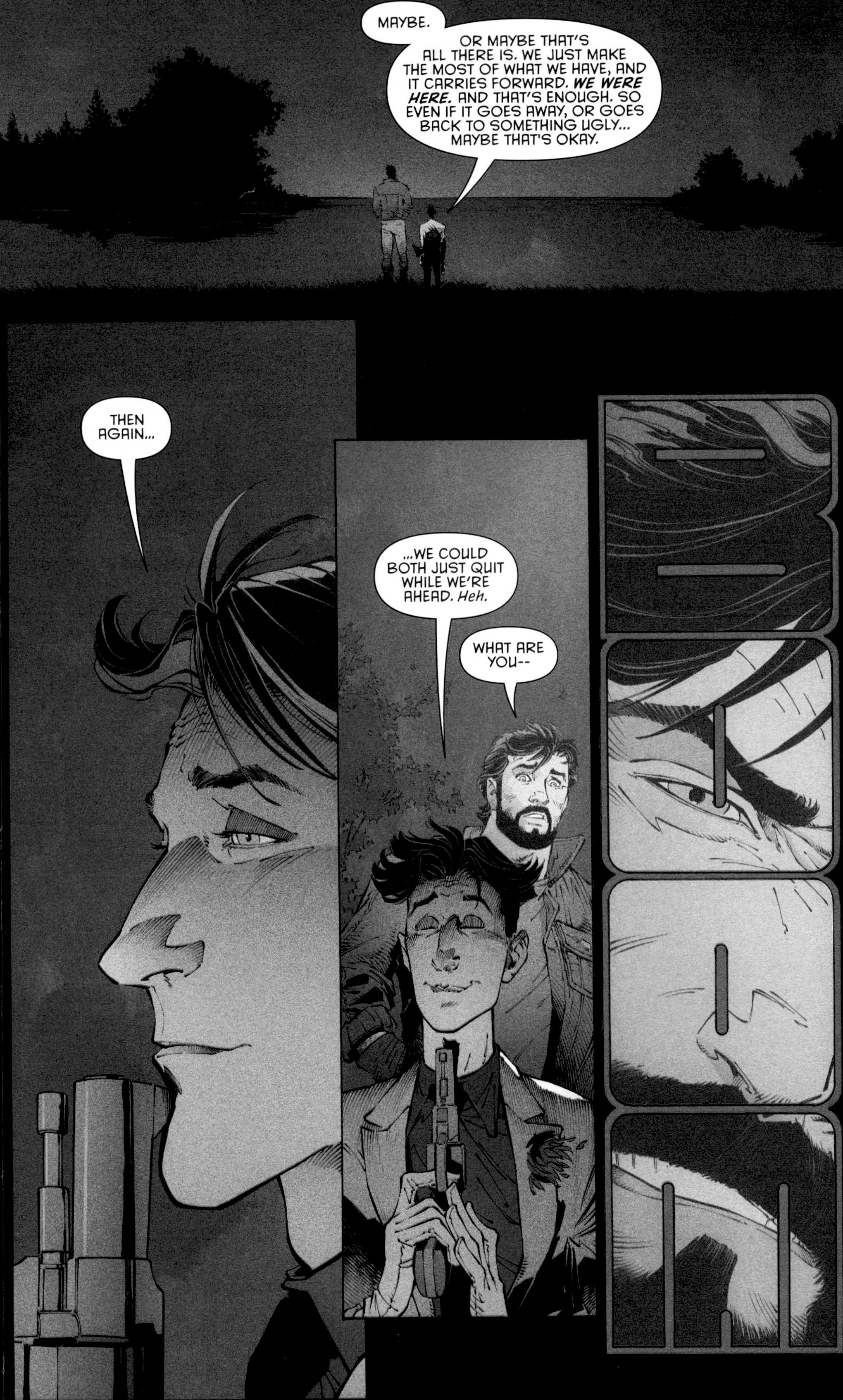
MAYBE.
OR MAYBE THAT'S ALL THERE IS. WE JUST MAKE THE MOST OF WHAT WE HAVE, AND IT CARRIES FORWARD. ***WE WERE HERE.*** AND THAT'S ENOUGH. SO EVEN IF IT GOES AWAY, OR GOES BACK TO SOMETHING UGLY... MAYBE THAT'S OKAY.
THEN AGAIN...
...WE COULD BOTH JUST QUIT WHILE WE'RE AHEAD. *Heh.*
WHAT ARE YOU--

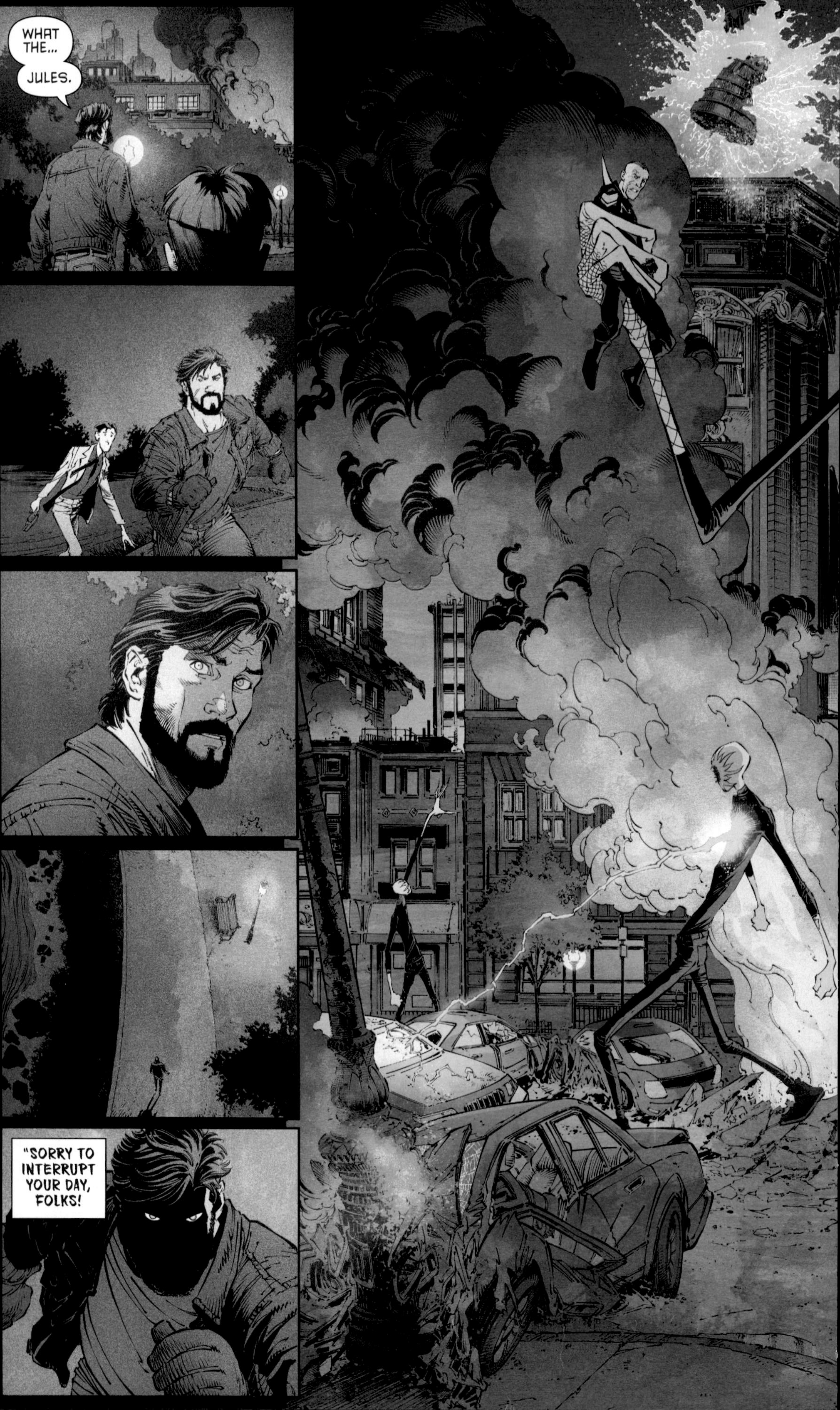
WHAT THE...
JULES.
"SORRY TO INTERRUPT YOUR DAY, FOLKS!

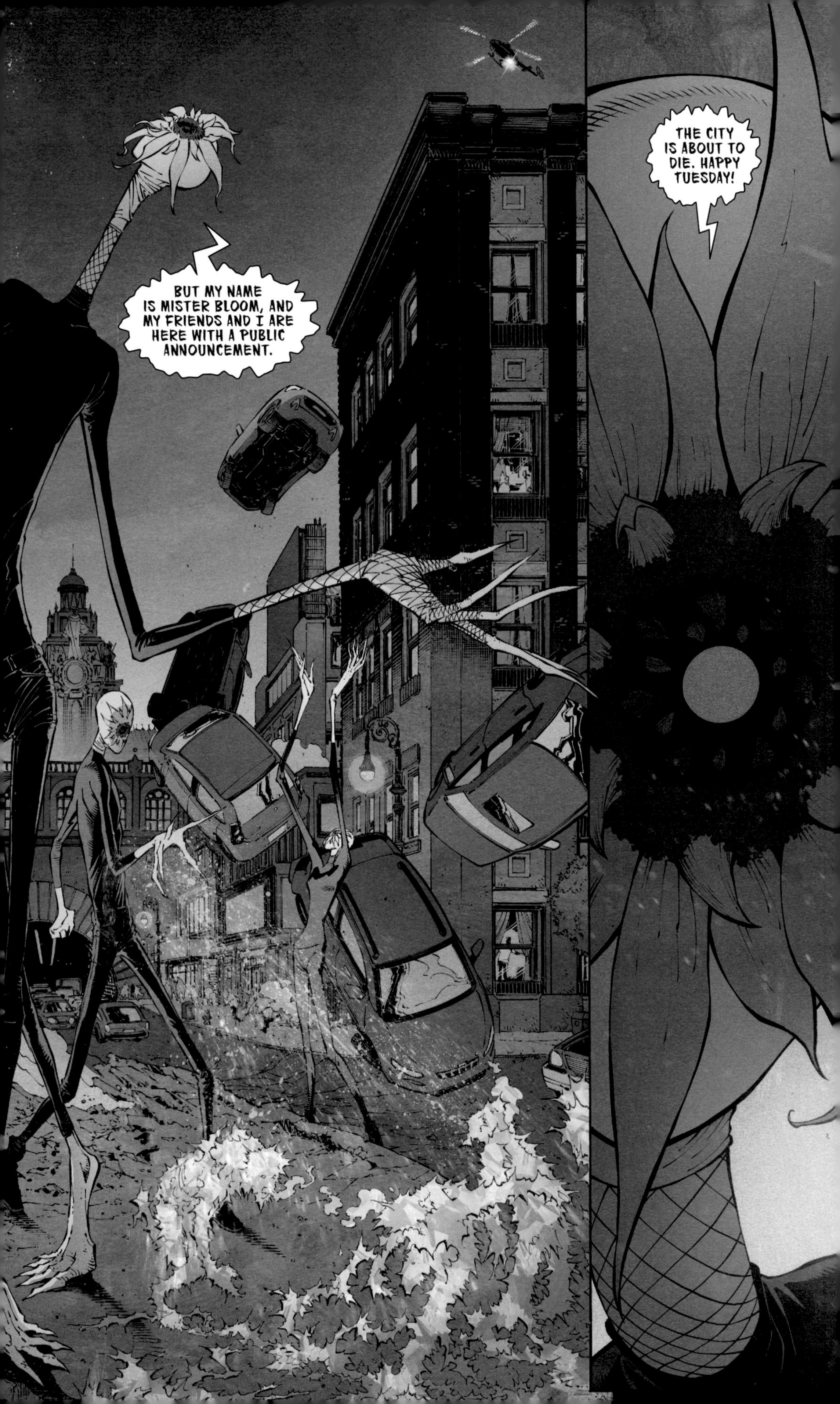
BUT MY NAME IS MISTER BLOOM, AND MY FRIENDS AND I ARE HERE WITH A PUBLIC ANNOUNCEMENT.
THE CITY IS ABOUT TO DIE. HAPPY TUESDAY!

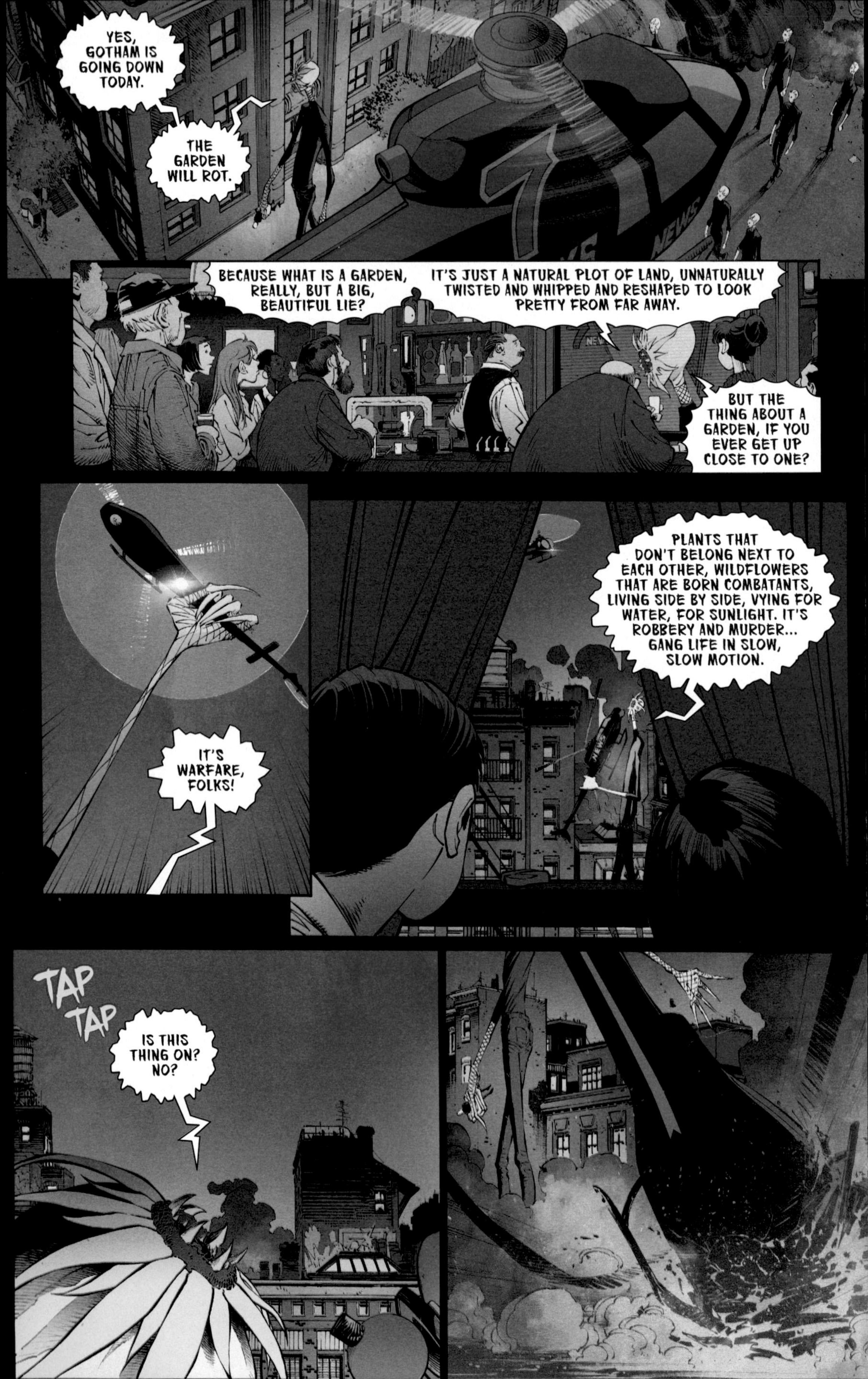
YES, GOTHAM IS GOING DOWN TODAY.
THE GARDEN WILL ROT.
BECAUSE WHAT IS A GARDEN, REALLY, BUT A BIG, BEAUTIFUL LIE?
IT'S JUST A NATURAL PLOT OF LAND, UNNATURALLY TWISTED AND WHIPPED AND RESHAPED TO LOOK PRETTY FROM FAR AWAY.
BUT THE THING ABOUT A GARDEN, IF YOU EVER GET UP CLOSE TO ONE?
IT'S WARFARE, FOLKS!
PLANTS THAT DON'T BELONG NEXT TO EACH OTHER, WILDFLOWERS THAT ARE BORN COMBATANTS, LIVING SIDE BY SIDE, VYING FOR WATER, FOR SUNLIGHT. IT'S ROBBERY AND MURDER... GANG LIFE IN SLOW, SLOW MOTION.
TAP TAP
IS THIS THING ON? NO?

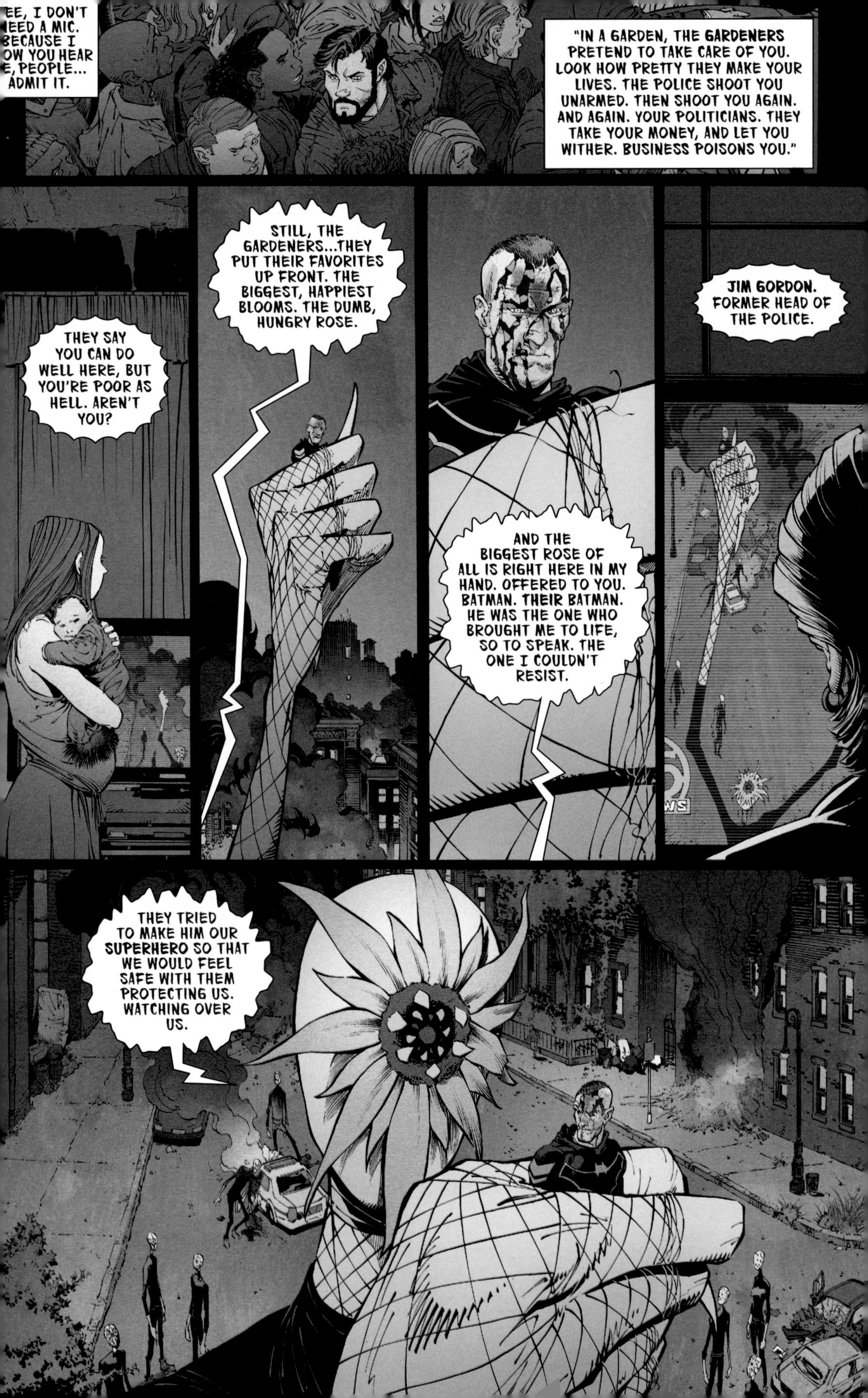

EE, I DON'T
IEED A MIC.
BECAUSE I
OW YOU HEAR
E, PEOPLE...
ADMIT IT.
"IN A GARDEN, THE GARDENERS PRETEND TO TAKE CARE OF YOU. LOOK HOW PRETTY THEY MAKE YOUR LIVES. THE POLICE SHOOT YOU UNARMED. THEN SHOOT YOU AGAIN. AND AGAIN. YOUR POLITICIANS. THEY TAKE YOUR MONEY, AND LET YOU WITHER. BUSINESS POISONS YOU."
THEY SAY YOU CAN DO WELL HERE, BUT YOU'RE POOR AS HELL. AREN'T YOU?
STILL, THE GARDENERS...THEY PUT THEIR FAVORITES UP FRONT. THE BIGGEST, HAPPIEST BLOOMS. THE DUMB, HUNGRY ROSE.
AND THE BIGGEST ROSE OF ALL IS RIGHT HERE IN MY HAND. OFFERED TO YOU. BATMAN. THEIR BATMAN. HE WAS THE ONE WHO BROUGHT ME TO LIFE, SO TO SPEAK. THE ONE I COULDN'T RESIST.
JIM GORDON. FORMER HEAD OF THE POLICE.
THEY TRIED TO MAKE HIM OUR SUPERHERO SO THAT WE WOULD FEEL SAFE WITH THEM PROTECTING US. WATCHING OVER US.

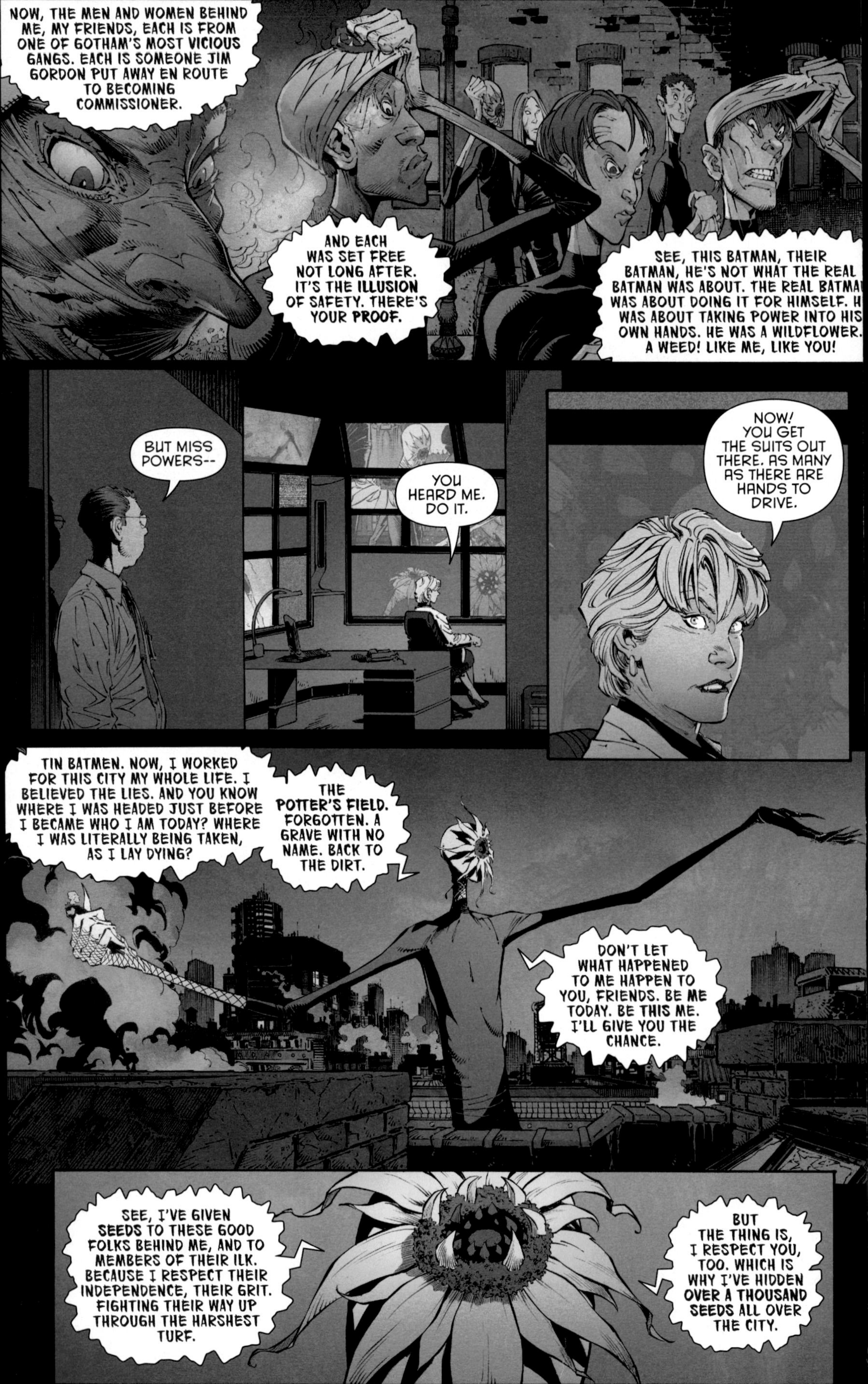
NOW, THE MEN AND WOMEN BEHIND ME, MY FRIENDS, EACH IS FROM ONE OF GOTHAM'S MOST VICIOUS GANGS. EACH IS SOMEONE JIM GORDON PUT AWAY EN ROUTE TO BECOMING COMMISSIONER.
AND EACH WAS SET FREE NOT LONG AFTER. IT'S THE ILLUSION OF SAFETY. THERE'S YOUR PROOF.
SEE, THIS BATMAN, THEIR BATMAN, HE'S NOT WHAT THE REAL BATMAN WAS ABOUT. THE REAL BATMA WAS ABOUT DOING IT FOR HIMSELF. H WAS ABOUT TAKING POWER INTO HIS OWN HANDS. HE WAS A WILDFLOWER. A WEED! LIKE ME, LIKE YOU!
BUT MISS POWERS--
YOU HEARD ME. DO IT.
NOW! YOU GET THE SUITS OUT THERE. AS MANY AS THERE ARE HANDS TO DRIVE.
TIN BATMEN. NOW, I WORKED FOR THIS CITY MY WHOLE LIFE. I BELIEVED THE LIES. AND YOU KNOW WHERE I WAS HEADED JUST BEFORE I BECAME WHO I AM TODAY? WHERE I WAS LITERALLY BEING TAKEN, AS I LAY DYING?
THE POTTER'S FIELD. FORGOTTEN. A GRAVE WITH NO NAME. BACK TO THE DIRT.
DON'T LET WHAT HAPPENED TO ME HAPPEN TO YOU, FRIENDS. BE ME TODAY. BE THIS ME. I'LL GIVE YOU THE CHANCE.
SEE, I'VE GIVEN SEEDS TO THESE GOOD FOLKS BEHIND ME, AND TO MEMBERS OF THEIR ILK. BECAUSE I RESPECT THEIR INDEPENDENCE, THEIR GRIT. FIGHTING THEIR WAY UP THROUGH THE HARSHEST TURF.
BUT THE THING IS, I RESPECT YOU, TOO. WHICH IS WHY I'VE HIDDEN OVER A THOUSAND SEEDS ALL OVER THE CITY.

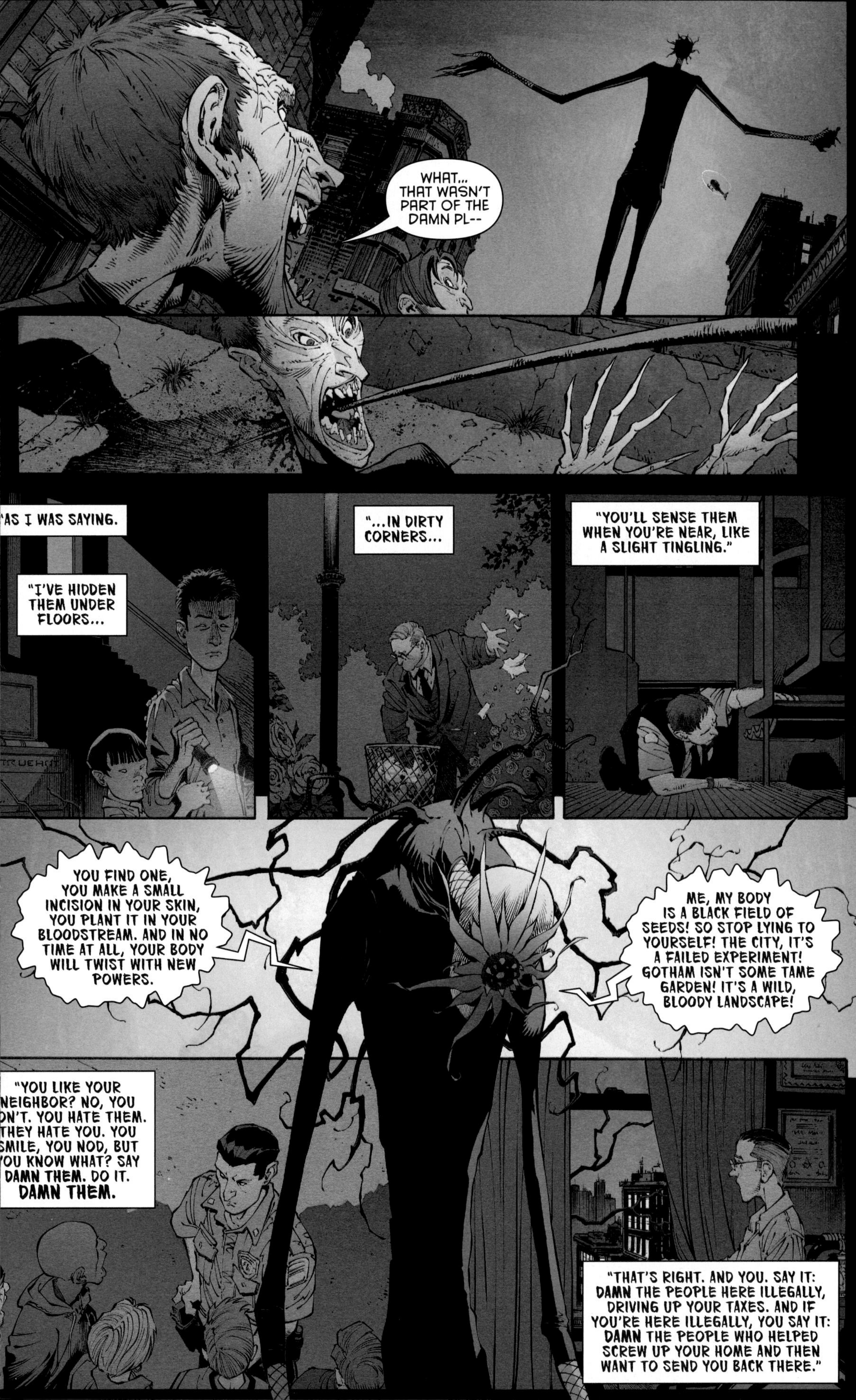

WHAT... THAT WASN'T PART OF THE DAMN PL--
"AS I WAS SAYING.
"I'VE HIDDEN THEM UNDER FLOORS...
"...IN DIRTY CORNERS...
"YOU'LL SENSE THEM WHEN YOU'RE NEAR, LIKE A SLIGHT TINGLING."
YOU FIND ONE, YOU MAKE A SMALL INCISION IN YOUR SKIN, YOU PLANT IT IN YOUR BLOODSTREAM. AND IN NO TIME AT ALL, YOUR BODY WILL TWIST WITH NEW POWERS.
ME, MY BODY IS A BLACK FIELD OF SEEDS! SO STOP LYING TO YOURSELF! THE CITY, IT'S A FAILED EXPERIMENT! GOTHAM ISN'T SOME TAME GARDEN! IT'S A WILD, BLOODY LANDSCAPE!
"YOU LIKE YOUR NEIGHBOR? NO, YOU ON'T. YOU HATE THEM. THEY HATE YOU. YOU SMILE, YOU NOD, BUT YOU KNOW WHAT? SAY DAMN THEM. DO IT. DAMN THEM.
"THAT'S RIGHT. AND YOU. SAY IT: DAMN THE PEOPLE HERE ILLEGALLY, DRIVING UP YOUR TAXES. AND IF YOU'RE HERE ILLEGALLY, YOU SAY IT: DAMN THE PEOPLE WHO HELPED SCREW UP YOUR HOME AND THEN WANT TO SEND YOU BACK THERE."

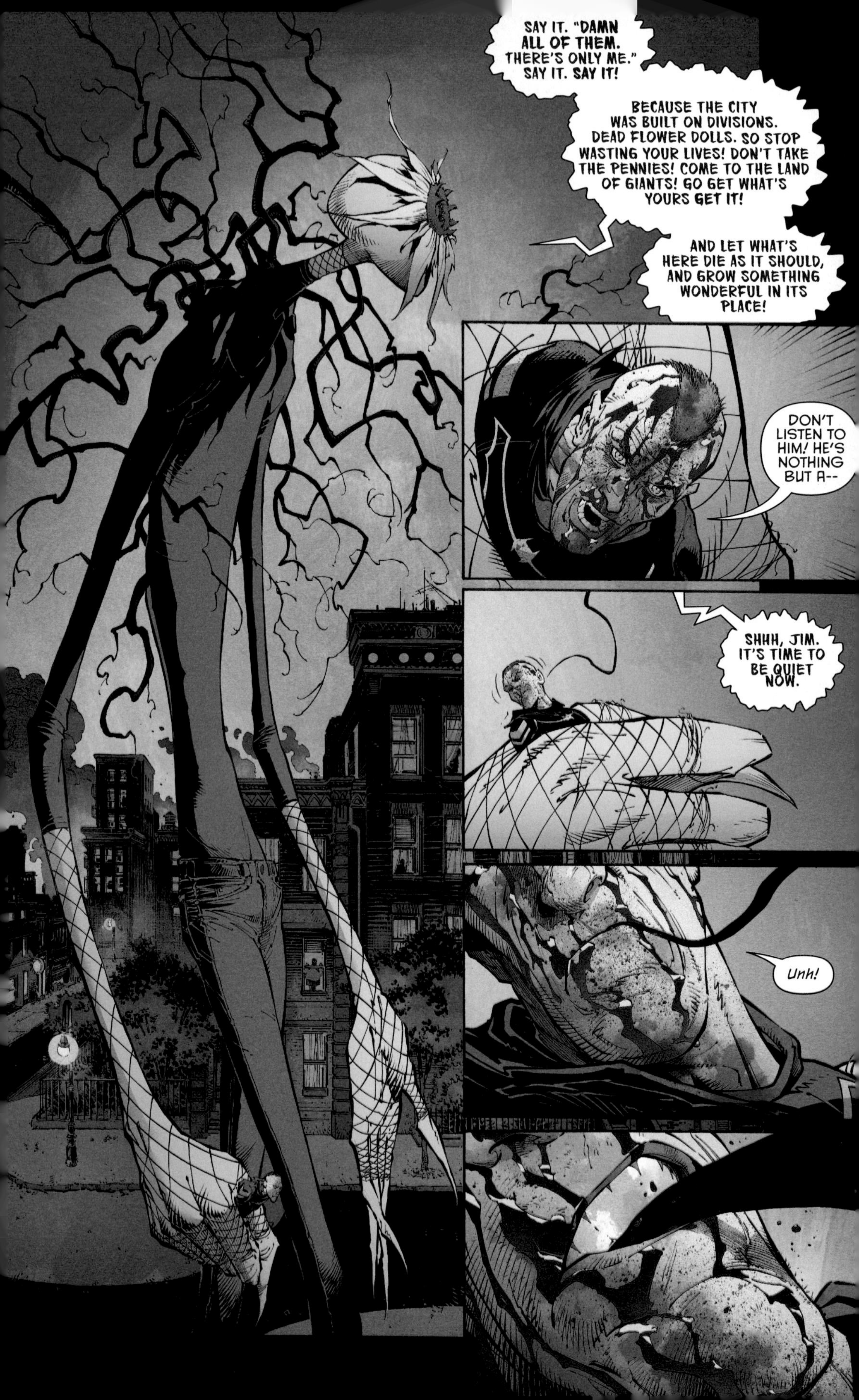
SAY IT. "DAMN ALL OF THEM. THERE'S ONLY ME." SAY IT. SAY IT!
BECAUSE THE CITY WAS BUILT ON DIVISIONS. DEAD FLOWER DOLLS. SO STOP WASTING YOUR LIVES! DON'T TAKE THE PENNIES! COME TO THE LAND OF GIANTS! GO GET WHAT'S YOURS GET IT!
AND LET WHAT'S HERE DIE AS IT SHOULD, AND GROW SOMETHING WONDERFUL IN ITS PLACE!
DON'T LISTEN TO HIM! HE'S NOTHING BUT A--
SHHH, JIM. IT'S TIME TO BE QUIET NOW.
Unh!

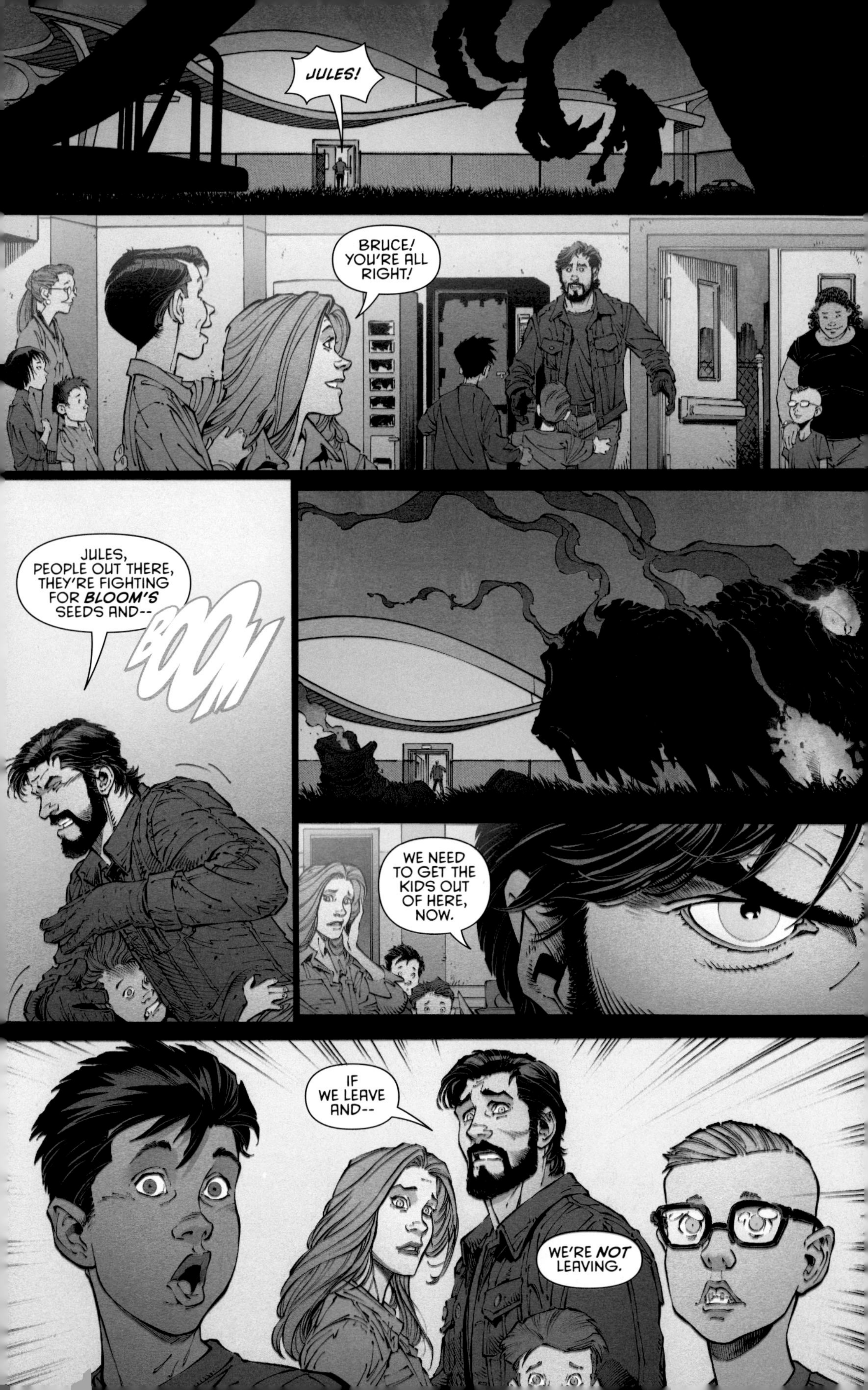
JULES!
BRUCE! YOU'RE ALL RIGHT!
JULES, PEOPLE OUT THERE, THEY'RE FIGHTING FOR BLOOM'S SEEDS AND--
BOOM
WE NEED TO GET THE KIDS OUT OF HERE, NOW.
IF WE LEAVE AND--
WE'RE NOT LEAVING.

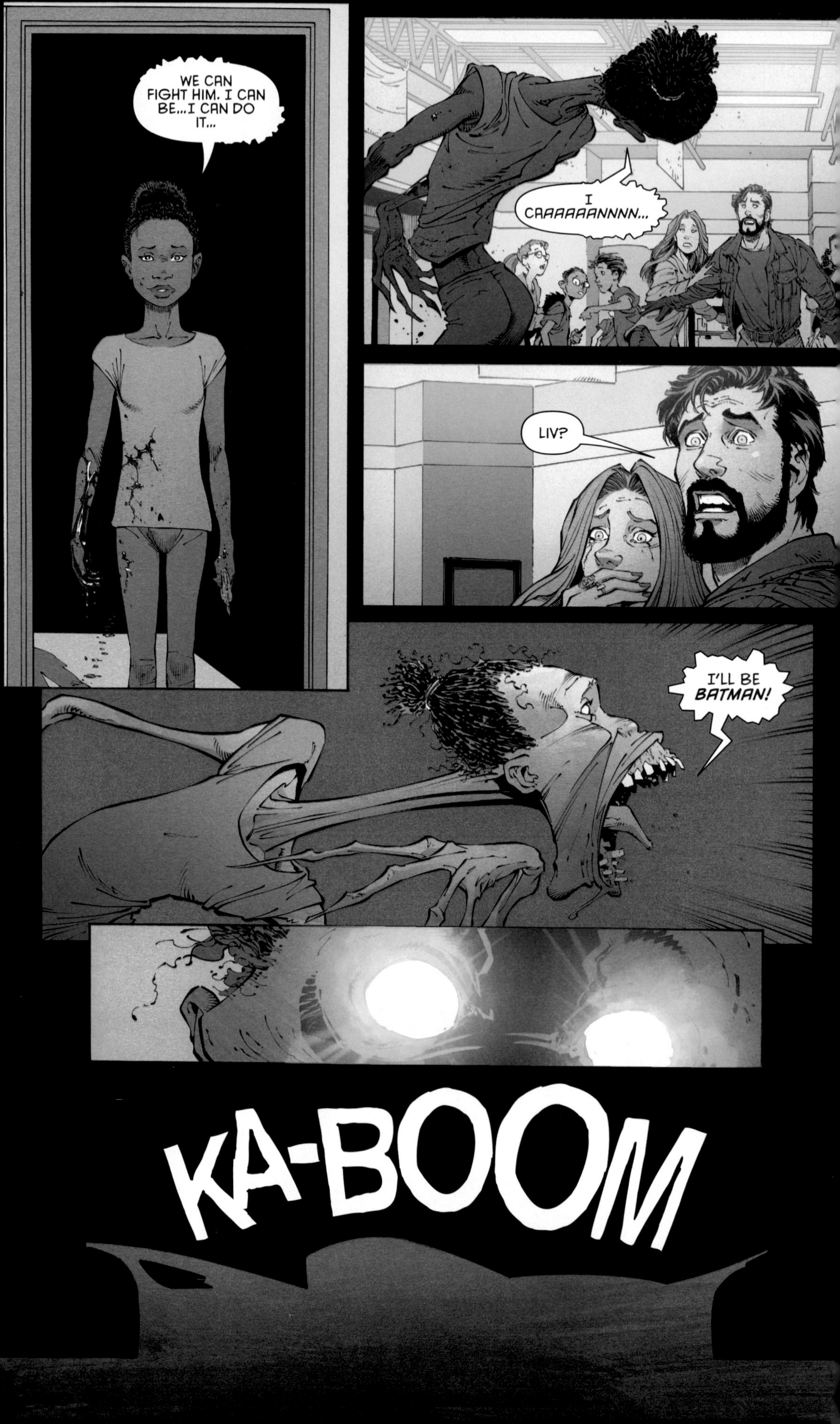
WE CAN FIGHT HIM. I CAN BE...I CAN DO IT...
I CAAAAAANNNN...
LIV?
I'LL BE BATMAN!
KA-BOOM

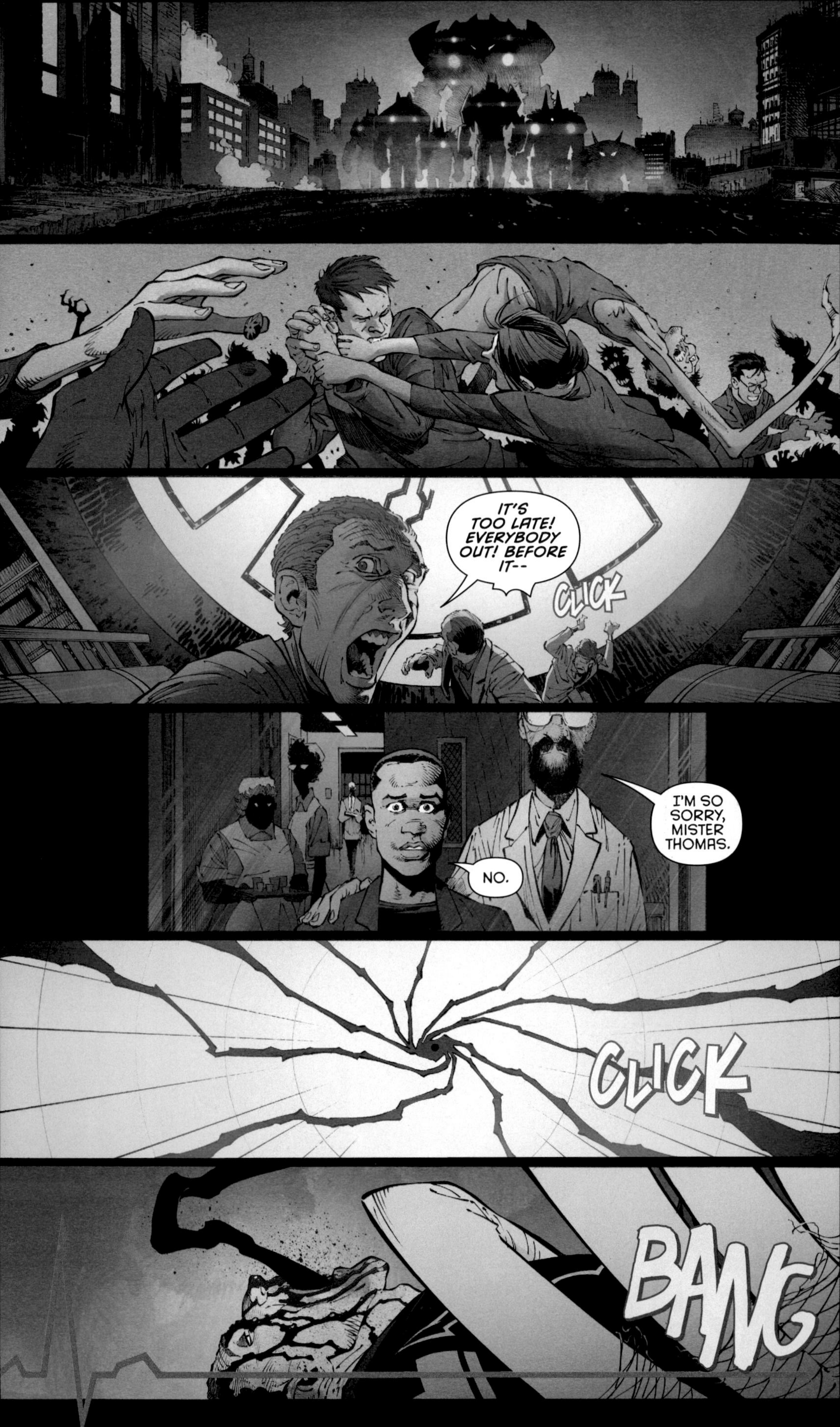
IT'S TOO LATE! EVERYBODY OUT! BEFORE IT--
CLICK
I'M SO SORRY, MISTER THOMAS.
NO.
CLICK
BANG

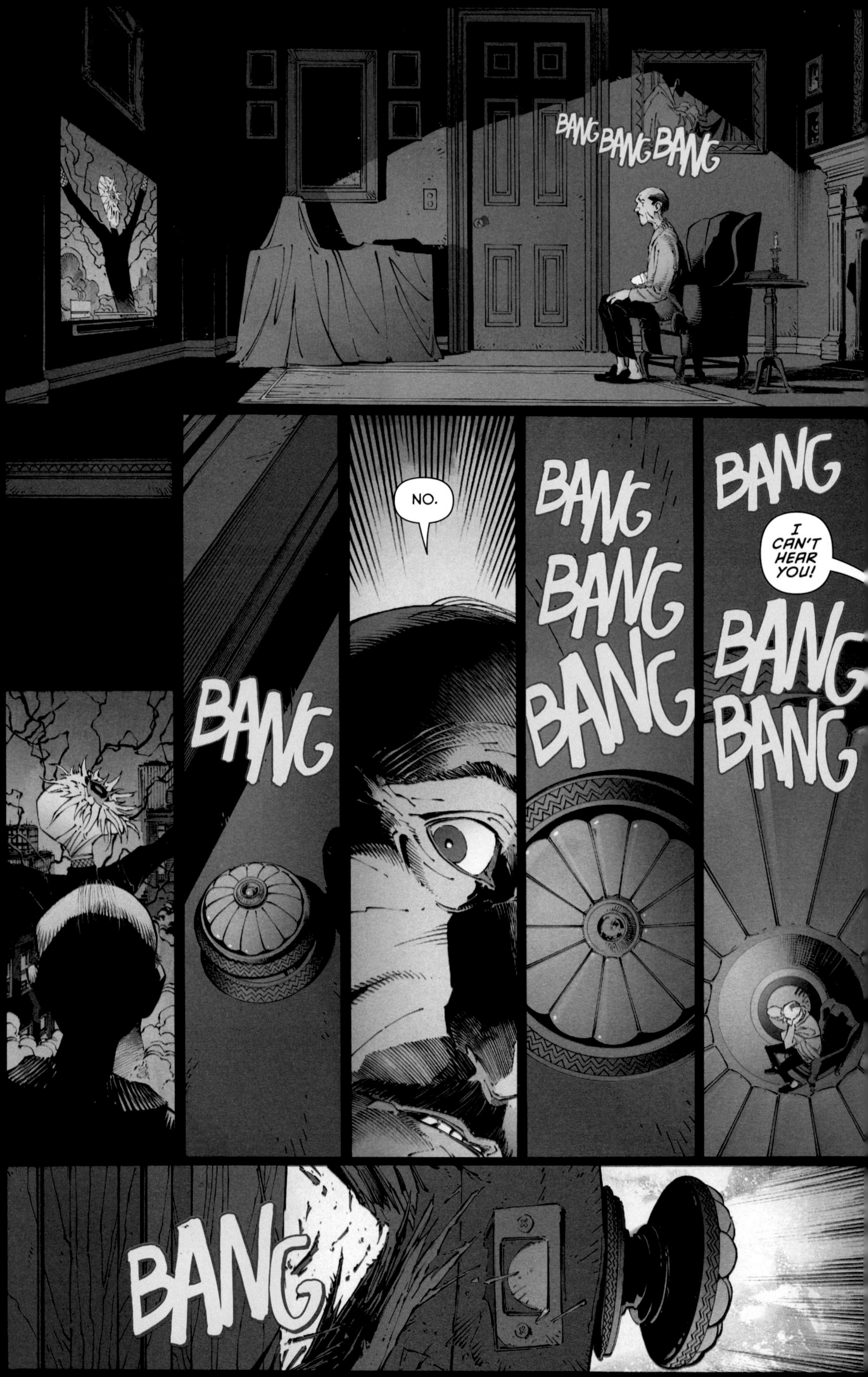
BANG BANG BANG
BANG
NO.
BANG BANG BANG
BANG
I CAN'T HEAR YOU!
BANG BANG
BANG

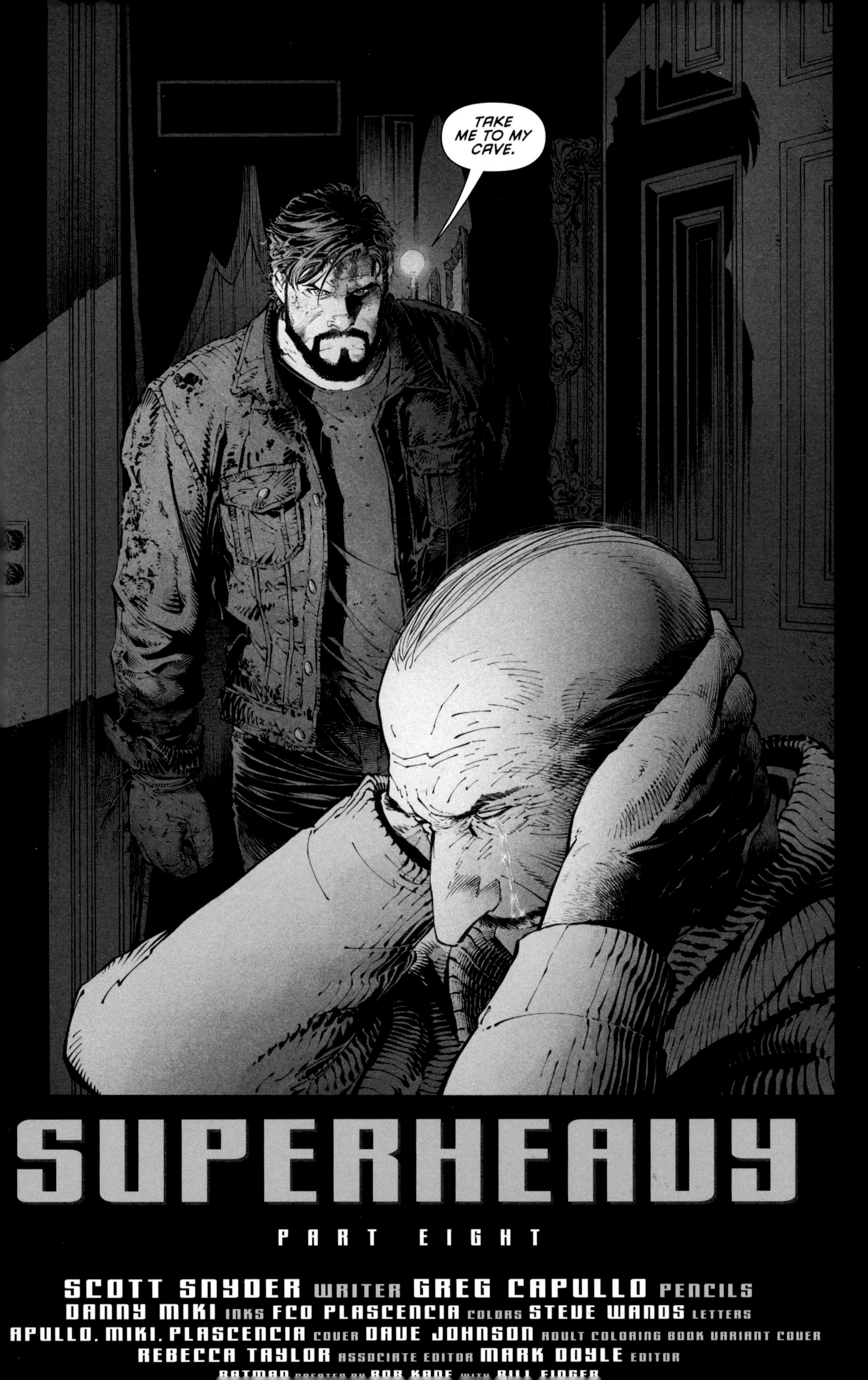
TAKE ME TO MY CAVE.

# SUPERHEAVY

## PART EIGHT

SCOTT SNYDER WRITER GREG CAPULLO PENCILS
DANNY MIKI INKS FCO PLASCENCIA COLORS STEVE WANDS LETTERS
APULLO, MIKI, PLASCENCIA COVER DAVE JOHNSON ADULT COLORING BOOK VARIANT COVER
REBECCA TAYLOR ASSOCIATE EDITOR MARK DOYLE EDITOR
BATMAN CREATED BY BOB KANE WITH BILL FINGER

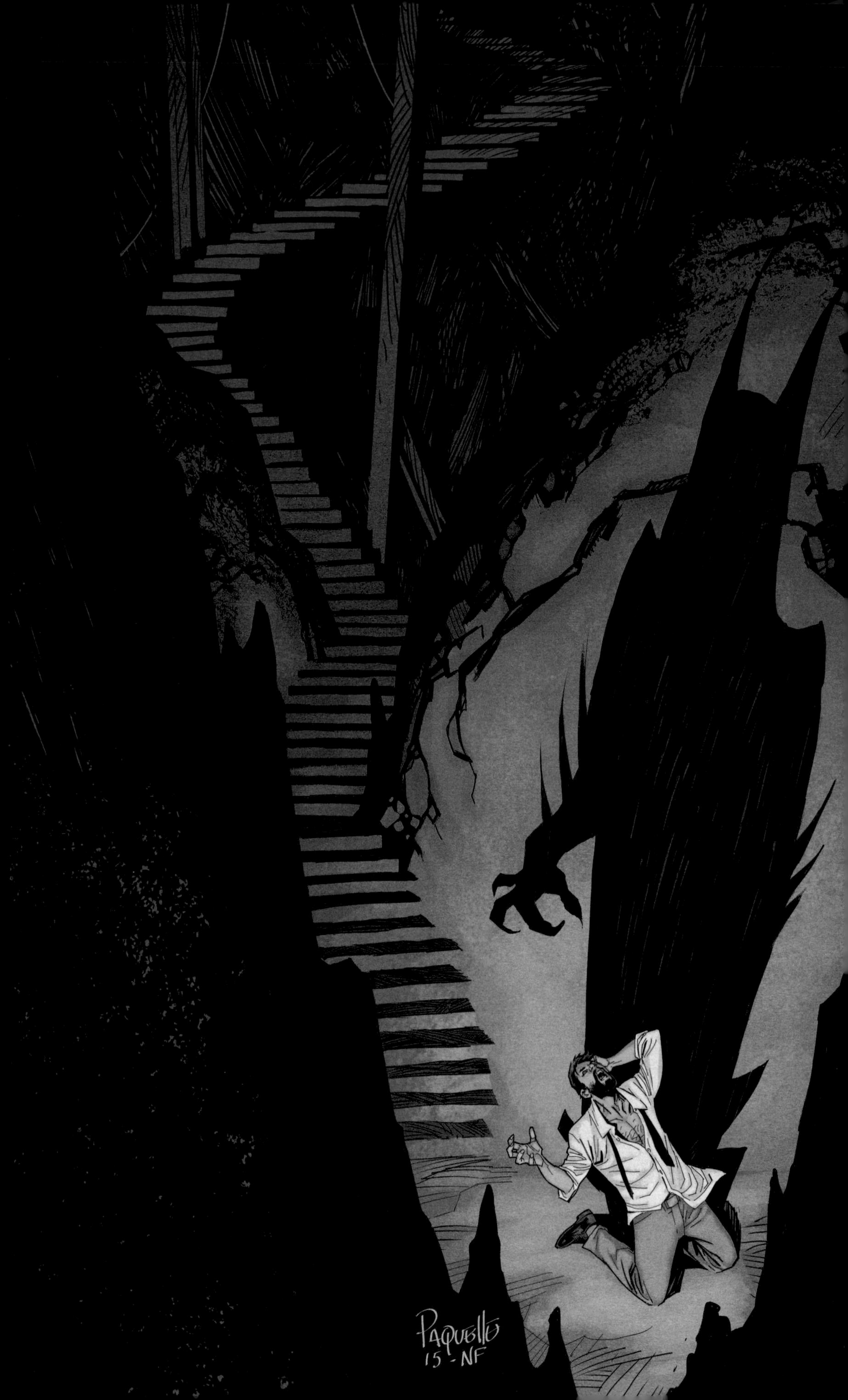
PAQUETTE
15 - NF

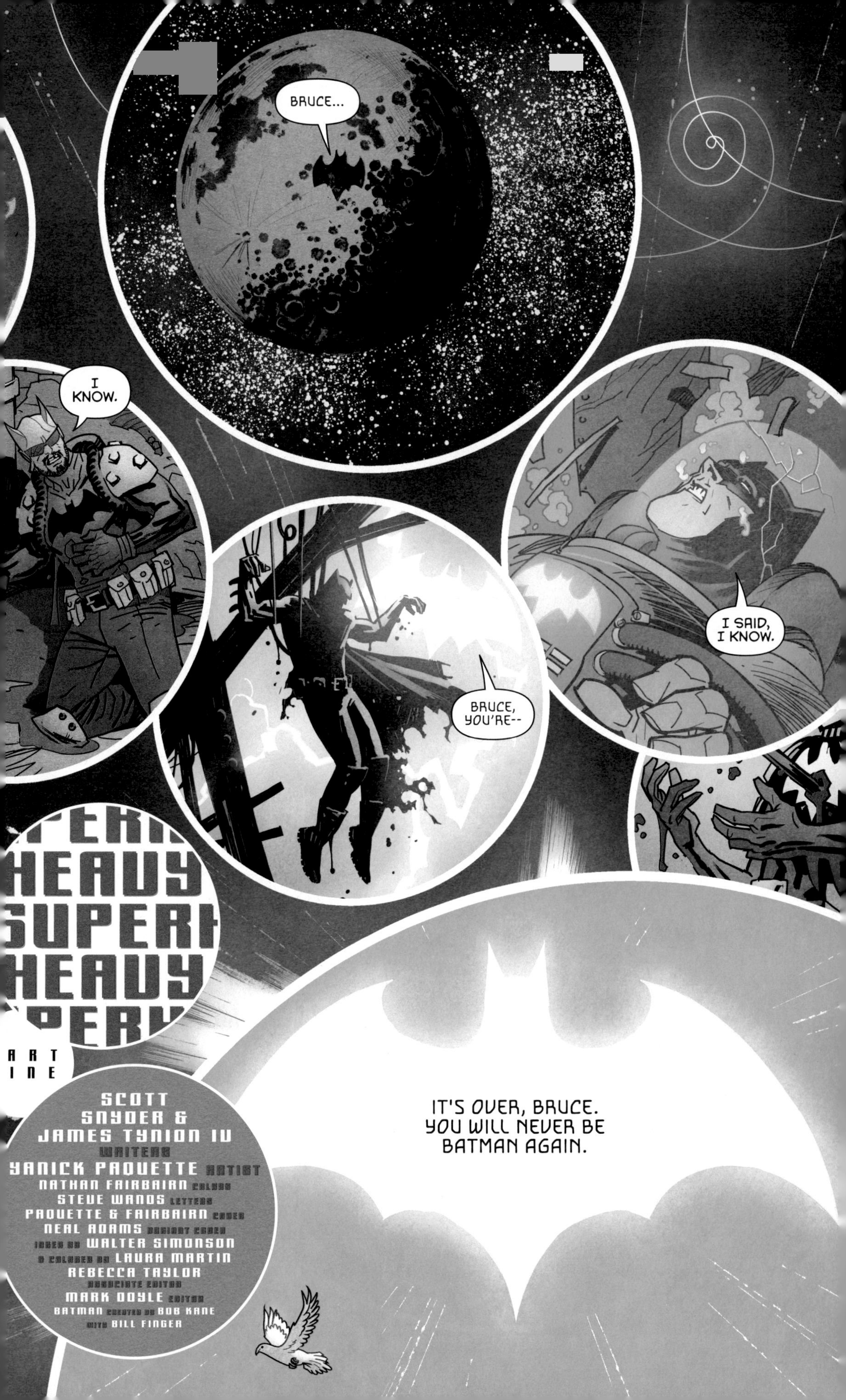
BRUCE...
I KNOW.
BRUCE, YOU'RE--
I SAID, I KNOW.
IT'S OVER, BRUCE. YOU WILL NEVER BE BATMAN AGAIN.
SCOTT SNYDER & JAMES TYNION IV WRITERS
YANICK PAQUETTE ARTIST
NATHAN FAIRBAIRN COLORS
STEVE WANDS LETTERS
PAQUETTE & FAIRBAIRN COVER
NEAL ADAMS VARIANT COVER
INKED BY WALTER SIMONSON
& COLORED BY LAURA MARTIN
REBECCA TAYLOR ASSOCIATE EDITOR
MARK DOYLE EDITOR
BATMAN CREATED BY BOB KANE WITH BILL FINGER

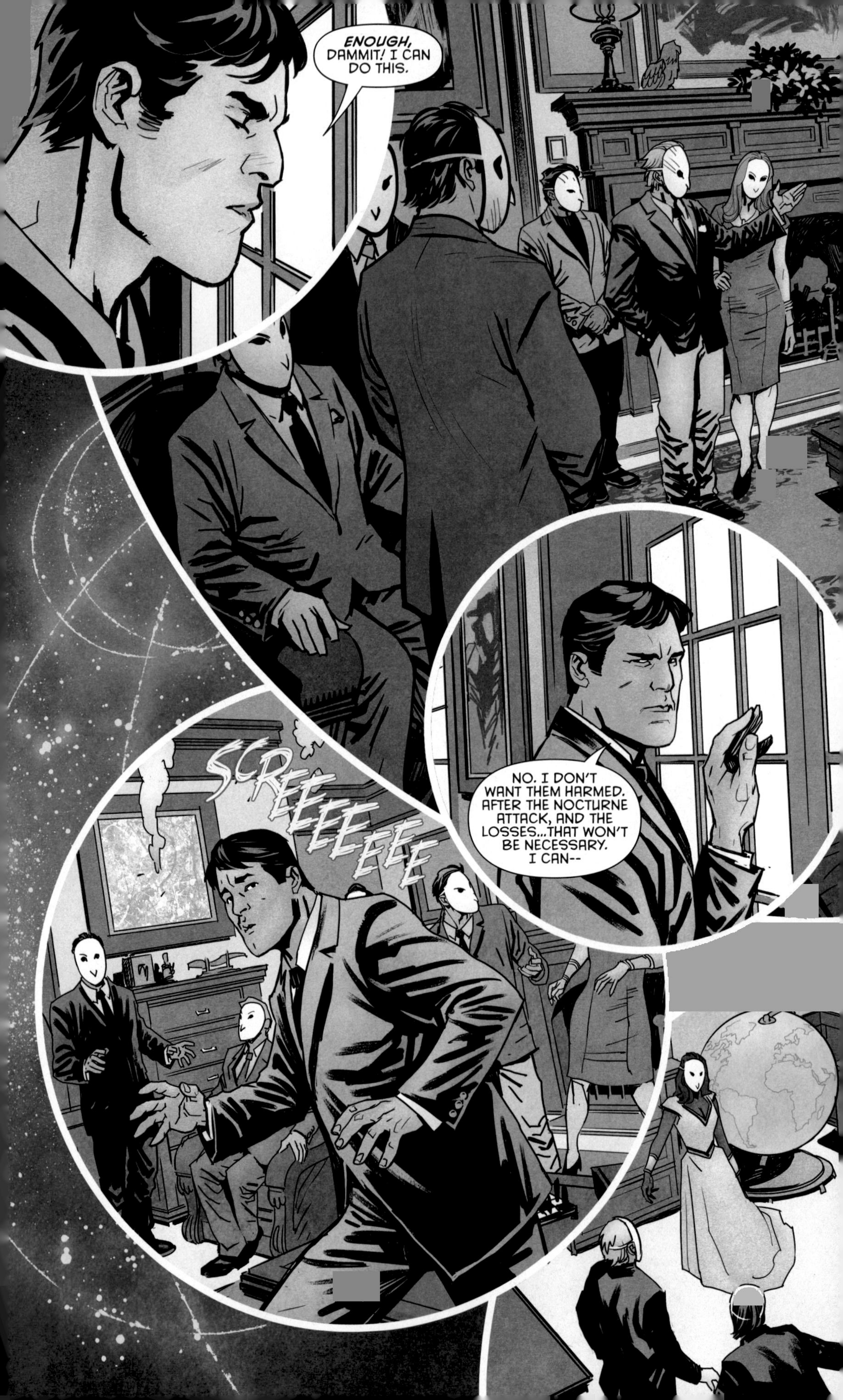
ENOUGH, DAMMIT! I CAN DO THIS.
NO. I DON'T WANT THEM HARMED. AFTER THE NOCTURNE ATTACK, AND THE LOSSES...THAT WON'T BE NECESSARY. I CAN--
SCREEEEEEEEE

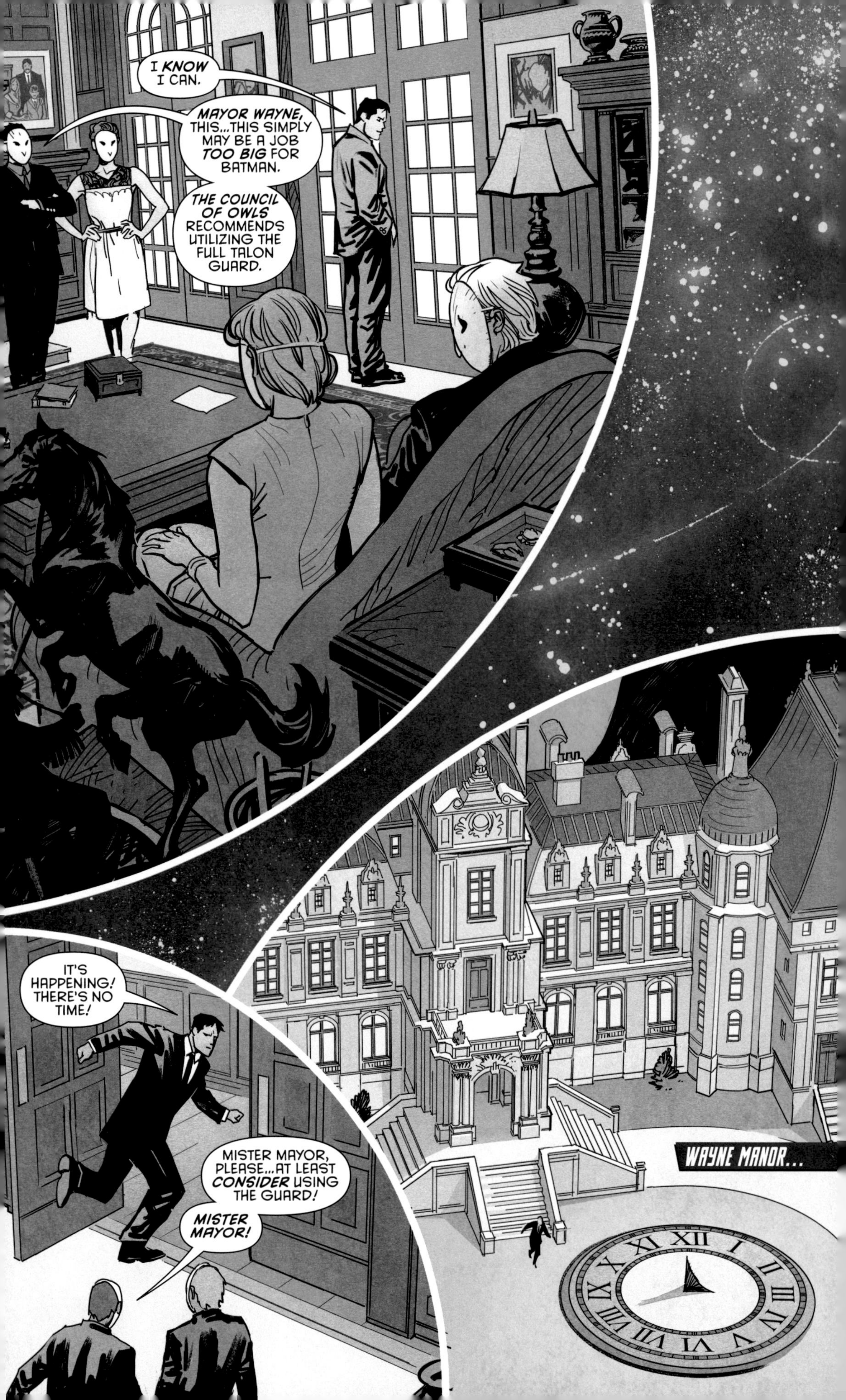
I KNOW I CAN.
MAYOR WAYNE, THIS...THIS SIMPLY MAY BE A JOB TOO BIG FOR BATMAN.
THE COUNCIL OF OWLS RECOMMENDS UTILIZING THE FULL TALON GUARD.
WAYNE MANOR...
IT'S HAPPENING! THERE'S NO TIME!
MISTER MAYOR, PLEASE...AT LEAST CONSIDER USING THE GUARD!
MISTER MAYOR!

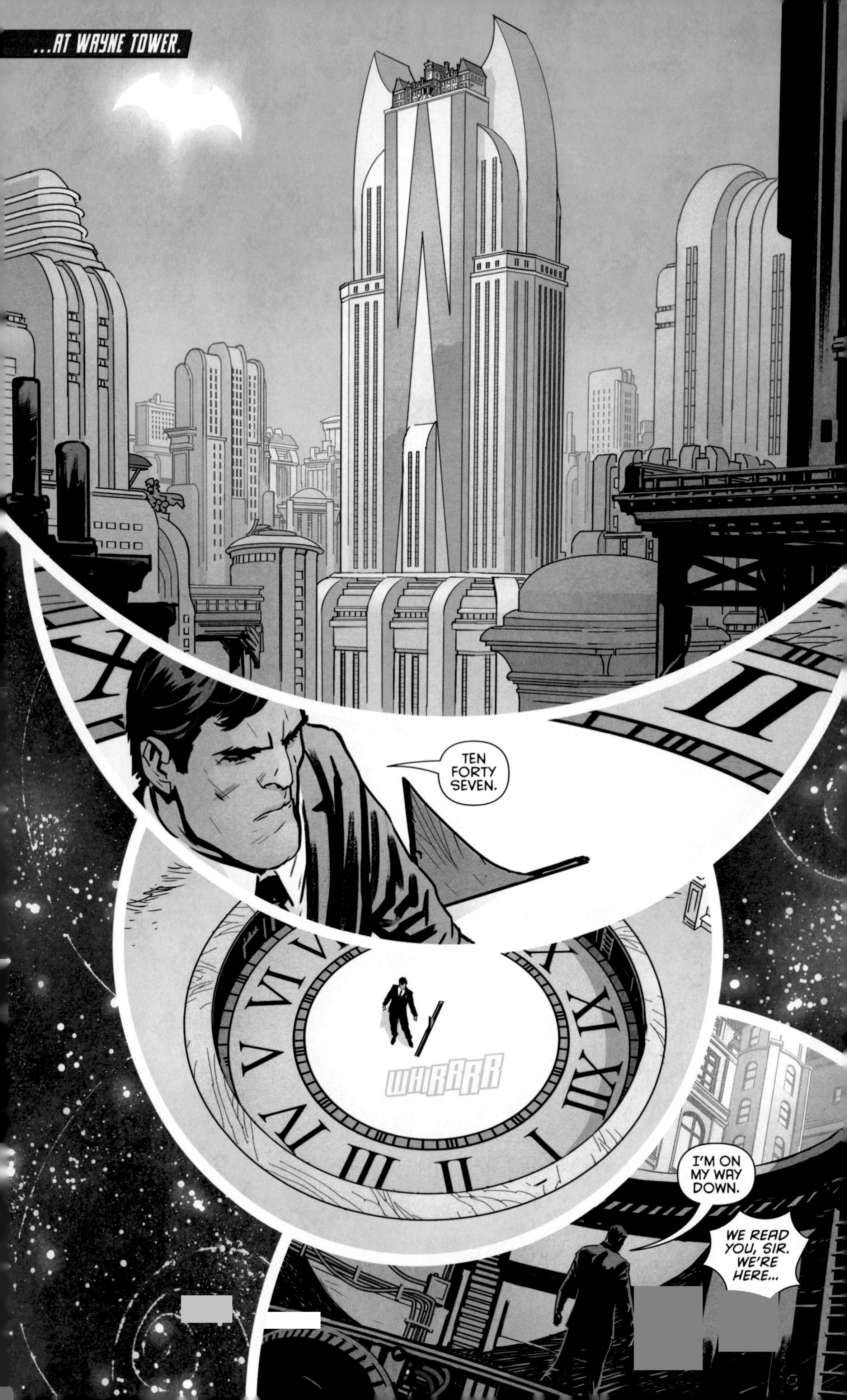
...AT WAYNE TOWER.
TEN FORTY SEVEN.
WHIRRRR
I'M ON MY WAY DOWN.
WE READ YOU, SIR. WE'RE HERE...

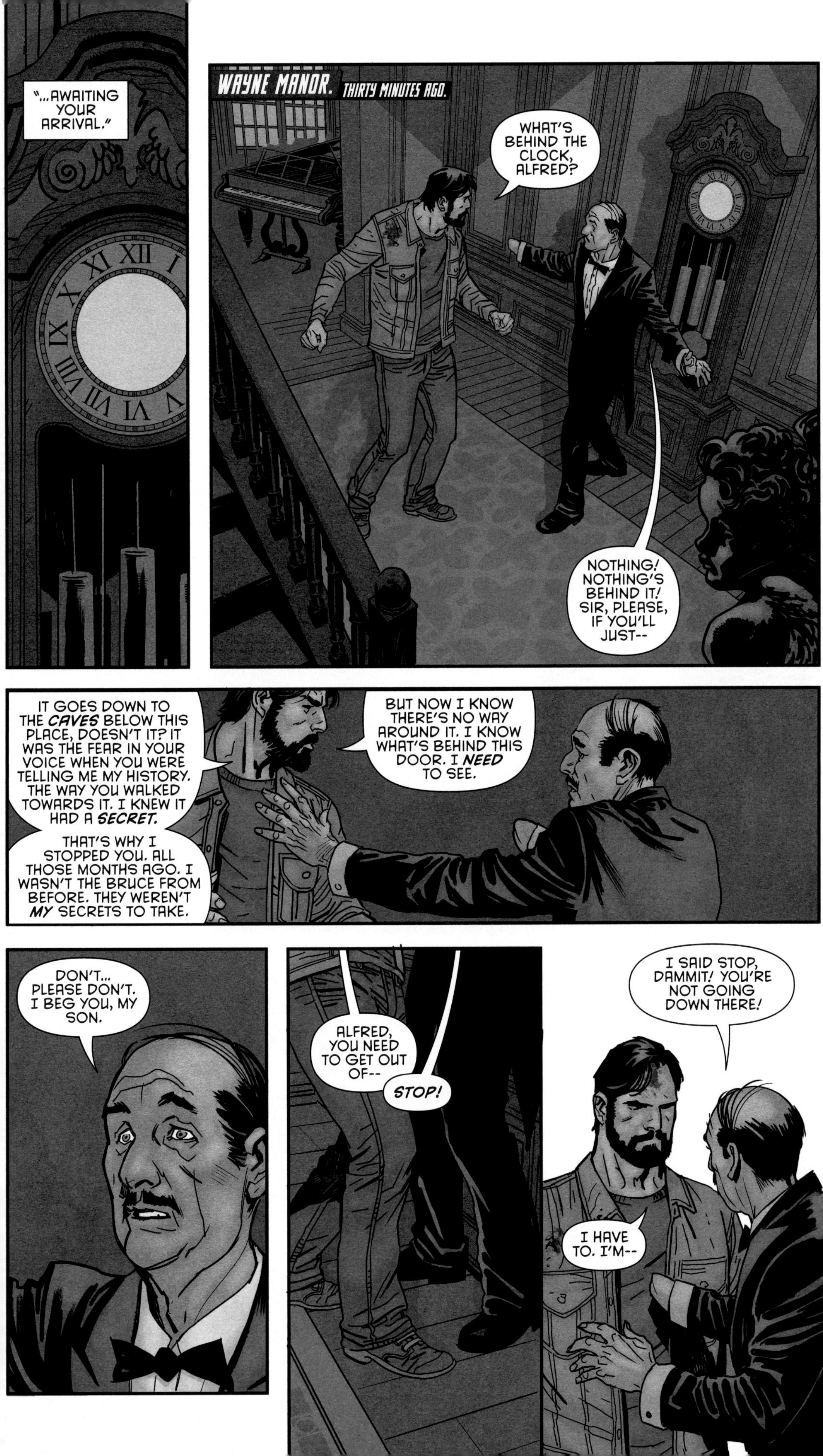
"...AWAITING YOUR ARRIVAL."
WAYNE MANOR. THIRTY MINUTES AGO.
WHAT'S BEHIND THE CLOCK, ALFRED?
NOTHING! NOTHING'S BEHIND IT! SIR, PLEASE, IF YOU'LL JUST--
IT GOES DOWN TO THE CAVES BELOW THIS PLACE, DOESN'T IT? IT WAS THE FEAR IN YOUR VOICE WHEN YOU WERE TELLING ME MY HISTORY. THE WAY YOU WALKED TOWARDS IT. I KNEW IT HAD A SECRET.
THAT'S WHY I STOPPED YOU. ALL THOSE MONTHS AGO. I WASN'T THE BRUCE FROM BEFORE. THEY WEREN'T MY SECRETS TO TAKE.
BUT NOW I KNOW THERE'S NO WAY AROUND IT. I KNOW WHAT'S BEHIND THIS DOOR. I NEED TO SEE.
DON'T... PLEASE DON'T. I BEG YOU, MY SON.
ALFRED, YOU NEED TO GET OUT OF--
STOP!
I SAID STOP, DAMMIT! YOU'RE NOT GOING DOWN THERE!
I HAVE TO. I'M--

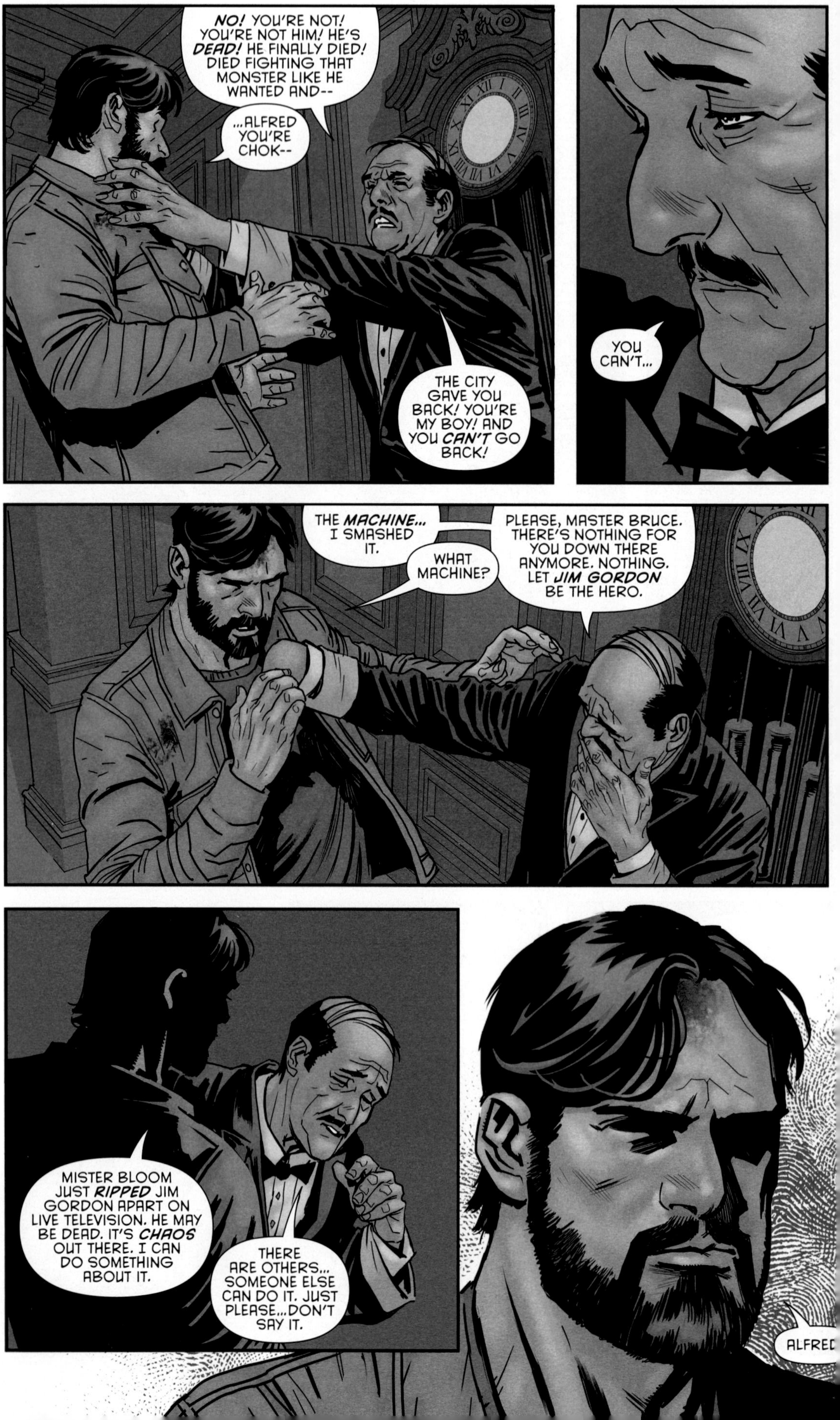
NO! YOU'RE NOT! YOU'RE NOT HIM! HE'S DEAD! HE FINALLY DIED! DIED FIGHTING THAT MONSTER LIKE HE WANTED AND--
...ALFRED YOU'RE CHOK--
THE CITY GAVE YOU BACK! YOU'RE MY BOY! AND YOU CAN'T GO BACK!
YOU CAN'T...
THE MACHINE... I SMASHED IT.
WHAT MACHINE?
PLEASE, MASTER BRUCE. THERE'S NOTHING FOR YOU DOWN THERE ANYMORE. NOTHING. LET JIM GORDON BE THE HERO.
MISTER BLOOM JUST RIPPED JIM GORDON APART ON LIVE TELEVISION. HE MAY BE DEAD. IT'S CHAOS OUT THERE. I CAN DO SOMETHING ABOUT IT.
THERE ARE OTHERS... SOMEONE ELSE CAN DO IT. JUST PLEASE...DON'T SAY IT.
ALFRED

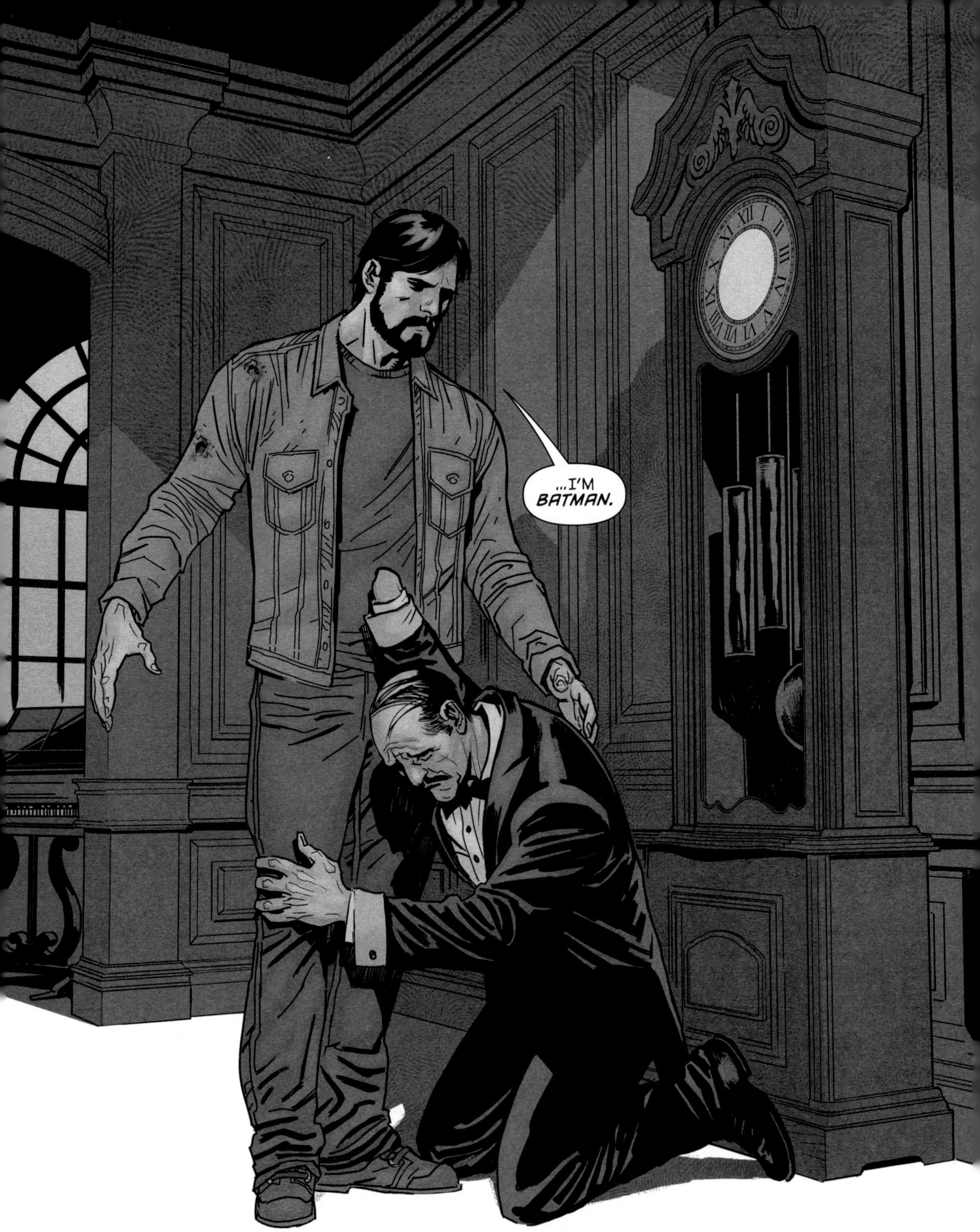
...I'M BATMAN.

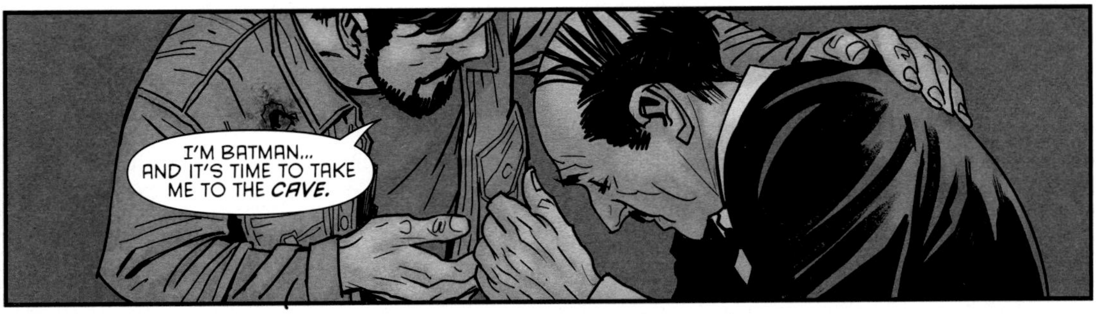
I'M BATMAN... AND IT'S TIME TO TAKE ME TO THE CAVE.

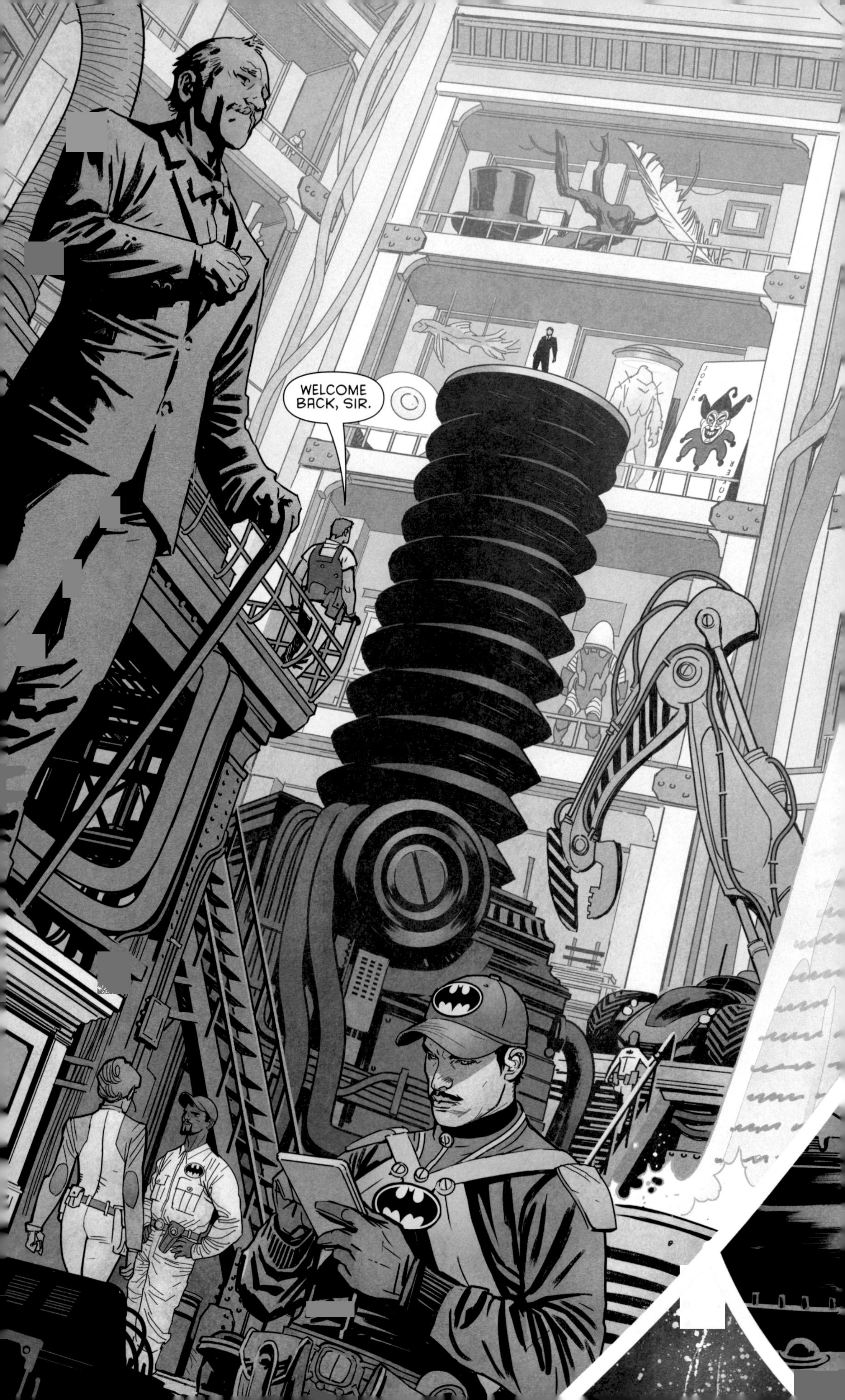
WELCOME BACK, SIR.

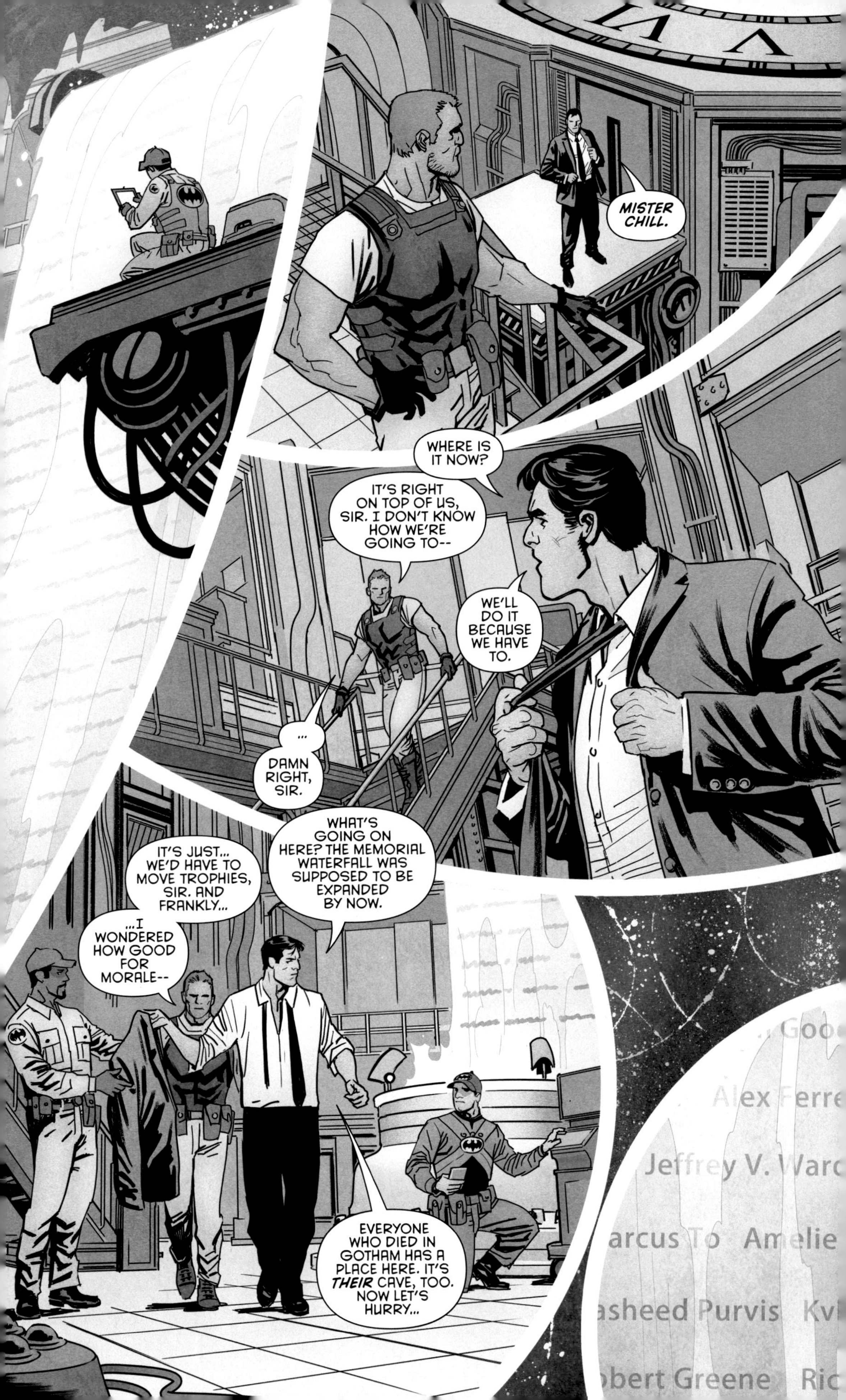
MISTER CHILL.
WHERE IS IT NOW?
IT'S RIGHT ON TOP OF US, SIR. I DON'T KNOW HOW WE'RE GOING TO--
WE'LL DO IT BECAUSE WE HAVE TO.
...
DAMN RIGHT, SIR.
WHAT'S GOING ON HERE? THE MEMORIAL WATERFALL WAS SUPPOSED TO BE EXPANDED BY NOW.
IT'S JUST... WE'D HAVE TO MOVE TROPHIES, SIR. AND FRANKLY...
...I WONDERED HOW GOOD FOR MORALE--
EVERYONE WHO DIED IN GOTHAM HAS A PLACE HERE. IT'S THEIR CAVE, TOO. NOW LET'S HURRY...
Alex Ferre
Jeffrey V. Ward
Amelie
asheed Purvis
obert Greene

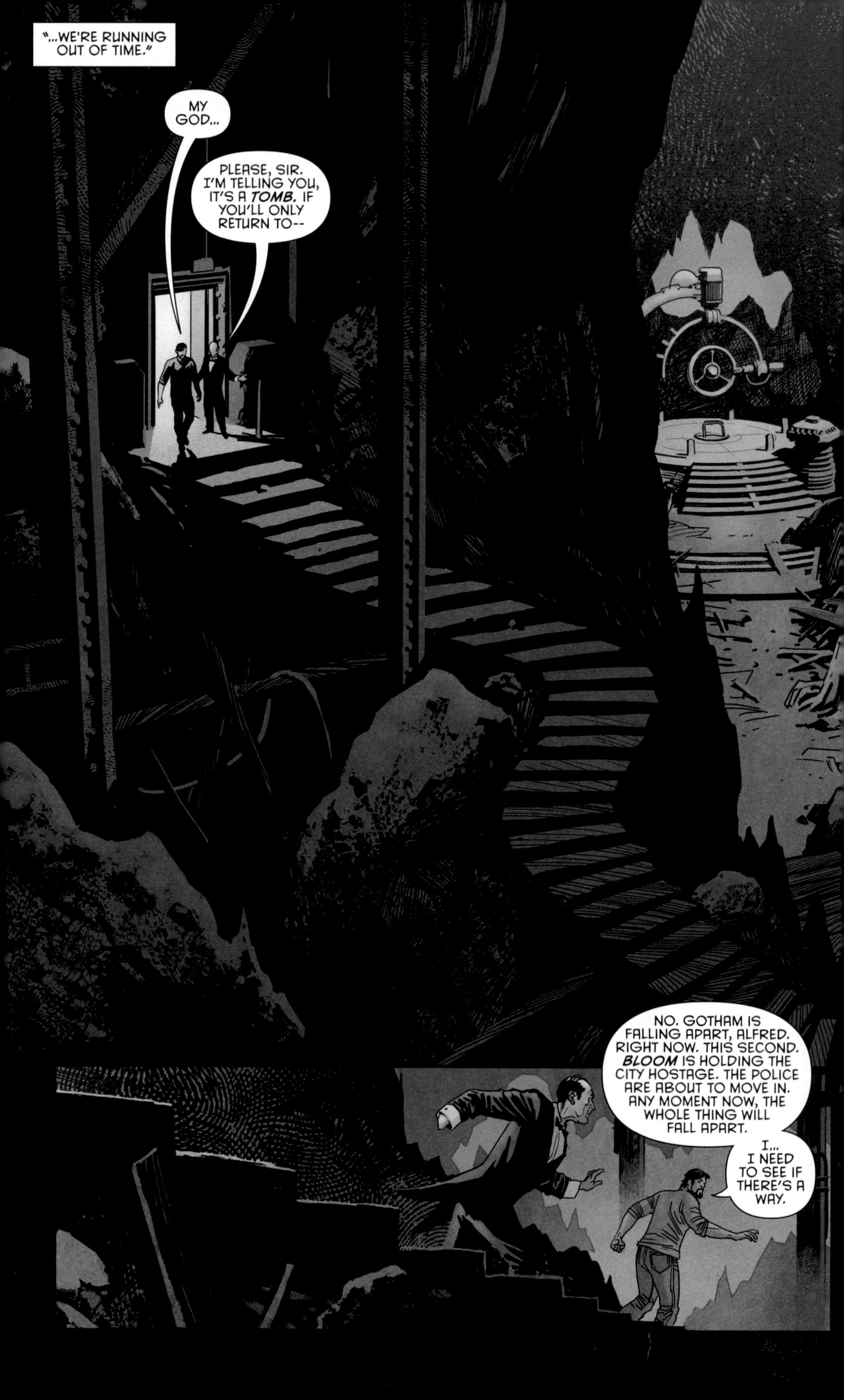
"...WE'RE RUNNING OUT OF TIME."
MY GOD...
PLEASE, SIR. I'M TELLING YOU, IT'S A TOMB. IF YOU'LL ONLY RETURN TO--
NO. GOTHAM IS FALLING APART, ALFRED. RIGHT NOW. THIS SECOND. BLOOM IS HOLDING THE CITY HOSTAGE. THE POLICE ARE ABOUT TO MOVE IN. ANY MOMENT NOW, THE WHOLE THING WILL FALL APART.
I... I NEED TO SEE IF THERE'S A WAY.

THERE. THAT'S IT. THE MACHINE YOU DESTROYED... THE ONE YOU SAID COULD MAKE ME *HIM* AGAIN. TELL ME HOW IT WORKED.

IT *DIDN'T*.

YOU...THE *OLD* BRUCE. HE HAD A TERRIBLE, FINAL DREAM. A NEVER-ENDING LINEAGE OF *BRUCE WAYNES*, IMPRINTED WITH BATMAN'S MEMORIES, HIS SKILLS, EACH SUCCEEDING THE PRIOR. BUT IT WAS NEVER COMPLETED. *CLONING* WASN'T THE PROBLEM. THE ISSUE WAS THE HUMAN *MIND*.

EVERY SIMULATION HE RAN, THE HOST DIED FROM THE SHOCK OF THE *TRAUMA* HE INFLICTED ON IT. BATMAN WAS TOO MUCH FOR ANOTHER LIVING MIND TO TAKE. THE PROJECT WAS A FAILURE.

AND THOSE MINDS WERE EMPTY, MASTER BRUCE. YOUR MIND...IT'S FULL WITH THIS NEW, *REAL* YOU. TO TRY TO ADD *BATMAN* TO IT, IT WOULD SURELY KILL YOU.

OR MAYBE IT WOULD MAKE SOMETHING *NEW*. A BATMAN WITHOUT THE TRAUMA. SOMETHING GREATER THAN HE EVER WAS BEFORE.

MASTER BRUCE, THERE IS *NO* WAY. I DESTROYED THE MACHINE'S SERVER. THE MEMORIES ARE *GONE*.

YOU KEEP SAYING THAT. BUT IF BATMAN WAS WHAT EVERYONE SAYS HE WAS, HE WOULD HAVE HAD A BACKUP. THERE WOULD HAVE BEEN A WAY TO ACTIVATE--

VOICE COMMAND RECOGNIZED. ACTIVATING FULL CAVE SYSTEMS.

WELCOME BACK, BATMAN.

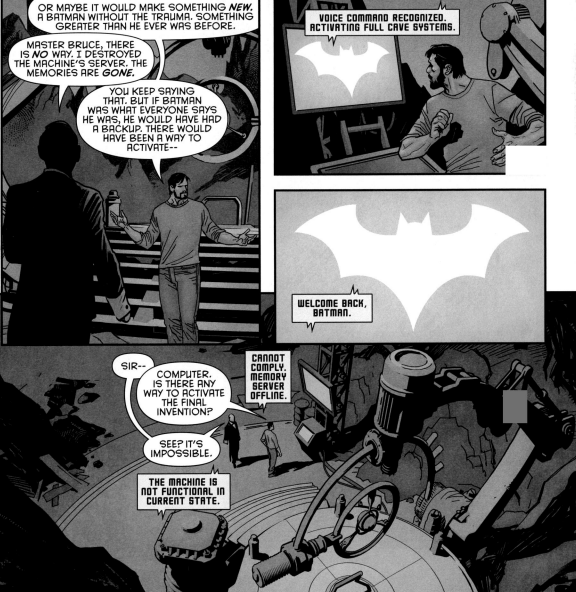

SIR--

COMPUTER. IS THERE ANY WAY TO ACTIVATE THE FINAL INVENTION?

CANNOT COMPLY. MEMORY SERVER OFFLINE.

SEE? IT'S IMPOSSIBLE.

THE MACHINE IS NOT FUNCTIONAL IN CURRENT STATE.

THERE HAS TO BE A WAY...I KNOW HE WOULD HAVE HAD A WAY OUT, EVEN FROM THIS. COMPUTER...ARE ANY OTHER SERVERS COMPATIBLE WITH THE MACHINE?

ONE RESULT FOUND.

SHALL I ACTIVATE THE ALFRED PROTOCOL?

ALF

WHAT ON EARTH?

ACTIVATE IT.

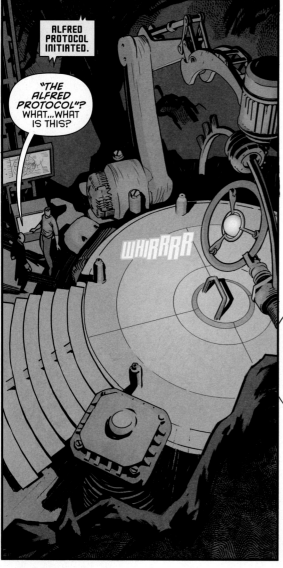

ALFRED PROTOCOL INITIATED.

"THE ALFRED PROTOCOL"? WHAT...WHAT IS THIS?

WHIRRRR

IT'S A FULL BACKUP OF THE MEMORY DRIVES...LOOK...THE LAST UPDATE WAS JUST BEFORE THE FINAL ATTACK WITH JOKER. HIS LAST MOMENT IN THE CAVE.

WHY WOULD HE NAME IT--

YOU'RE THE ONE WHO WOULD ALWAYS PATCH HIM UP AND MAKE HIM NEW WHEN HE FELL. WHO ELSE WOULD HE ENTRUST THE WHOLE OF BATMAN TO?

MAYBE THE ALFRED STANDING IN FRONT OF ME WOULDN'T DO IT, BUT I THINK THERE ARE TWO *GHOSTS* DOWN IN THIS CAVE. THE MAN I WAS, AND THE ONE PERSON HE TRUSTED MORE THAN ANYONE TO FATHER EACH GENERATION OF BATMAN.

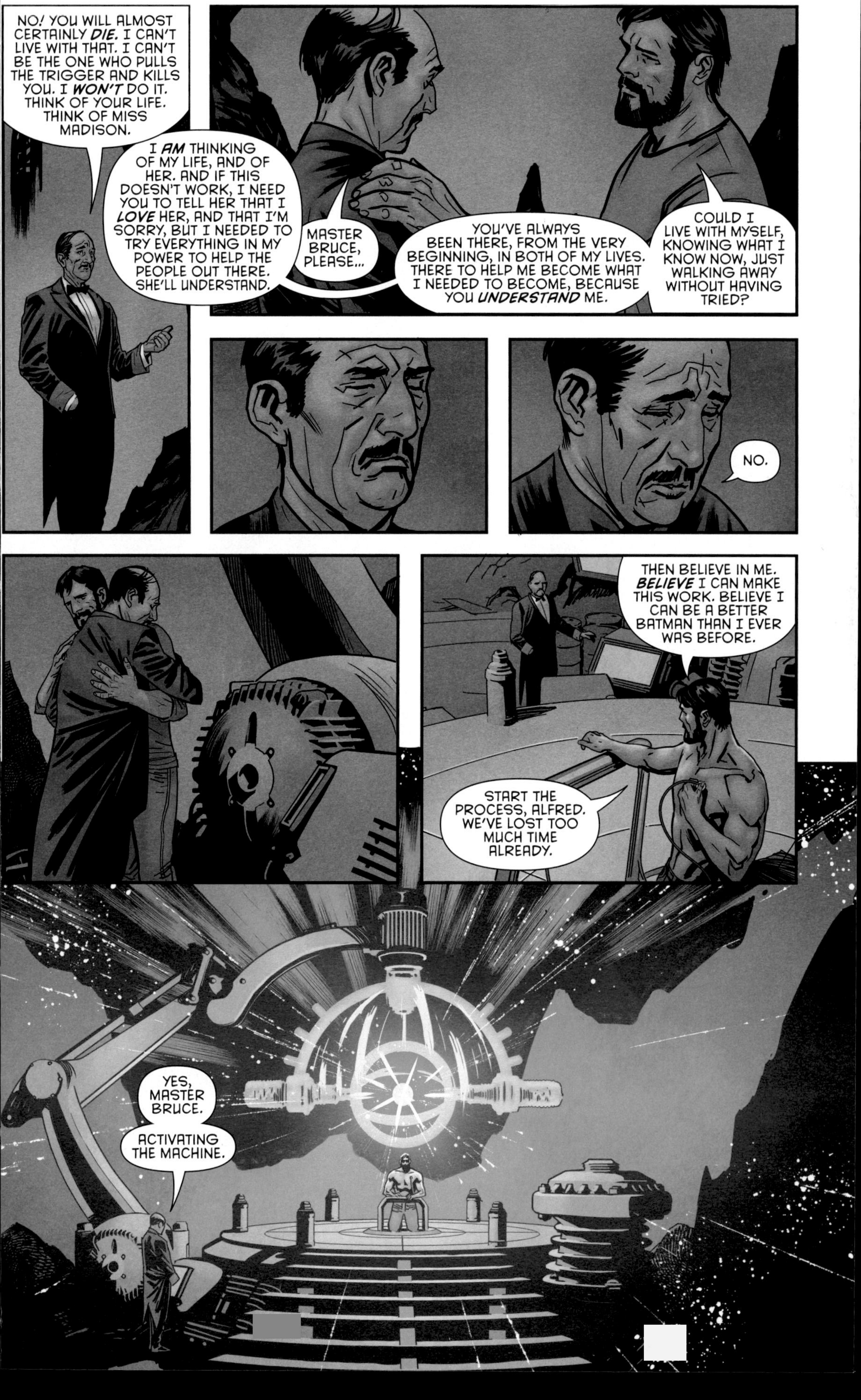
NO! YOU WILL ALMOST CERTAINLY DIE. I CAN'T LIVE WITH THAT. I CAN'T BE THE ONE WHO PULLS THE TRIGGER AND KILLS YOU. I WON'T DO IT. THINK OF YOUR LIFE. THINK OF MISS MADISON.
I AM THINKING OF MY LIFE, AND OF HER. AND IF THIS DOESN'T WORK, I NEED YOU TO TELL HER THAT I LOVE HER, AND THAT I'M SORRY, BUT I NEEDED TO TRY EVERYTHING IN MY POWER TO HELP THE PEOPLE OUT THERE. SHE'LL UNDERSTAND.
MASTER BRUCE, PLEASE...
YOU'VE ALWAYS BEEN THERE, FROM THE VERY BEGINNING, IN BOTH OF MY LIVES. THERE TO HELP ME BECOME WHAT I NEEDED TO BECOME, BECAUSE YOU UNDERSTAND ME.
COULD I LIVE WITH MYSELF, KNOWING WHAT I KNOW NOW, JUST WALKING AWAY WITHOUT HAVING TRIED?
NO.
THEN BELIEVE IN ME. BELIEVE I CAN MAKE THIS WORK. BELIEVE I CAN BE A BETTER BATMAN THAN I EVER WAS BEFORE.
START THE PROCESS, ALFRED. WE'VE LOST TOO MUCH TIME ALREADY.
YES, MASTER BRUCE.
ACTIVATING THE MACHINE.

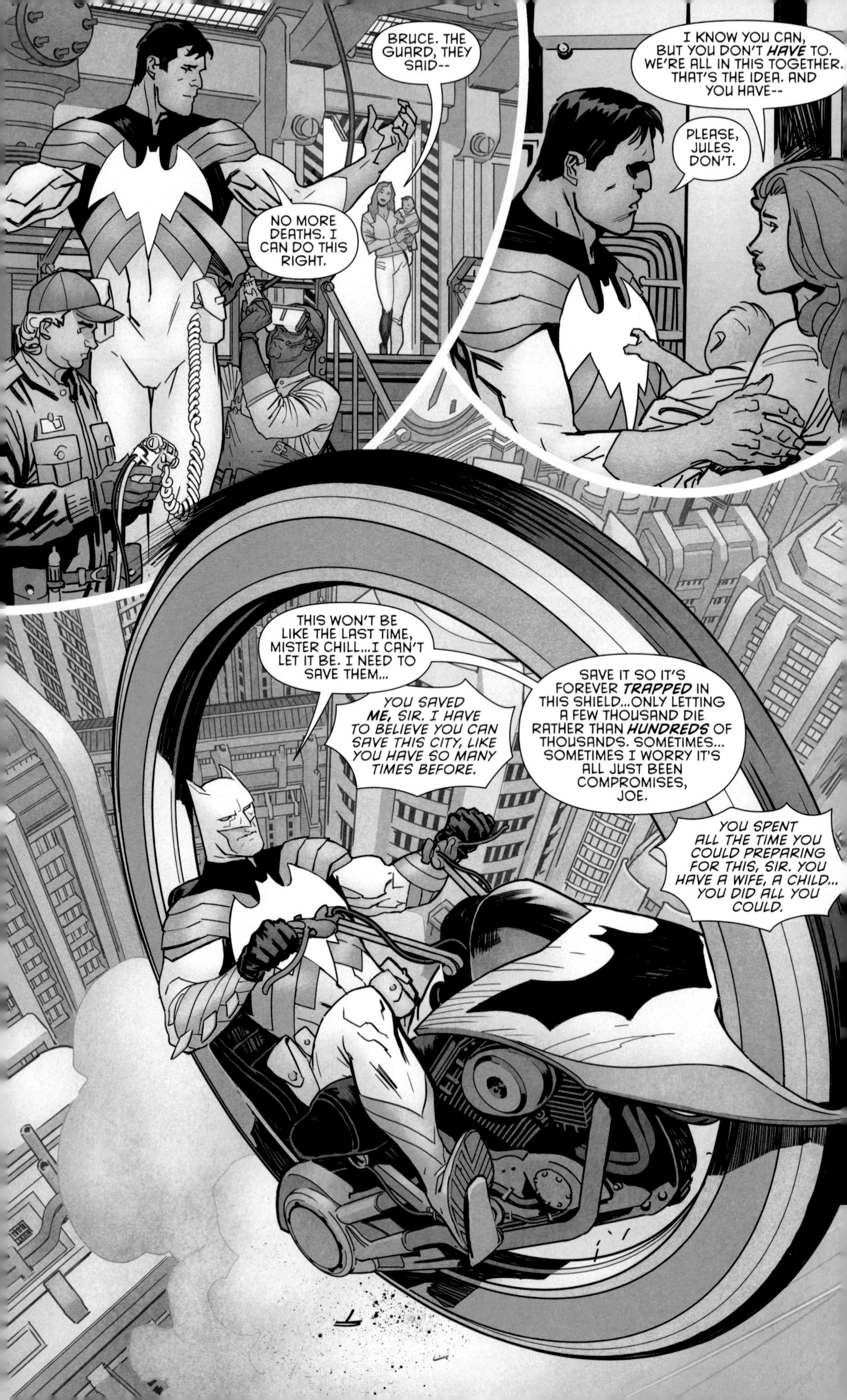
BRUCE. THE GUARD, THEY SAID--
NO MORE DEATHS. I CAN DO THIS RIGHT.
I KNOW YOU CAN, BUT YOU DON'T *HAVE* TO. WE'RE ALL IN THIS TOGETHER. THAT'S THE IDEA. AND YOU HAVE--
PLEASE, JULES. DON'T.
THIS WON'T BE LIKE THE LAST TIME, MISTER CHILL...I CAN'T LET IT BE. I NEED TO SAVE THEM...
*YOU SAVED **ME,** SIR. I HAVE TO BELIEVE YOU CAN SAVE THIS CITY, LIKE YOU HAVE SO MANY TIMES BEFORE.*
SAVE IT SO IT'S FOREVER ***TRAPPED*** IN THIS SHIELD...ONLY LETTING A FEW THOUSAND DIE RATHER THAN ***HUNDREDS*** OF THOUSANDS. SOMETIMES... SOMETIMES I WORRY IT'S ALL JUST BEEN COMPROMISES, JOE.
*YOU SPENT ALL THE TIME YOU COULD PREPARING FOR THIS, SIR. YOU HAVE A WIFE, A CHILD... YOU DID ALL YOU COULD.*

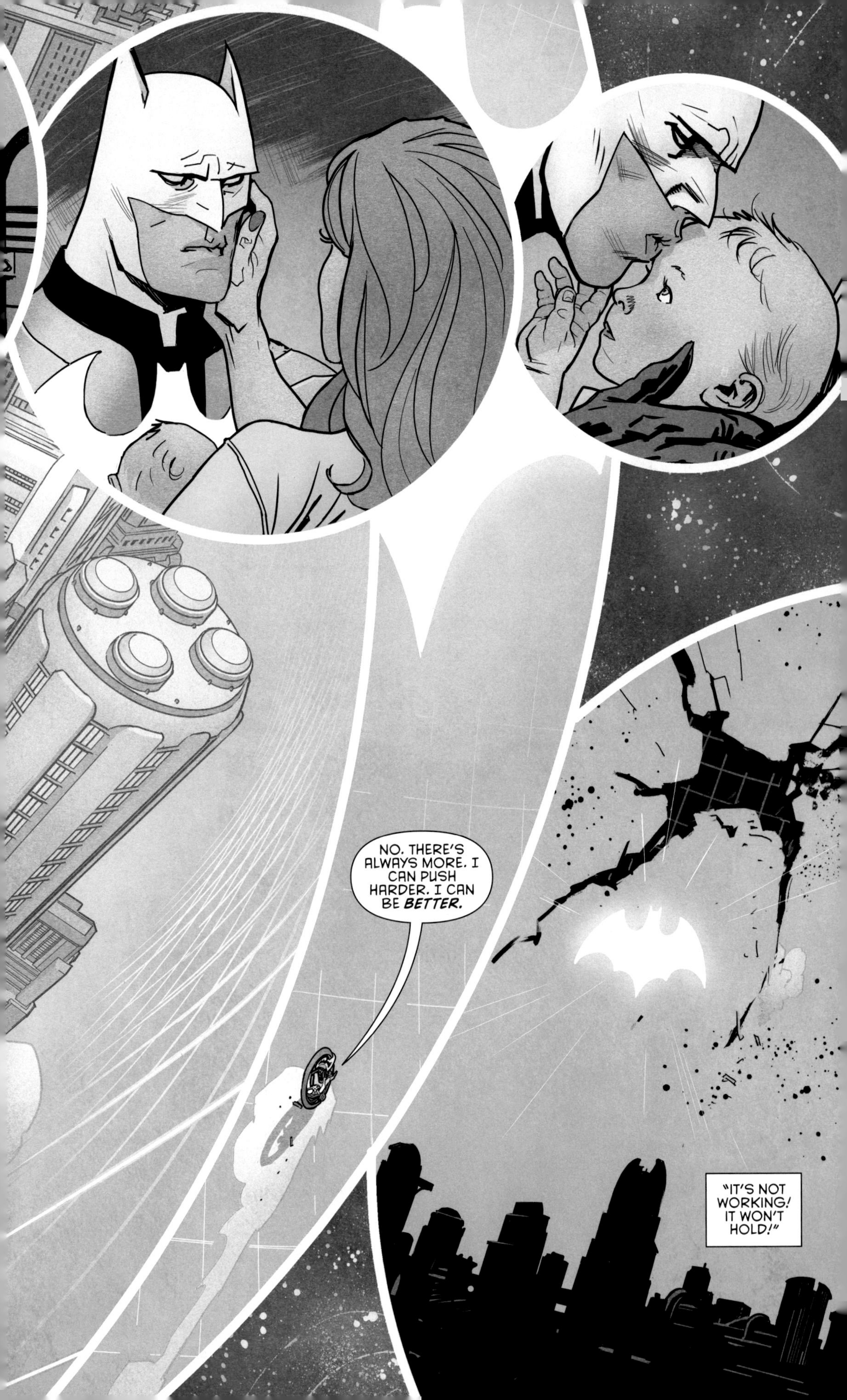
NO. THERE'S ALWAYS MORE. I CAN PUSH HARDER. I CAN BE *BETTER.*
"IT'S NOT WORKING! IT WON'T HOLD!"

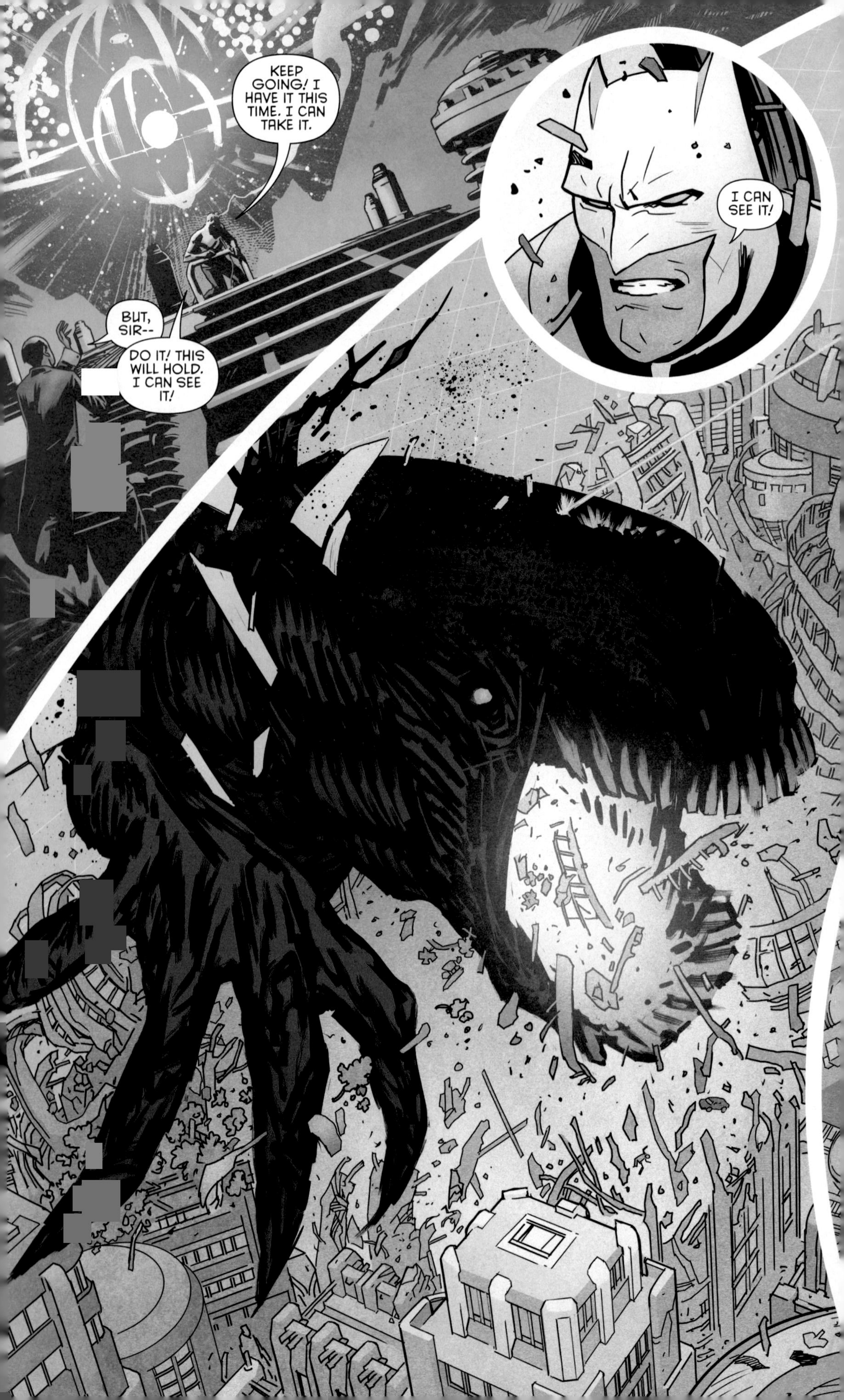

KEEP GOING! I HAVE IT THIS TIME. I CAN TAKE IT.
BUT, SIR--
DO IT! THIS WILL HOLD. I CAN SEE IT!
I CAN SEE IT!

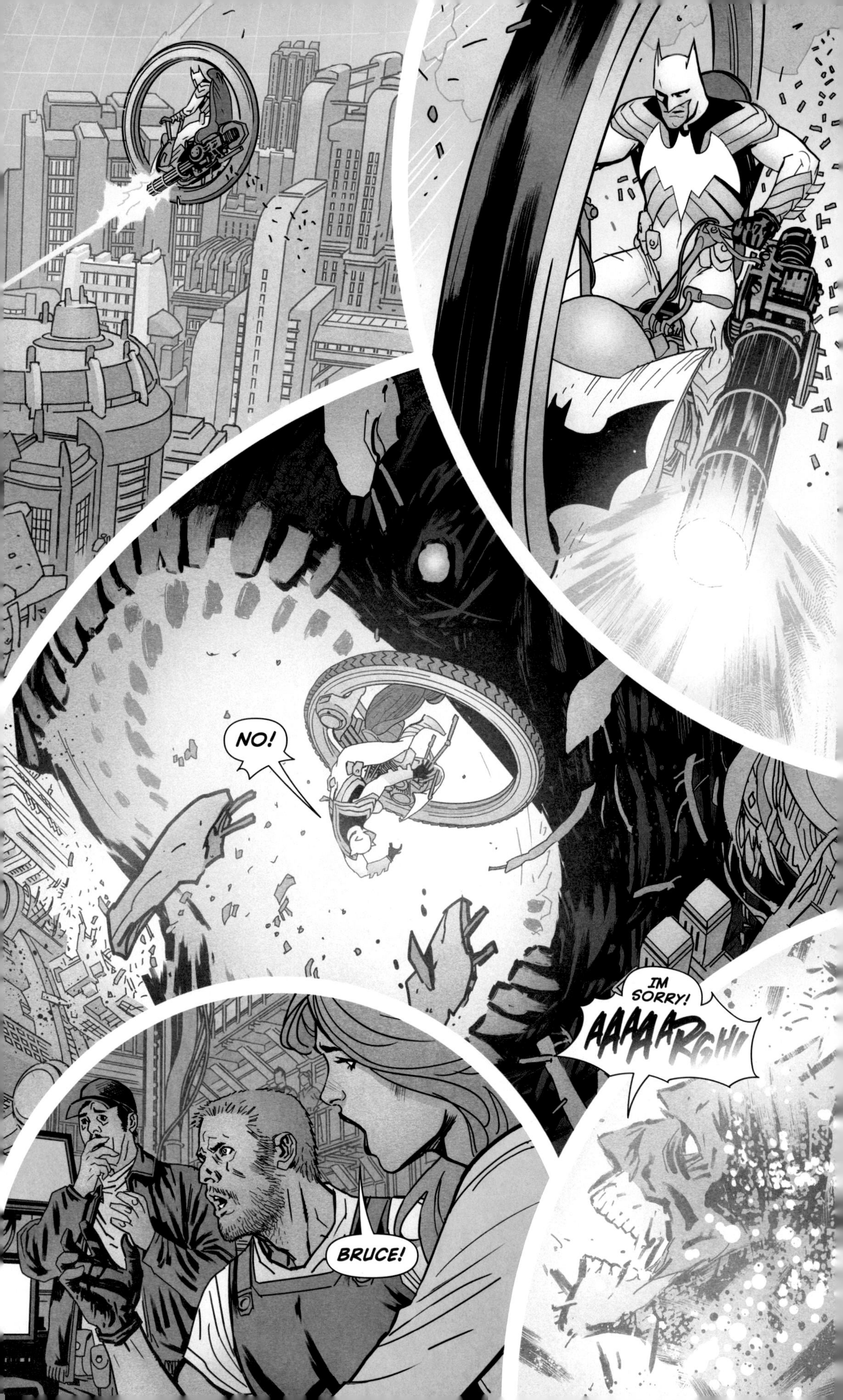
NO!
IM SORRY!
AAAAARGH!
BRUCE!

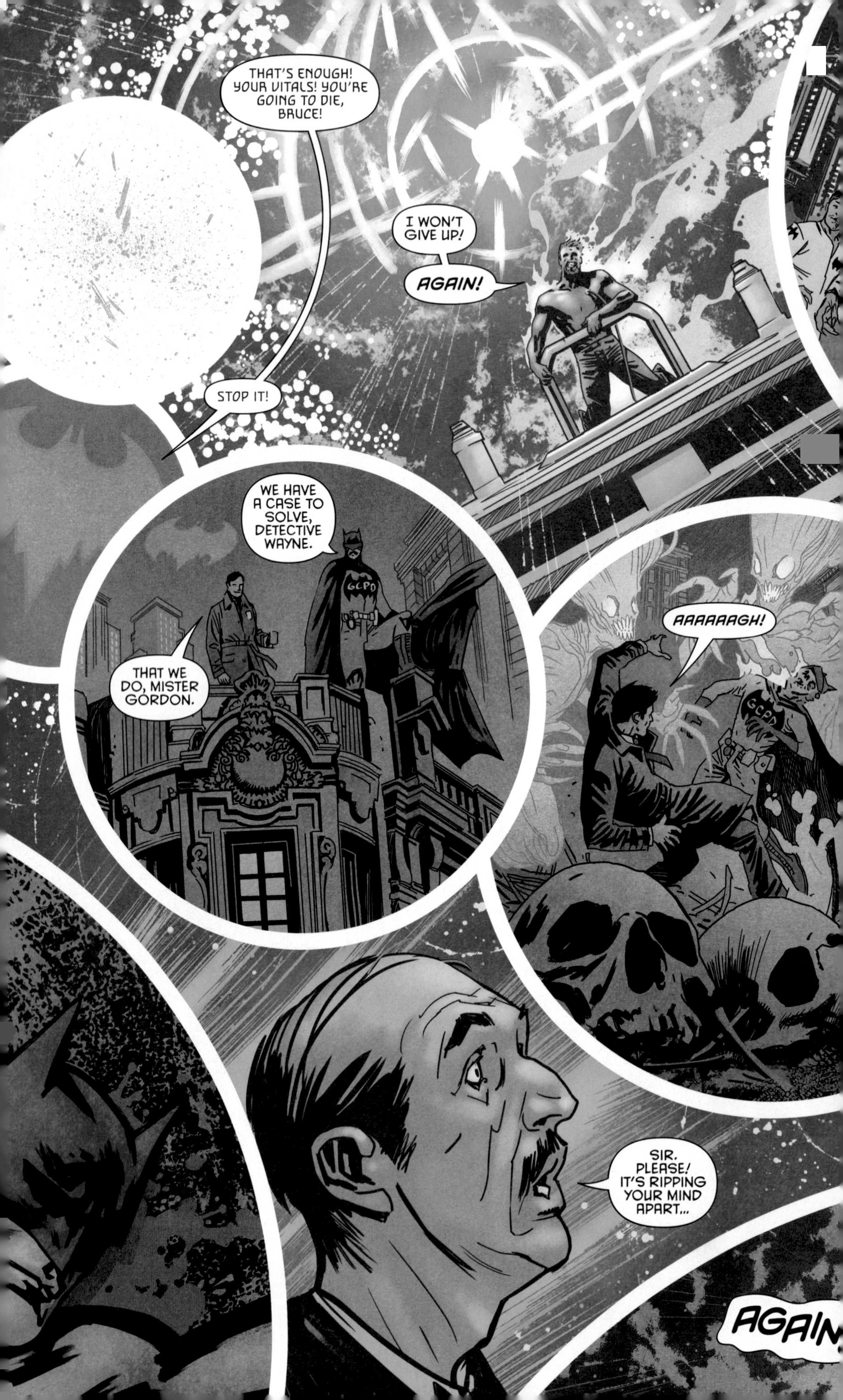
THAT'S ENOUGH! YOUR VITALS! YOU'RE GOING TO DIE, BRUCE!
STOP IT!
I WON'T GIVE UP!
AGAIN!
WE HAVE A CASE TO SOLVE, DETECTIVE WAYNE.
THAT WE DO, MISTER GORDON.
AAAAAAGH!
SIR. PLEASE! IT'S RIPPING YOUR MIND APART...
AGAIN

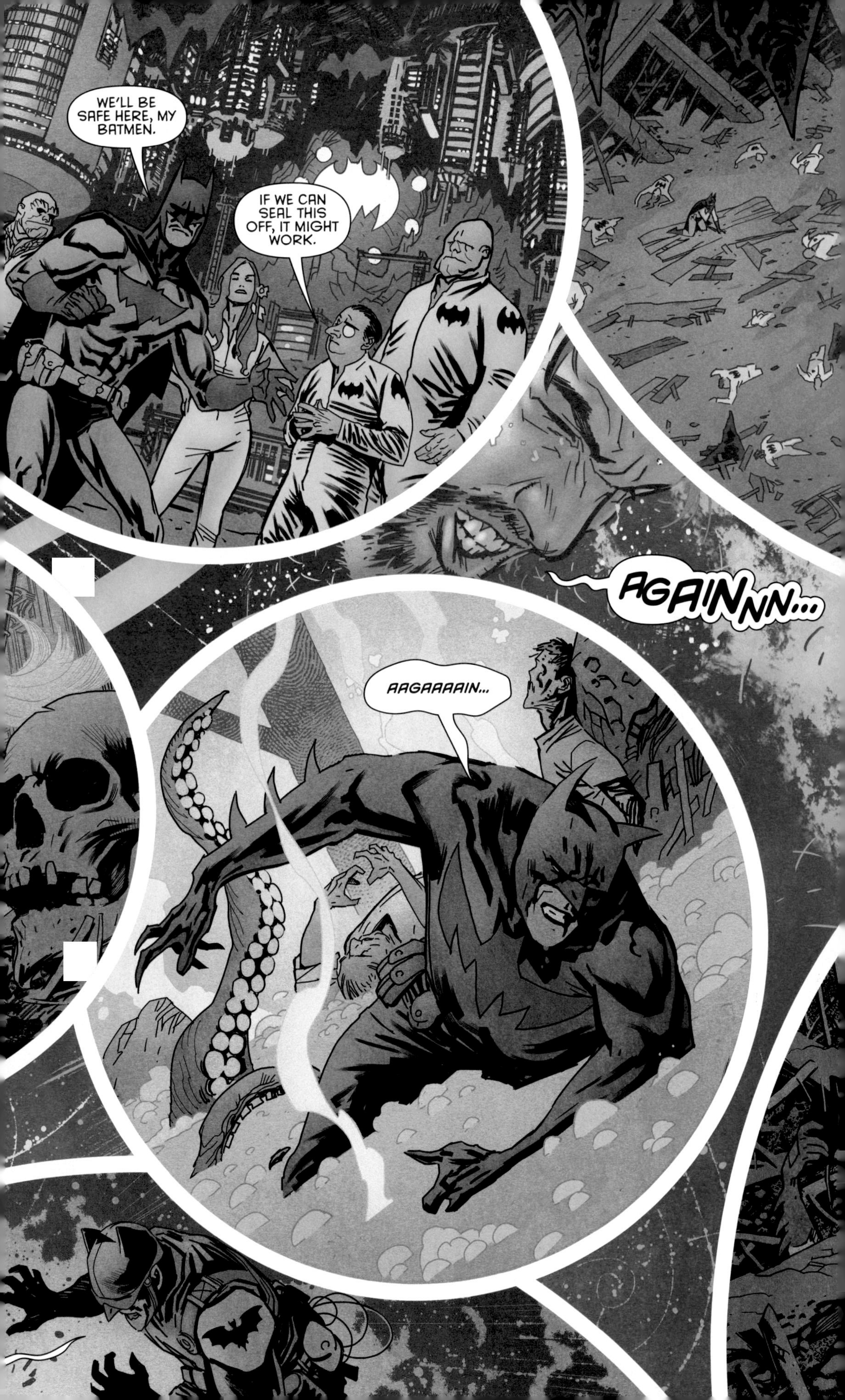
WE'LL BE SAFE HERE, MY BATMEN.
IF WE CAN SEAL THIS OFF, IT MIGHT WORK.
AGAINnnn...
AAGAAAAIN...

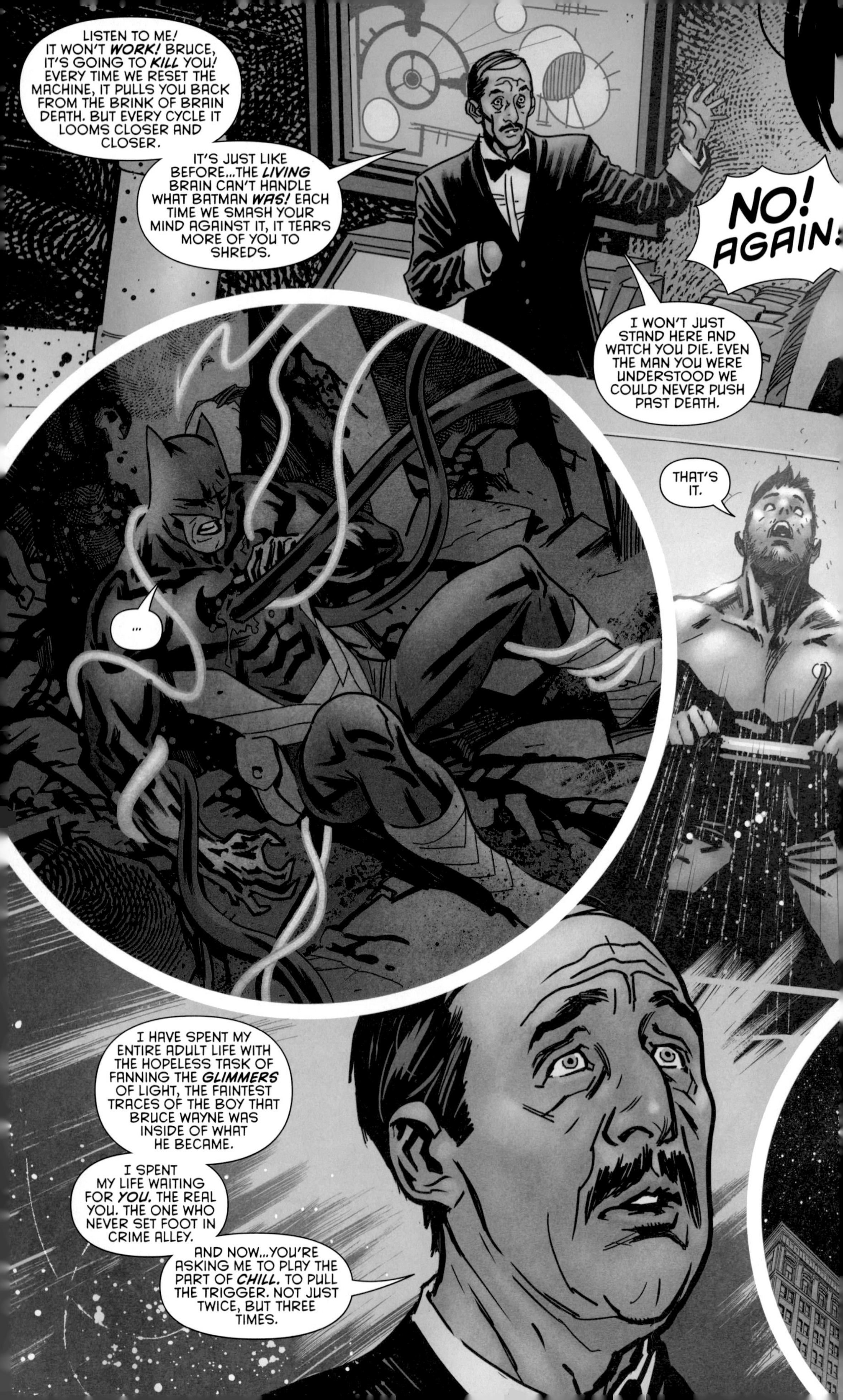
LISTEN TO ME! IT WON'T WORK! BRUCE, IT'S GOING TO KILL YOU! EVERY TIME WE RESET THE MACHINE, IT PULLS YOU BACK FROM THE BRINK OF BRAIN DEATH. BUT EVERY CYCLE IT LOOMS CLOSER AND CLOSER.
IT'S JUST LIKE BEFORE...THE LIVING BRAIN CAN'T HANDLE WHAT BATMAN WAS! EACH TIME WE SMASH YOUR MIND AGAINST IT, IT TEARS MORE OF YOU TO SHREDS.
NO! AGAIN!
I WON'T JUST STAND HERE AND WATCH YOU DIE. EVEN THE MAN YOU WERE UNDERSTOOD WE COULD NEVER PUSH PAST DEATH.
...
THAT'S IT.
I HAVE SPENT MY ENTIRE ADULT LIFE WITH THE HOPELESS TASK OF FANNING THE GLIMMERS OF LIGHT, THE FAINTEST TRACES OF THE BOY THAT BRUCE WAYNE WAS INSIDE OF WHAT HE BECAME.
I SPENT MY LIFE WAITING FOR YOU. THE REAL YOU. THE ONE WHO NEVER SET FOOT IN CRIME ALLEY.
AND NOW...YOU'RE ASKING ME TO PLAY THE PART OF CHILL. TO PULL THE TRIGGER. NOT JUST TWICE, BUT THREE TIMES.

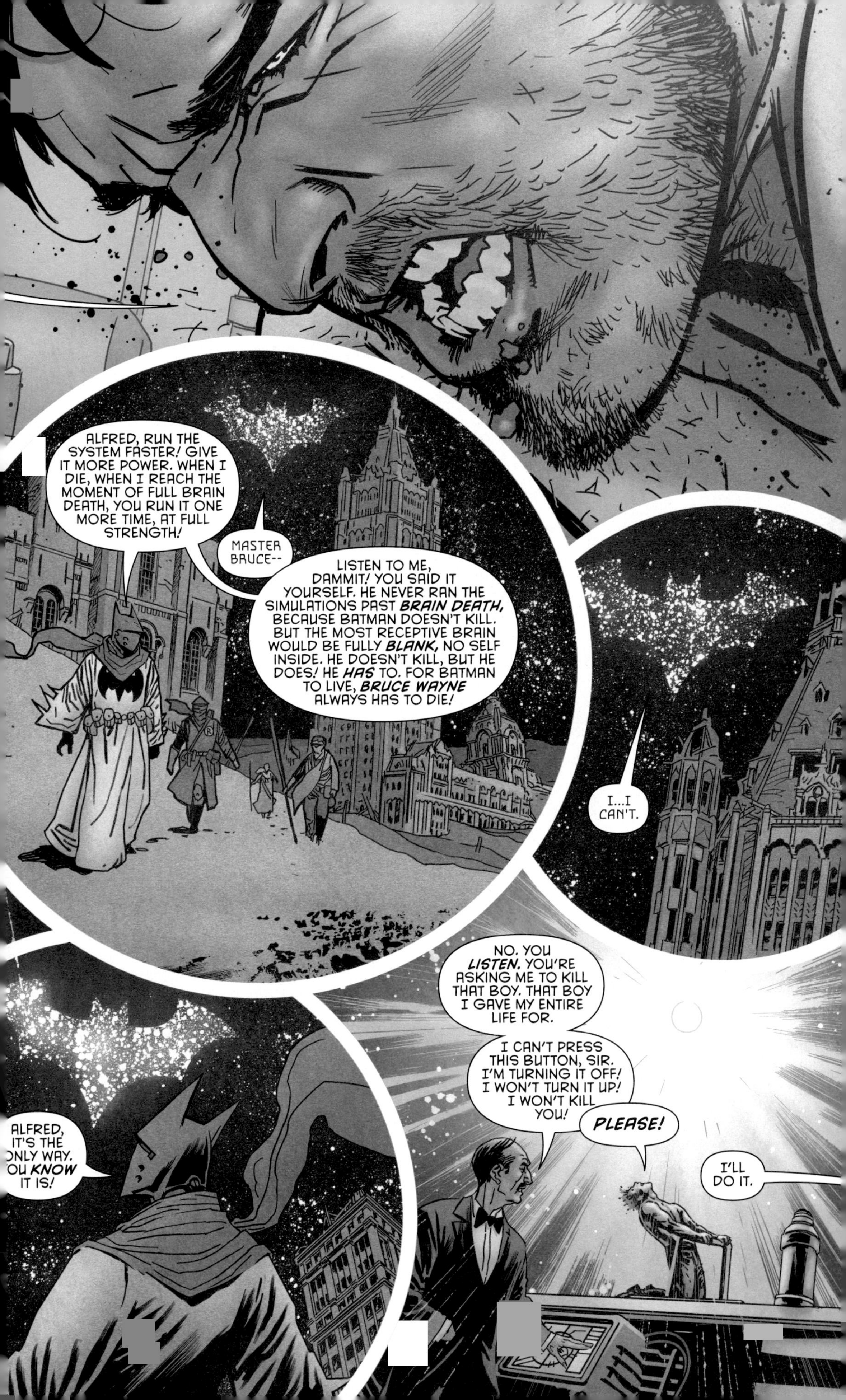
ALFRED, RUN THE SYSTEM FASTER! GIVE IT MORE POWER. WHEN I DIE, WHEN I REACH THE MOMENT OF FULL BRAIN DEATH, YOU RUN IT ONE MORE TIME, AT FULL STRENGTH!
MASTER BRUCE--
LISTEN TO ME, DAMMIT! YOU SAID IT YOURSELF. HE NEVER RAN THE SIMULATIONS PAST *BRAIN DEATH,* BECAUSE BATMAN DOESN'T KILL. BUT THE MOST RECEPTIVE BRAIN WOULD BE FULLY *BLANK,* NO SELF INSIDE. HE DOESN'T KILL, BUT HE DOES! HE *HAS* TO. FOR BATMAN TO LIVE, *BRUCE WAYNE* ALWAYS HAS TO DIE!
I...I CAN'T.
ALFRED, IT'S THE ONLY WAY. YOU *KNOW* IT IS!
NO. YOU *LISTEN.* YOU'RE ASKING ME TO KILL THAT BOY. THAT BOY I GAVE MY ENTIRE LIFE FOR.
I CAN'T PRESS THIS BUTTON, SIR. I'M TURNING IT OFF! I WON'T TURN IT UP! I WON'T KILL YOU!
*PLEASE!*
I'LL DO IT.

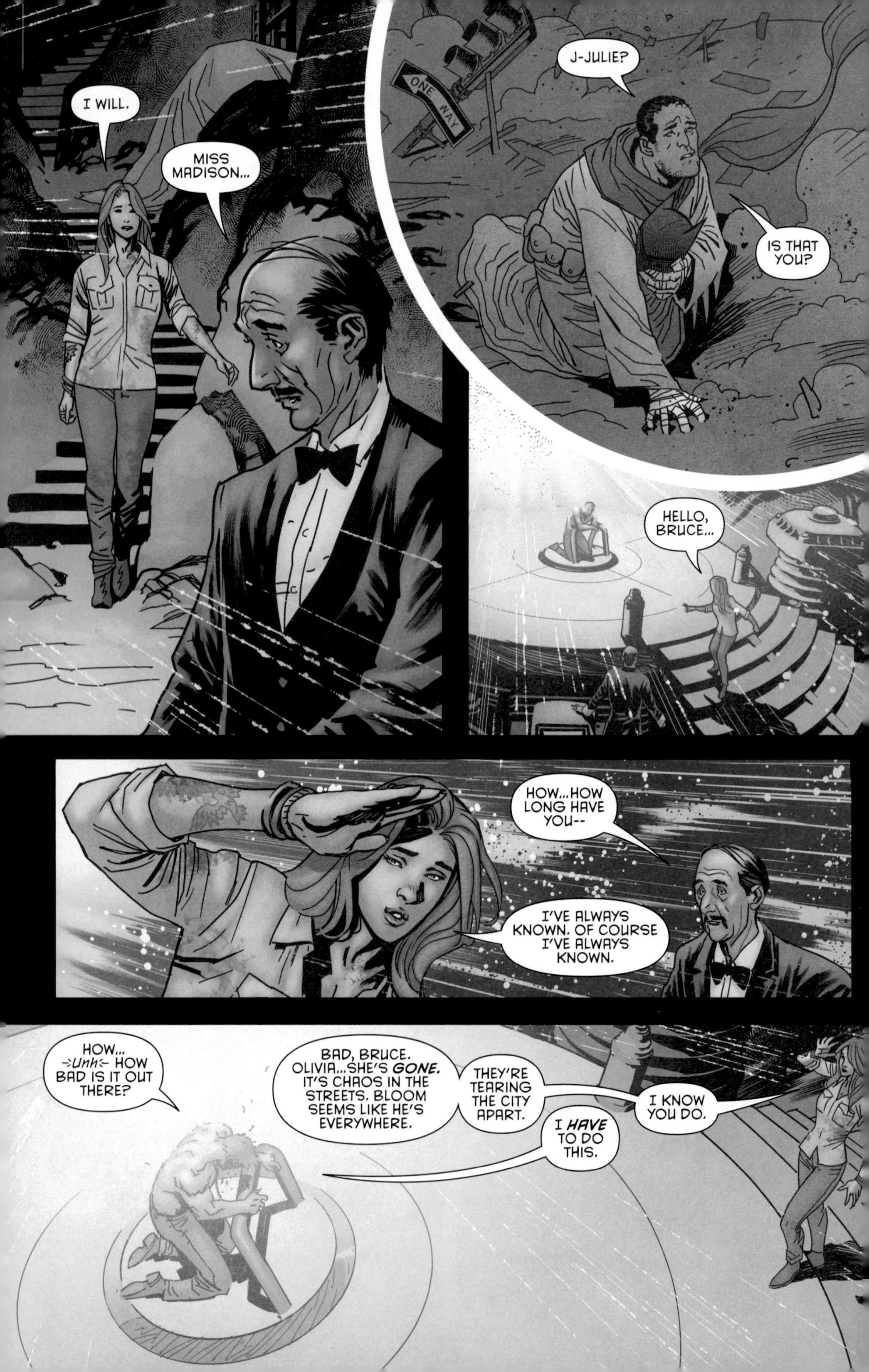
I WILL.
MISS MADISON...
J-JULIE?
IS THAT YOU?
HELLO, BRUCE...
HOW...HOW LONG HAVE YOU--
I'VE ALWAYS KNOWN. OF COURSE I'VE ALWAYS KNOWN.
HOW... ~Unh~ HOW BAD IS IT OUT THERE?
BAD, BRUCE. OLIVIA...SHE'S GONE. IT'S CHAOS IN THE STREETS. BLOOM SEEMS LIKE HE'S EVERYWHERE.
THEY'RE TEARING THE CITY APART.
I KNOW YOU DO.
I HAVE TO DO THIS.

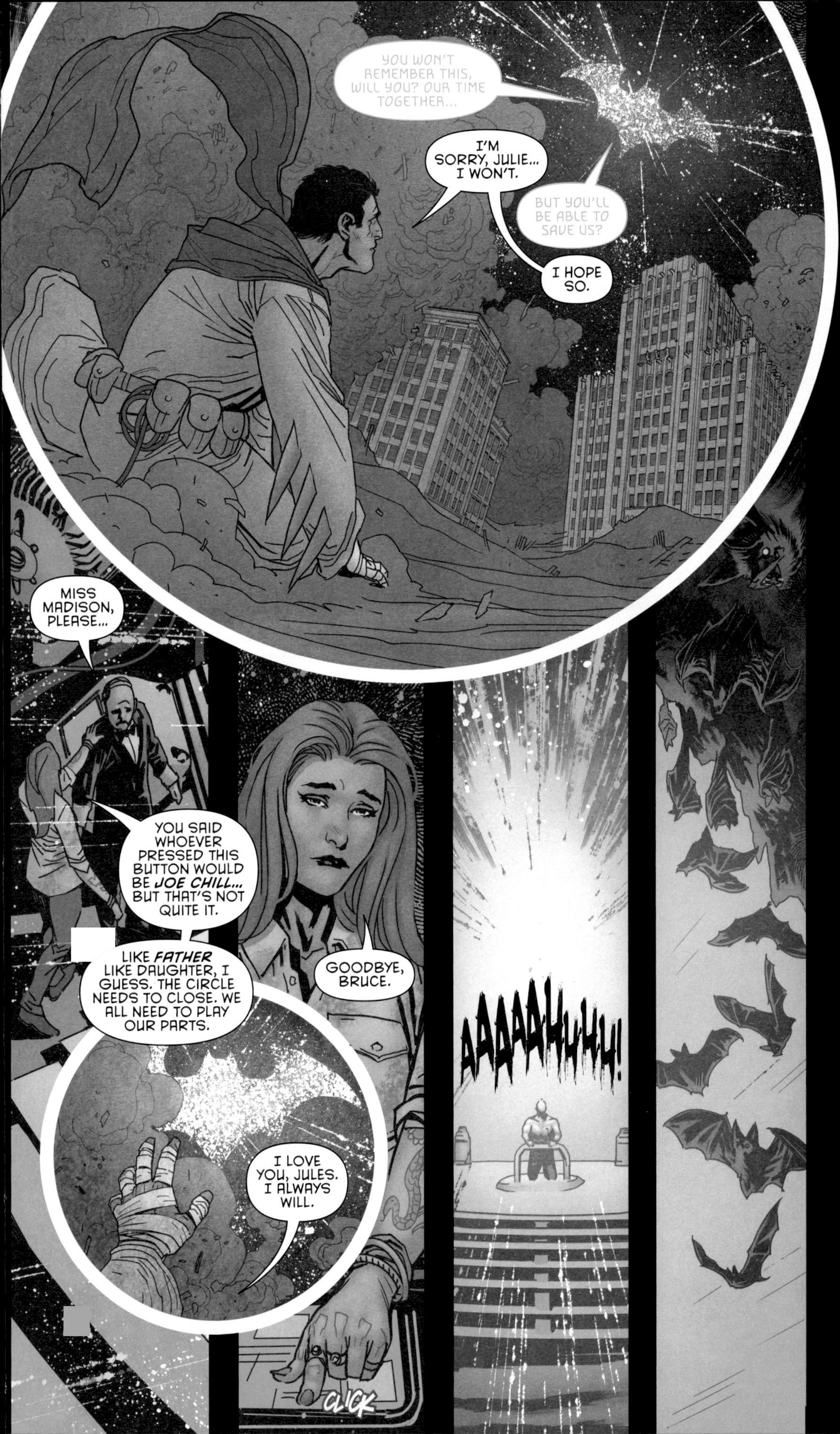

YOU WON'T REMEMBER THIS, WILL YOU? OUR TIME TOGETHER...
I'M SORRY, JULIE... I WON'T.
BUT YOU'LL BE ABLE TO SAVE US?
I HOPE SO.
MISS MADISON, PLEASE...
YOU SAID WHOEVER PRESSED THIS BUTTON WOULD BE *JOE CHILL*... BUT THAT'S NOT QUITE IT.
LIKE *FATHER* LIKE DAUGHTER, I GUESS. THE CIRCLE NEEDS TO CLOSE. WE ALL NEED TO PLAY OUR PARTS.
GOODBYE, BRUCE.
I LOVE YOU, JULES. I ALWAYS WILL.
CLICK
AAAAAHHHH!

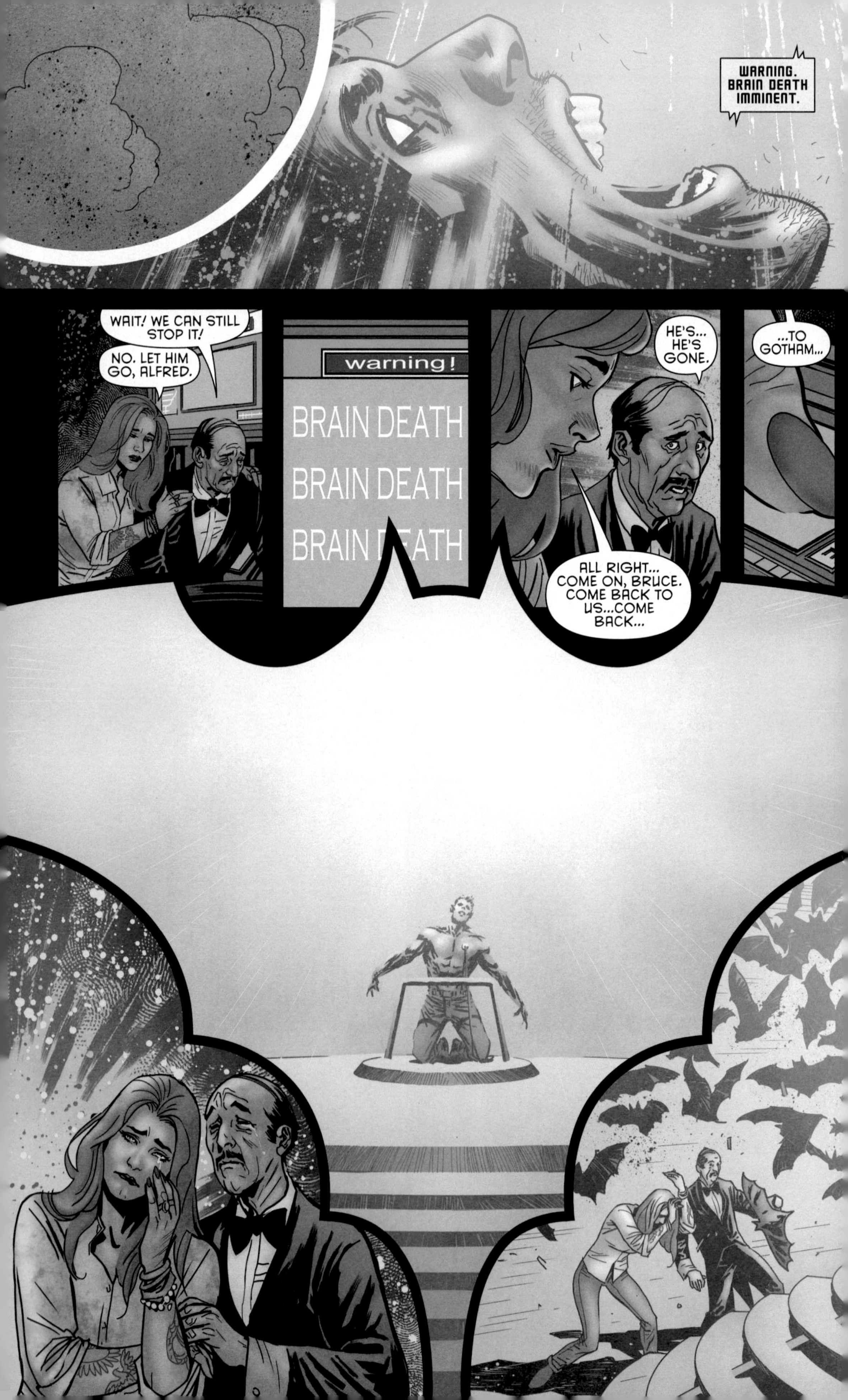
WARNING. BRAIN DEATH IMMINENT.
WAIT! WE CAN STILL STOP IT!
NO. LET HIM GO, ALFRED.
warning!
BRAIN DEATH
BRAIN DEATH
BRAIN DEATH
HE'S... HE'S GONE.
ALL RIGHT... COME ON, BRUCE. COME BACK TO US...COME BACK...
...TO GOTHAM...

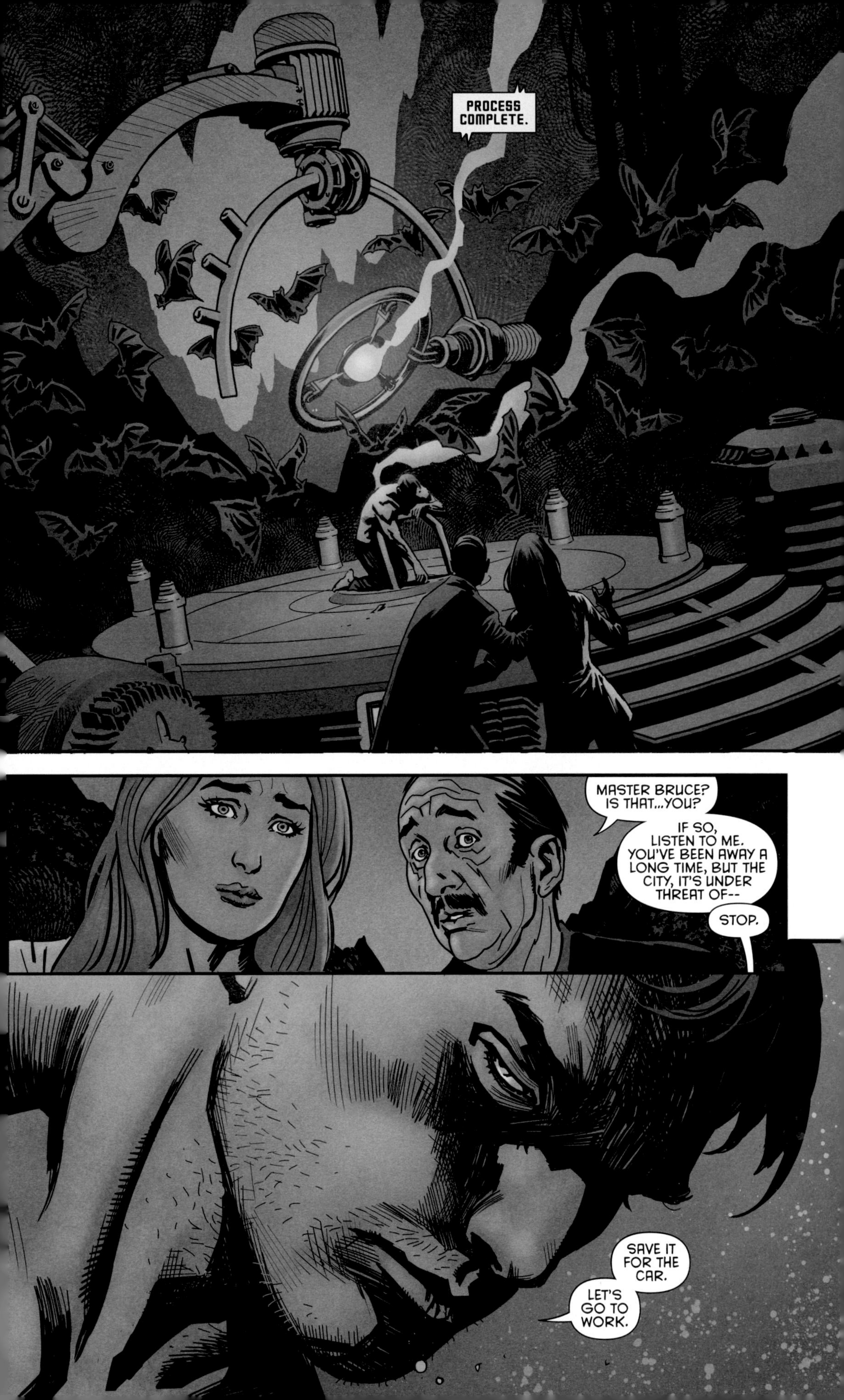
PROCESS COMPLETE.
MASTER BRUCE? IS THAT...YOU?
IF SO, LISTEN TO ME. YOU'VE BEEN AWAY A LONG TIME, BUT THE CITY, IT'S UNDER THREAT OF--
STOP.
SAVE IT FOR THE CAR.
LET'S GO TO WORK.

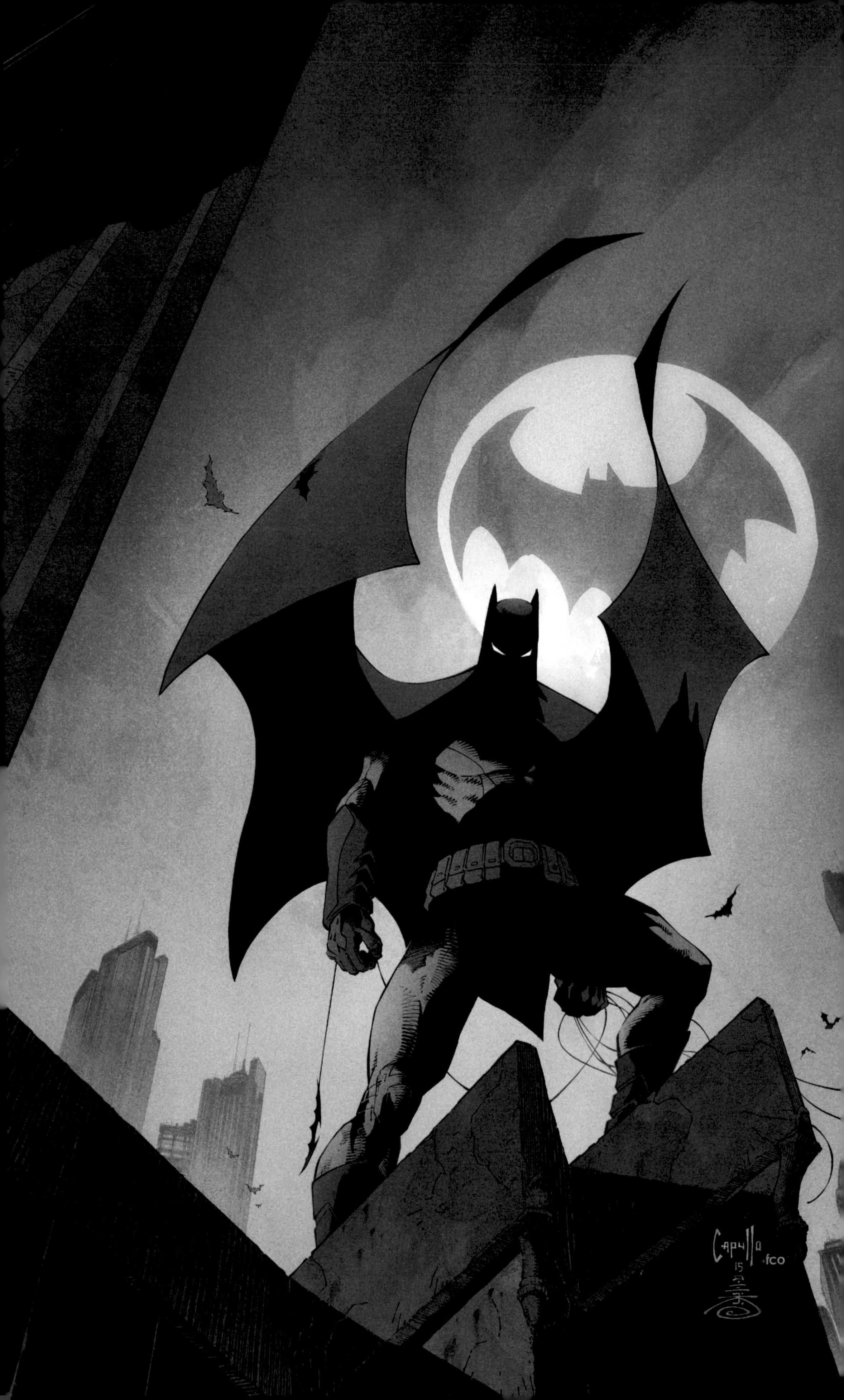

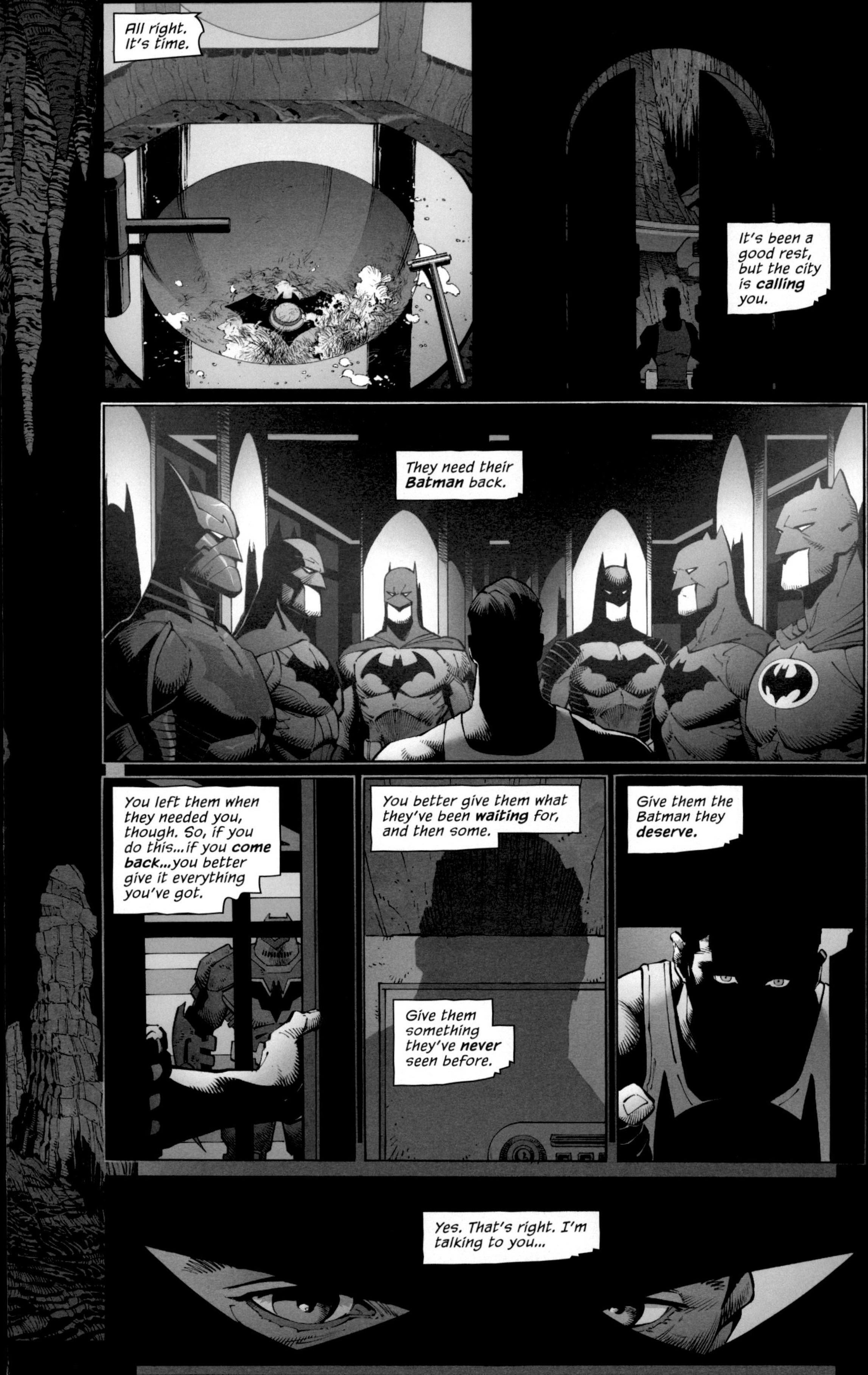
All right. It's time.
It's been a good rest, but the city is calling you.
They need their Batman back.
You left them when they needed you, though. So, if you do this...if you come back...you better give it everything you've got.
You better give them what they've been waiting for, and then some.
Give them something they've never seen before.
Give them the Batman they deserve.
Yes. That's right. I'm talking to you...

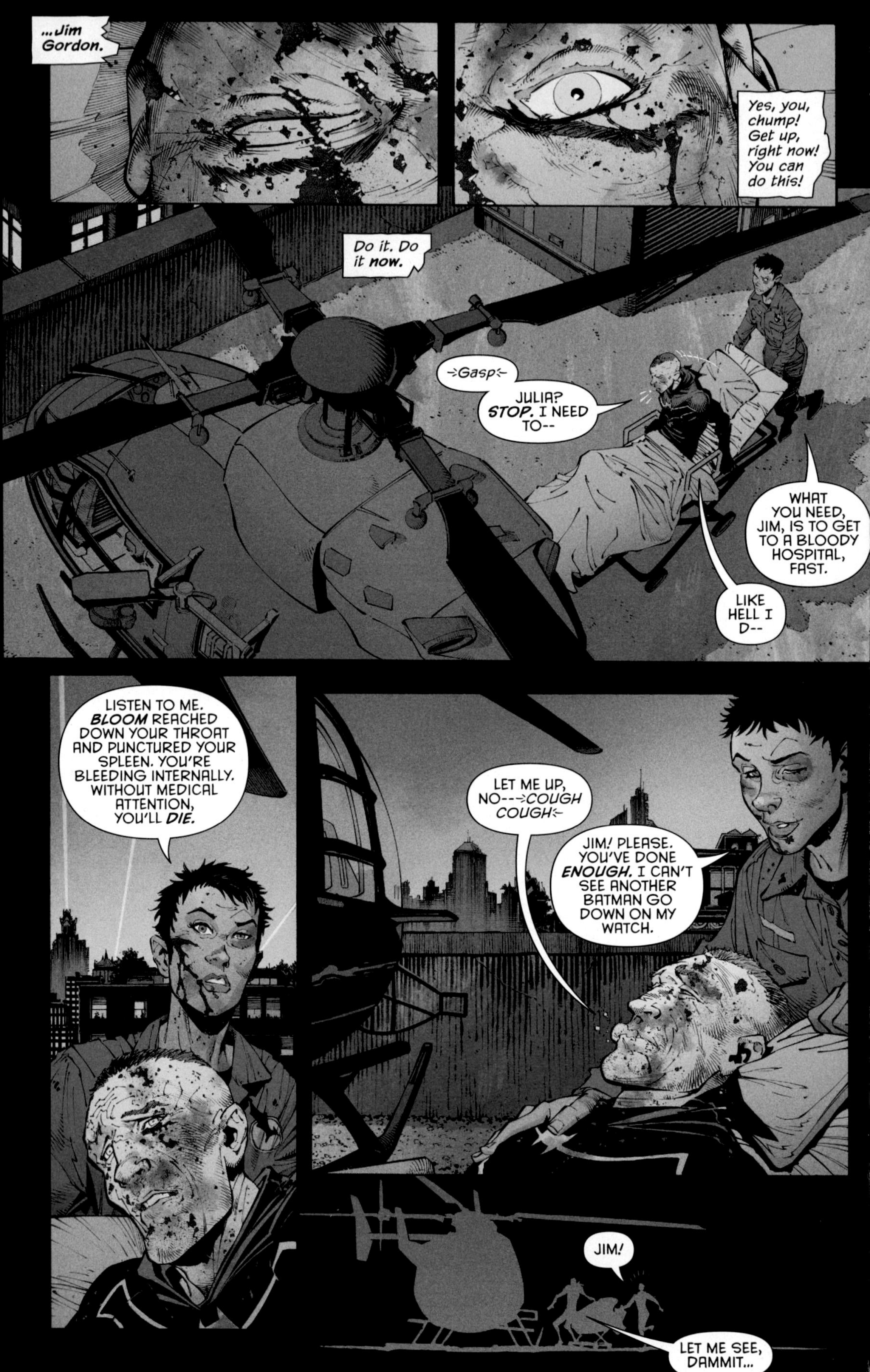
...Jim Gordon.
Yes, you, chump! Get up, right now! You can do this!
Do it. Do it now.
Gasp
JULIA? STOP. I NEED TO--
WHAT YOU NEED, JIM, IS TO GET TO A BLOODY HOSPITAL, FAST.
LIKE HELL I D--
LISTEN TO ME. BLOOM REACHED DOWN YOUR THROAT AND PUNCTURED YOUR SPLEEN. YOU'RE BLEEDING INTERNALLY. WITHOUT MEDICAL ATTENTION, YOU'LL DIE.
LET ME UP, NO--COUGH COUGH
JIM! PLEASE. YOU'VE DONE ENOUGH. I CAN'T SEE ANOTHER BATMAN GO DOWN ON MY WATCH.
JIM!
LET ME SEE, DAMMIT...

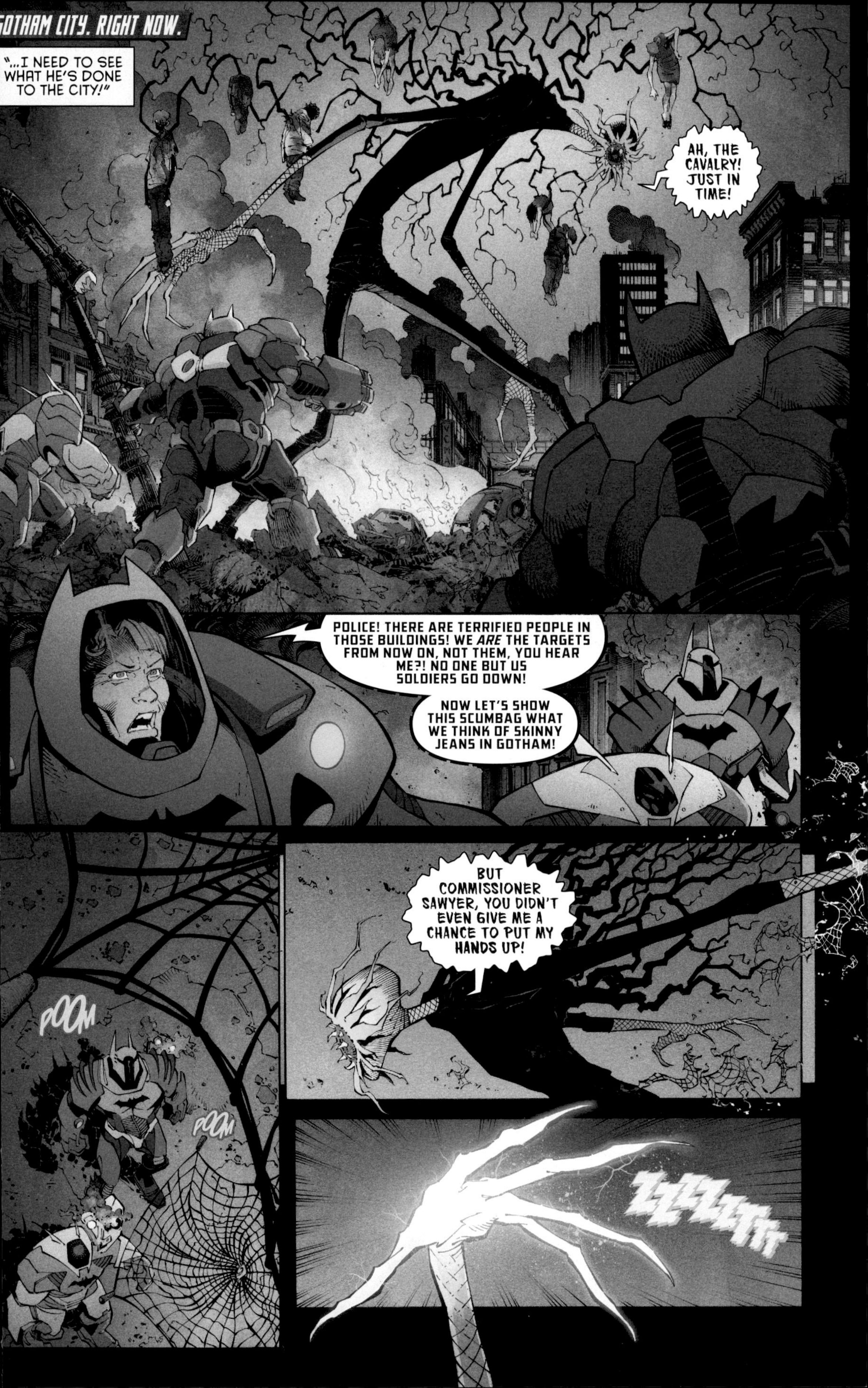
GOTHAM CITY. RIGHT NOW.
"...I NEED TO SEE WHAT HE'S DONE TO THE CITY!"
AH, THE CAVALRY! JUST IN TIME!
POLICE! THERE ARE TERRIFIED PEOPLE IN THOSE BUILDINGS! WE *ARE* THE TARGETS FROM NOW ON, NOT THEM, YOU HEAR ME?! NO ONE BUT US SOLDIERS GO DOWN!
NOW LET'S SHOW THIS SCUMBAG WHAT WE THINK OF SKINNY JEANS IN GOTHAM!
BUT COMMISSIONER SAWYER, YOU DIDN'T EVEN GIVE ME A CHANCE TO PUT MY HANDS UP!
POOM
POOM
ZZZZZZTTTT

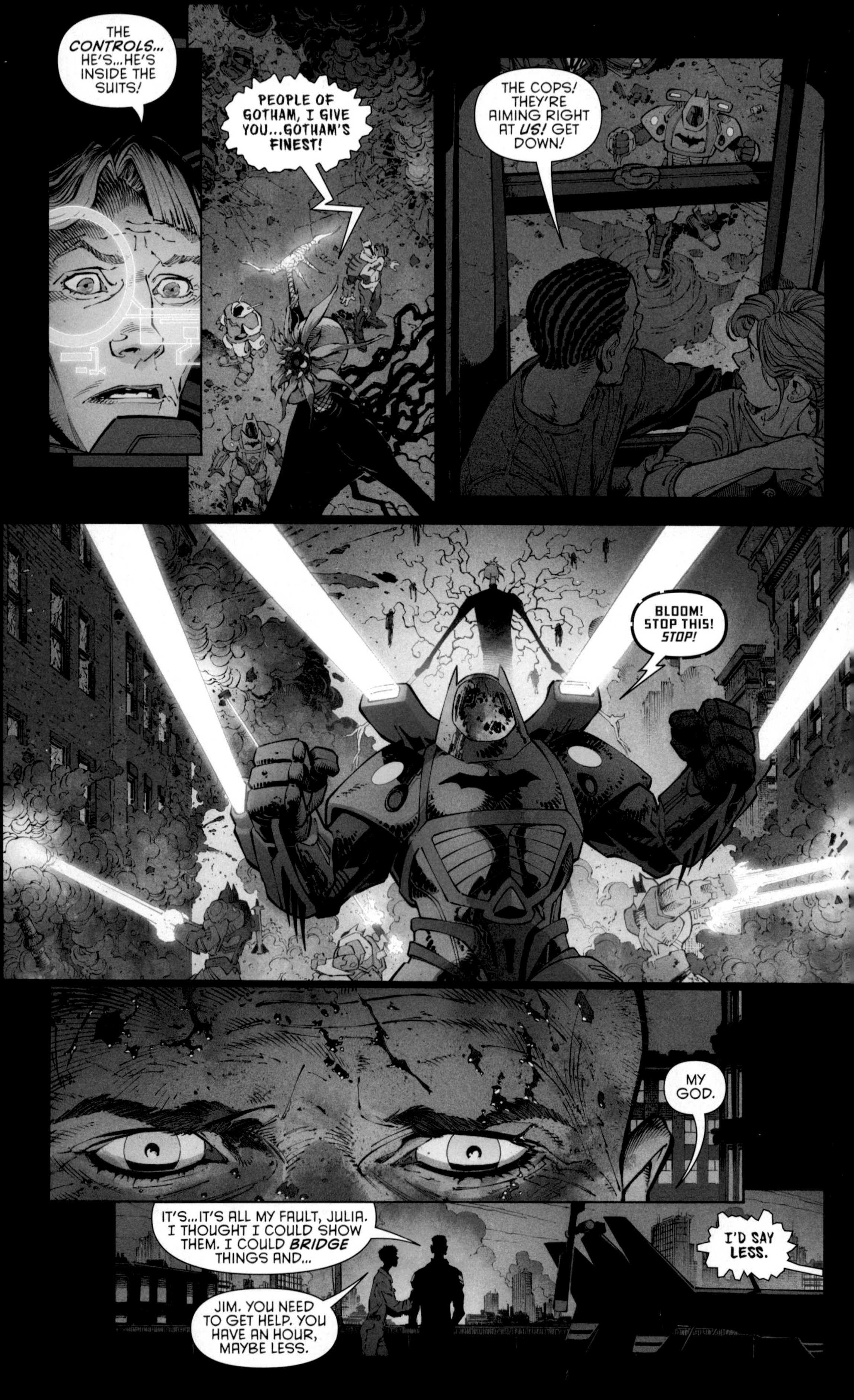
THE CONTROLS... HE'S...HE'S INSIDE THE SUITS!
PEOPLE OF GOTHAM, I GIVE YOU...GOTHAM'S FINEST!
THE COPS! THEY'RE AIMING RIGHT AT US! GET DOWN!
BLOOM! STOP THIS! STOP!
MY GOD.
IT'S...IT'S ALL MY FAULT, JULIA. I THOUGHT I COULD SHOW THEM. I COULD BRIDGE THINGS AND...
JIM. YOU NEED TO GET HELP. YOU HAVE AN HOUR, MAYBE LESS.
I'D SAY LESS.

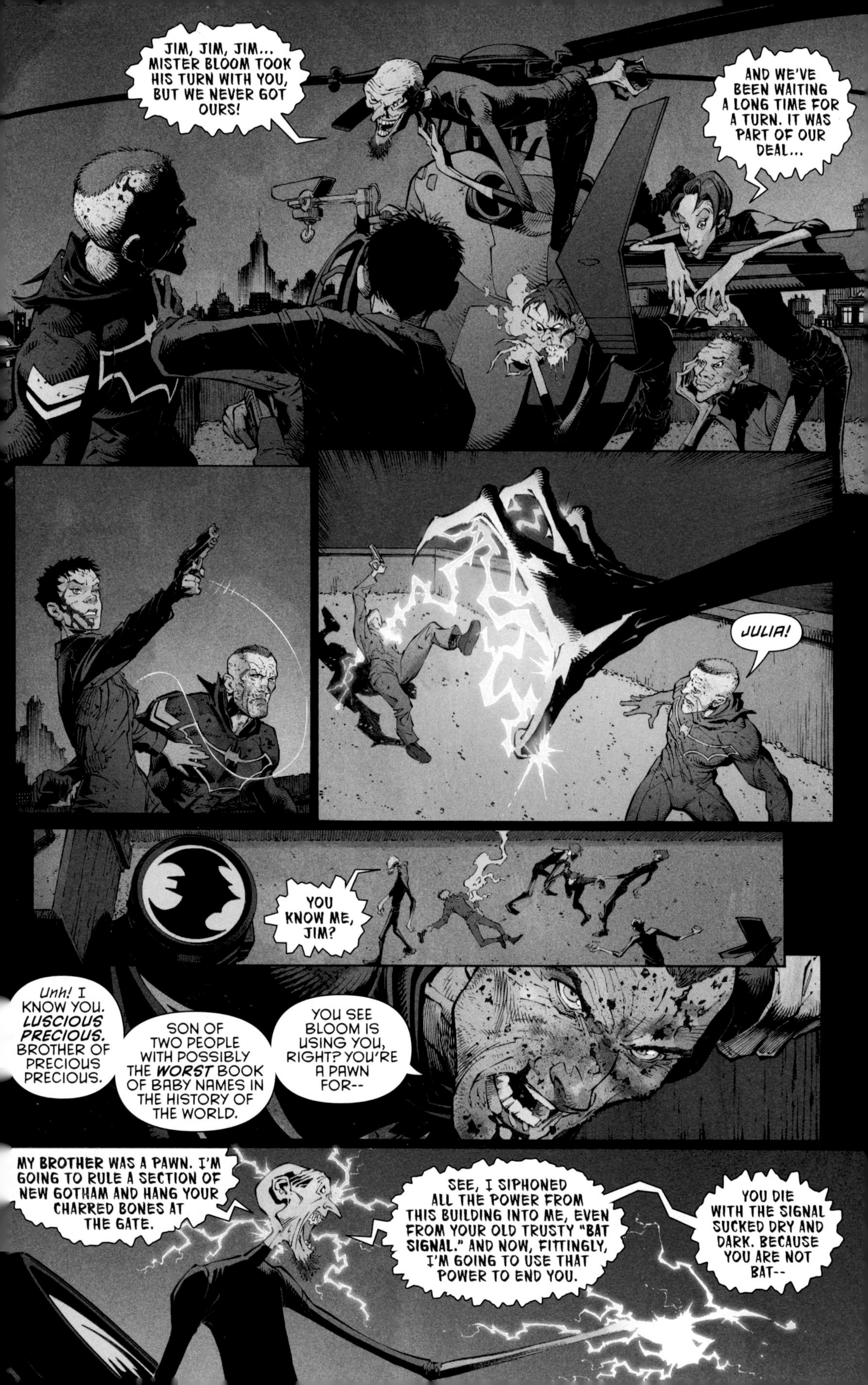

JIM, JIM, JIM... MISTER BLOOM TOOK HIS TURN WITH YOU, BUT WE NEVER GOT OURS!
AND WE'VE BEEN WAITING A LONG TIME FOR A TURN. IT WAS PART OF OUR DEAL...
JULIA!
YOU KNOW ME, JIM?
Unh! I KNOW YOU. LUSCIOUS PRECIOUS. BROTHER OF PRECIOUS PRECIOUS.
SON OF TWO PEOPLE WITH POSSIBLY THE WORST BOOK OF BABY NAMES IN THE HISTORY OF THE WORLD.
YOU SEE BLOOM IS USING YOU, RIGHT? YOU'RE A PAWN FOR--
MY BROTHER WAS A PAWN. I'M GOING TO RULE A SECTION OF NEW GOTHAM AND HANG YOUR CHARRED BONES AT THE GATE.
SEE, I SIPHONED ALL THE POWER FROM THIS BUILDING INTO ME, EVEN FROM YOUR OLD TRUSTY "BAT SIGNAL." AND NOW, FITTINGLY, I'M GOING TO USE THAT POWER TO END YOU.
YOU DIE WITH THE SIGNAL SUCKED DRY AND DARK. BECAUSE YOU ARE NOT BAT--

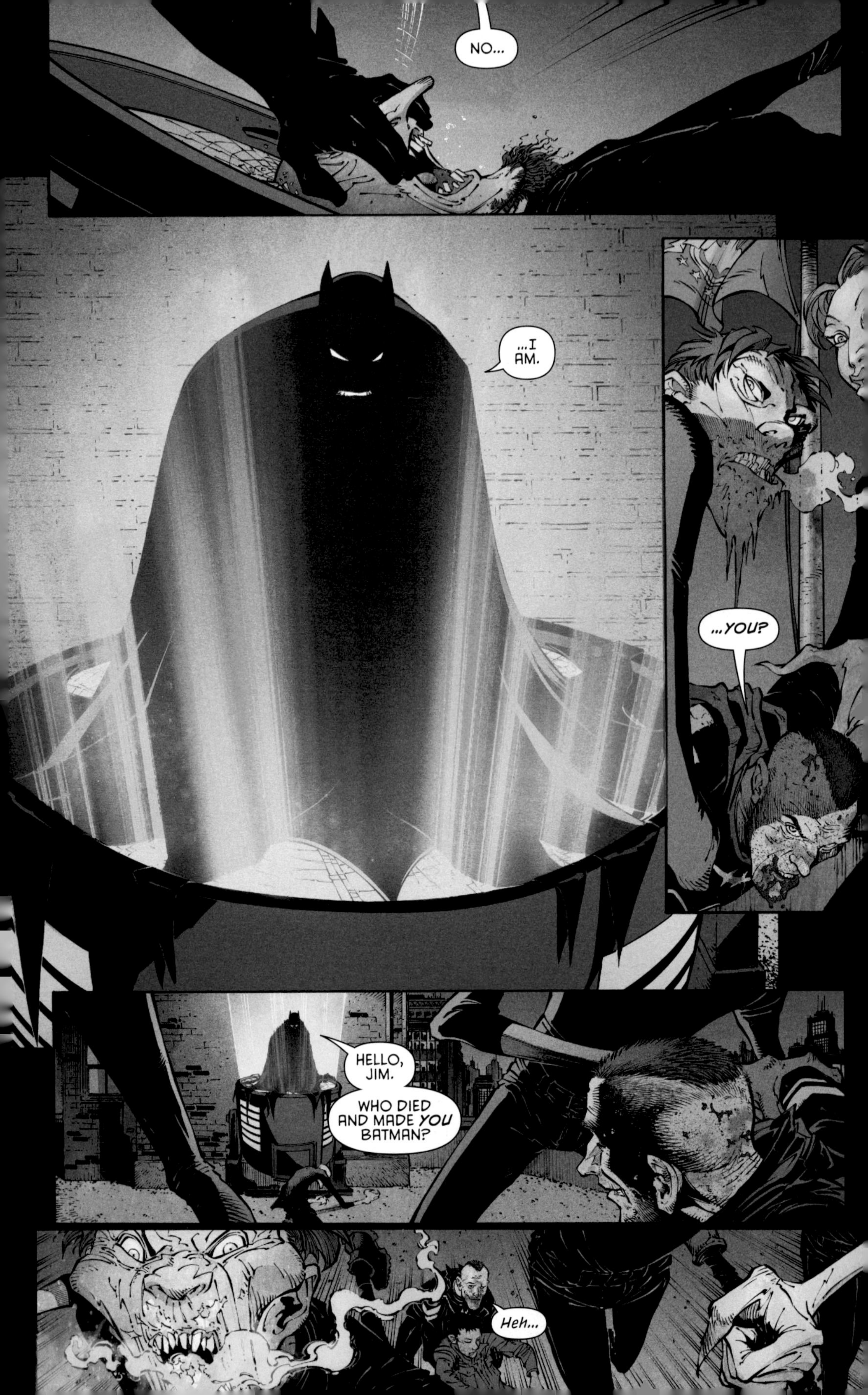
NO...
...I AM.
...YOU?
HELLO, JIM.
WHO DIED AND MADE *YOU* BATMAN?
Heh...

# SUPERHEAVY

## PART TEN

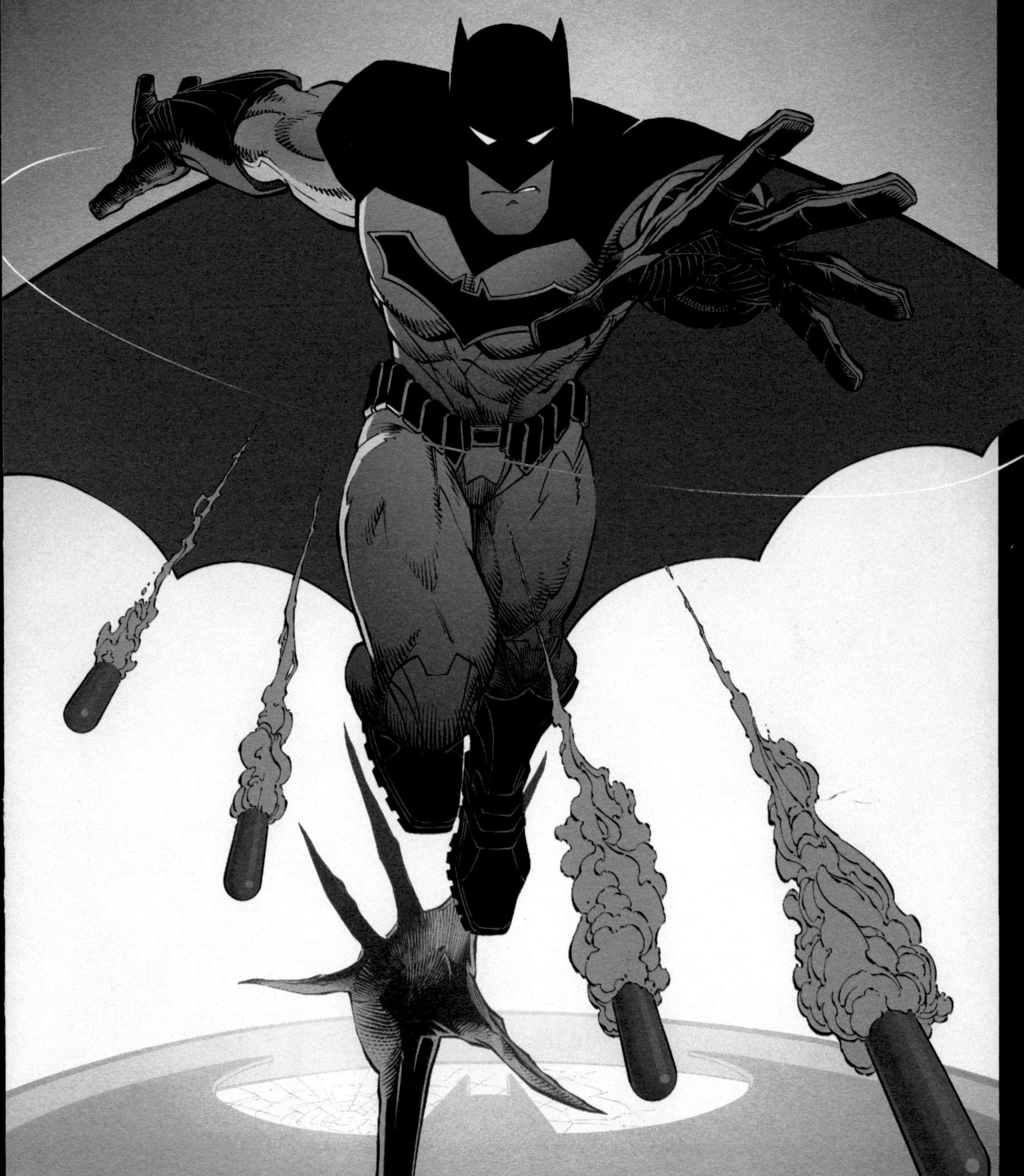

SCOTT SNYDER writer GREG CAPULLO pencils
DANNY MIKI inks FCO PLASCENCIA colors
YANICK PAQUETTE epilogue art NATHAN FAIRBAIRN epilogue colors
STEVE WANDS letters CAPULLO, MIKI, PLASCENCIA cover
BATMAN V SUPERMAN VARIANT COVERS BY
HRIS DAUGHTRY, JIM LEE & ALEX SINCLAIR; DAVE JOHNSON & DAVE MCCAIG
REBECCA TAYLOR associate editor MARK DOYLE editor
BATMAN created by BOB KANE with BILL FINGER

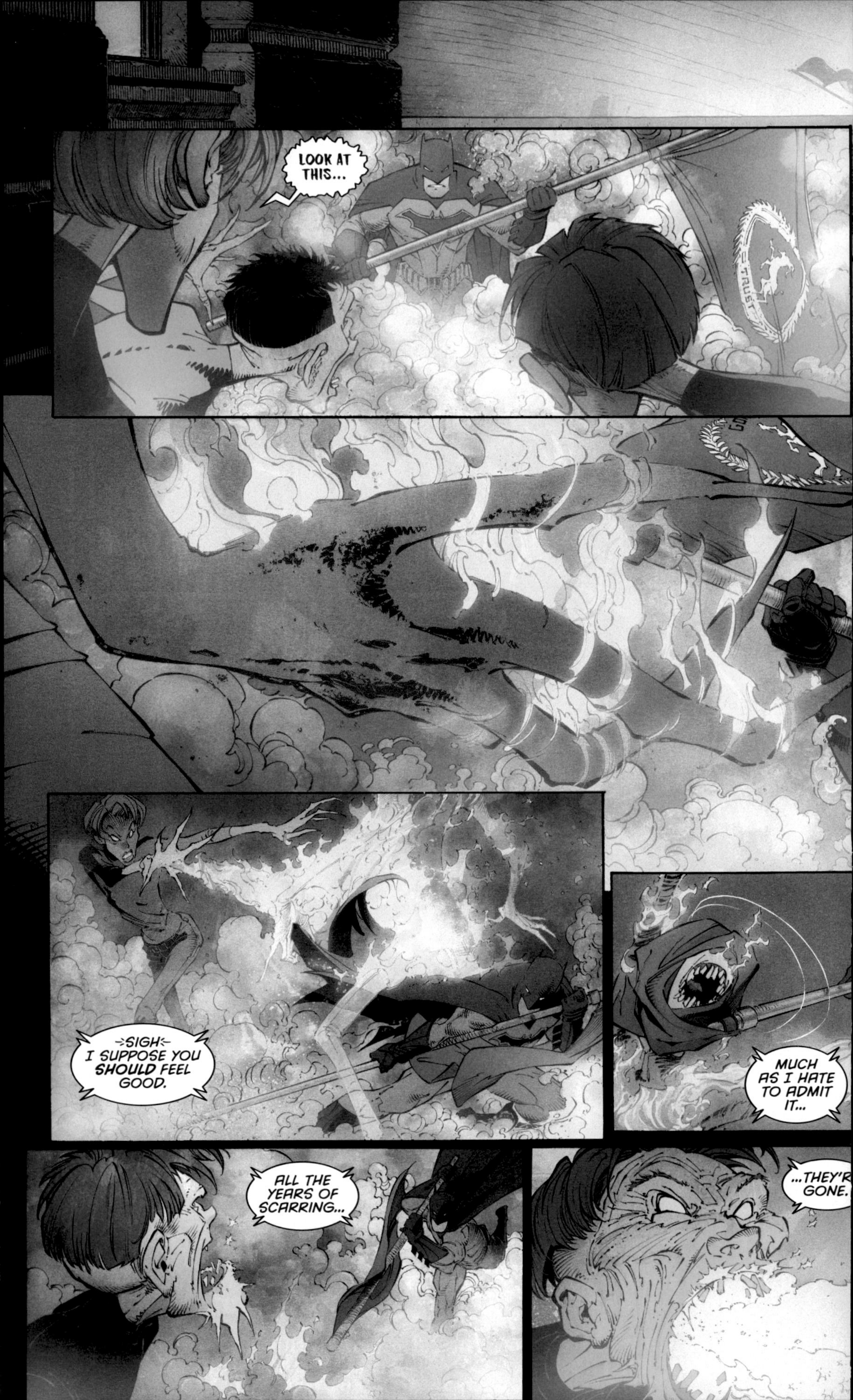
LOOK AT THIS...
SIGH I SUPPOSE YOU SHOULD FEEL GOOD.
MUCH AS I HATE TO ADMIT IT...
ALL THE YEARS OF SCARRING...
...THEY'R GONE.

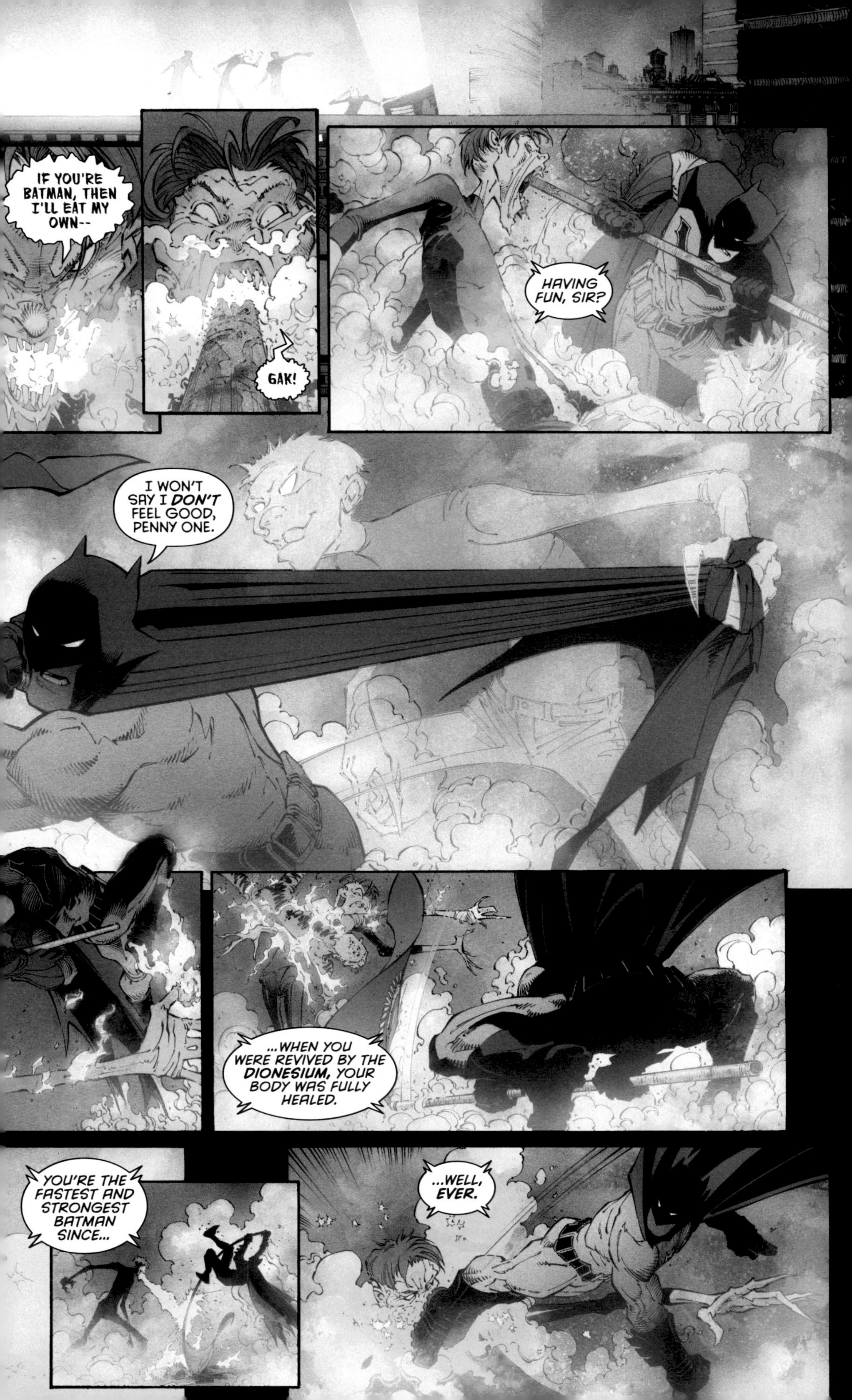
IF YOU'RE BATMAN, THEN I'LL EAT MY OWN--
GAK!
HAVING FUN, SIR?
I WON'T SAY I DON'T FEEL GOOD, PENNY ONE.
...WHEN YOU WERE REVIVED BY THE DIONESIUM, YOUR BODY WAS FULLY HEALED.
YOU'RE THE FASTEST AND STRONGEST BATMAN SINCE...
...WELL, EVER.

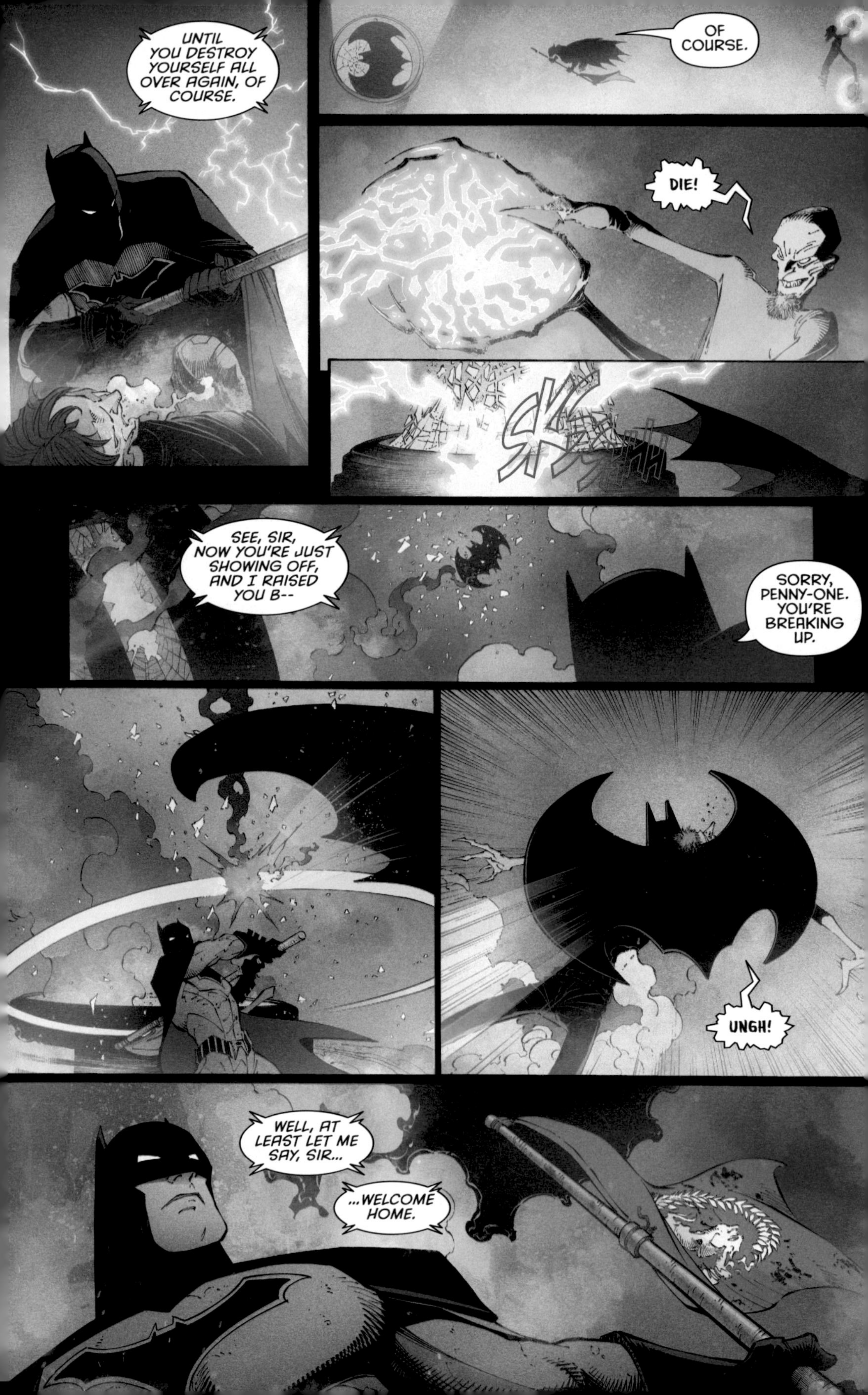
UNTIL YOU DESTROY YOURSELF ALL OVER AGAIN, OF COURSE.
OF COURSE.
DIE!
SEE, SIR, NOW YOU'RE JUST SHOWING OFF, AND I RAISED YOU B--
SORRY, PENNY-ONE. YOU'RE BREAKING UP.
UNGH!
WELL, AT LEAST LET ME SAY, SIR...
...WELCOME HOME.

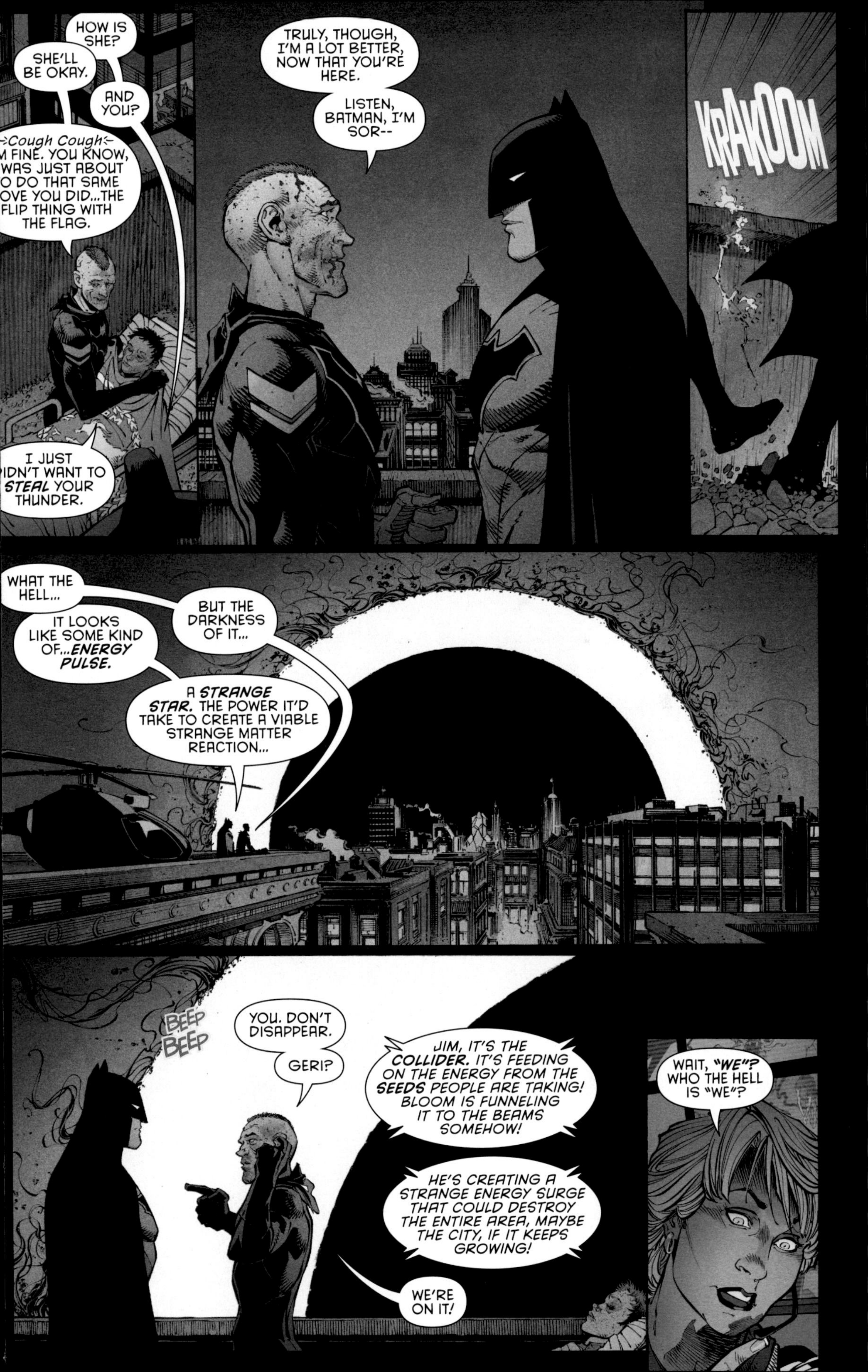
HOW IS SHE?
SHE'LL BE OKAY.
AND YOU?
⇒Cough Cough⇐ I'M FINE. YOU KNOW, I WAS JUST ABOUT TO DO THAT SAME MOVE YOU DID...THE FLIP THING WITH THE FLAG.
I JUST DIDN'T WANT TO STEAL YOUR THUNDER.
TRULY, THOUGH, I'M A LOT BETTER, NOW THAT YOU'RE HERE.
LISTEN, BATMAN, I'M SOR--
KRAKOOM
WHAT THE HELL...
IT LOOKS LIKE SOME KIND OF...ENERGY PULSE.
BUT THE DARKNESS OF IT...
A STRANGE STAR. THE POWER IT'D TAKE TO CREATE A VIABLE STRANGE MATTER REACTION...
BEEP BEEP
YOU. DON'T DISAPPEAR.
GERI?
JIM, IT'S THE COLLIDER. IT'S FEEDING ON THE ENERGY FROM THE SEEDS PEOPLE ARE TAKING! BLOOM IS FUNNELING IT TO THE BEAMS SOMEHOW!
HE'S CREATING A STRANGE ENERGY SURGE THAT COULD DESTROY THE ENTIRE AREA, MAYBE THE CITY, IF IT KEEPS GROWING!
WE'RE ON IT!
WAIT, "WE"? WHO THE HELL IS "WE"?

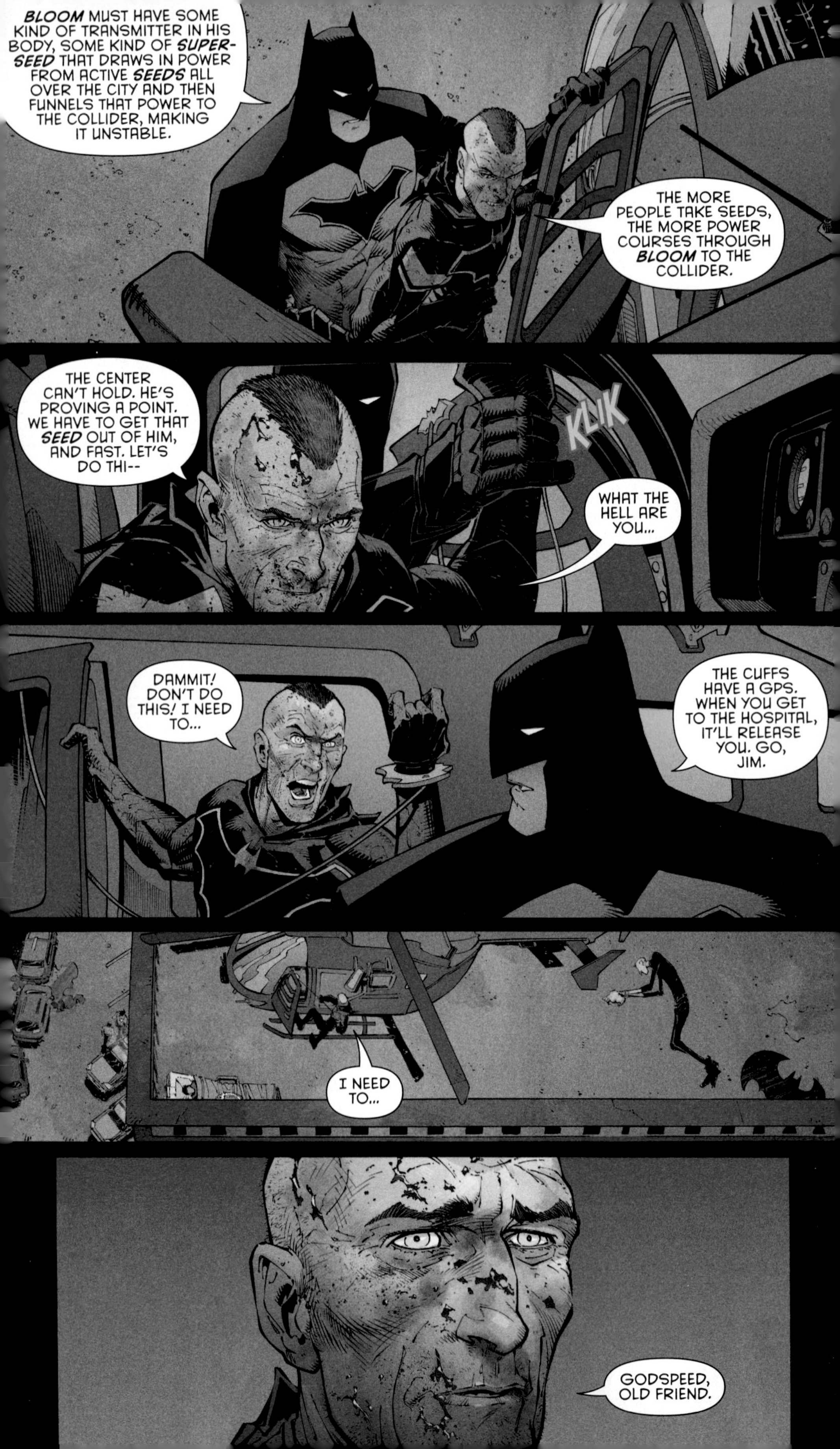
BLOOM MUST HAVE SOME KIND OF TRANSMITTER IN HIS BODY, SOME KIND OF SUPER-SEED THAT DRAWS IN POWER FROM ACTIVE SEEDS ALL OVER THE CITY AND THEN FUNNELS THAT POWER TO THE COLLIDER, MAKING IT UNSTABLE.
THE MORE PEOPLE TAKE SEEDS, THE MORE POWER COURSES THROUGH BLOOM TO THE COLLIDER.
THE CENTER CAN'T HOLD. HE'S PROVING A POINT. WE HAVE TO GET THAT SEED OUT OF HIM, AND FAST. LET'S DO THI--
KLIK
WHAT THE HELL ARE YOU...
DAMMIT! DON'T DO THIS! I NEED TO...
THE CUFFS HAVE A GPS. WHEN YOU GET TO THE HOSPITAL, IT'LL RELEASE YOU. GO, JIM.
I NEED TO...
GODSPEED, OLD FRIEND.

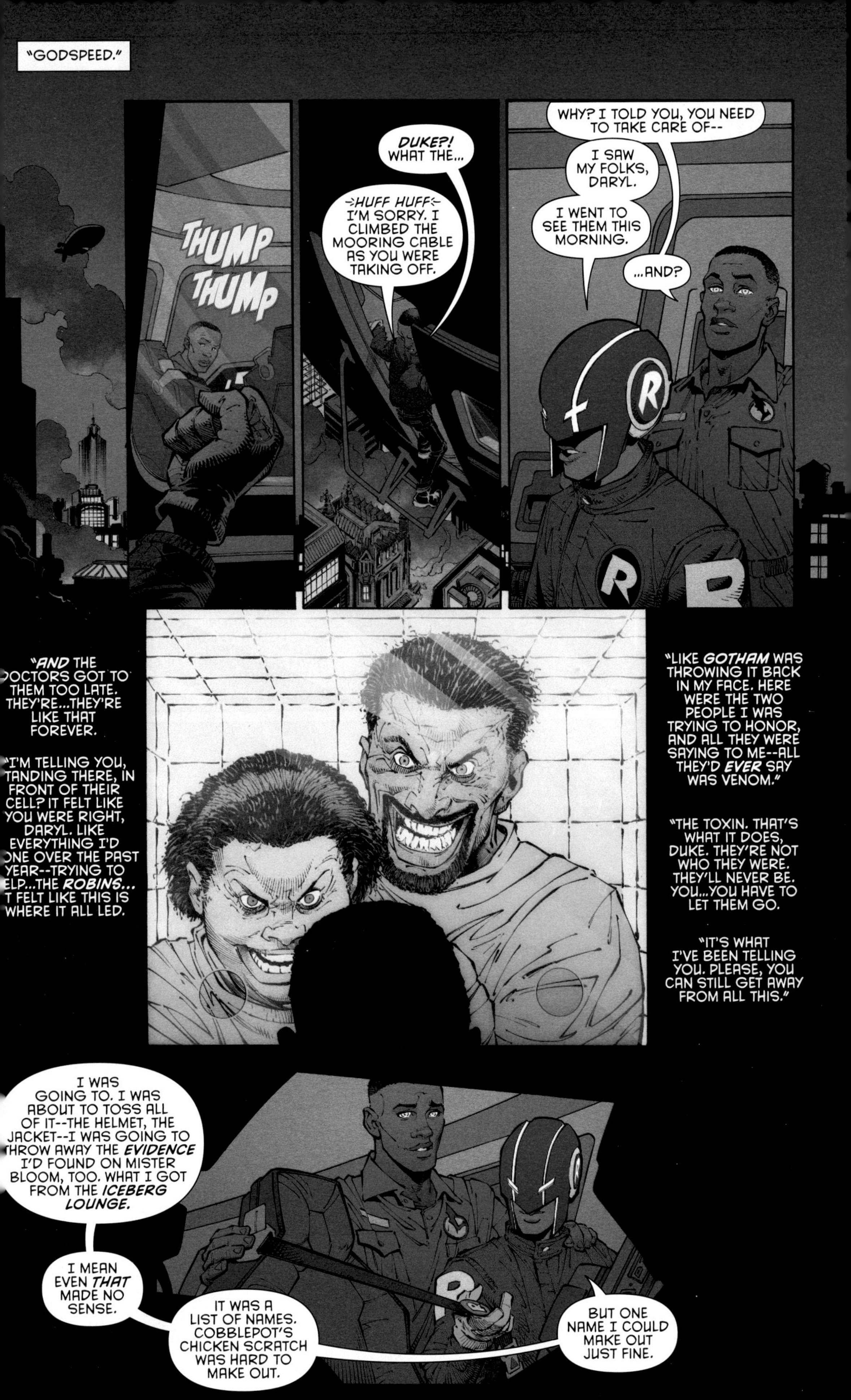

"GODSPEED."
THUMP THUMP
DUKE?! WHAT THE...
HUFF HUFF I'M SORRY. I CLIMBED THE MOORING CABLE AS YOU WERE TAKING OFF.
WHY? I TOLD YOU, YOU NEED TO TAKE CARE OF--
I SAW MY FOLKS, DARYL.
I WENT TO SEE THEM THIS MORNING.
...AND?
"AND THE OCTORS GOT TO THEM TOO LATE. THEY'RE...THEY'RE LIKE THAT FOREVER.
"I'M TELLING YOU, TANDING THERE, IN FRONT OF THEIR CELL? IT FELT LIKE YOU WERE RIGHT, DARYL. LIKE EVERYTHING I'D ONE OVER THE PAST YEAR--TRYING TO ELP...THE ROBINS... T FELT LIKE THIS IS WHERE IT ALL LED.
"LIKE GOTHAM WAS THROWING IT BACK IN MY FACE. HERE WERE THE TWO PEOPLE I WAS TRYING TO HONOR, AND ALL THEY WERE SAYING TO ME--ALL THEY'D EVER SAY WAS VENOM."
"THE TOXIN. THAT'S WHAT IT DOES, DUKE. THEY'RE NOT WHO THEY WERE. THEY'LL NEVER BE. YOU...YOU HAVE TO LET THEM GO.
"IT'S WHAT I'VE BEEN TELLING YOU. PLEASE, YOU CAN STILL GET AWAY FROM ALL THIS."
I WAS GOING TO. I WAS ABOUT TO TOSS ALL OF IT--THE HELMET, THE JACKET--I WAS GOING TO THROW AWAY THE EVIDENCE I'D FOUND ON MISTER BLOOM, TOO. WHAT I GOT FROM THE ICEBERG LOUNGE.
I MEAN EVEN THAT MADE NO SENSE.
IT WAS A LIST OF NAMES. COBBLEPOT'S CHICKEN SCRATCH WAS HARD TO MAKE OUT.
BUT ONE NAME I COULD MAKE OUT JUST FINE.

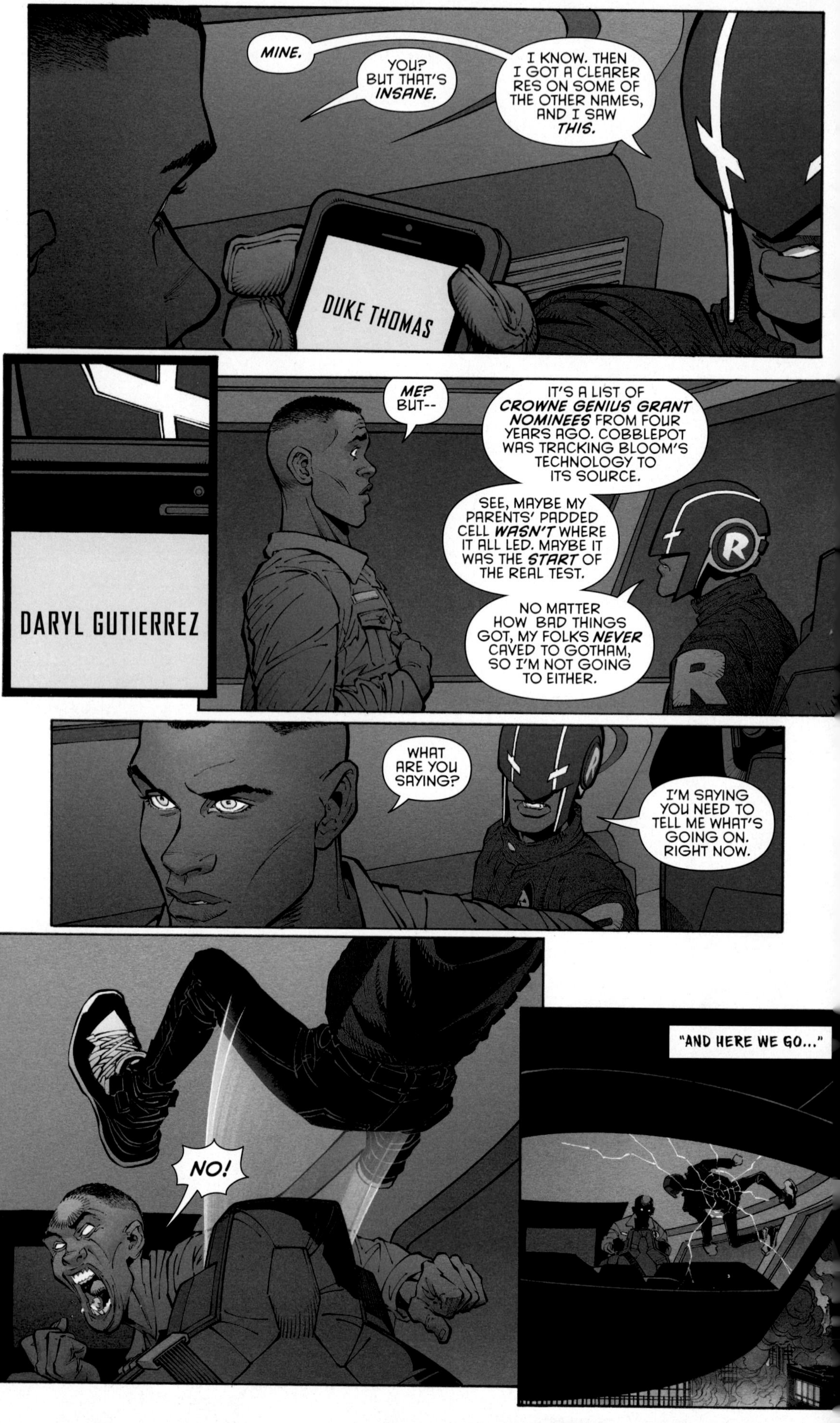
MINE.
YOU? BUT THAT'S INSANE.
I KNOW. THEN I GOT A CLEARER RES ON SOME OF THE OTHER NAMES, AND I SAW THIS.
DUKE THOMAS
DARYL GUTIERREZ
ME? BUT--
IT'S A LIST OF CROWNE GENIUS GRANT NOMINEES FROM FOUR YEARS AGO. COBBLEPOT WAS TRACKING BLOOM'S TECHNOLOGY TO ITS SOURCE.
SEE, MAYBE MY PARENTS' PADDED CELL WASN'T WHERE IT ALL LED. MAYBE IT WAS THE START OF THE REAL TEST.
NO MATTER HOW BAD THINGS GOT, MY FOLKS NEVER CAVED TO GOTHAM, SO I'M NOT GOING TO EITHER.
WHAT ARE YOU SAYING?
I'M SAYING YOU NEED TO TELL ME WHAT'S GOING ON. RIGHT NOW.
NO!
"AND HERE WE GO..."

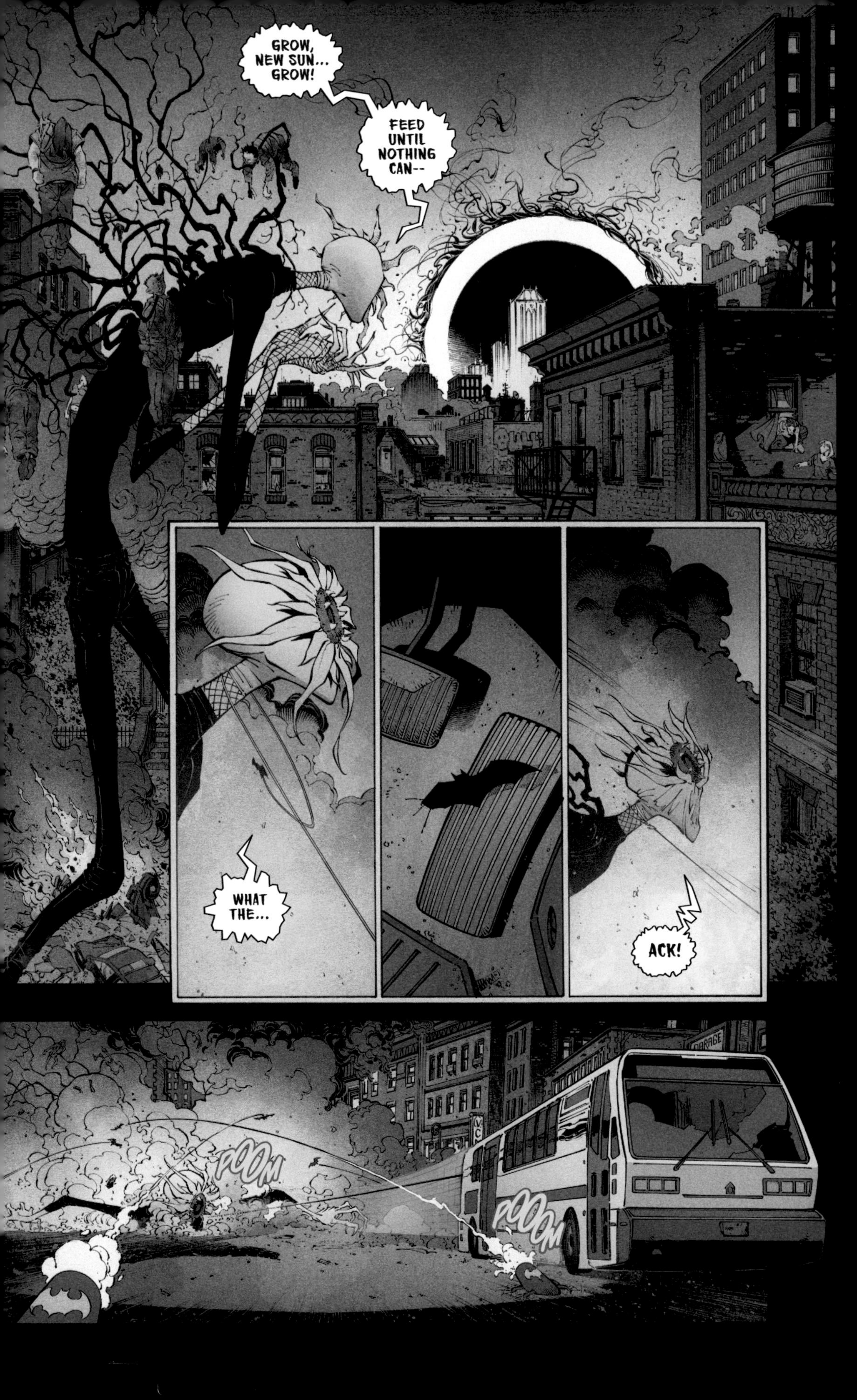
GROW, NEW SUN... GROW!
FEED UNTIL NOTHING CAN--
WHAT THE...
ACK!
POOM
POOOM

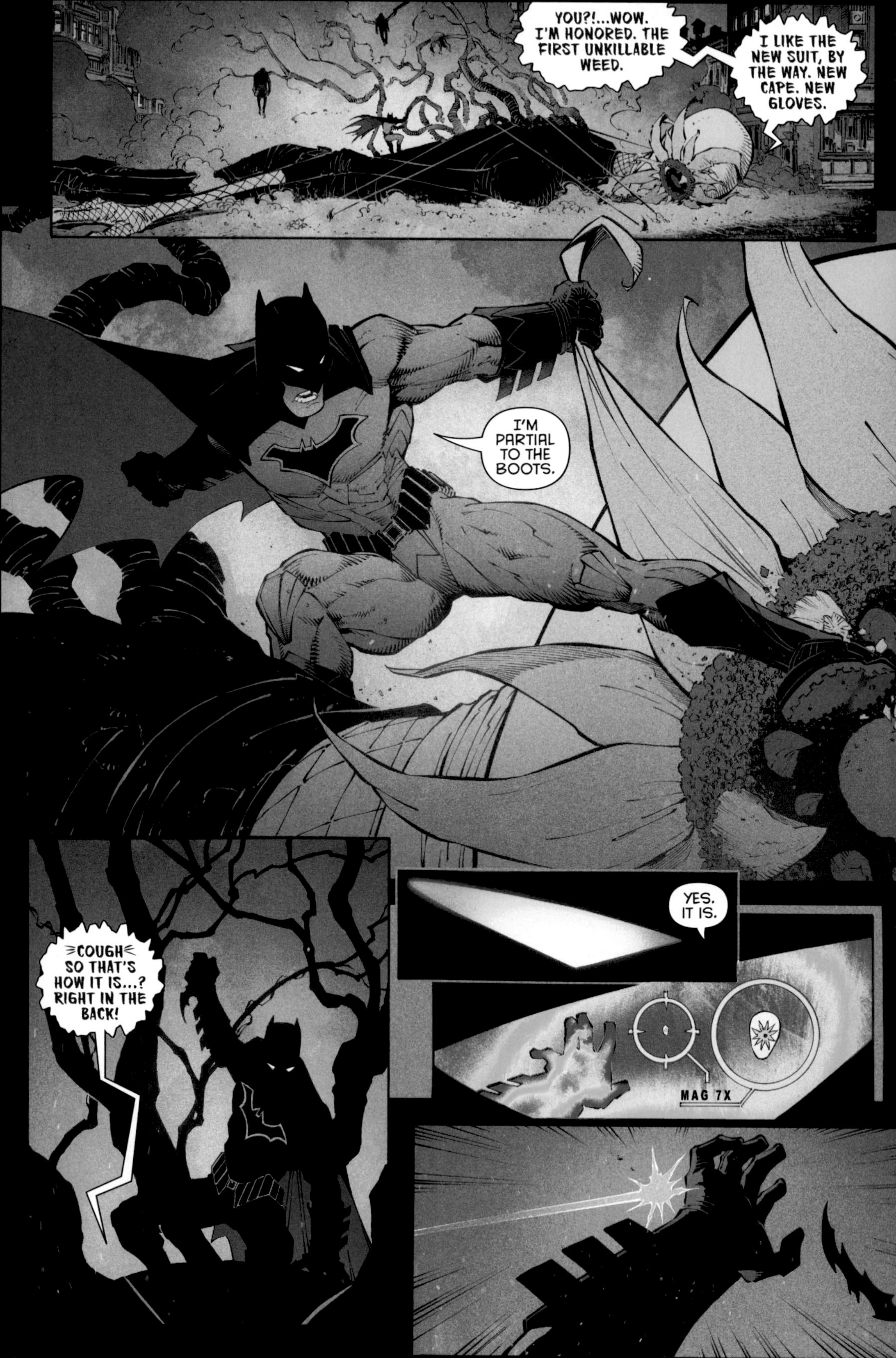
YOU?!...WOW. I'M HONORED. THE FIRST UNKILLABLE WEED.
I LIKE THE NEW SUIT, BY THE WAY. NEW CAPE. NEW GLOVES.
I'M PARTIAL TO THE BOOTS.
COUGH SO THAT'S HOW IT IS...? RIGHT IN THE BACK!
YES. IT IS.
MAG 7X

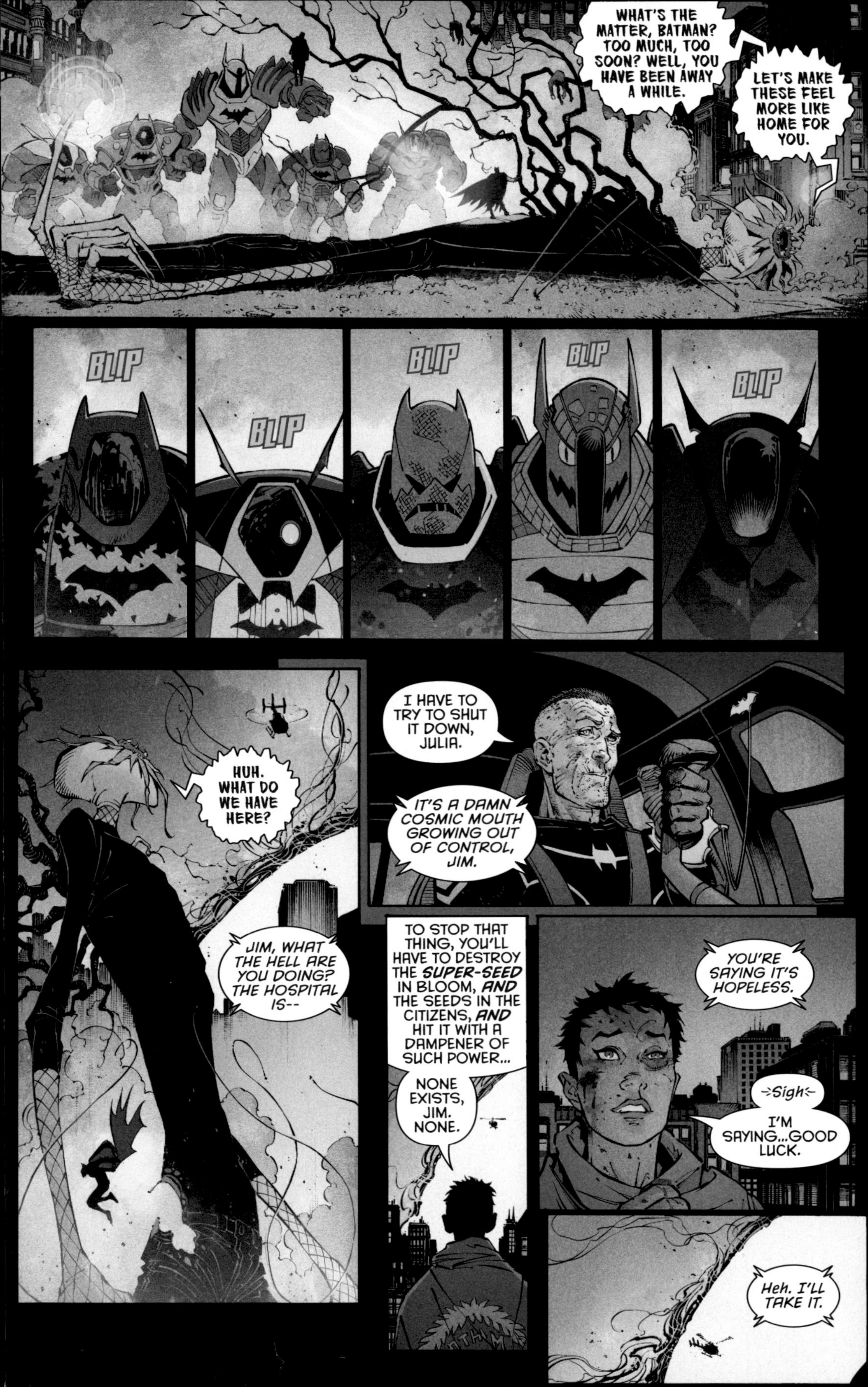

WHAT'S THE MATTER, BATMAN? TOO MUCH, TOO SOON? WELL, YOU HAVE BEEN AWAY A WHILE.
LET'S MAKE THESE FEEL MORE LIKE HOME FOR YOU.
BLIP
BLIP
BLIP
BLIP
BLIP
HUH. WHAT DO WE HAVE HERE?
JIM, WHAT THE HELL ARE YOU DOING? THE HOSPITAL IS--
I HAVE TO TRY TO SHUT IT DOWN, JULIA.
IT'S A DAMN COSMIC MOUTH GROWING OUT OF CONTROL, JIM.
TO STOP THAT THING, YOU'LL HAVE TO DESTROY THE SUPER-SEED IN BLOOM, AND THE SEEDS IN THE CITIZENS, AND HIT IT WITH A DAMPENER OF SUCH POWER...
NONE EXISTS, JIM. NONE.
YOU'RE SAYING IT'S HOPELESS.
Sigh
I'M SAYING...GOOD LUCK.
Heh. I'LL TAKE IT.

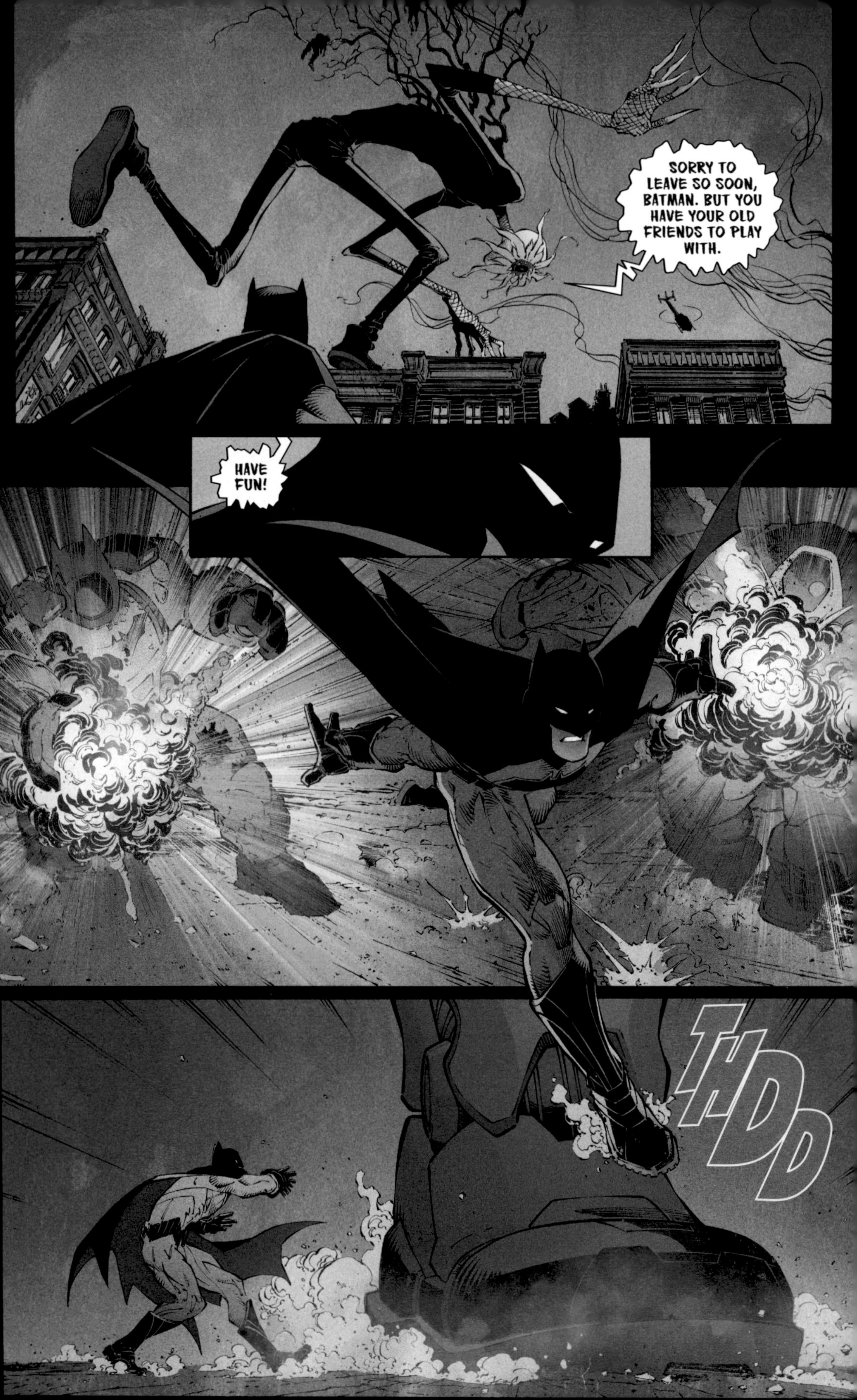
SORRY TO LEAVE SO SOON, BATMAN. BUT YOU HAVE YOUR OLD FRIENDS TO PLAY WITH.
HAVE FUN!
THDD

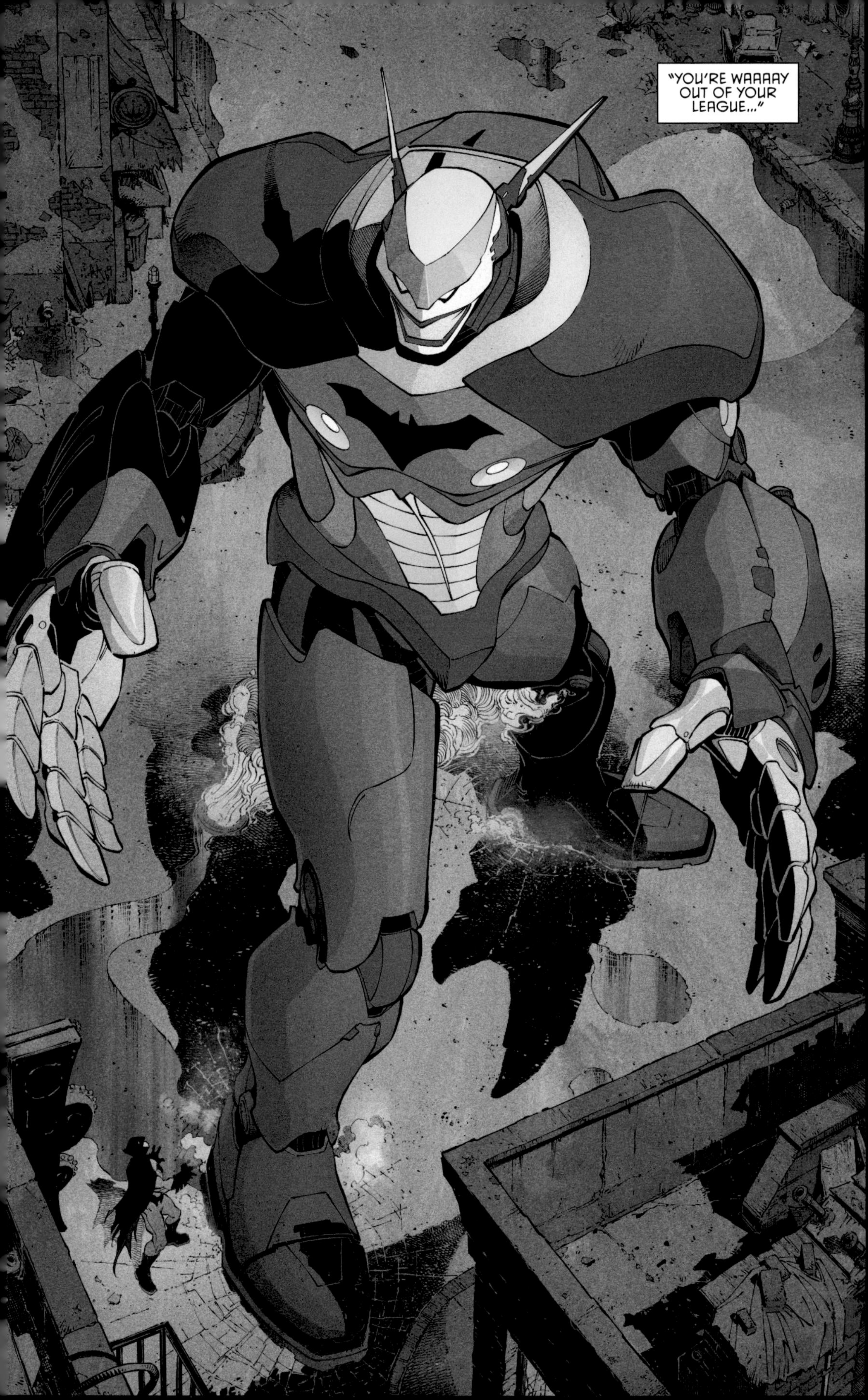
"YOU'RE WAAAAY OUT OF YOUR LEAGUE..."

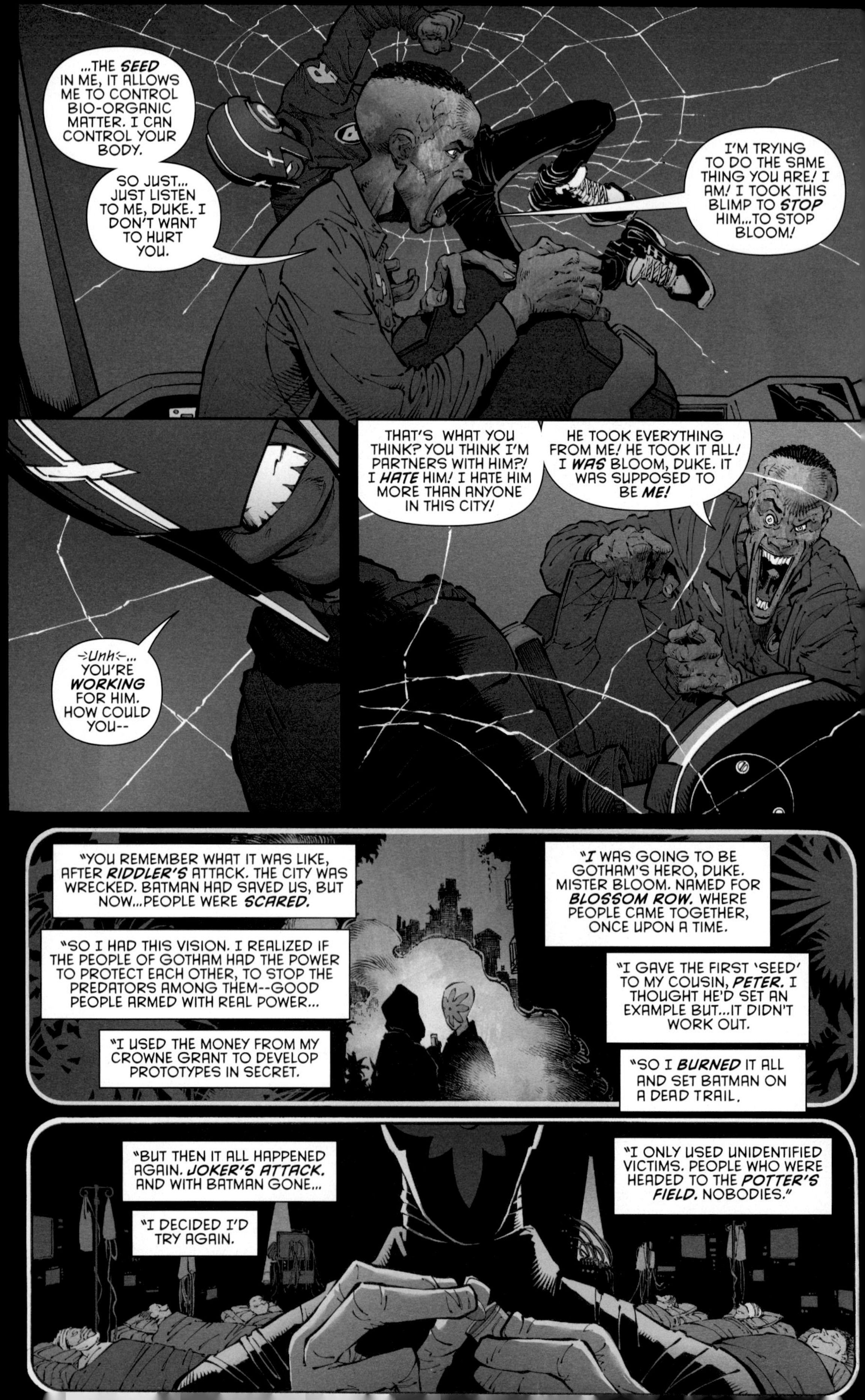
...THE SEED IN ME, IT ALLOWS ME TO CONTROL BIO-ORGANIC MATTER. I CAN CONTROL YOUR BODY.
SO JUST... JUST LISTEN TO ME, DUKE. I DON'T WANT TO HURT YOU.
I'M TRYING TO DO THE SAME THING YOU ARE! I AM! I TOOK THIS BLIMP TO STOP HIM...TO STOP BLOOM!
-Unh-... YOU'RE WORKING FOR HIM. HOW COULD YOU--
THAT'S WHAT YOU THINK? YOU THINK I'M PARTNERS WITH HIM?! I HATE HIM! I HATE HIM MORE THAN ANYONE IN THIS CITY!
HE TOOK EVERYTHING FROM ME! HE TOOK IT ALL! I WAS BLOOM, DUKE. IT WAS SUPPOSED TO BE ME!
"YOU REMEMBER WHAT IT WAS LIKE, AFTER RIDDLER'S ATTACK. THE CITY WAS WRECKED. BATMAN HAD SAVED US, BUT NOW...PEOPLE WERE SCARED.
"SO I HAD THIS VISION. I REALIZED IF THE PEOPLE OF GOTHAM HAD THE POWER TO PROTECT EACH OTHER, TO STOP THE PREDATORS AMONG THEM--GOOD PEOPLE ARMED WITH REAL POWER...
"I USED THE MONEY FROM MY CROWNE GRANT TO DEVELOP PROTOTYPES IN SECRET.
"I WAS GOING TO BE GOTHAM'S HERO, DUKE. MISTER BLOOM. NAMED FOR BLOSSOM ROW. WHERE PEOPLE CAME TOGETHER, ONCE UPON A TIME.
"I GAVE THE FIRST 'SEED' TO MY COUSIN, PETER. I THOUGHT HE'D SET AN EXAMPLE BUT...IT DIDN'T WORK OUT.
"SO I BURNED IT ALL AND SET BATMAN ON A DEAD TRAIL.
"BUT THEN IT ALL HAPPENED AGAIN. JOKER'S ATTACK. AND WITH BATMAN GONE...
"I DECIDED I'D TRY AGAIN.
"I ONLY USED UNIDENTIFIED VICTIMS. PEOPLE WHO WERE HEADED TO THE POTTER'S FIELD. NOBODIES."

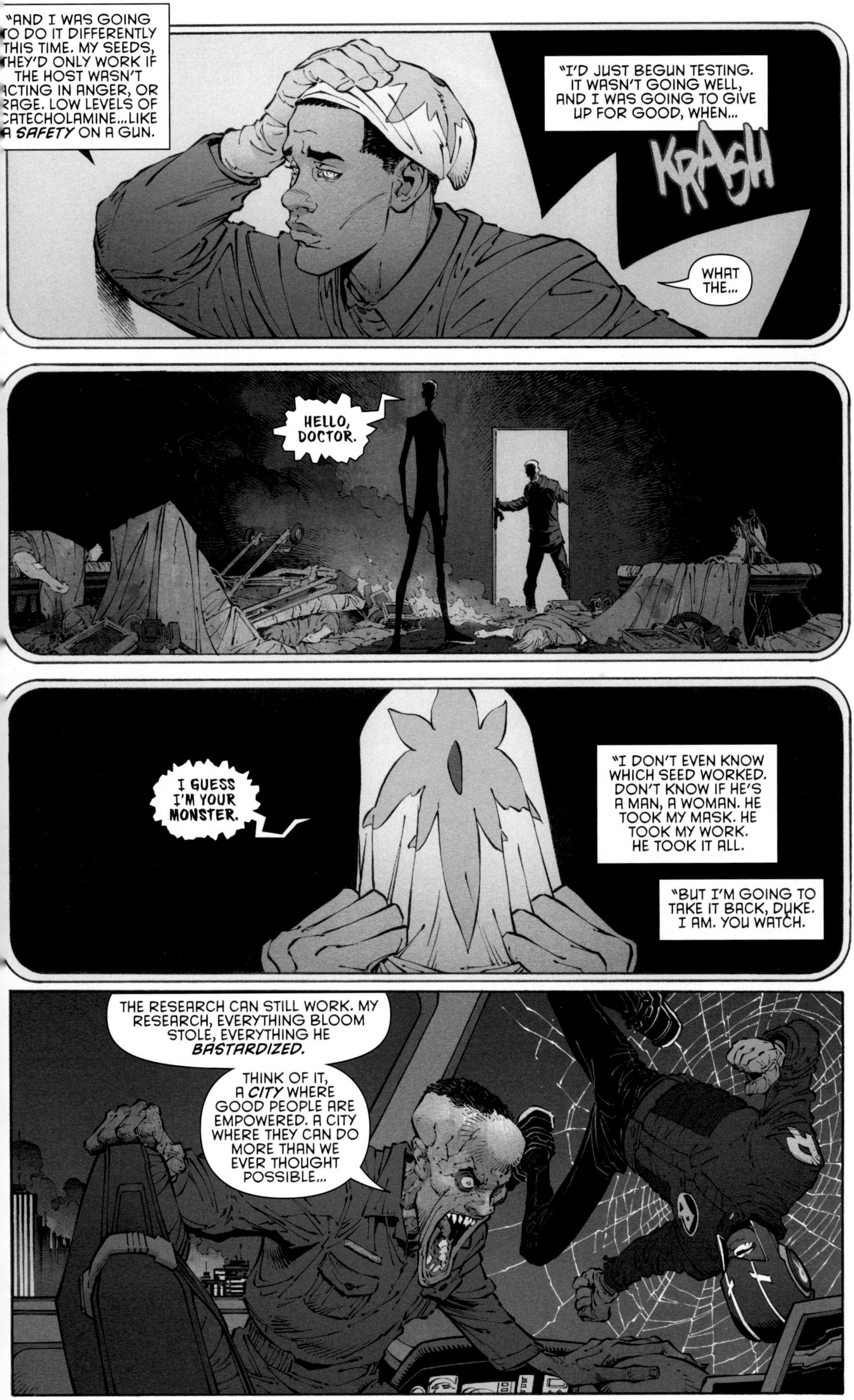
"AND I WAS GOING TO DO IT DIFFERENTLY THIS TIME. MY SEEDS, THEY'D ONLY WORK IF THE HOST WASN'T ACTING IN ANGER, OR RAGE. LOW LEVELS OF CATECHOLAMINE...LIKE A *SAFETY* ON A GUN.
"I'D JUST BEGUN TESTING. IT WASN'T GOING WELL, AND I WAS GOING TO GIVE UP FOR GOOD, WHEN...
KRASH
WHAT THE...
HELLO, DOCTOR.
I GUESS I'M YOUR MONSTER.
"I DON'T EVEN KNOW WHICH SEED WORKED. DON'T KNOW IF HE'S A MAN, A WOMAN. HE TOOK MY MASK. HE TOOK MY WORK. HE TOOK IT ALL.
"BUT I'M GOING TO TAKE IT BACK, DUKE. I AM. YOU WATCH.
THE RESEARCH CAN STILL WORK. MY RESEARCH, EVERYTHING BLOOM STOLE, EVERYTHING HE *BASTARDIZED.*
THINK OF IT, A *CITY* WHERE GOOD PEOPLE ARE EMPOWERED. A CITY WHERE THEY CAN DO MORE THAN WE EVER THOUGHT POSSIBLE...

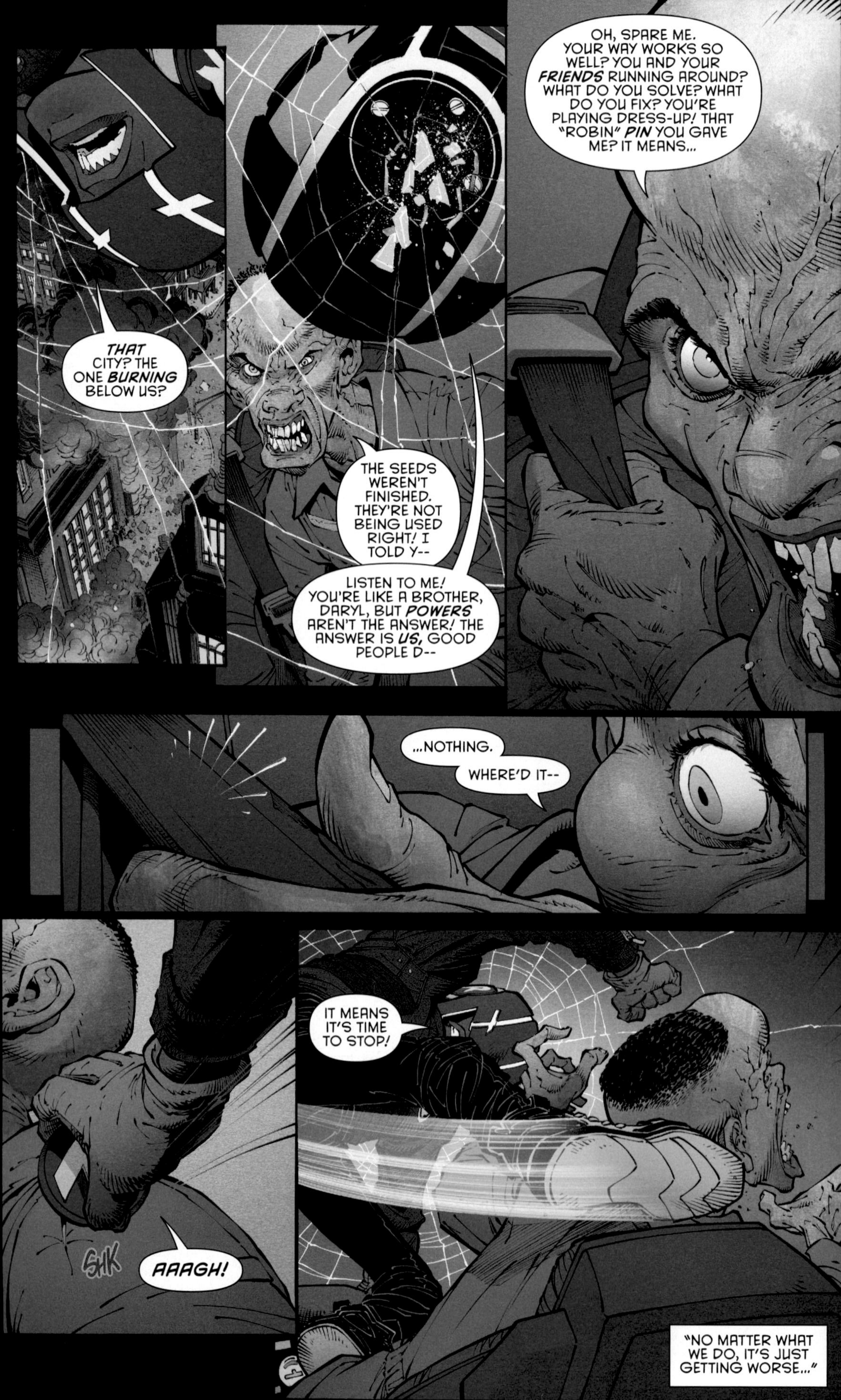
THAT CITY? THE ONE BURNING BELOW US?
THE SEEDS WEREN'T FINISHED. THEY'RE NOT BEING USED RIGHT! I TOLD Y--
LISTEN TO ME! YOU'RE LIKE A BROTHER, DARYL, BUT POWERS AREN'T THE ANSWER! THE ANSWER IS US, GOOD PEOPLE D--
OH, SPARE ME. YOUR WAY WORKS SO WELL? YOU AND YOUR FRIENDS RUNNING AROUND? WHAT DO YOU SOLVE? WHAT DO YOU FIX? YOU'RE PLAYING DRESS-UP! THAT "ROBIN" PIN YOU GAVE ME? IT MEANS...
...NOTHING.
WHERE'D IT--
SHK
AAAGH!
IT MEANS IT'S TIME TO STOP!
"NO MATTER WHAT WE DO, IT'S JUST GETTING WORSE..."

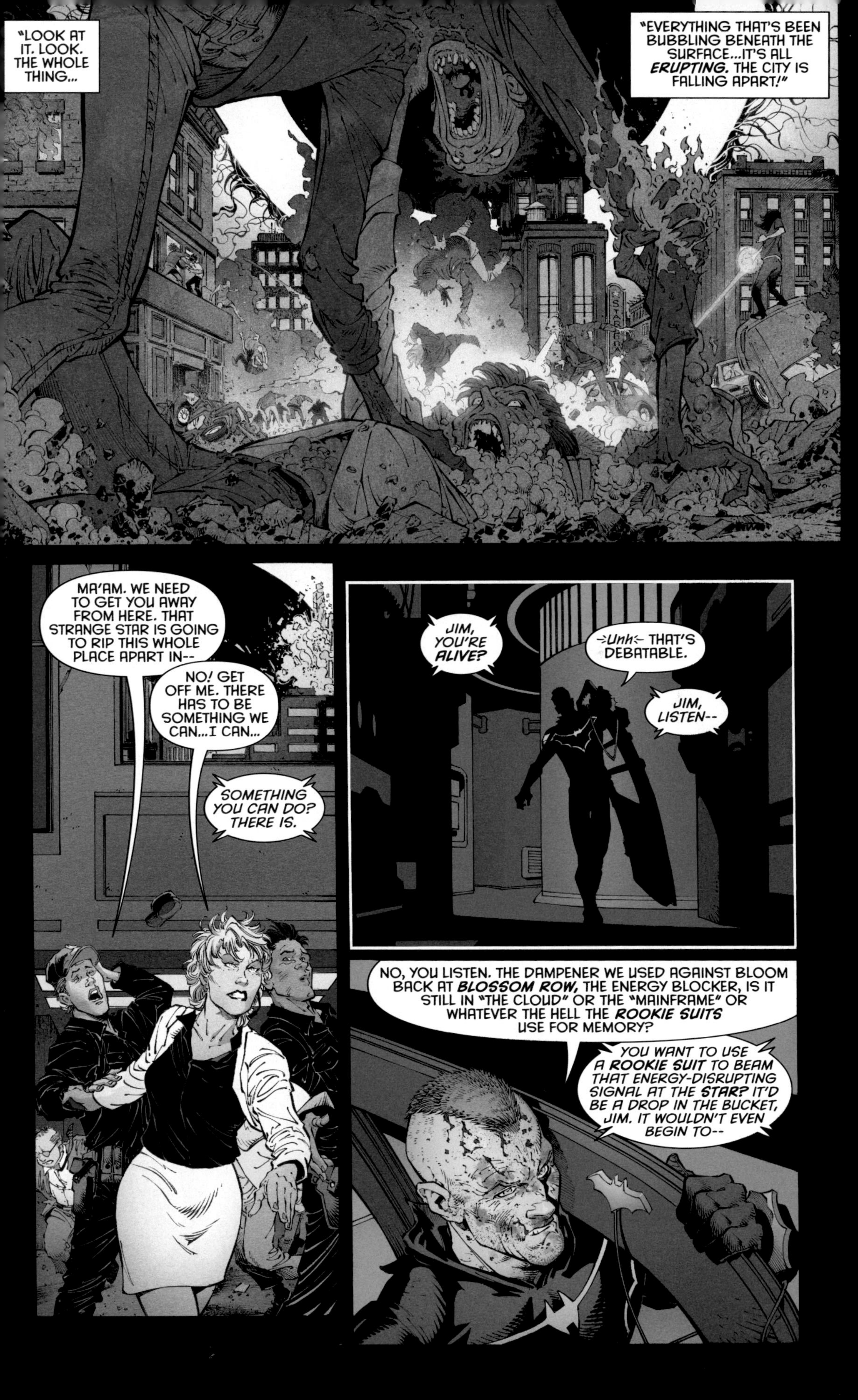
"LOOK AT IT. LOOK. THE WHOLE THING...
"EVERYTHING THAT'S BEEN BUBBLING BENEATH THE SURFACE...IT'S ALL ERUPTING. THE CITY IS FALLING APART!"
MA'AM. WE NEED TO GET YOU AWAY FROM HERE. THAT STRANGE STAR IS GOING TO RIP THIS WHOLE PLACE APART IN--
NO! GET OFF ME. THERE HAS TO BE SOMETHING WE CAN...I CAN...
SOMETHING YOU CAN DO? THERE IS.
JIM, YOU'RE ALIVE?
-Unh- THAT'S DEBATABLE.
JIM, LISTEN--
NO, YOU LISTEN. THE DAMPENER WE USED AGAINST BLOOM BACK AT BLOSSOM ROW, THE ENERGY BLOCKER, IS IT STILL IN "THE CLOUD" OR THE "MAINFRAME" OR WHATEVER THE HELL THE ROOKIE SUITS USE FOR MEMORY?
YOU WANT TO USE A ROOKIE SUIT TO BEAM THAT ENERGY-DISRUPTING SIGNAL AT THE STAR? IT'D BE A DROP IN THE BUCKET, JIM. IT WOULDN'T EVEN BEGIN TO--

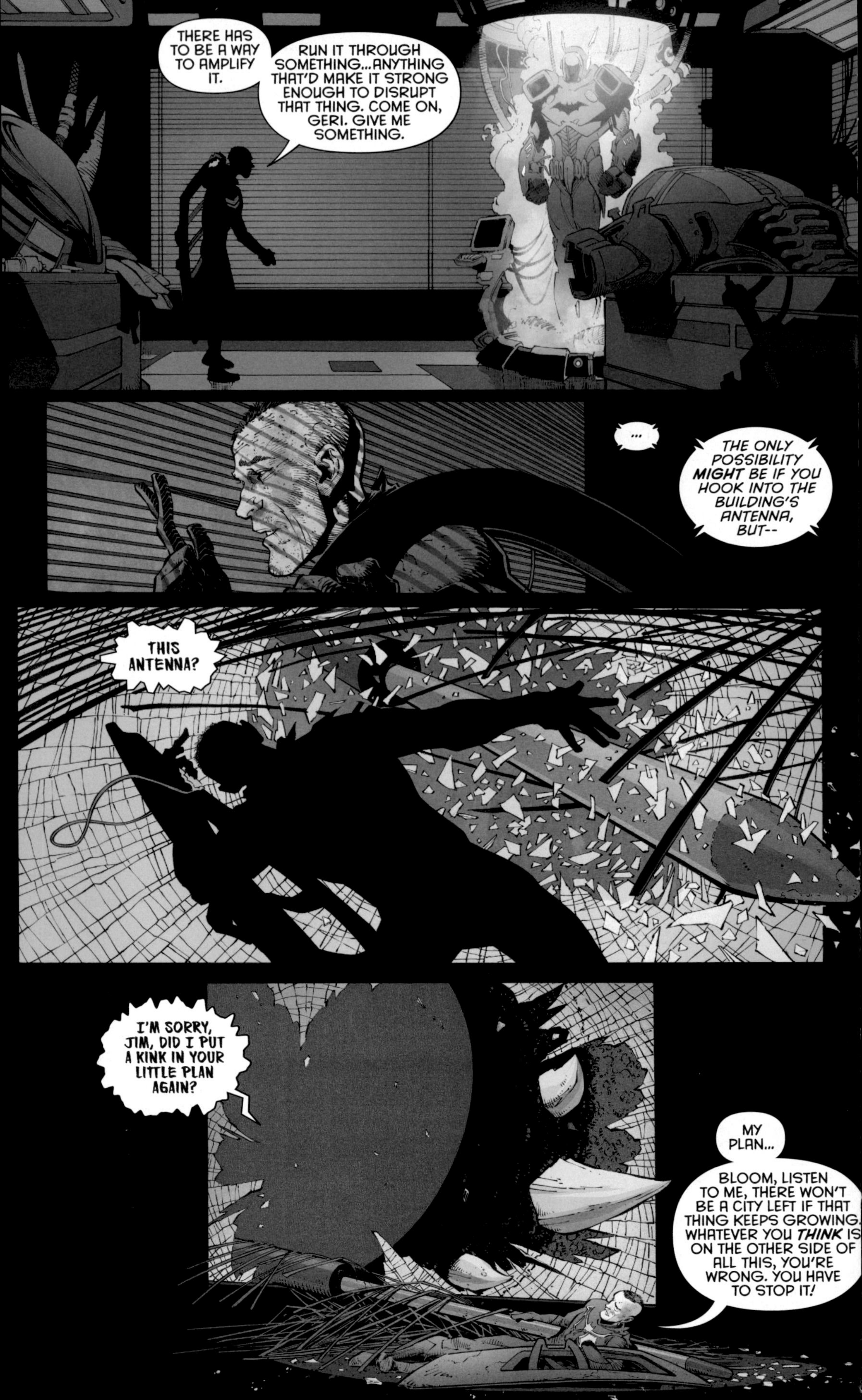
THERE HAS TO BE A WAY TO AMPLIFY IT.
RUN IT THROUGH SOMETHING...ANYTHING THAT'D MAKE IT STRONG ENOUGH TO DISRUPT THAT THING. COME ON, GERI. GIVE ME SOMETHING.
...
THE ONLY POSSIBILITY MIGHT BE IF YOU HOOK INTO THE BUILDING'S ANTENNA, BUT--
THIS ANTENNA?
I'M SORRY, JIM, DID I PUT A KINK IN YOUR LITTLE PLAN AGAIN?
MY PLAN...
BLOOM, LISTEN TO ME, THERE WON'T BE A CITY LEFT IF THAT THING KEEPS GROWING. WHATEVER YOU THINK IS ON THE OTHER SIDE OF ALL THIS, YOU'RE WRONG. YOU HAVE TO STOP IT!

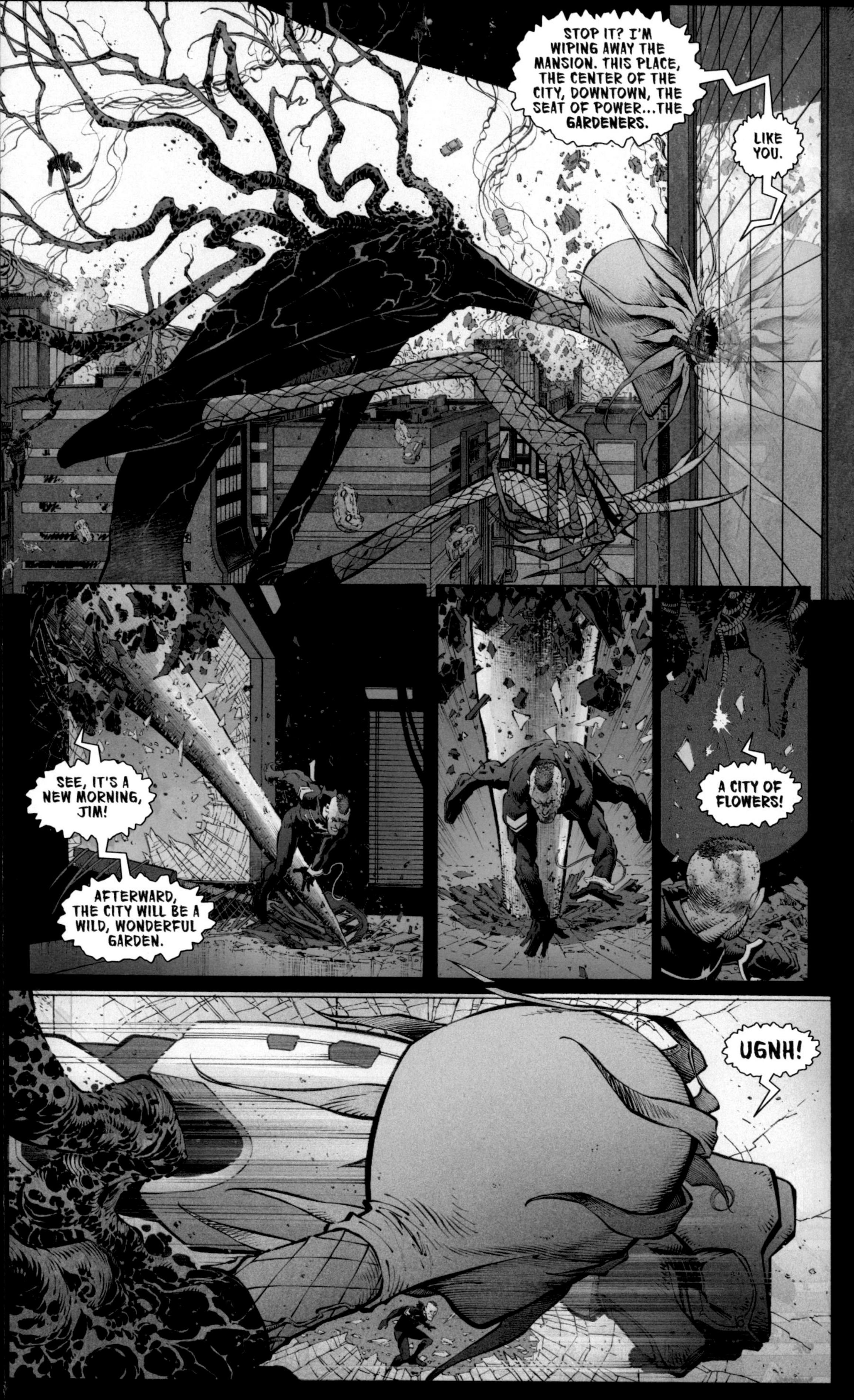
STOP IT? I'M WIPING AWAY THE MANSION. THIS PLACE, THE CENTER OF THE CITY, DOWNTOWN, THE SEAT OF POWER...THE GARDENERS.
LIKE YOU.
SEE, IT'S A NEW MORNING, JIM!
AFTERWARD, THE CITY WILL BE A WILD, WONDERFUL GARDEN.
A CITY OF FLOWERS!
UGNH!

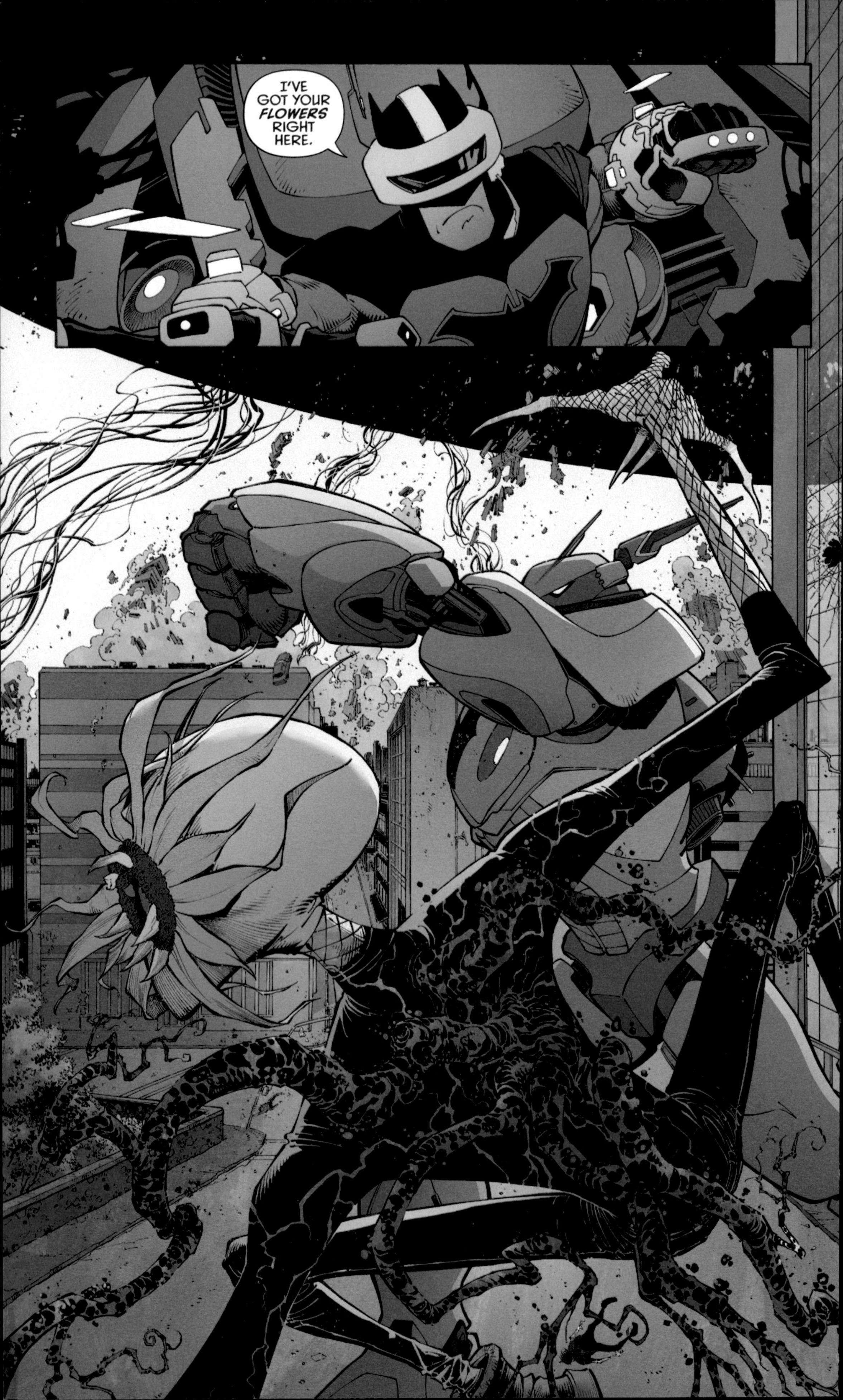
I'VE GOT YOUR *FLOWERS* RIGHT HERE.

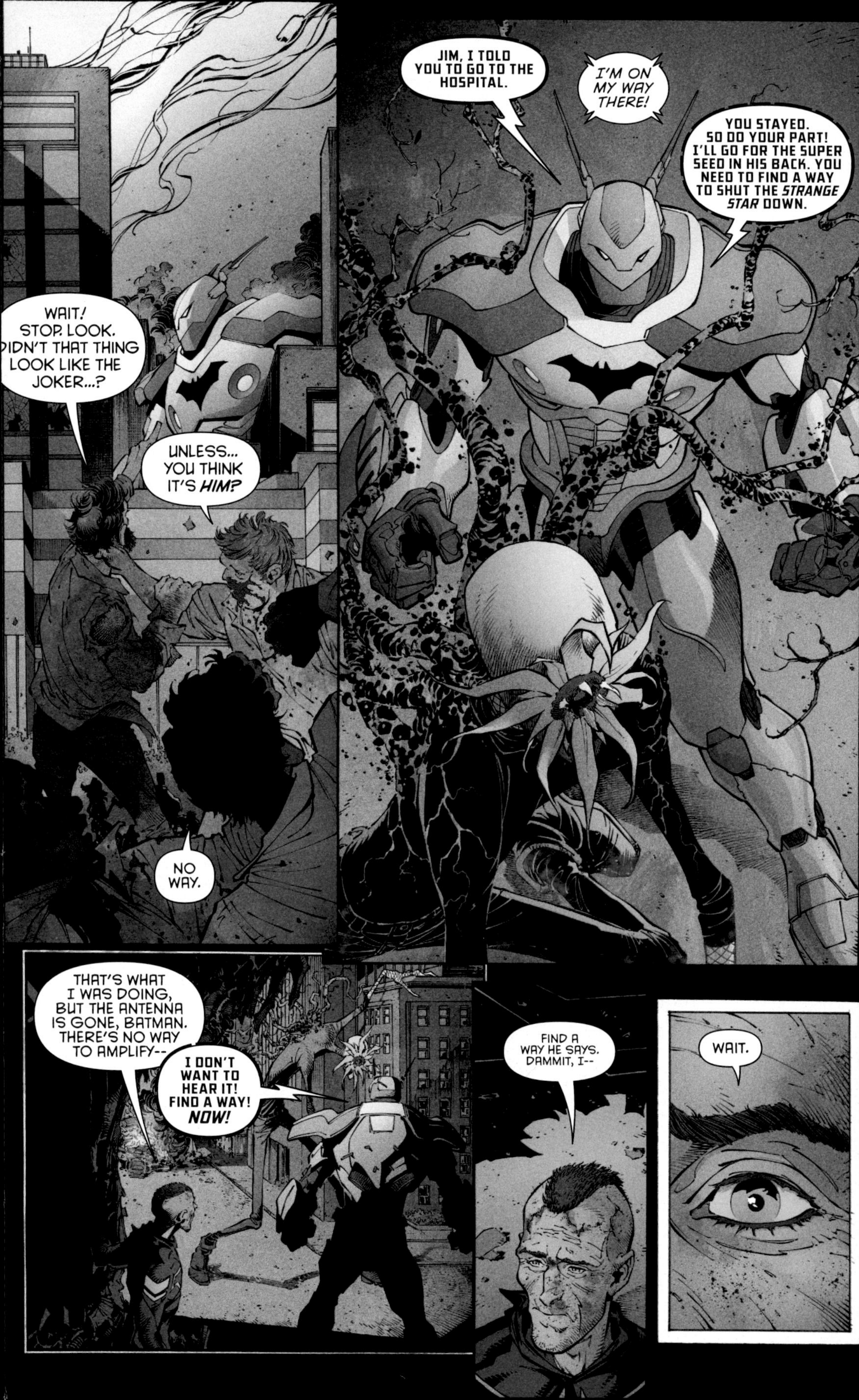
WAIT! STOP. LOOK. DIDN'T THAT THING LOOK LIKE THE JOKER...?
UNLESS... YOU THINK IT'S HIM?
NO WAY.
JIM, I TOLD YOU TO GO TO THE HOSPITAL.
I'M ON MY WAY THERE!
YOU STAYED. SO DO YOUR PART! I'LL GO FOR THE SUPER SEED IN HIS BACK. YOU NEED TO FIND A WAY TO SHUT THE STRANGE STAR DOWN.
THAT'S WHAT I WAS DOING, BUT THE ANTENNA IS GONE, BATMAN. THERE'S NO WAY TO AMPLIFY--
I DON'T WANT TO HEAR IT! FIND A WAY! NOW!
FIND A WAY HE SAYS. DAMMIT, I--
WAIT.

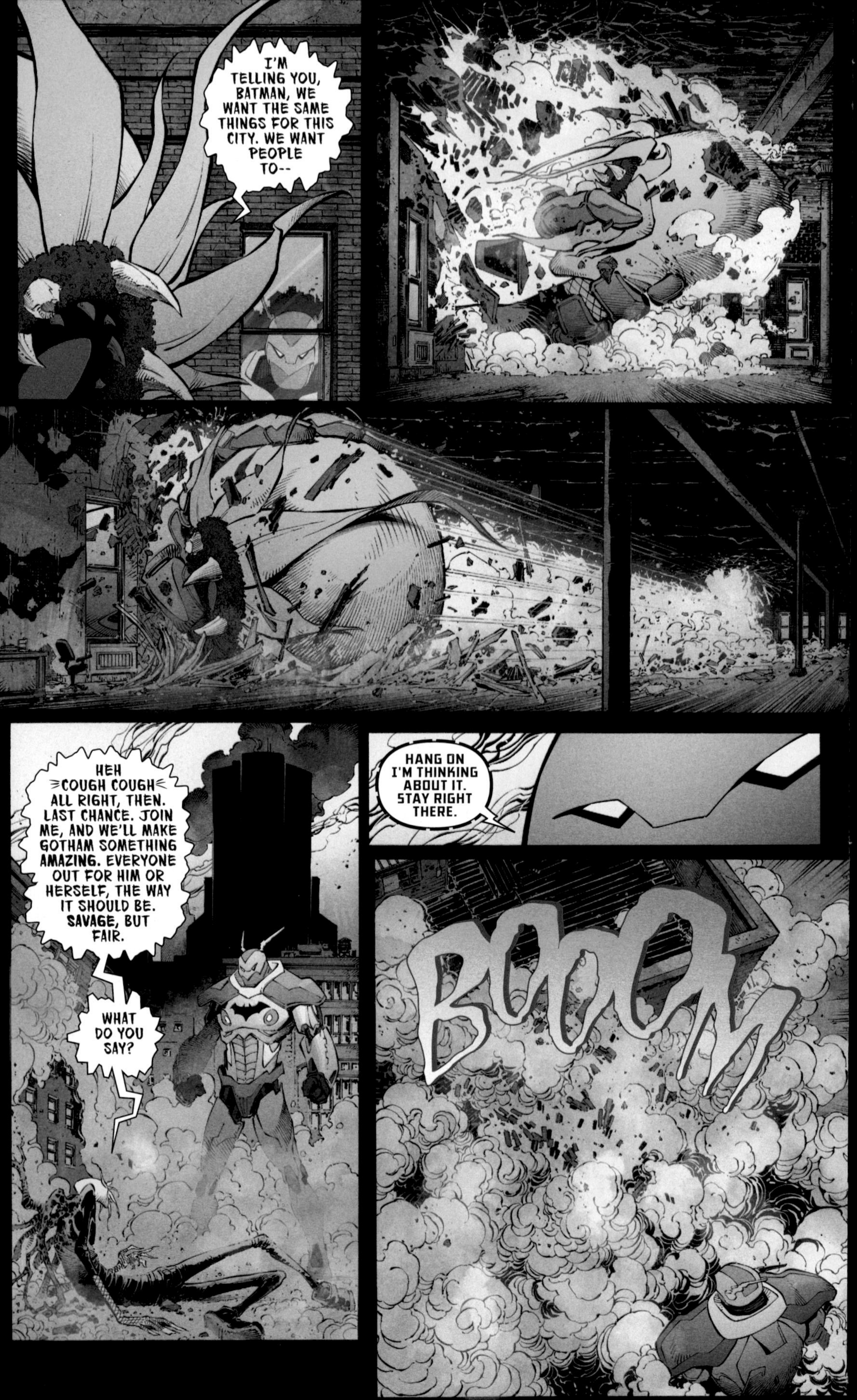
I'M TELLING YOU, BATMAN, WE WANT THE SAME THINGS FOR THIS CITY. WE WANT PEOPLE TO--
HEH
COUGH COUGH
ALL RIGHT, THEN. LAST CHANCE. JOIN ME, AND WE'LL MAKE GOTHAM SOMETHING AMAZING. EVERYONE OUT FOR HIM OR HERSELF, THE WAY IT SHOULD BE. SAVAGE, BUT FAIR.
WHAT DO YOU SAY?
HANG ON I'M THINKING ABOUT IT. STAY RIGHT THERE.
BOOOM

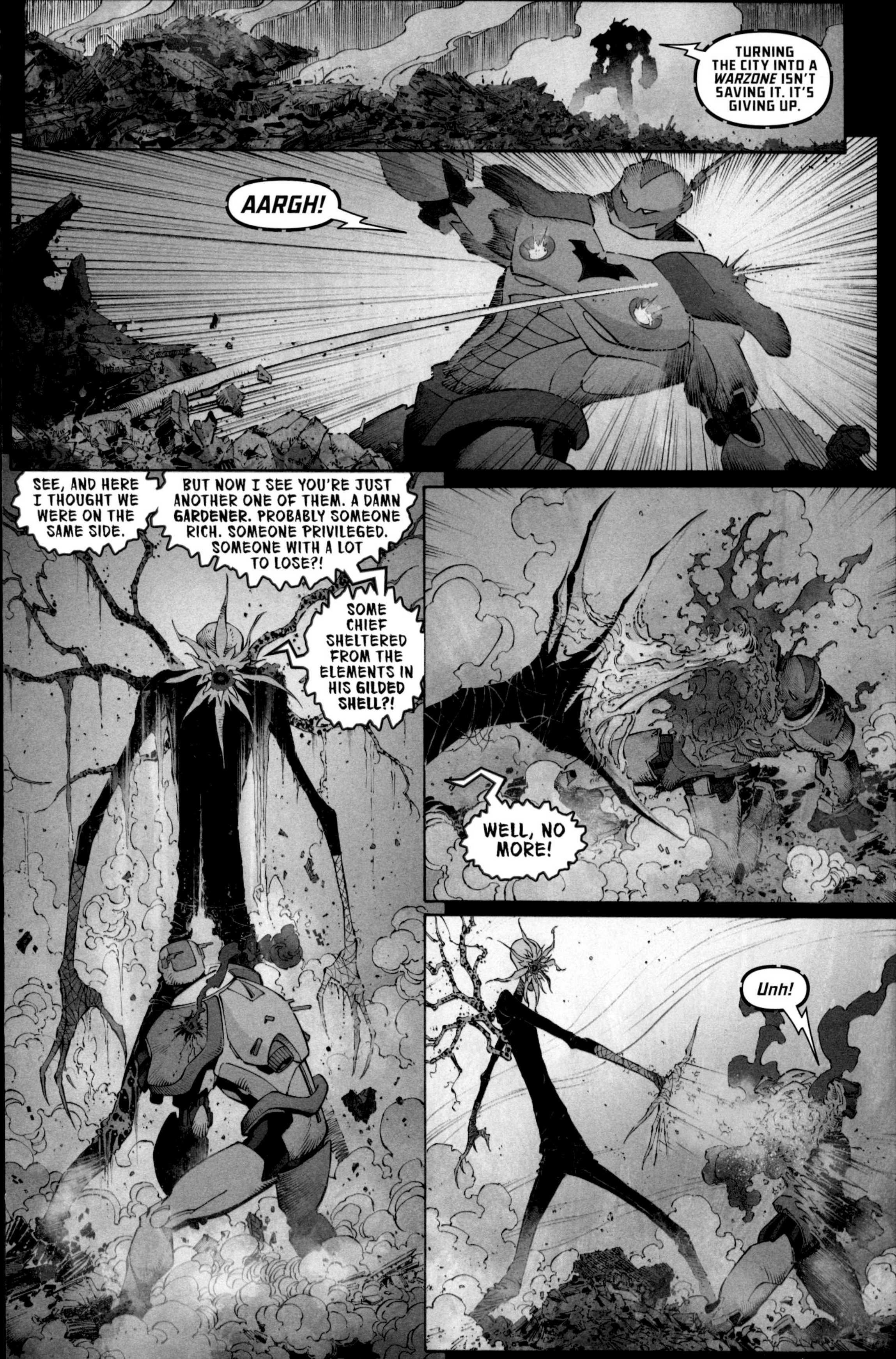

TURNING THE CITY INTO A *WARZONE* ISN'T SAVING IT. IT'S GIVING UP.
*AARGH!*
SEE, AND HERE I THOUGHT WE WERE ON THE SAME SIDE.
BUT NOW I SEE YOU'RE JUST ANOTHER ONE OF THEM. A DAMN GARDENER. PROBABLY SOMEONE RICH. SOMEONE PRIVILEGED. SOMEONE WITH A LOT TO LOSE?!
SOME CHIEF SHELTERED FROM THE ELEMENTS IN HIS GILDED SHELL?!
WELL, NO MORE!
*Unh!*

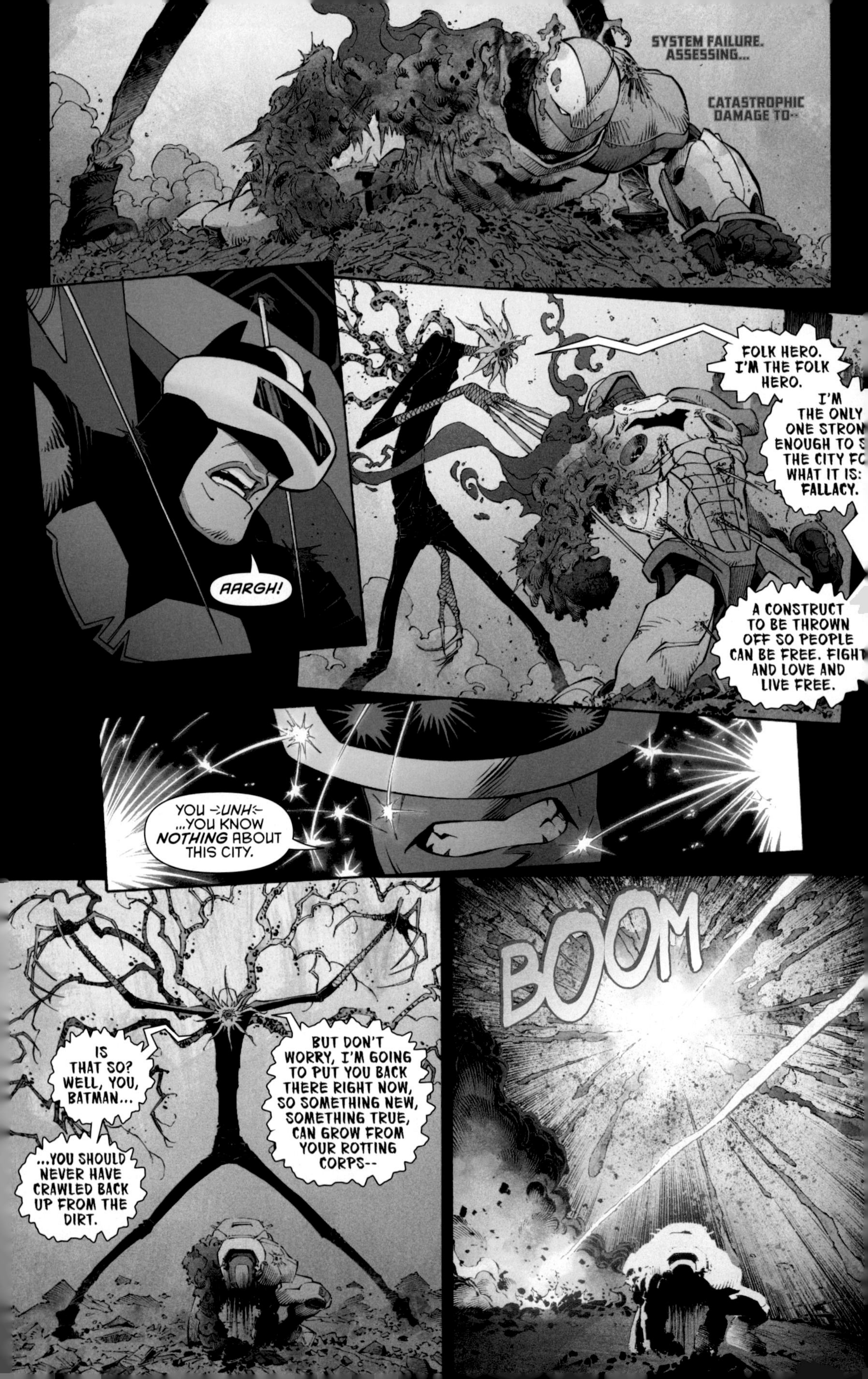
SYSTEM FAILURE. ASSESSING...
CATASTROPHIC DAMAGE TO--
AARGH!
FOLK HERO. I'M THE FOLK HERO.
I'M THE ONLY ONE STRON ENOUGH TO S THE CITY FO WHAT IT IS: FALLACY.
A CONSTRUCT TO BE THROWN OFF SO PEOPLE CAN BE FREE. FIGHT AND LOVE AND LIVE FREE.
YOU -UNH- ...YOU KNOW NOTHING ABOUT THIS CITY.
IS THAT SO? WELL, YOU, BATMAN...
...YOU SHOULD NEVER HAVE CRAWLED BACK UP FROM THE DIRT.
BUT DON'T WORRY, I'M GOING TO PUT YOU BACK THERE RIGHT NOW, SO SOMETHING NEW, SOMETHING TRUE, CAN GROW FROM YOUR ROTTING CORPS--
BOOM

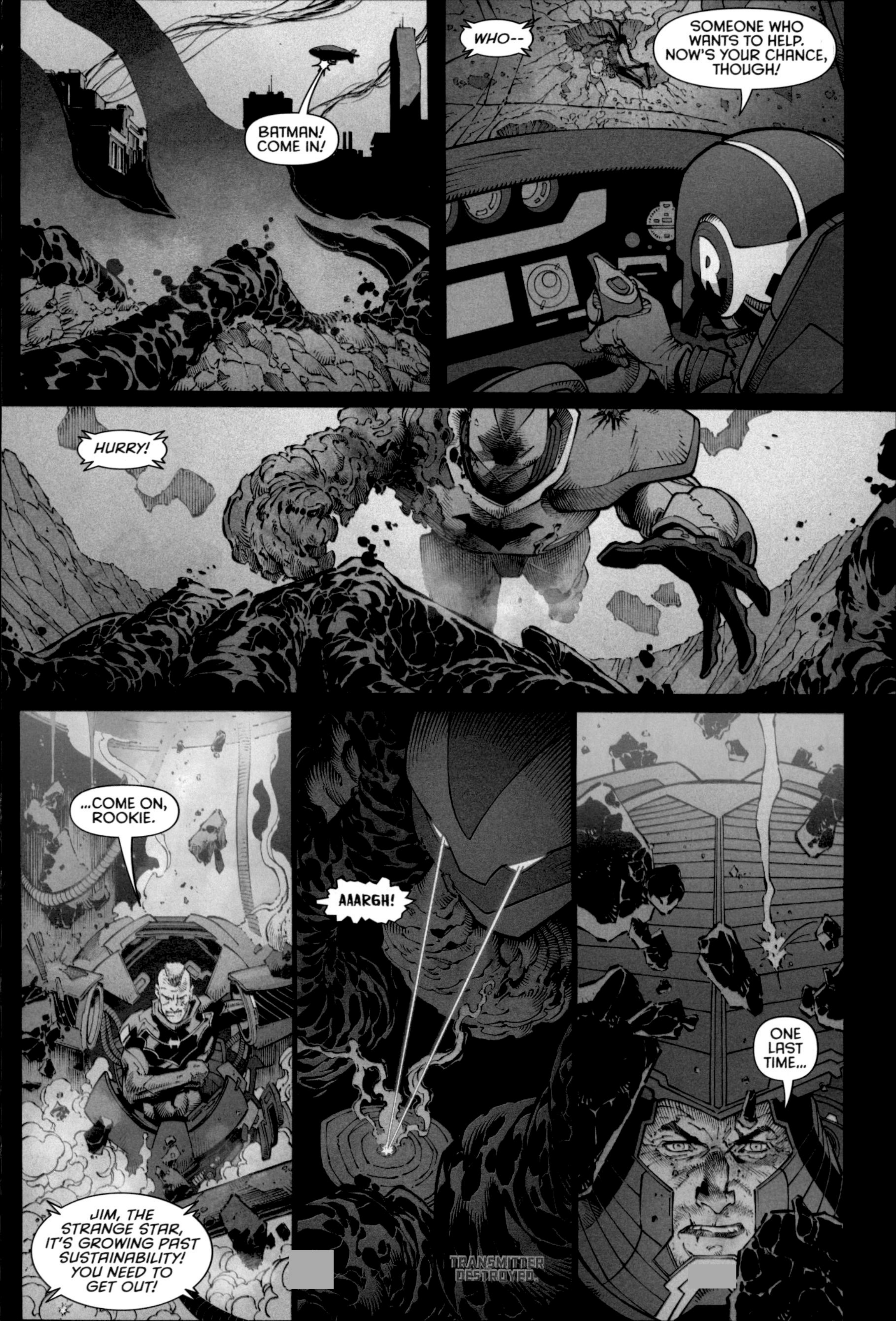
BATMAN! COME IN!
WHO--
SOMEONE WHO WANTS TO HELP. NOW'S YOUR CHANCE, THOUGH!
HURRY!
...COME ON, ROOKIE.
JIM, THE STRANGE STAR, IT'S GROWING PAST SUSTAINABILITY! YOU NEED TO GET OUT!
AAARGH!
TRANSMITTER DESTROYED.
ONE LAST TIME...

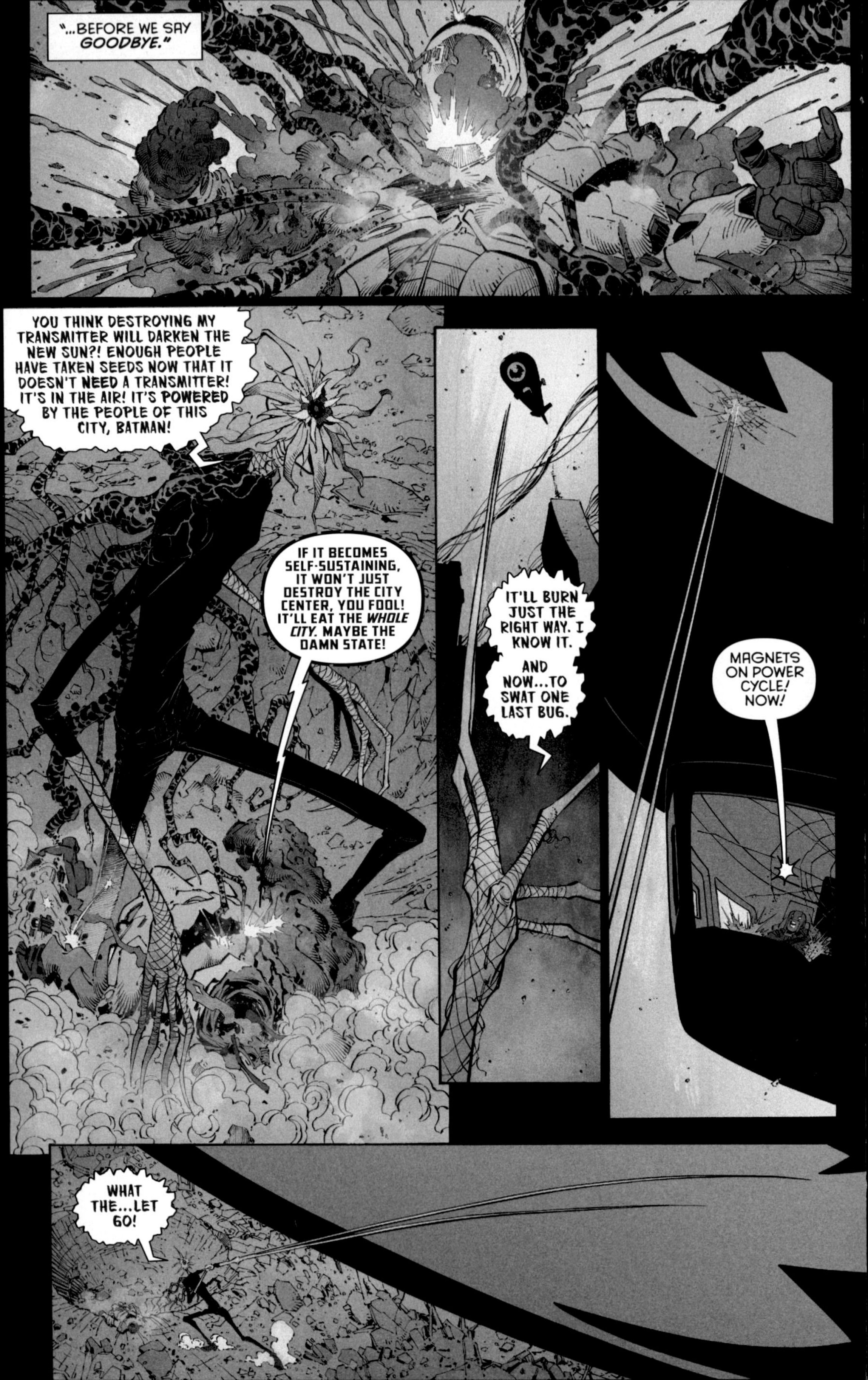
"...BEFORE WE SAY GOODBYE."
YOU THINK DESTROYING MY TRANSMITTER WILL DARKEN THE NEW SUN?! ENOUGH PEOPLE HAVE TAKEN SEEDS NOW THAT IT DOESN'T NEED A TRANSMITTER! IT'S IN THE AIR! IT'S POWERED BY THE PEOPLE OF THIS CITY, BATMAN!
IF IT BECOMES SELF-SUSTAINING, IT WON'T JUST DESTROY THE CITY CENTER, YOU FOOL! IT'LL EAT THE WHOLE CITY. MAYBE THE DAMN STATE!
IT'LL BURN JUST THE RIGHT WAY. I KNOW IT.
AND NOW...TO SWAT ONE LAST BUG.
MAGNETS ON POWER CYCLE! NOW!
WHAT THE...LET GO!

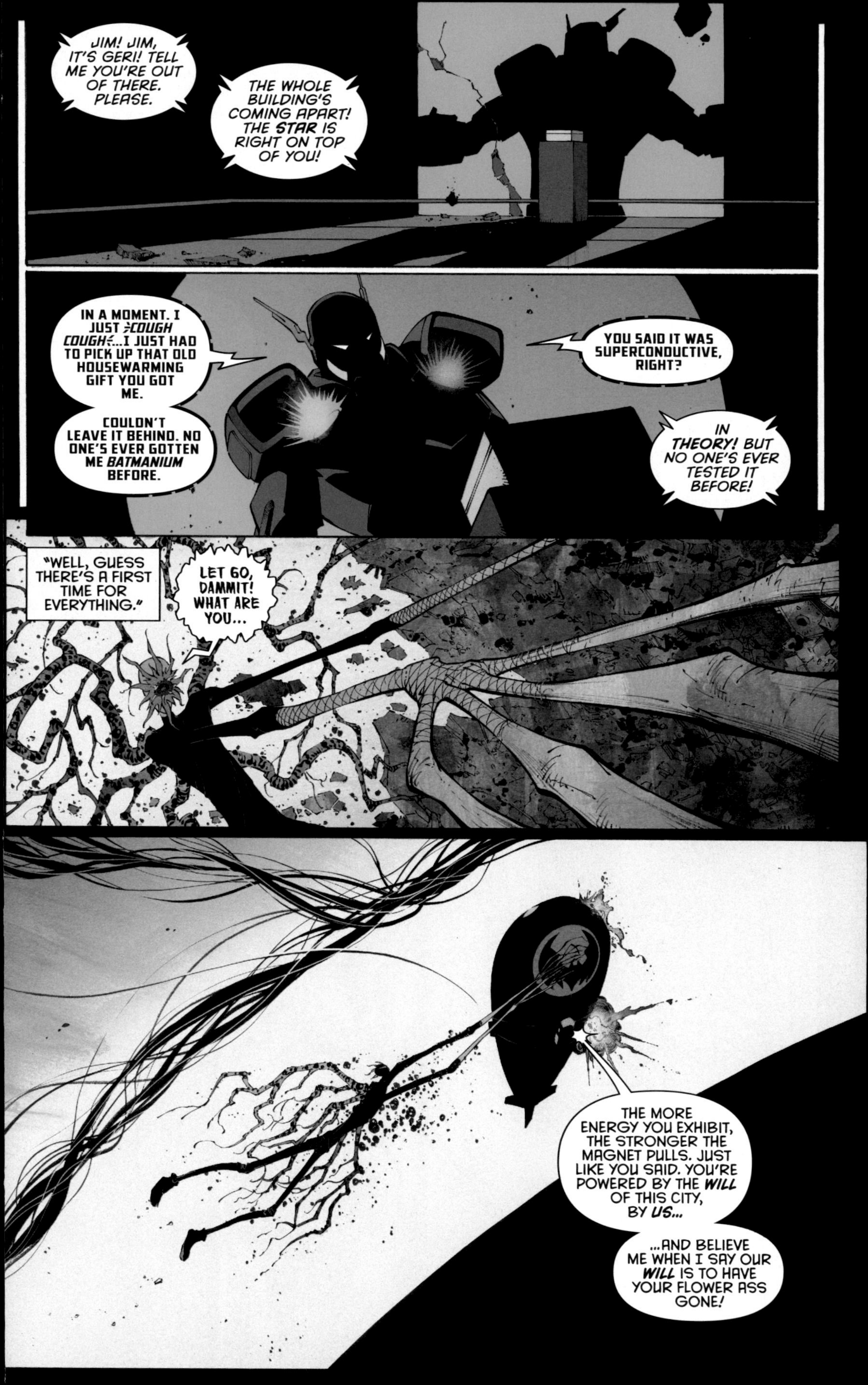
JIM! JIM, IT'S GERI! TELL ME YOU'RE OUT OF THERE. PLEASE.
THE WHOLE BUILDING'S COMING APART! THE STAR IS RIGHT ON TOP OF YOU!
IN A MOMENT. I JUST ≠COUGH COUGH≠...I JUST HAD TO PICK UP THAT OLD HOUSEWARMING GIFT YOU GOT ME.
COULDN'T LEAVE IT BEHIND. NO ONE'S EVER GOTTEN ME BATMANIUM BEFORE.
YOU SAID IT WAS SUPERCONDUCTIVE, RIGHT?
IN THEORY! BUT NO ONE'S EVER TESTED IT BEFORE!
"WELL, GUESS THERE'S A FIRST TIME FOR EVERYTHING."
LET GO, DAMMIT! WHAT ARE YOU...
THE MORE ENERGY YOU EXHIBIT, THE STRONGER THE MAGNET PULLS. JUST LIKE YOU SAID. YOU'RE POWERED BY THE WILL OF THIS CITY, BY US...
...AND BELIEVE ME WHEN I SAY OUR WILL IS TO HAVE YOUR FLOWER ASS GONE!

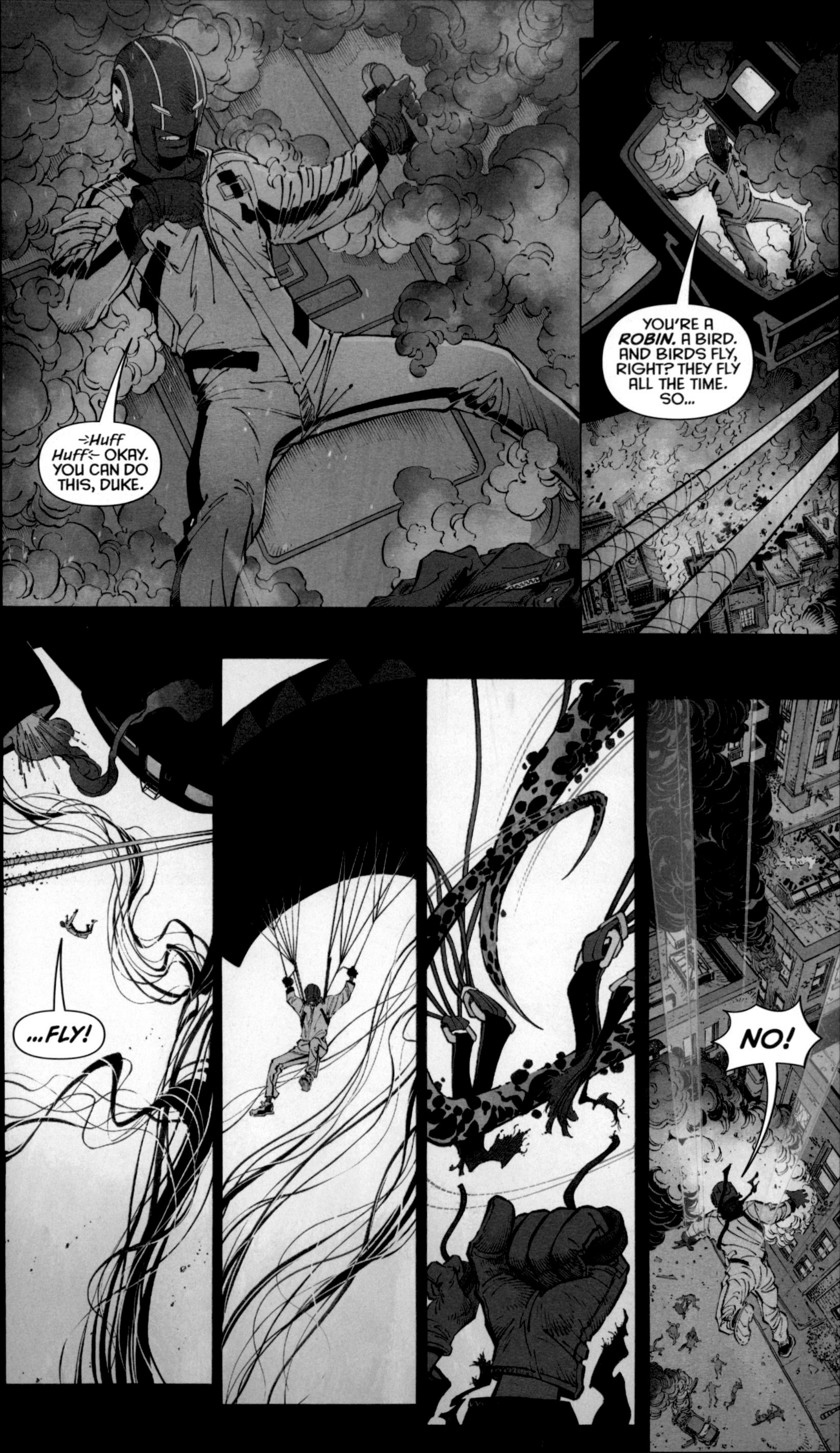

YOU'RE A ROBIN. A BIRD. AND BIRDS FLY, RIGHT? THEY FLY ALL THE TIME. SO...
~Huff Huff~ OKAY. YOU CAN DO THIS, DUKE.
...FLY!
NO!

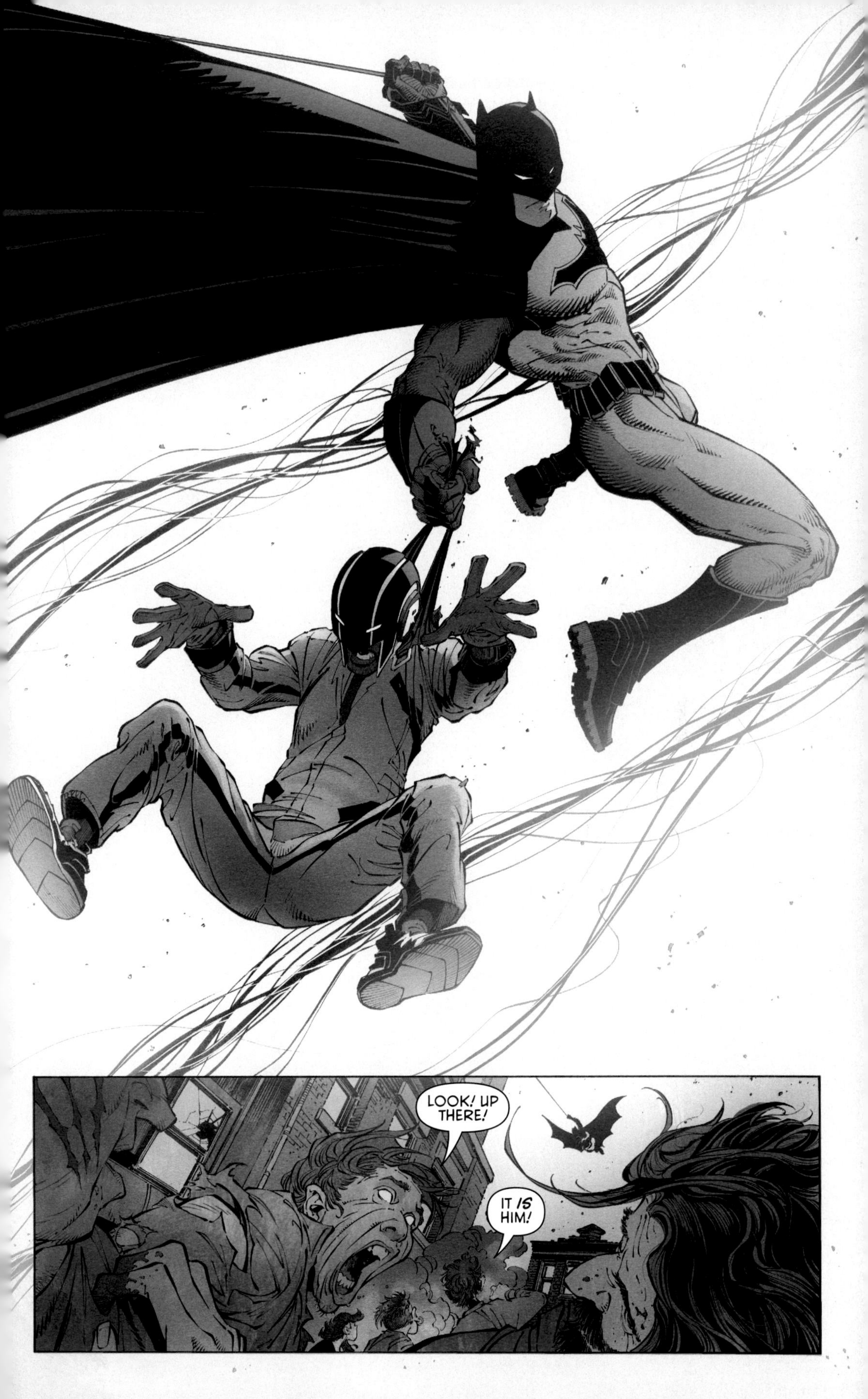
LOOK! UP THERE!
IT IS HIM!

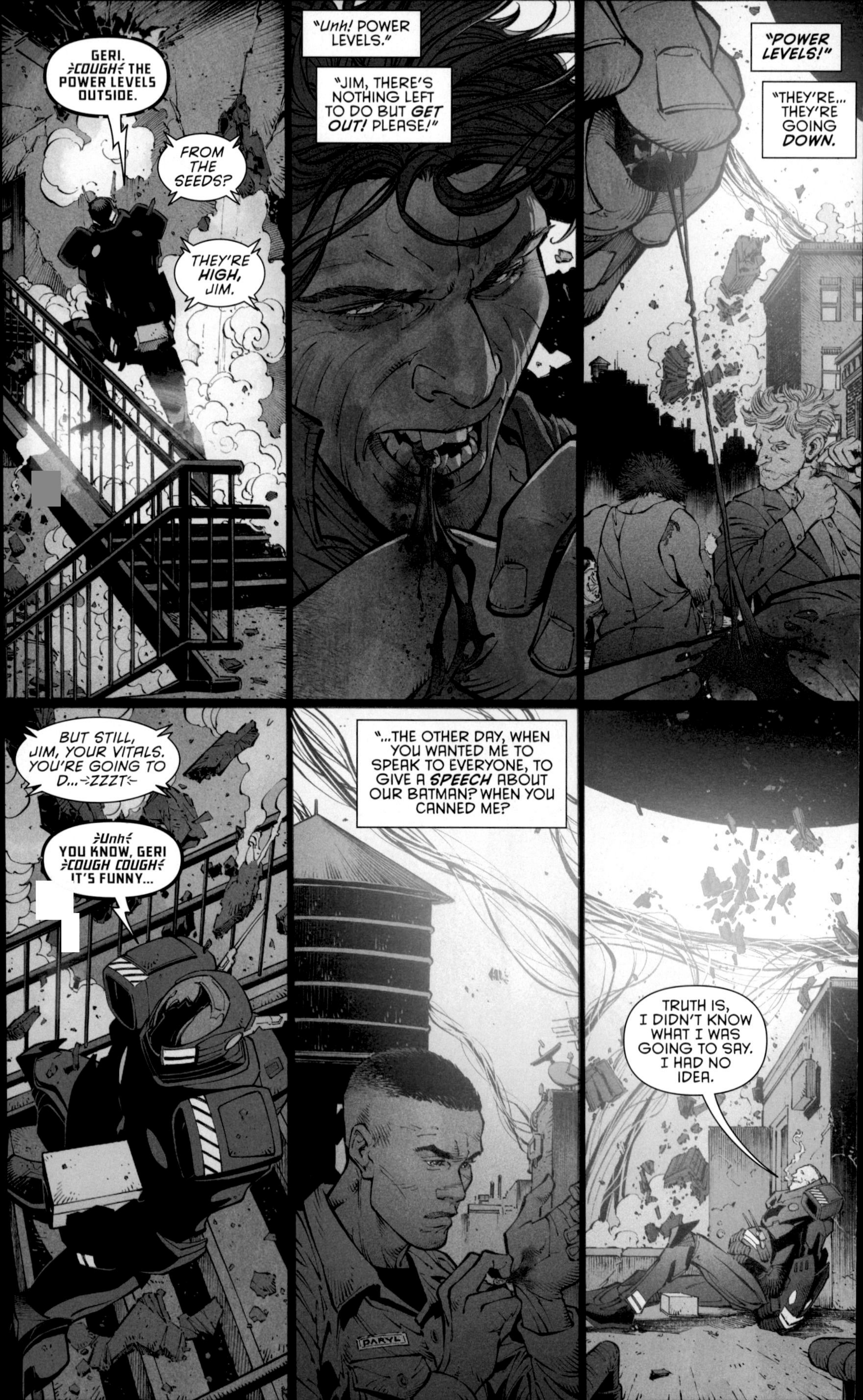
GERI. ⚡COUGH⚡ THE POWER LEVELS OUTSIDE.
FROM THE SEEDS?
THEY'RE HIGH, JIM.
"Unh! POWER LEVELS."
"JIM, THERE'S NOTHING LEFT TO DO BUT GET OUT! PLEASE!"
"POWER LEVELS!"
"THEY'RE... THEY'RE GOING DOWN.
BUT STILL, JIM, YOUR VITALS. YOU'RE GOING TO D... ⚡ZZZT⚡
⚡Unh⚡ YOU KNOW, GERI ⚡COUGH COUGH⚡ IT'S FUNNY...
"...THE OTHER DAY, WHEN YOU WANTED ME TO SPEAK TO EVERYONE, TO GIVE A SPEECH ABOUT OUR BATMAN? WHEN YOU CANNED ME?
DARYL
TRUTH IS, I DIDN'T KNOW WHAT I WAS GOING TO SAY. I HAD NO IDEA.

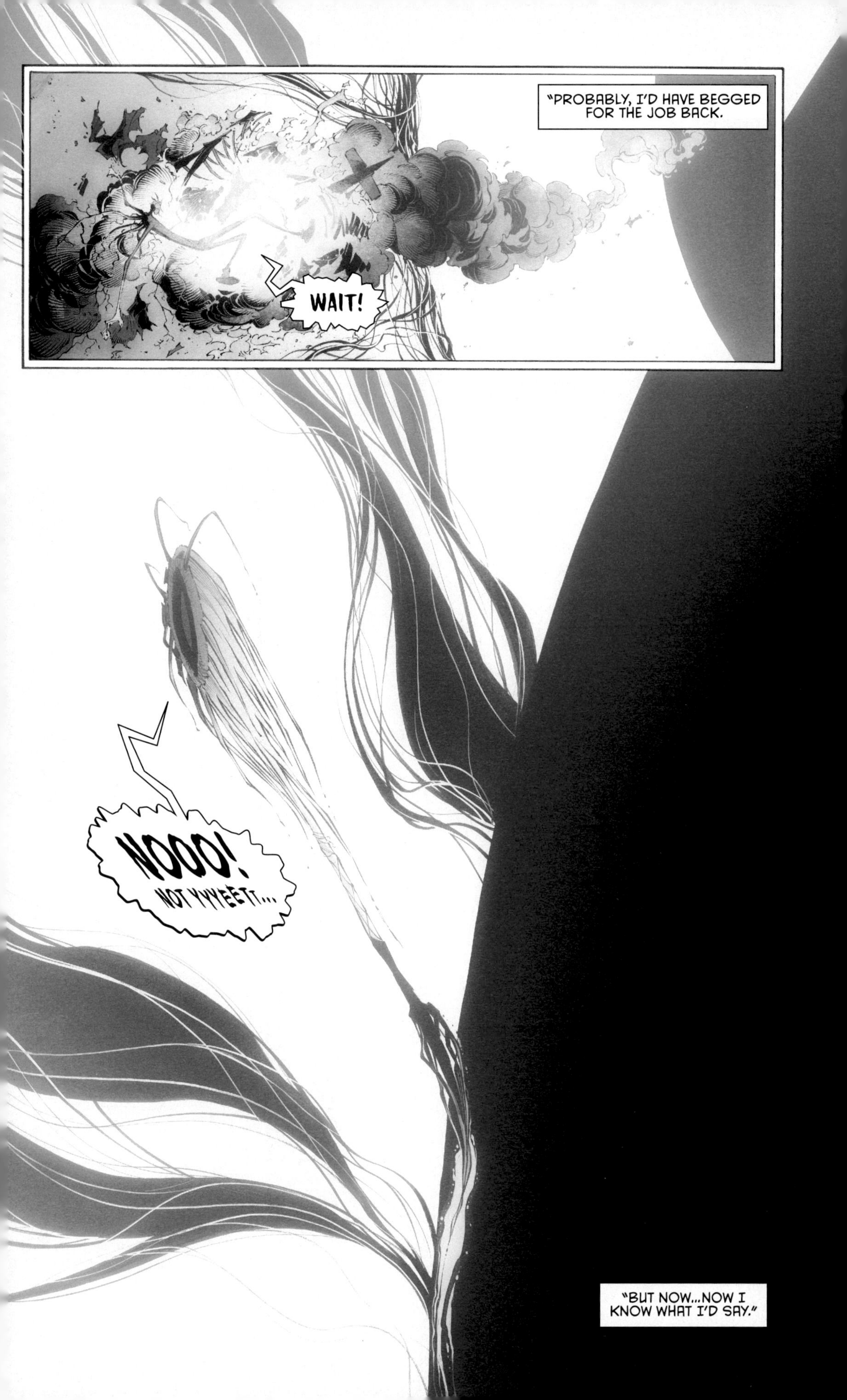
"PROBABLY, I'D HAVE BEGGED FOR THE JOB BACK.
WAIT!
NOOO! NOT YYYEEETT...
"BUT NOW...NOW I KNOW WHAT I'D SAY."

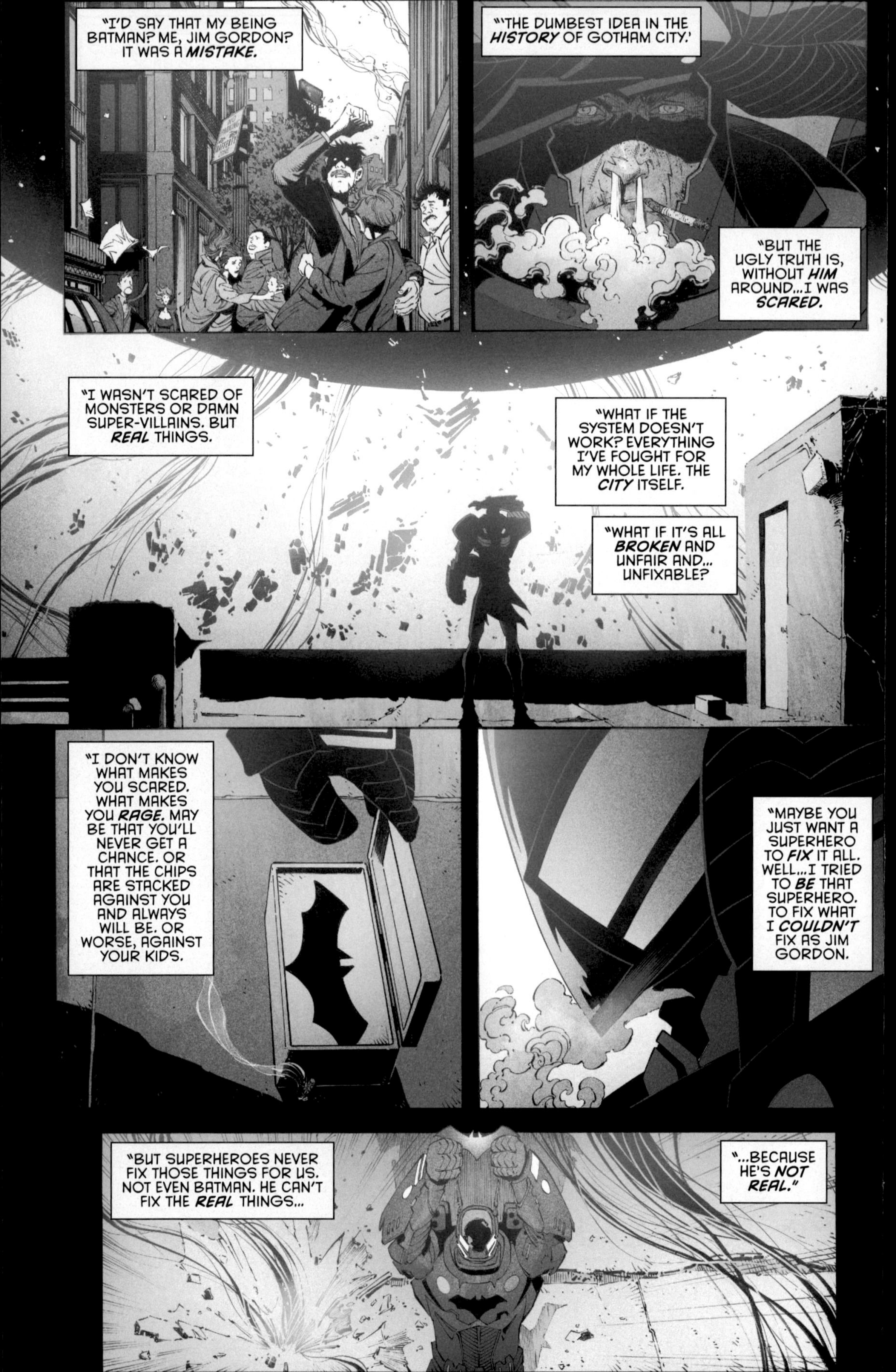
"I'D SAY THAT MY BEING BATMAN? ME, JIM GORDON? IT WAS A MISTAKE.
"'THE DUMBEST IDEA IN THE HISTORY OF GOTHAM CITY.'
"BUT THE UGLY TRUTH IS, WITHOUT HIM AROUND...I WAS SCARED.
"I WASN'T SCARED OF MONSTERS OR DAMN SUPER-VILLAINS. BUT REAL THINGS.
"WHAT IF THE SYSTEM DOESN'T WORK? EVERYTHING I'VE FOUGHT FOR MY WHOLE LIFE. THE CITY ITSELF.
"WHAT IF IT'S ALL BROKEN AND UNFAIR AND... UNFIXABLE?
"I DON'T KNOW WHAT MAKES YOU SCARED. WHAT MAKES YOU RAGE. MAY BE THAT YOU'LL NEVER GET A CHANCE. OR THAT THE CHIPS ARE STACKED AGAINST YOU AND ALWAYS WILL BE. OR WORSE, AGAINST YOUR KIDS.
"MAYBE YOU JUST WANT A SUPERHERO TO FIX IT ALL. WELL...I TRIED TO BE THAT SUPERHERO. TO FIX WHAT I COULDN'T FIX AS JIM GORDON.
"BUT SUPERHEROES NEVER FIX THOSE THINGS FOR US. NOT EVEN BATMAN. HE CAN'T FIX THE REAL THINGS...
"...BECAUSE HE'S NOT REAL."

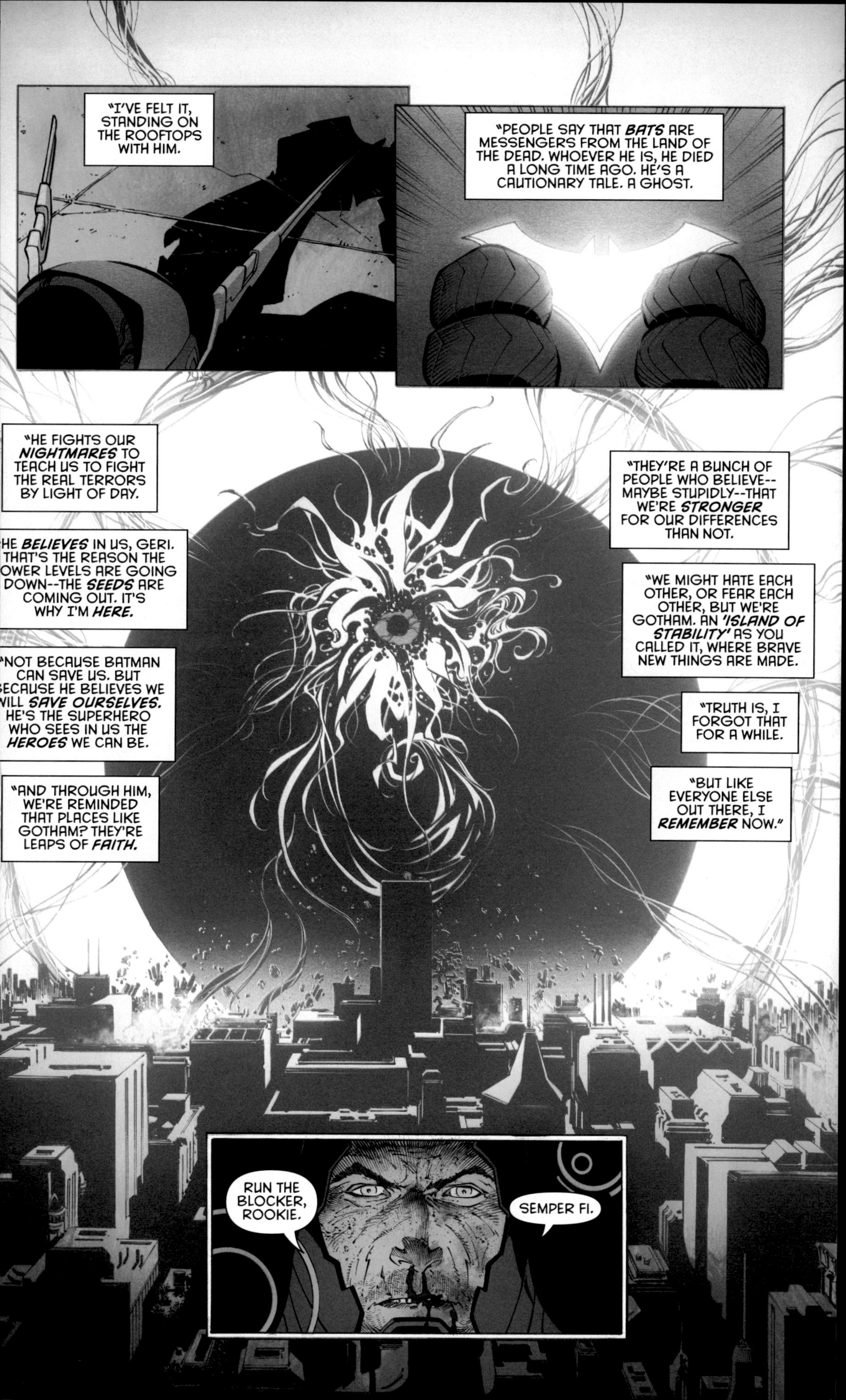

"I'VE FELT IT, STANDING ON THE ROOFTOPS WITH HIM.
"PEOPLE SAY THAT BATS ARE MESSENGERS FROM THE LAND OF THE DEAD. WHOEVER HE IS, HE DIED A LONG TIME AGO. HE'S A CAUTIONARY TALE. A GHOST.
"HE FIGHTS OUR NIGHTMARES TO TEACH US TO FIGHT THE REAL TERRORS BY LIGHT OF DAY.
HE BELIEVES IN US, GERI. THAT'S THE REASON THE OWER LEVELS ARE GOING DOWN--THE SEEDS ARE COMING OUT. IT'S WHY I'M HERE.
"NOT BECAUSE BATMAN CAN SAVE US. BUT BECAUSE HE BELIEVES WE WILL SAVE OURSELVES. HE'S THE SUPERHERO WHO SEES IN US THE HEROES WE CAN BE.
"AND THROUGH HIM, WE'RE REMINDED THAT PLACES LIKE GOTHAM? THEY'RE LEAPS OF FAITH.
"THEY'RE A BUNCH OF PEOPLE WHO BELIEVE-- MAYBE STUPIDLY--THAT WE'RE STRONGER FOR OUR DIFFERENCES THAN NOT.
"WE MIGHT HATE EACH OTHER, OR FEAR EACH OTHER, BUT WE'RE GOTHAM. AN 'ISLAND OF STABILITY' AS YOU CALLED IT, WHERE BRAVE NEW THINGS ARE MADE.
"TRUTH IS, I FORGOT THAT FOR A WHILE.
"BUT LIKE EVERYONE ELSE OUT THERE, I REMEMBER NOW."
RUN THE BLOCKER, ROOKIE.
SEMPER FI.

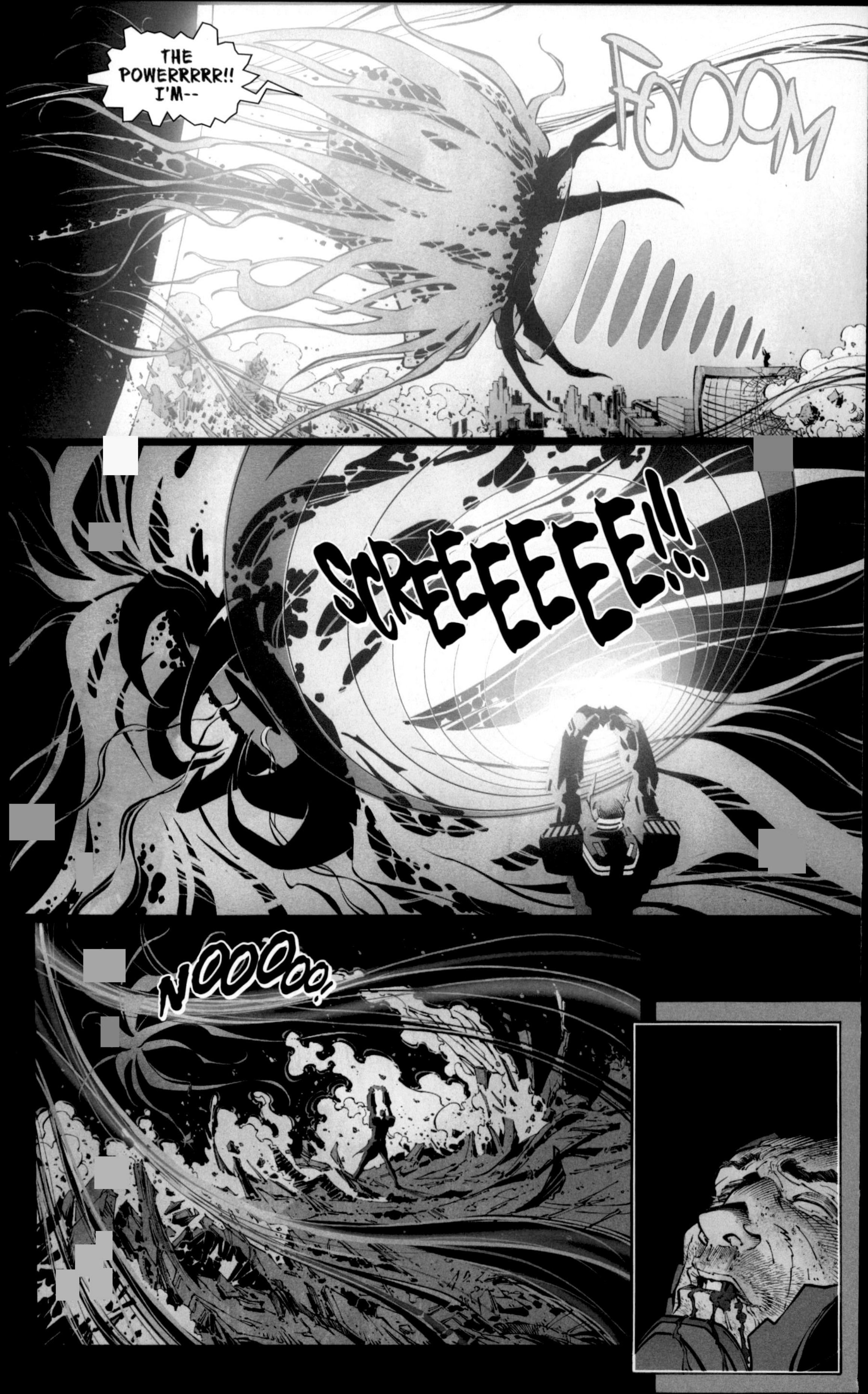
THE POWERRRRR!! I'M--
FOOOM
SCREEEEEE!!!
NOOOoo

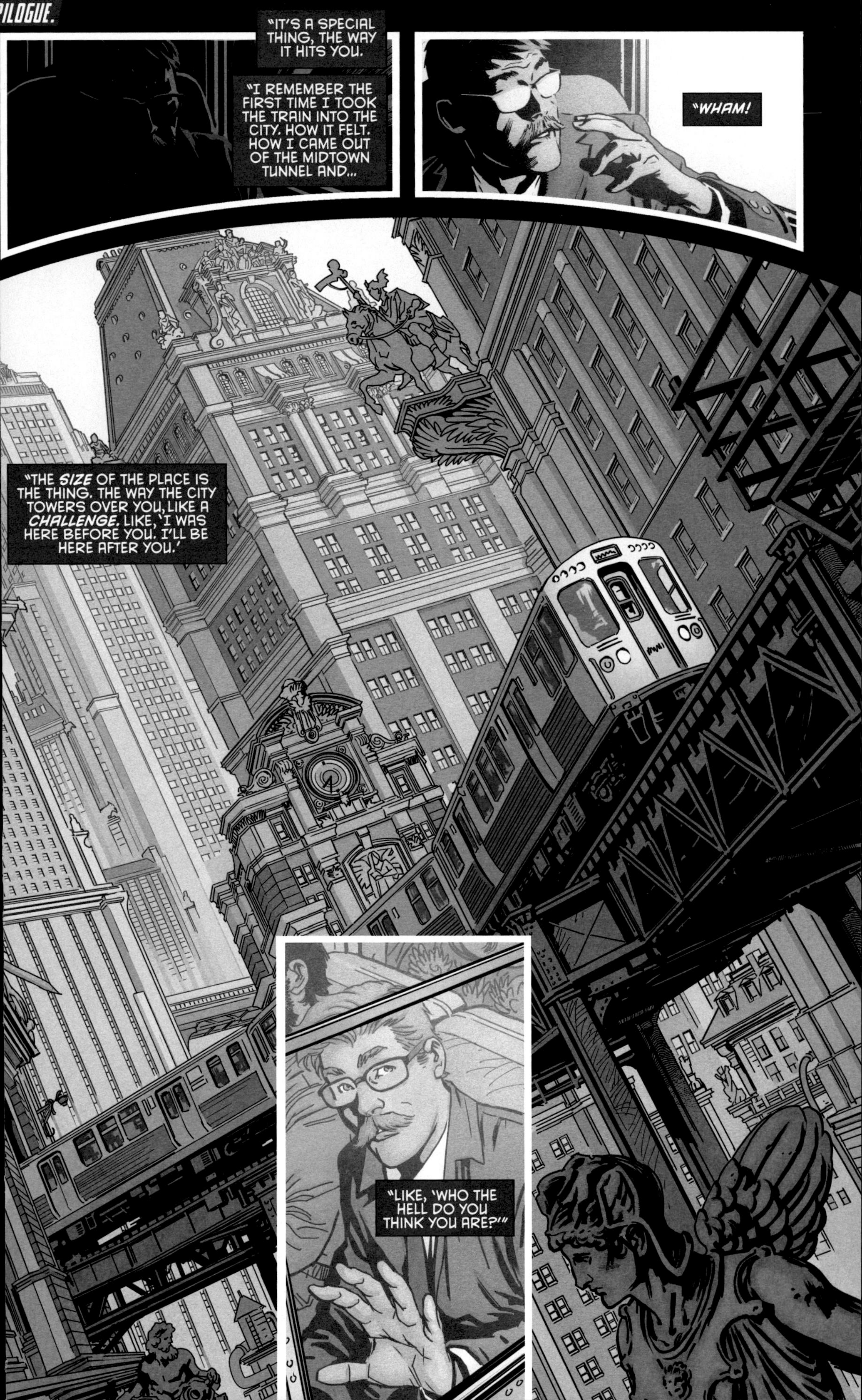
PILOGUE.
"IT'S A SPECIAL THING, THE WAY IT HITS YOU.
"I REMEMBER THE FIRST TIME I TOOK THE TRAIN INTO THE CITY. HOW IT FELT. HOW I CAME OUT OF THE MIDTOWN TUNNEL AND...
"WHAM!
"THE SIZE OF THE PLACE IS THE THING. THE WAY THE CITY TOWERS OVER YOU, LIKE A CHALLENGE. LIKE, 'I WAS HERE BEFORE YOU. I'LL BE HERE AFTER YOU.'
"LIKE, 'WHO THE HELL DO YOU THINK YOU ARE?'"

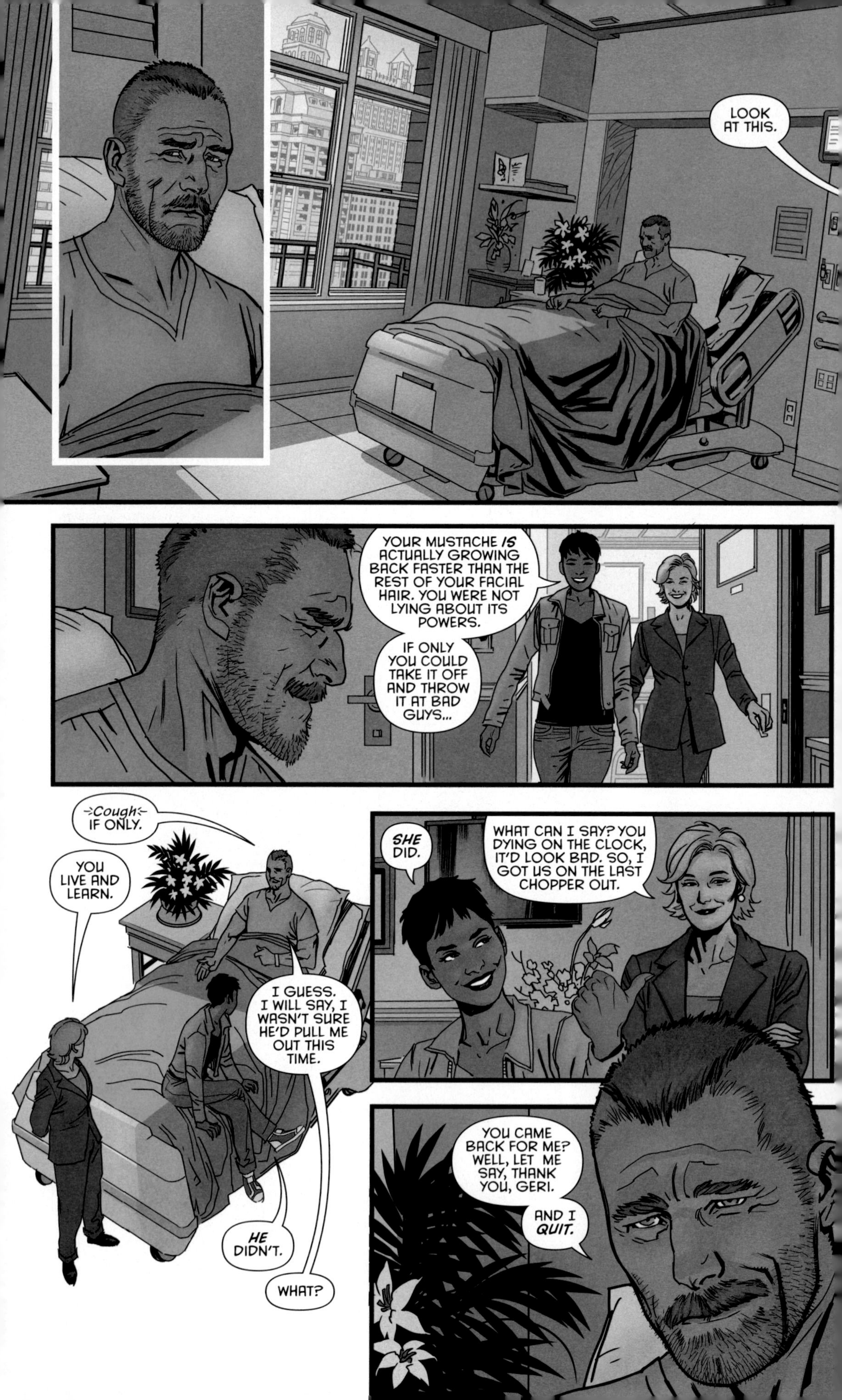

LOOK AT THIS.
YOUR MUSTACHE IS ACTUALLY GROWING BACK FASTER THAN THE REST OF YOUR FACIAL HAIR. YOU WERE NOT LYING ABOUT ITS POWERS.
IF ONLY YOU COULD TAKE IT OFF AND THROW IT AT BAD GUYS...
Cough IF ONLY.
YOU LIVE AND LEARN.
I GUESS. I WILL SAY, I WASN'T SURE HE'D PULL ME OUT THIS TIME.
HE DIDN'T.
WHAT?
SHE DID.
WHAT CAN I SAY? YOU DYING ON THE CLOCK, IT'D LOOK BAD. SO, I GOT US ON THE LAST CHOPPER OUT.
YOU CAME BACK FOR ME? WELL, LET ME SAY, THANK YOU, GERI.
AND I QUIT.

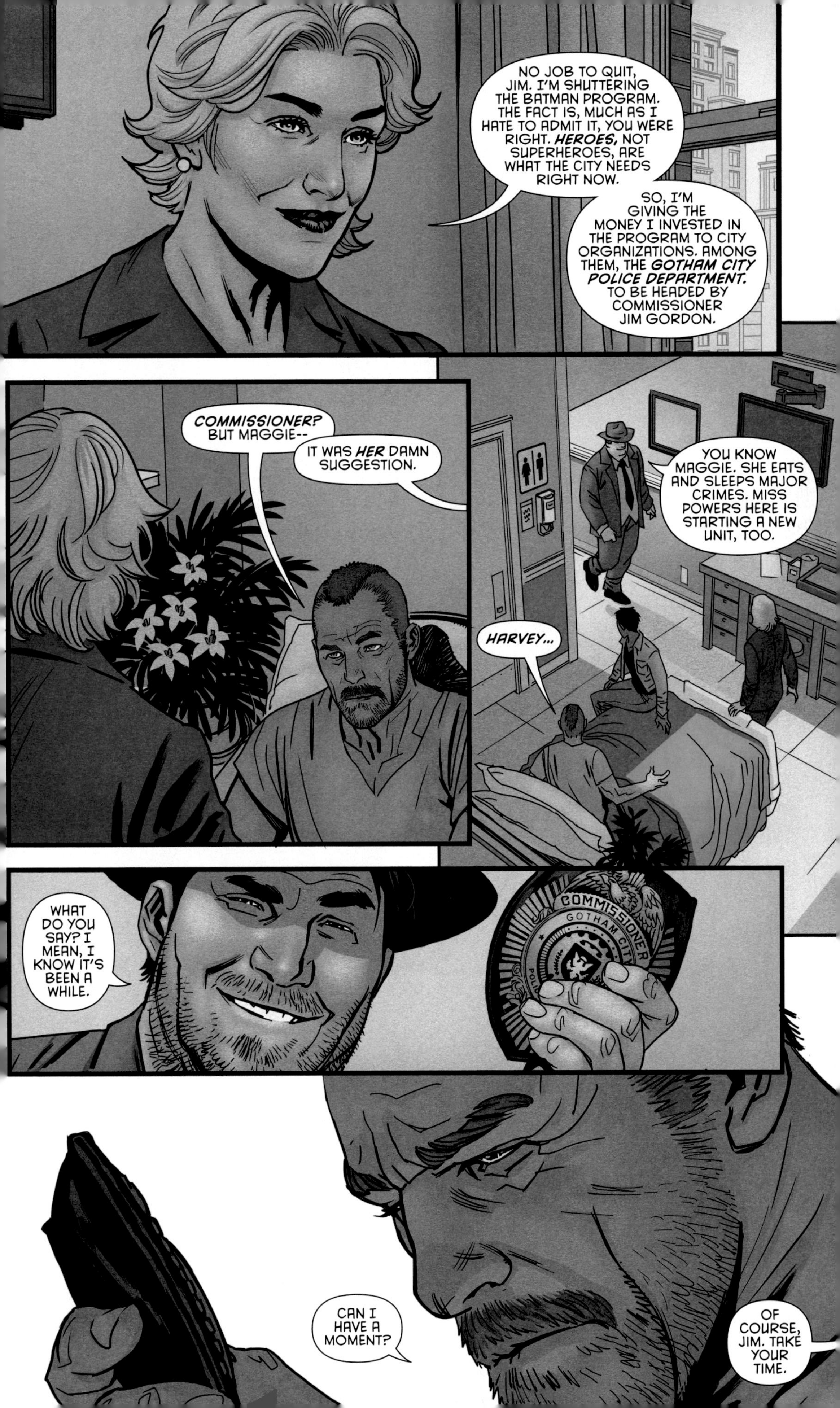

NO JOB TO QUIT, JIM. I'M SHUTTERING THE BATMAN PROGRAM. THE FACT IS, MUCH AS I HATE TO ADMIT IT, YOU WERE RIGHT. *HEROES,* NOT SUPERHEROES, ARE WHAT THE CITY NEEDS RIGHT NOW.
SO, I'M GIVING THE MONEY I INVESTED IN THE PROGRAM TO CITY ORGANIZATIONS. AMONG THEM, THE *GOTHAM CITY POLICE DEPARTMENT.* TO BE HEADED BY COMMISSIONER JIM GORDON.
*COMMISSIONER?* BUT MAGGIE--
IT WAS *HER* DAMN SUGGESTION.
YOU KNOW MAGGIE. SHE EATS AND SLEEPS MAJOR CRIMES. MISS POWERS HERE IS STARTING A NEW UNIT, TOO.
*HARVEY...*
WHAT DO YOU SAY? I MEAN, I KNOW IT'S BEEN A WHILE.
COMMISSIONER
GOTHAM CITY
CAN I HAVE A MOMENT?
OF COURSE, JIM. TAKE YOUR TIME.

WE HAVE WORK TO DO, JIM. YOU KNOW AS WELL AS I DO THAT RIGHT NOW IS THE MOST DANGEROUS TIME, WHEN ALL THE WOUNDS ARE OPEN. WHEN THINGS ARE HURTING.

I KNOW.

AND...AND I JUST WANT TO SAY I'M *SORRY,* OLD FRIEND. I CAN'T HELP BUT FEEL IT'S MY FAULT. TRYING TO BE YOU, TO TAKE YOUR PLACE...

...IT ALLOWED FOR BLOOM TO RISE UP AND BLOW THIS PLACE TO HELL ALL OVER AGAIN, JUST LIKE *JOKER* DID AND--

NO. NOT LIKE JOKER.

THE JOKER...THE DARKNESS IN HIM... NO ONE COULD BE HIM. BUT BLOOM, *ANYONE* CAN BECOME BLOOM IF THEY LOSE HOPE IN THIS PLACE.

WHAT I'M SAYING IS, HE WAS *YOUR* MONSTER, JIM, AND YOU STOPPED HIM, NOT ME. YOU AND THE PEOPLE OF THIS CITY.

SO THANK YOU. FOR KEEPING THE CITY SAFE WHILE I WAS GONE.

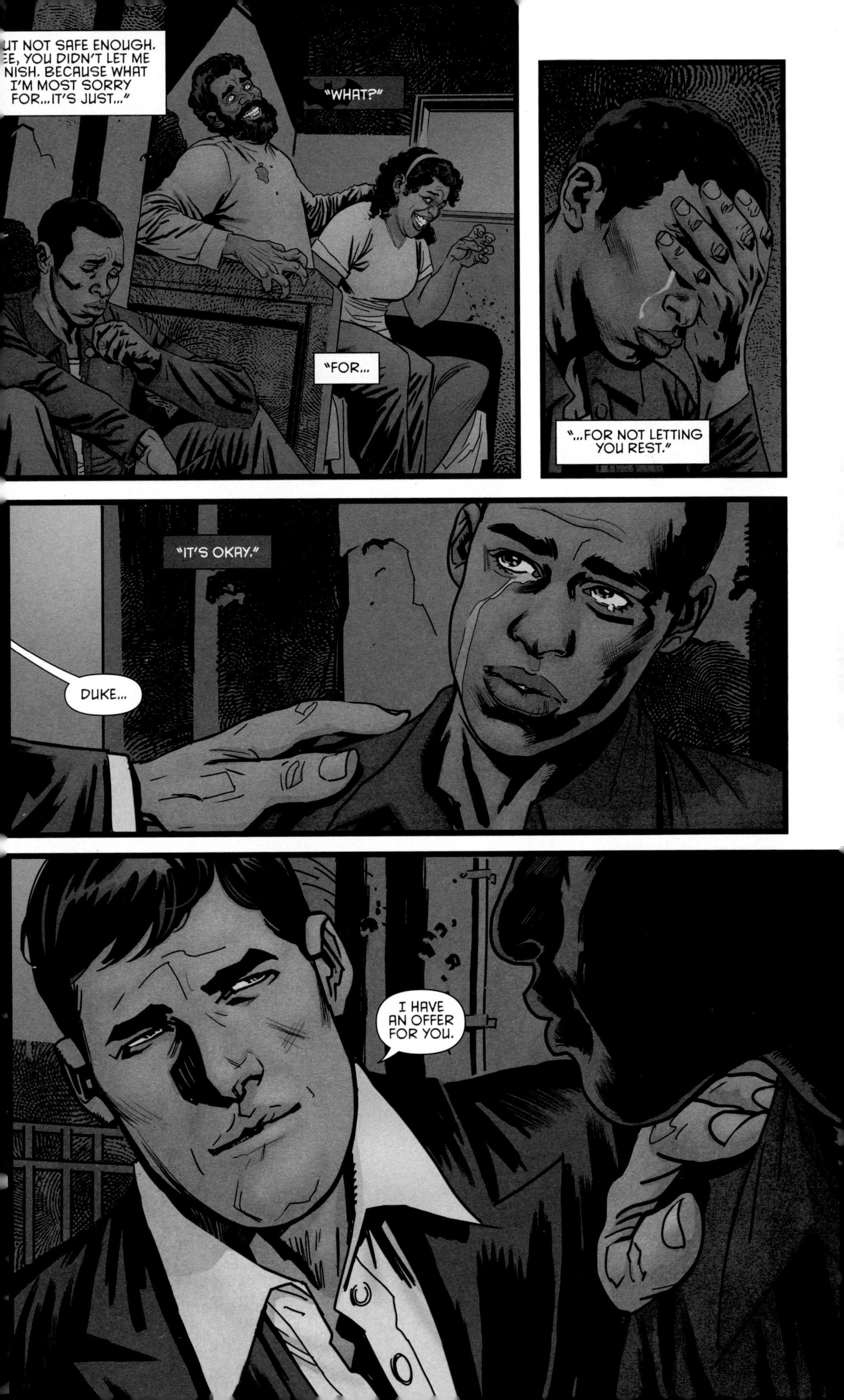
UT NOT SAFE ENOUGH.
EE, YOU DIDN'T LET ME
NISH. BECAUSE WHAT
I'M MOST SORRY
FOR...IT'S JUST..."
"WHAT?"
"FOR...
"...FOR NOT LETTING
YOU REST."
"IT'S OKAY."
DUKE...
I HAVE
AN OFFER
FOR YOU.

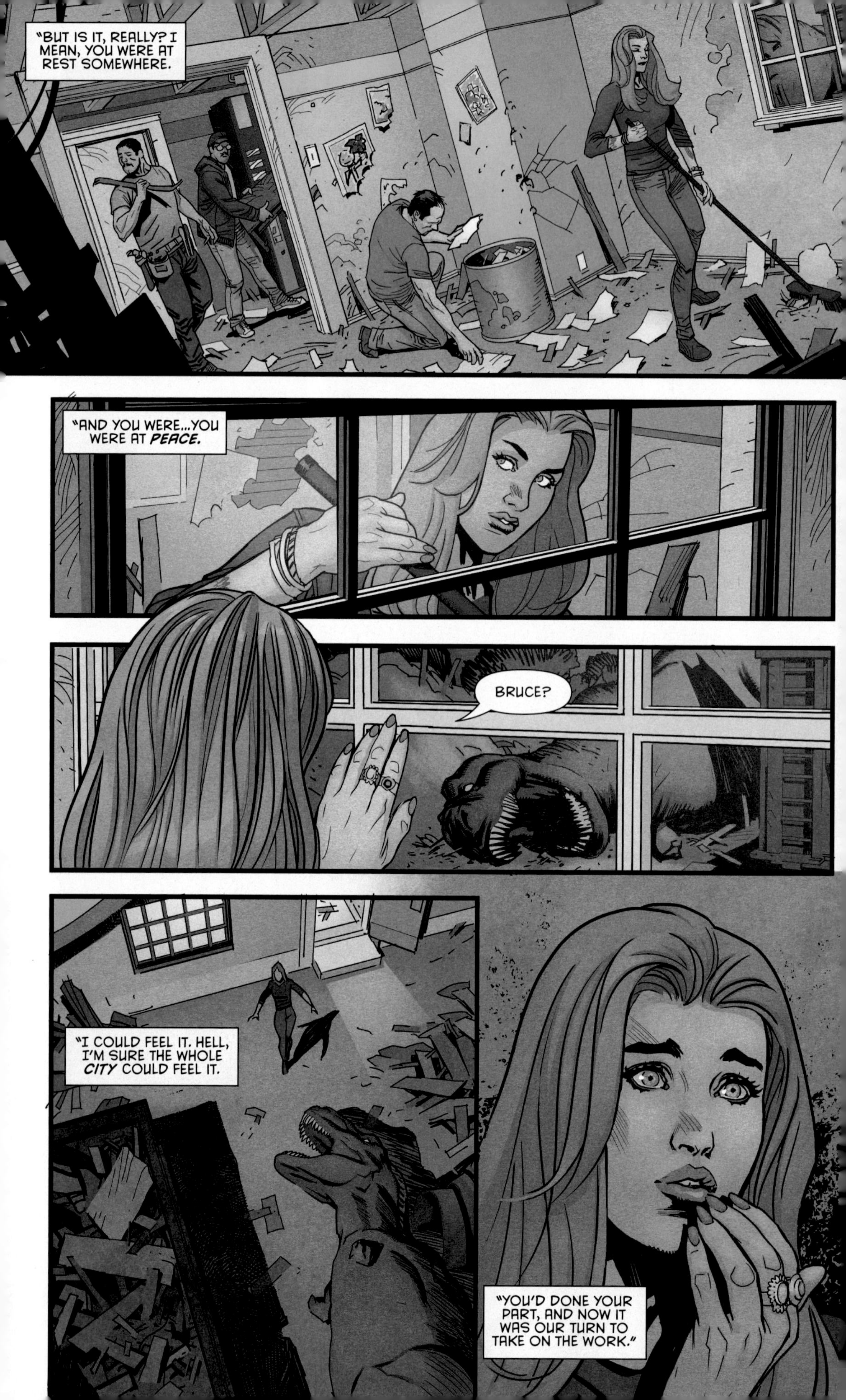
"BUT IS IT, REALLY? I MEAN, YOU WERE AT REST SOMEWHERE.
"AND YOU WERE...YOU WERE AT *PEACE.*
BRUCE?
"I COULD FEEL IT. HELL, I'M SURE THE WHOLE *CITY* COULD FEEL IT.
"YOU'D DONE YOUR PART, AND NOW IT WAS OUR TURN TO TAKE ON THE WORK."

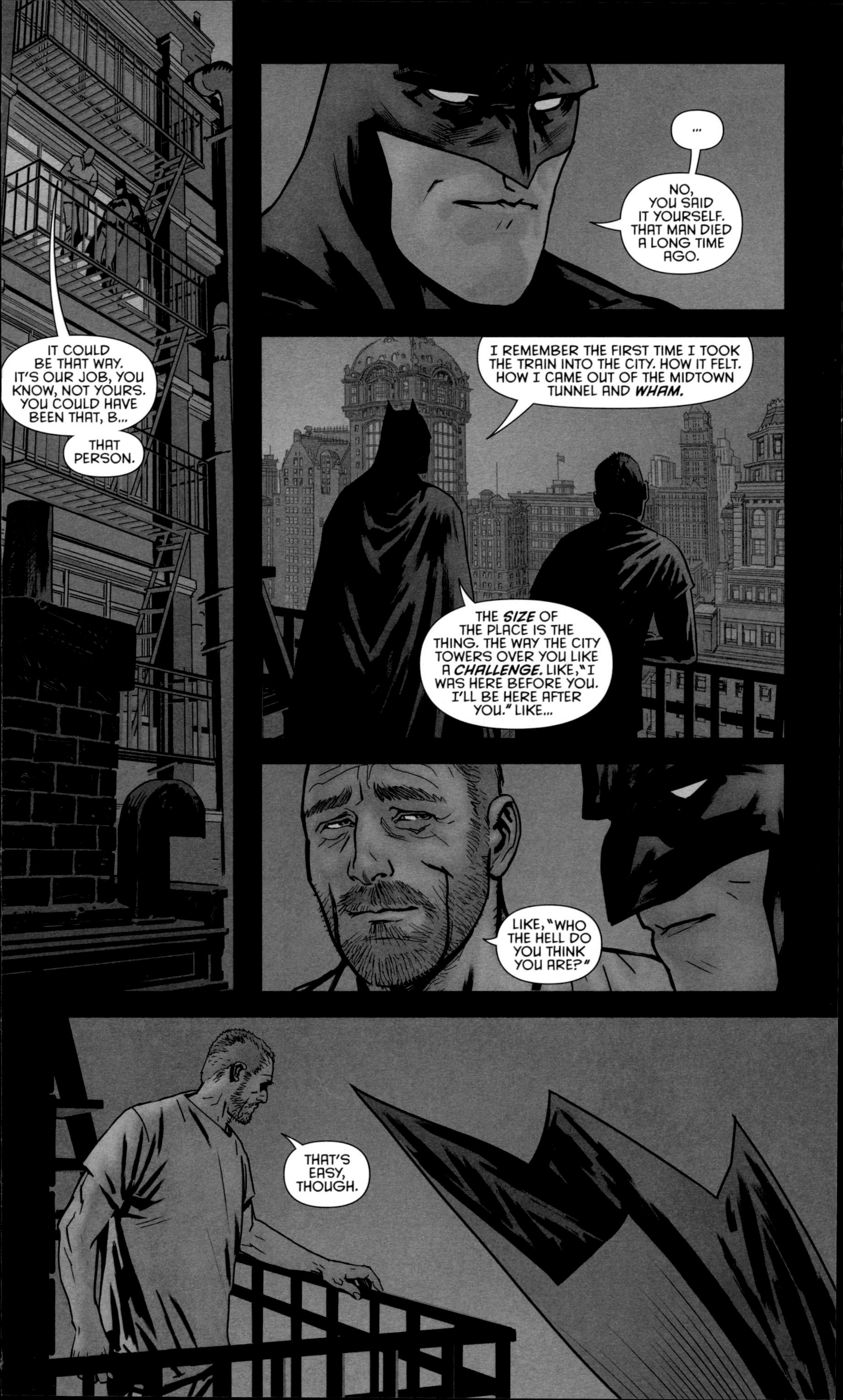

IT COULD BE THAT WAY. IT'S OUR JOB, YOU KNOW, NOT YOURS. YOU COULD HAVE BEEN THAT, B...
THAT PERSON.
...
NO, YOU SAID IT YOURSELF. THAT MAN DIED A LONG TIME AGO.
I REMEMBER THE FIRST TIME I TOOK THE TRAIN INTO THE CITY. HOW IT FELT. HOW I CAME OUT OF THE MIDTOWN TUNNEL AND *WHAM.*
THE *SIZE* OF THE PLACE IS THE THING. THE WAY THE CITY TOWERS OVER YOU LIKE A *CHALLENGE.* LIKE, "I WAS HERE BEFORE YOU. I'LL BE HERE AFTER YOU." LIKE...
LIKE, "WHO THE HELL DO YOU THINK YOU ARE?"
THAT'S EASY, THOUGH.

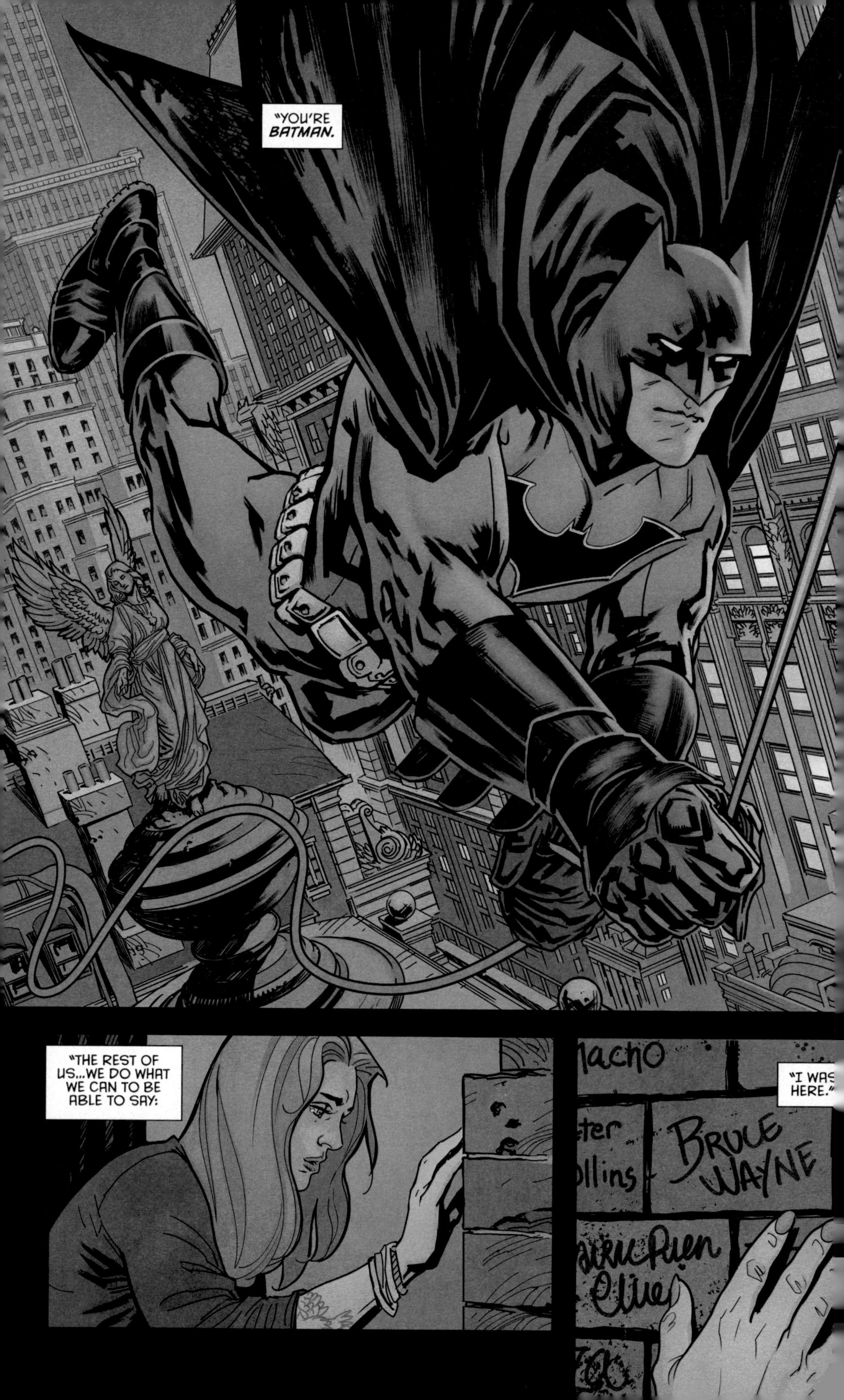
"YOU'RE BATMAN.
"THE REST OF US...WE DO WHAT WE CAN TO BE ABLE TO SAY:
BRUCE WAYNE
"I WAS HERE."

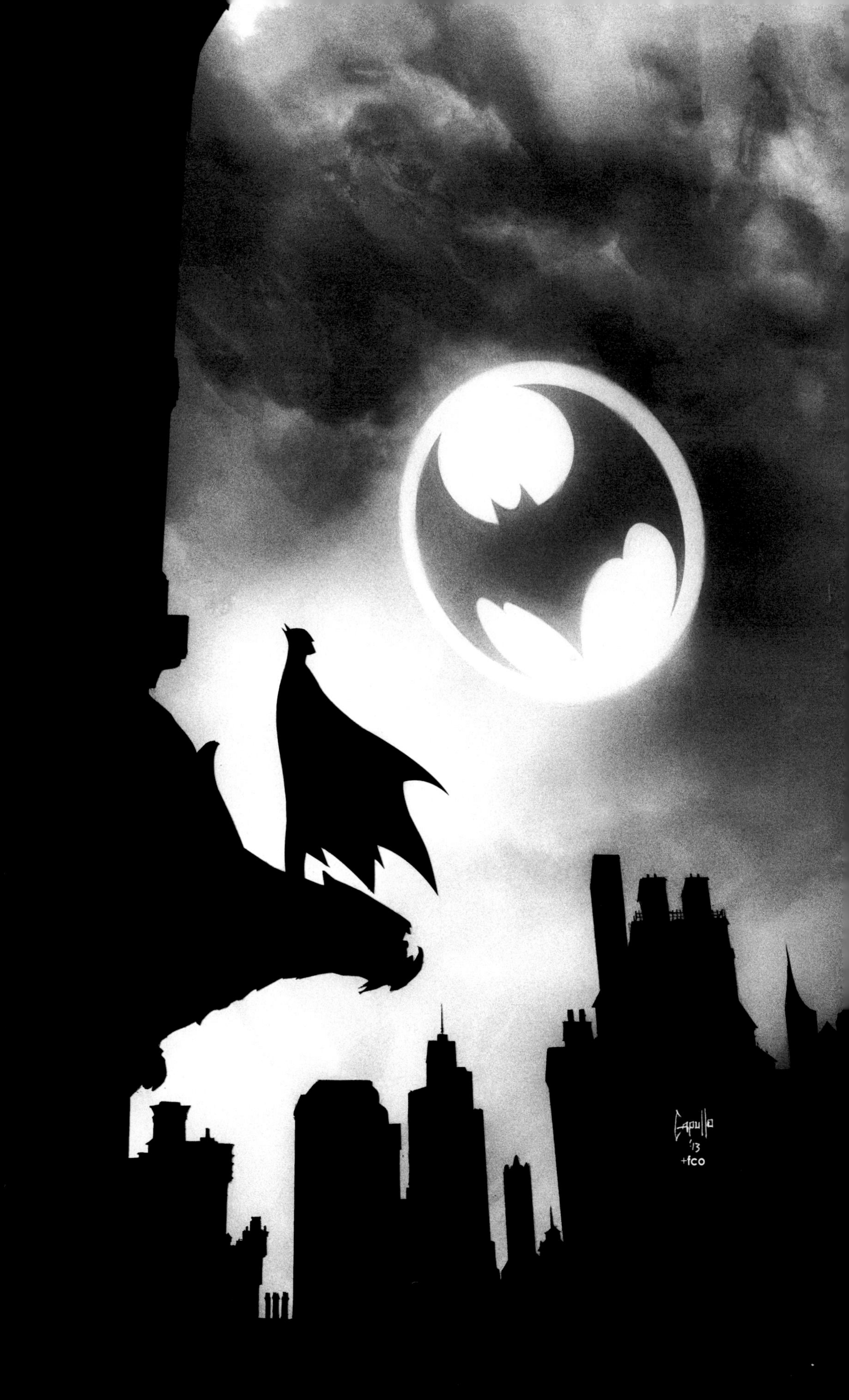
Capullo '13
+fco

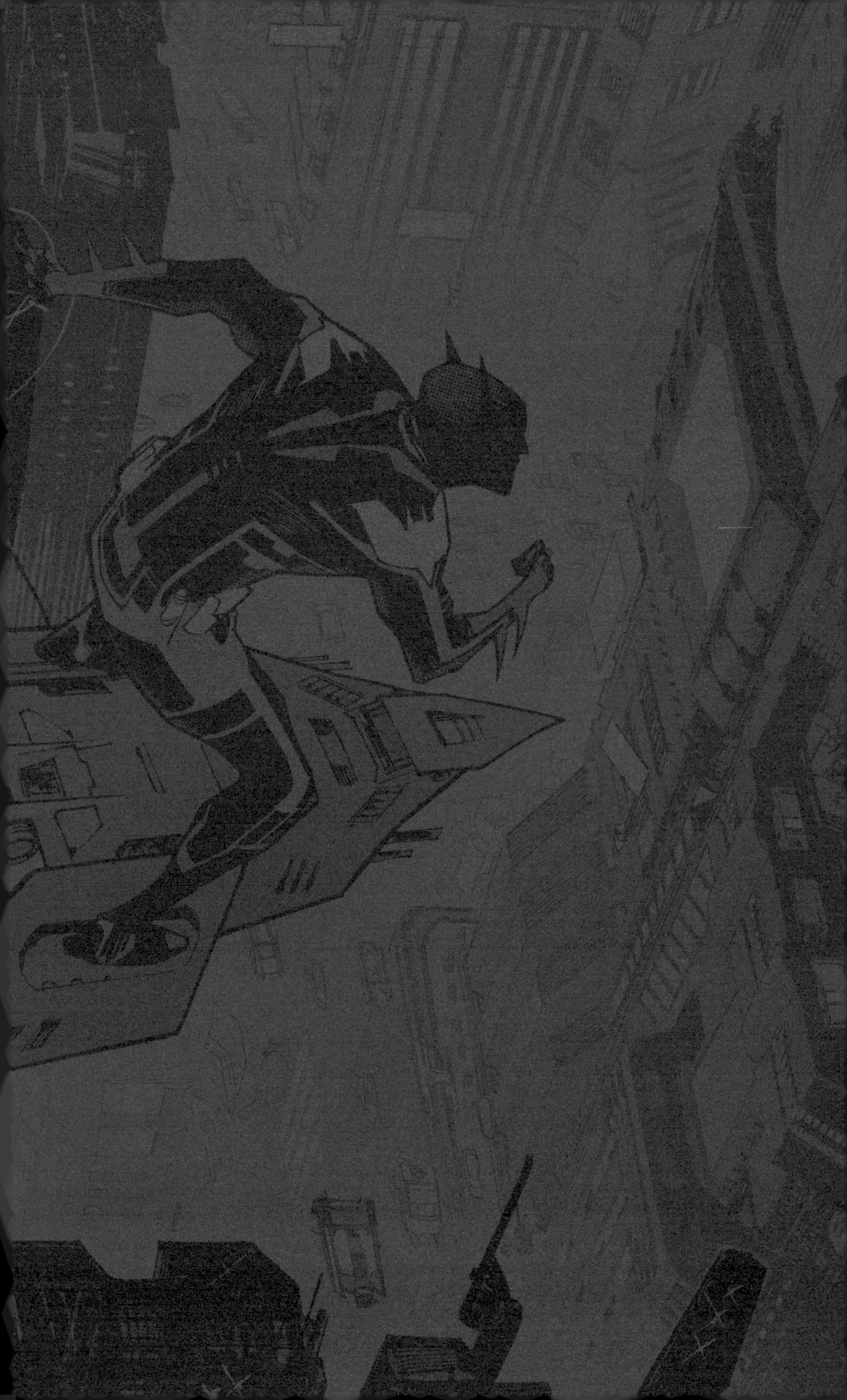

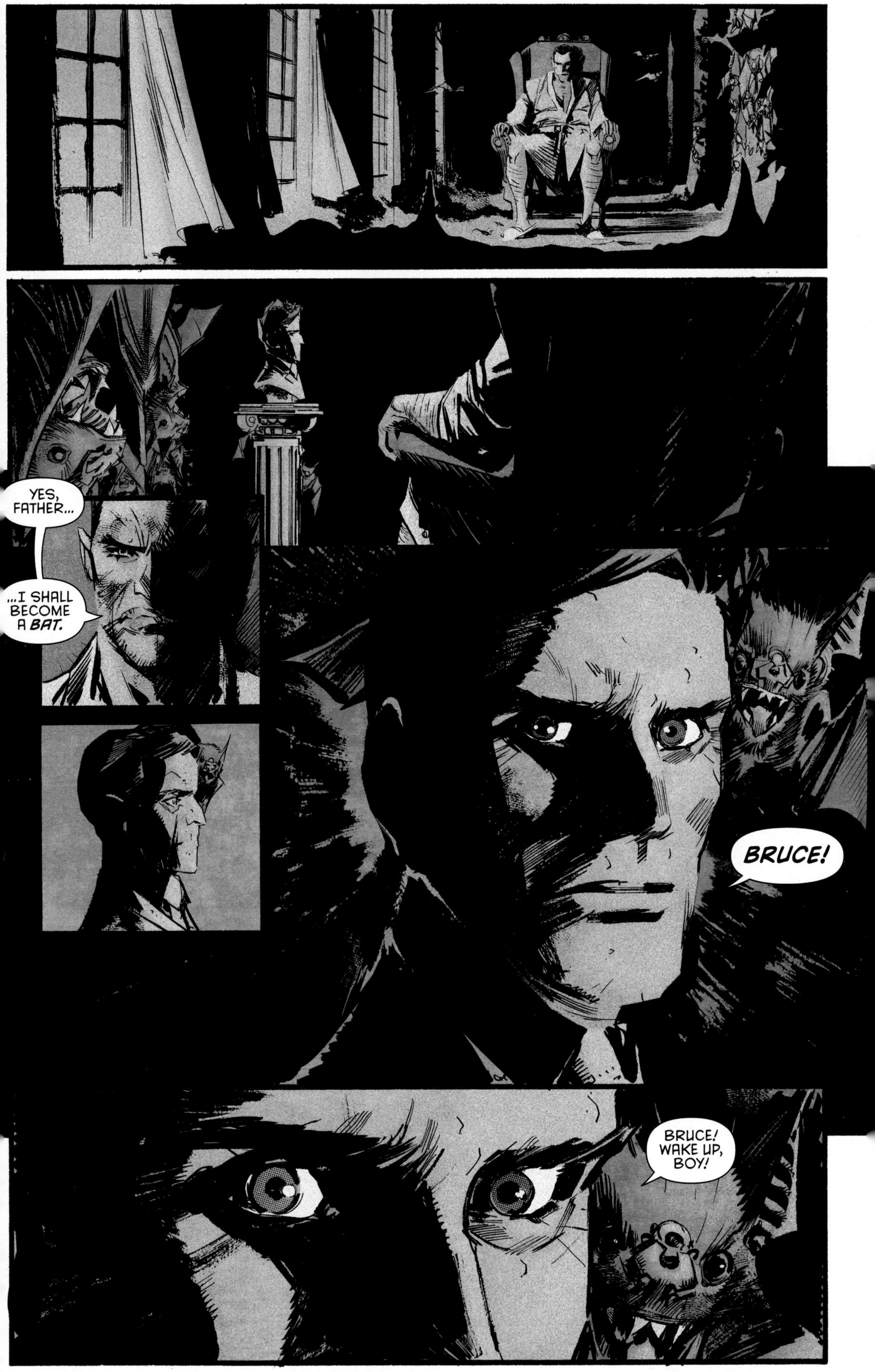
YES, FATHER...
...I SHALL BECOME A BAT.
BRUCE!
BRUCE! WAKE UP, BOY!

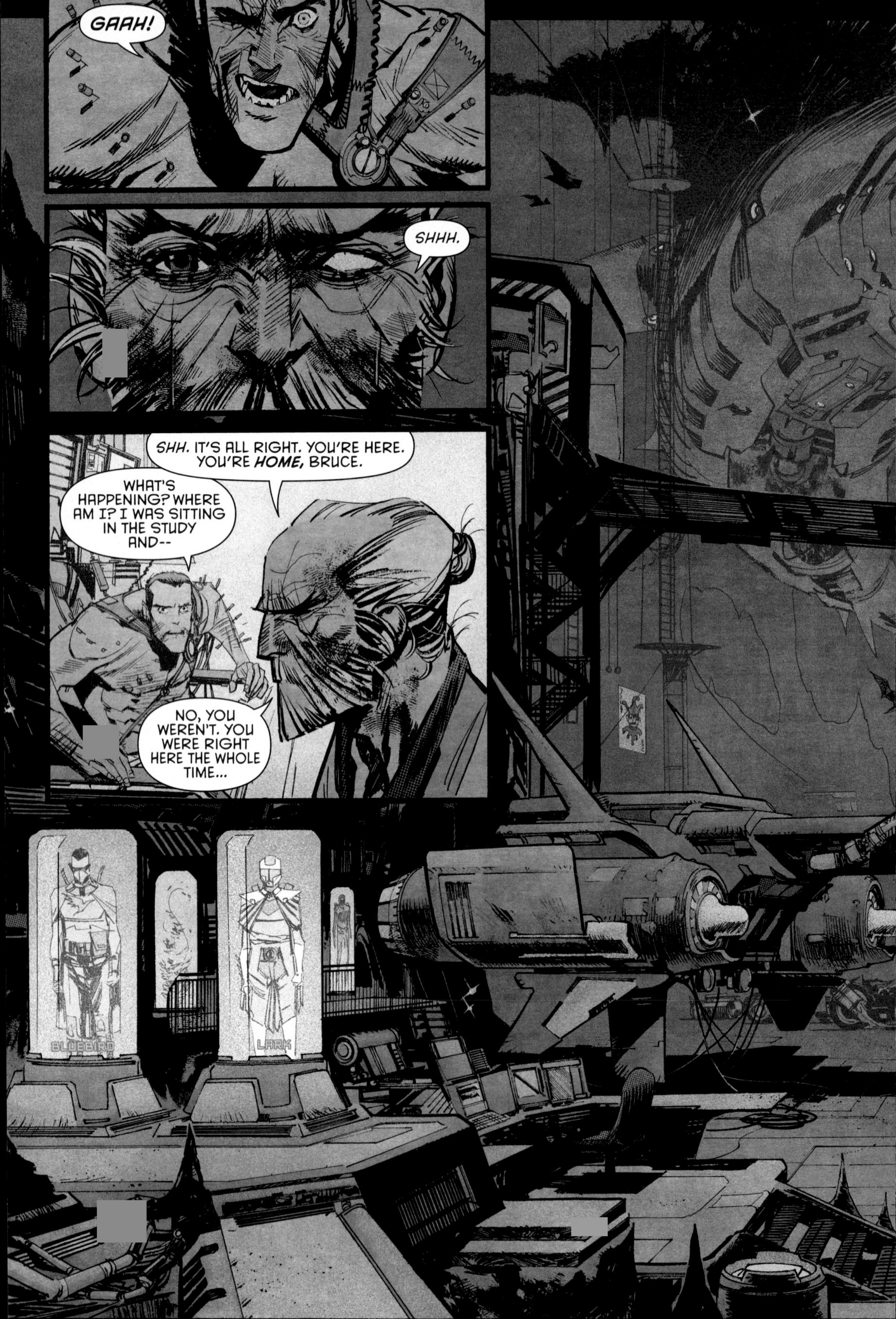
GAAH!
SHHH.
SHH. IT'S ALL RIGHT. YOU'RE HERE. YOU'RE HOME, BRUCE.
WHAT'S HAPPENING? WHERE AM I? I WAS SITTING IN THE STUDY AND--
NO, YOU WEREN'T. YOU WERE RIGHT HERE THE WHOLE TIME...
BLUEBIRD
LARK

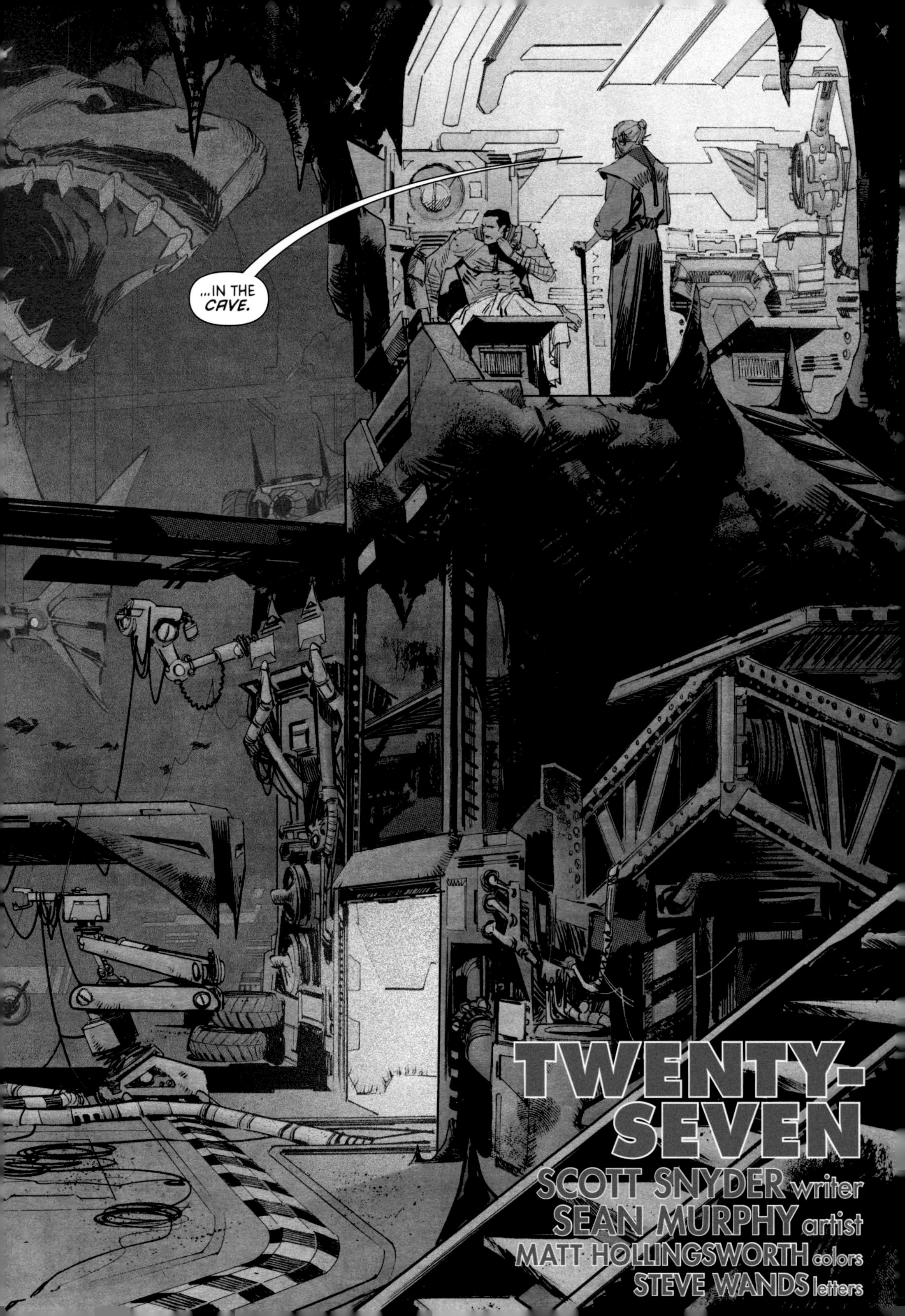
...IN THE CAVE.
TWENTY-SEVEN
SCOTT SNYDER writer
SEAN MURPHY artist
MATT HOLLINGSWORTH colors
STEVE WANDS letters

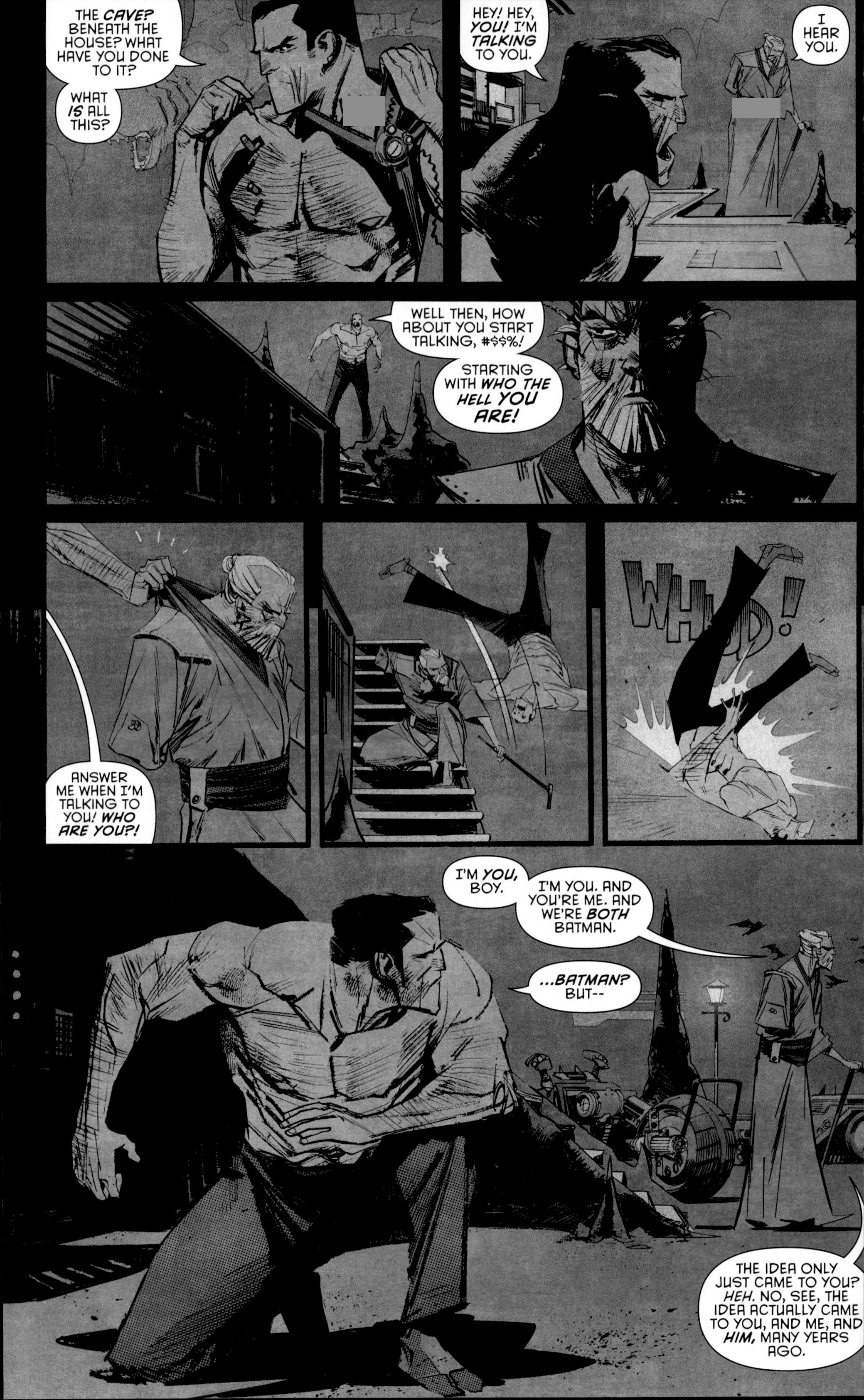

THE *CAVE?* BENEATH THE HOUSE? WHAT HAVE YOU DONE TO IT?
WHAT *IS* ALL THIS?
HEY! HEY, *YOU!* I'M *TALKING* TO YOU.
I HEAR YOU.
WELL THEN, HOW ABOUT YOU START TALKING, #$$%!
STARTING WITH ***WHO THE HELL YOU ARE!***
ANSWER ME WHEN I'M TALKING TO YOU! ***WHO ARE YOU?!***
WHUD!
I'M *YOU,* BOY.
I'M YOU. AND YOU'RE ME. AND WE'RE *BOTH* BATMAN.
*...BATMAN?* BUT--
THE IDEA ONLY JUST CAME TO YOU? *HEH.* NO, SEE, THE IDEA ACTUALLY CAME TO YOU, AND ME, AND *HIM,* MANY YEARS AGO.

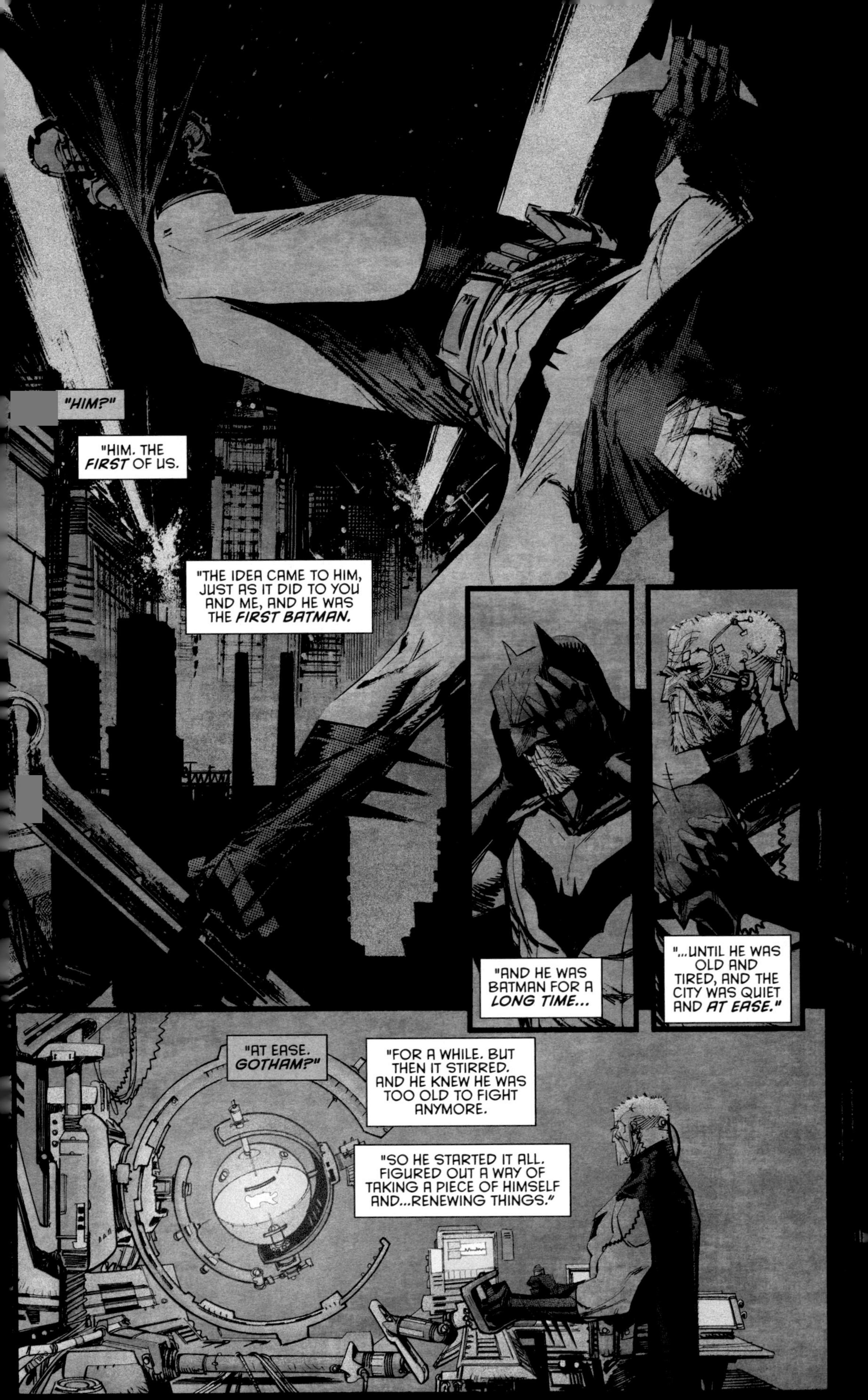
"HIM?"
"HIM. THE FIRST OF US.
"THE IDEA CAME TO HIM, JUST AS IT DID TO YOU AND ME, AND HE WAS THE FIRST BATMAN.
"AND HE WAS BATMAN FOR A LONG TIME...
"...UNTIL HE WAS OLD AND TIRED, AND THE CITY WAS QUIET AND AT EASE."
"AT EASE. GOTHAM?"
"FOR A WHILE. BUT THEN IT STIRRED. AND HE KNEW HE WAS TOO OLD TO FIGHT ANYMORE.
"SO HE STARTED IT ALL. FIGURED OUT A WAY OF TAKING A PIECE OF HIMSELF AND...RENEWING THINGS."

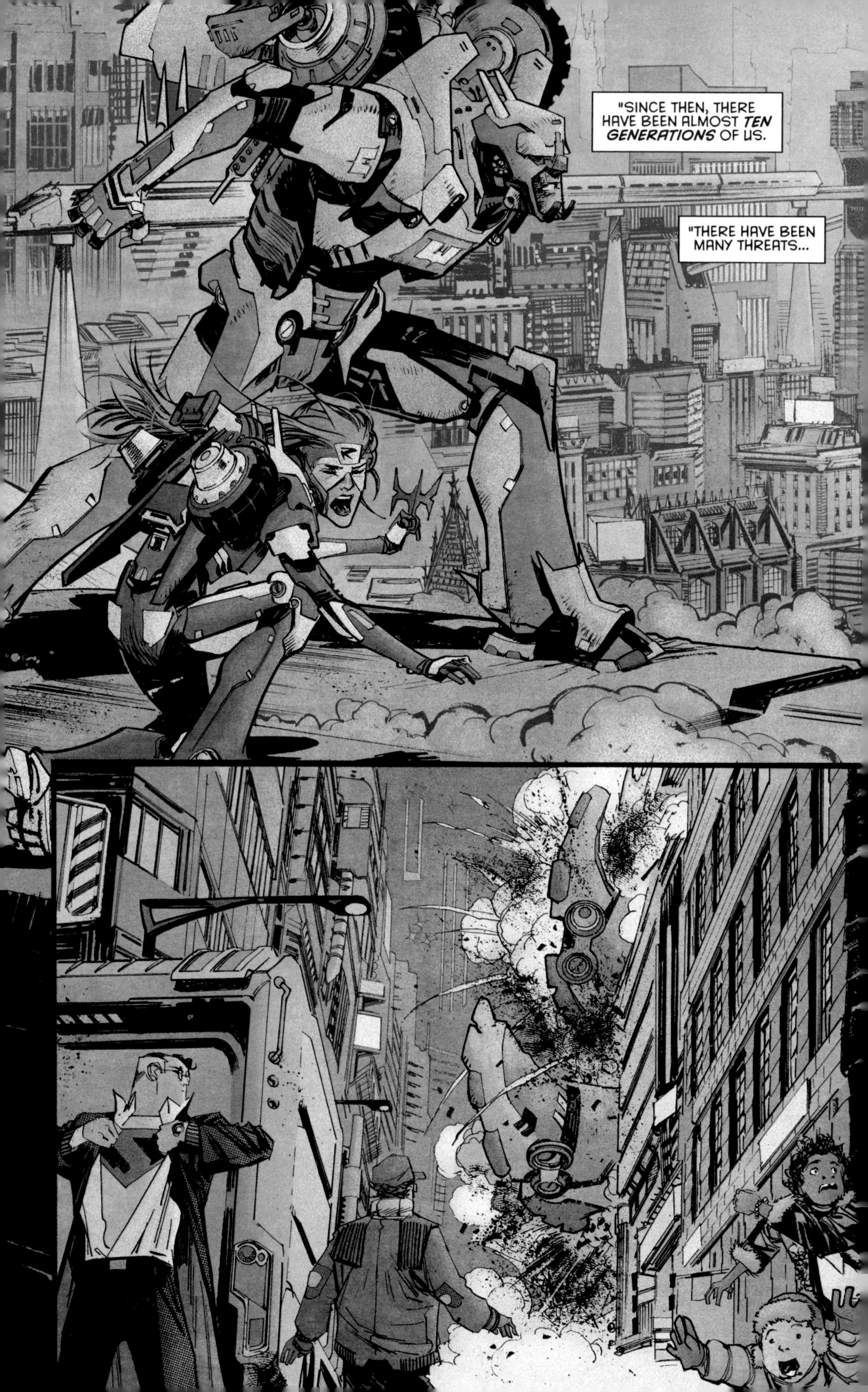
"SINCE THEN, THERE HAVE BEEN ALMOST *TEN GENERATIONS* OF US.
"THERE HAVE BEEN MANY THREATS...

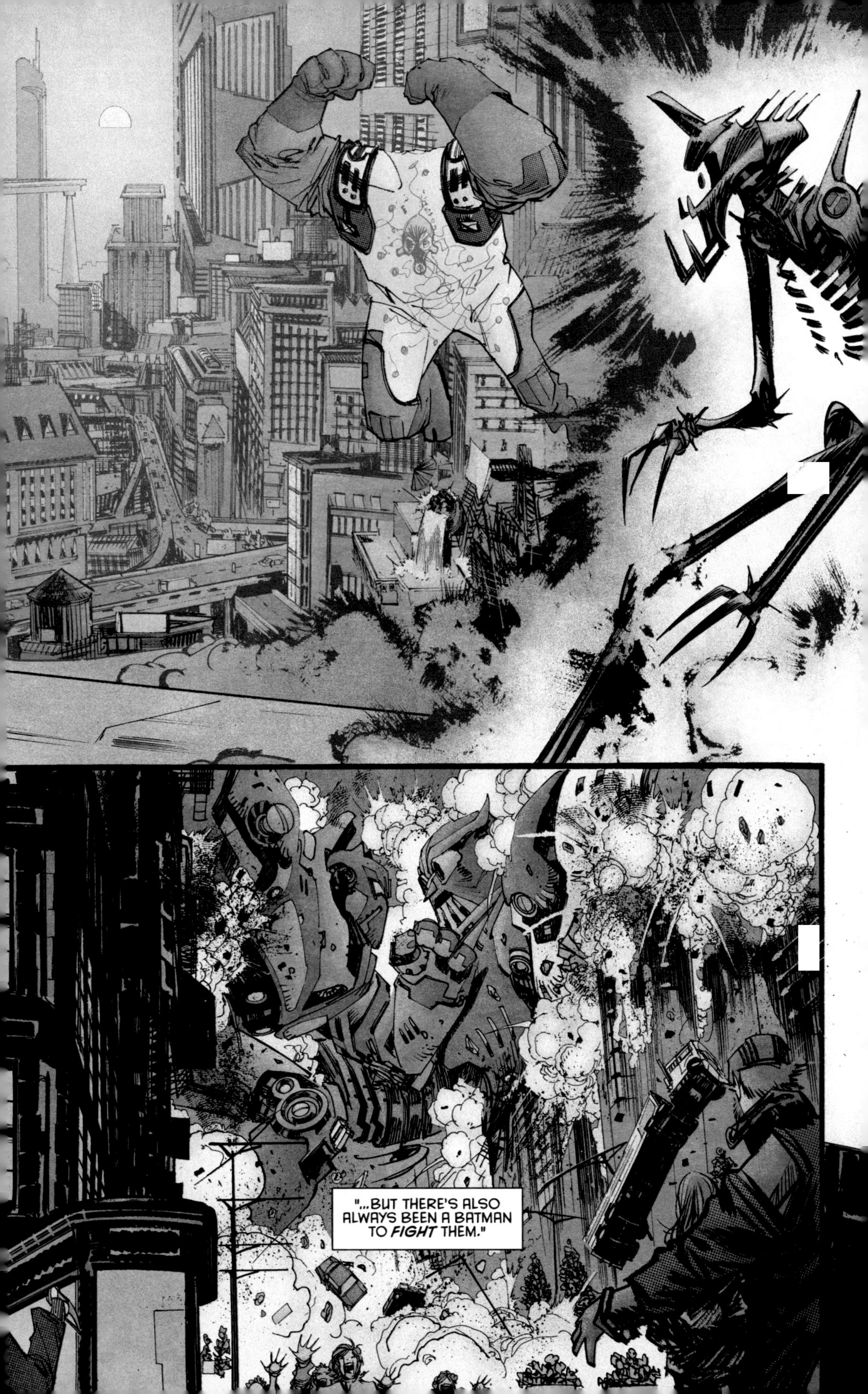
"...BUT THERE'S ALSO
ALWAYS BEEN A BATMAN
TO *FIGHT* THEM."

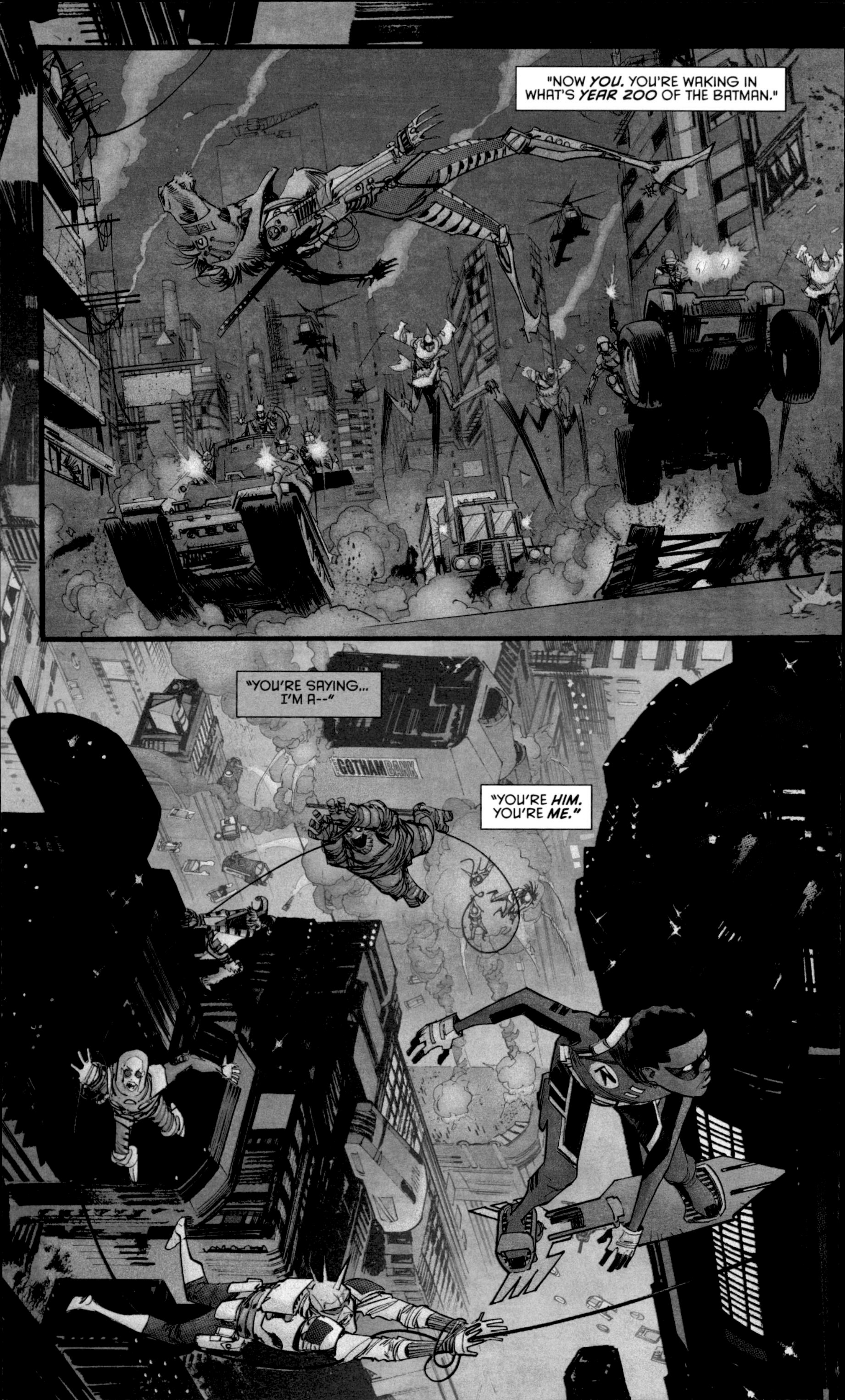
"NOW *YOU.* YOU'RE WAKING IN WHAT'S *YEAR 200* OF THE BATMAN."
"YOU'RE SAYING... I'M A--"
GOTHAM BANK
"YOU'RE *HIM.* YOU'RE *ME.*"

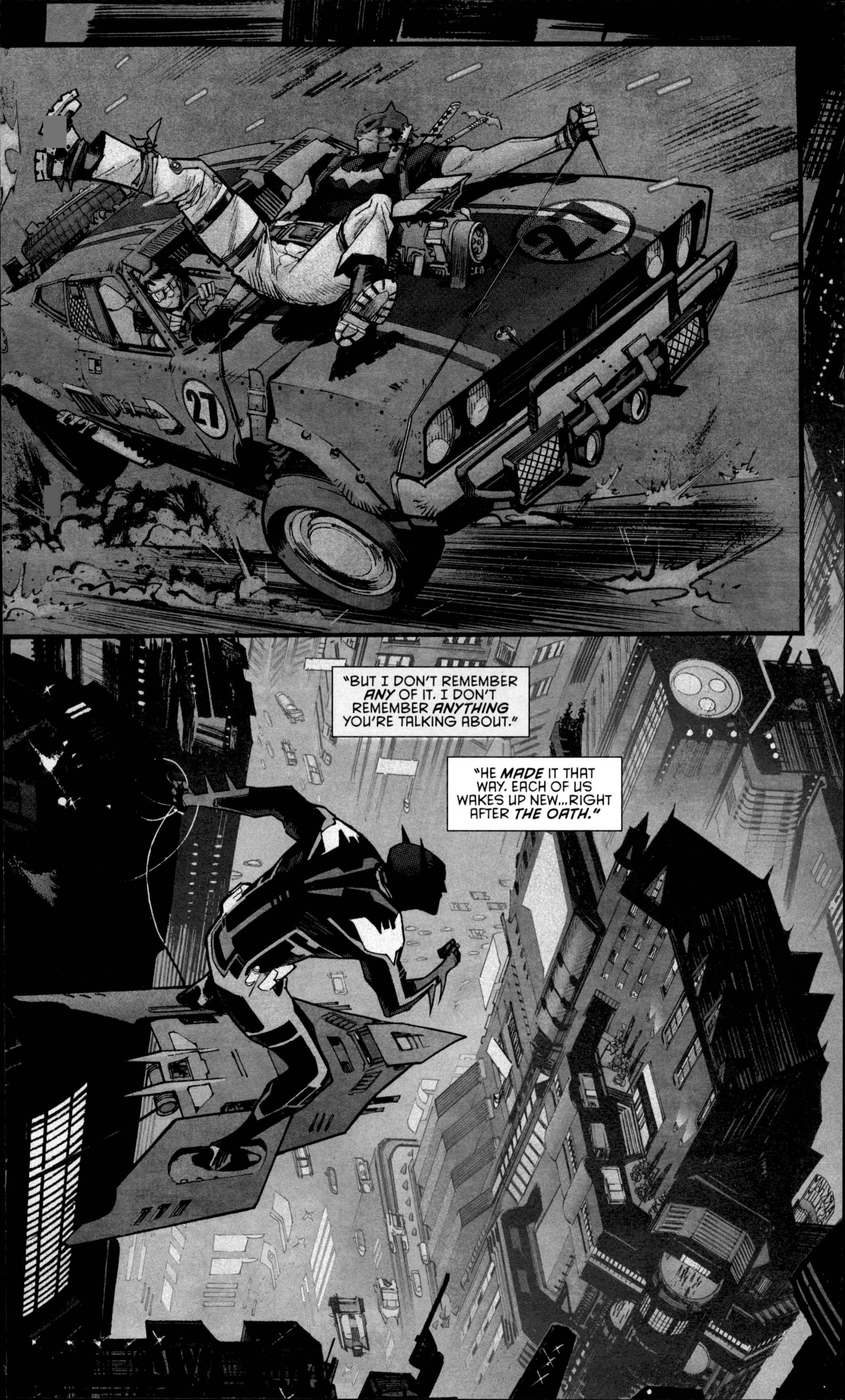
27
"BUT I DON'T REMEMBER ANY OF IT. I DON'T REMEMBER ANYTHING YOU'RE TALKING ABOUT."
"HE MADE IT THAT WAY. EACH OF US WAKES UP NEW...RIGHT AFTER THE OATH."

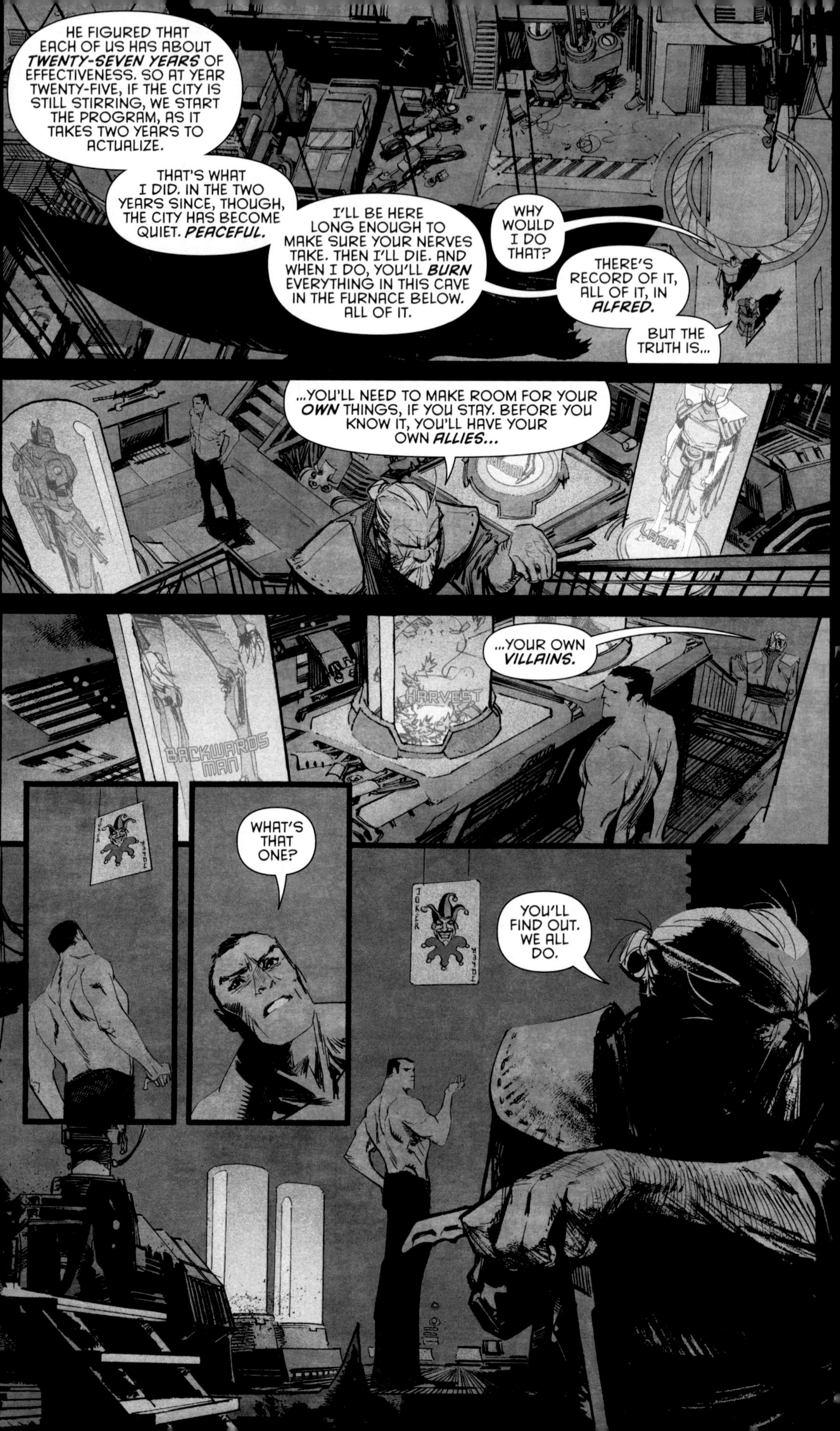
HE FIGURED THAT EACH OF US HAS ABOUT TWENTY-SEVEN YEARS OF EFFECTIVENESS. SO AT YEAR TWENTY-FIVE, IF THE CITY IS STILL STIRRING, WE START THE PROGRAM, AS IT TAKES TWO YEARS TO ACTUALIZE.
THAT'S WHAT I DID. IN THE TWO YEARS SINCE, THOUGH, THE CITY HAS BECOME QUIET. PEACEFUL.
WHY WOULD I DO THAT?
I'LL BE HERE LONG ENOUGH TO MAKE SURE YOUR NERVES TAKE. THEN I'LL DIE. AND WHEN I DO, YOU'LL BURN EVERYTHING IN THIS CAVE IN THE FURNACE BELOW. ALL OF IT.
THERE'S RECORD OF IT, ALL OF IT, IN ALFRED.
BUT THE TRUTH IS...
...YOU'LL NEED TO MAKE ROOM FOR YOUR OWN THINGS, IF YOU STAY. BEFORE YOU KNOW IT, YOU'LL HAVE YOUR OWN ALLIES...
LARK
...YOUR OWN VILLAINS.
HARVEST
BACKWARDS MAN
WHAT'S THAT ONE?
JOKER
YOU'LL FIND OUT. WE ALL DO.

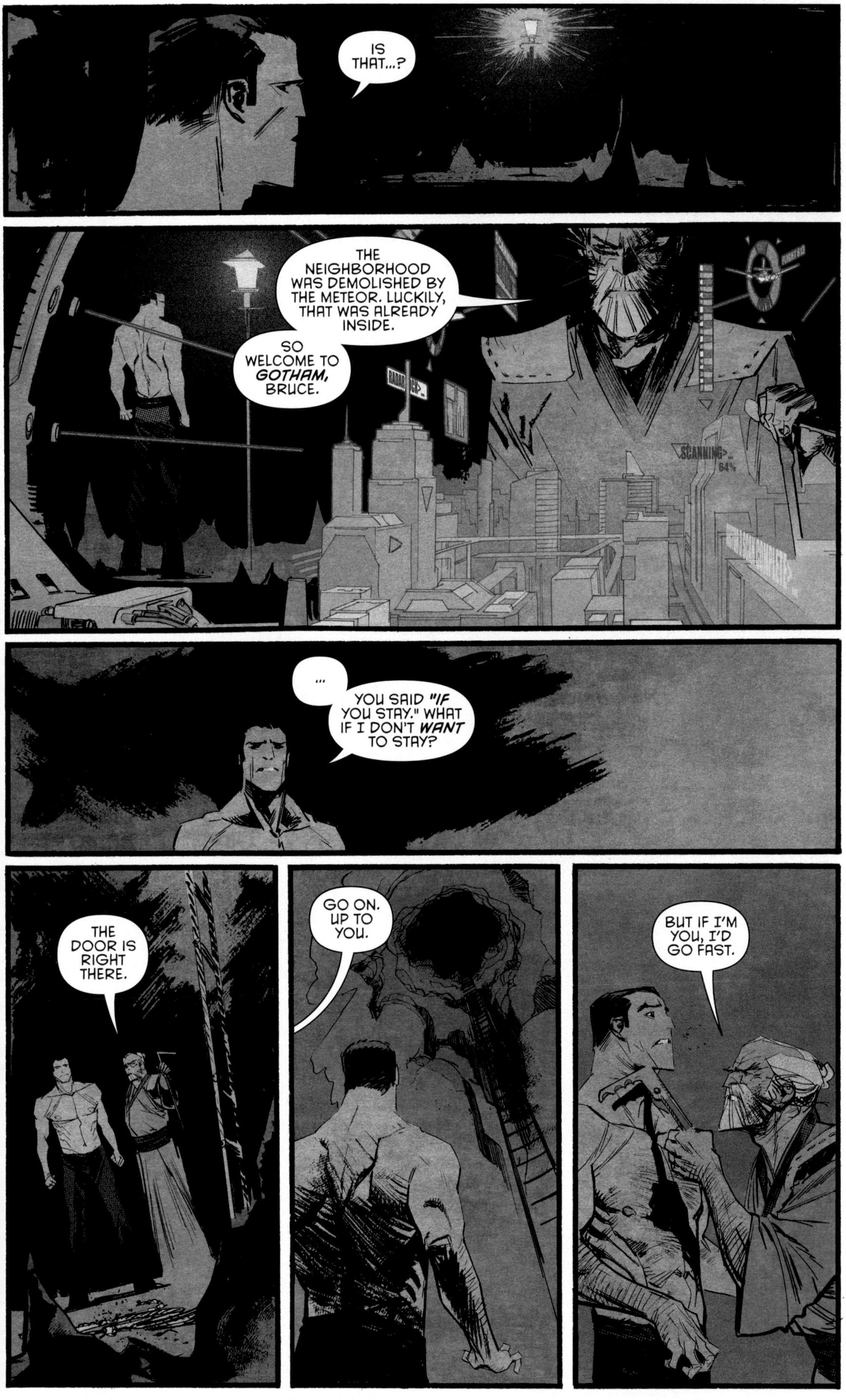

IS THAT...?
THE NEIGHBORHOOD WAS DEMOLISHED BY THE METEOR. LUCKILY, THAT WAS ALREADY INSIDE.
SO WELCOME TO *GOTHAM,* BRUCE.
SCANNING>_ 64%
...
YOU SAID *"IF* YOU STAY." WHAT IF I DON'T *WANT* TO STAY?
THE DOOR IS RIGHT THERE.
GO ON. UP TO YOU.
BUT IF I'M YOU, I'D GO FAST.

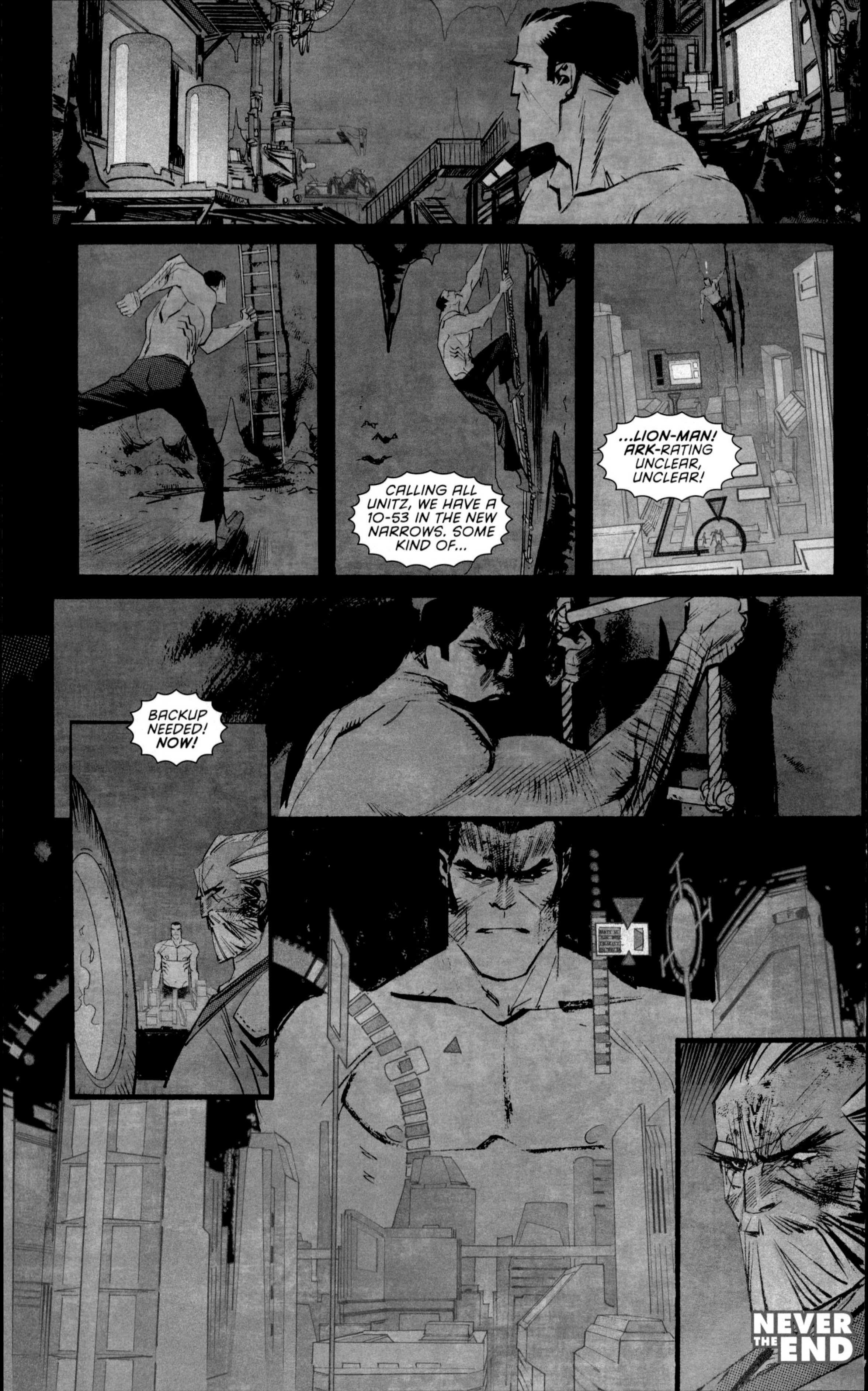
CALLING ALL UNITZ, WE HAVE A 10-53 IN THE NEW NARROWS. SOME KIND OF...
...LION-MAN! ARK-RATING UNCLEAR, UNCLEAR!
BACKUP NEEDED! NOW!
NEVER THE END

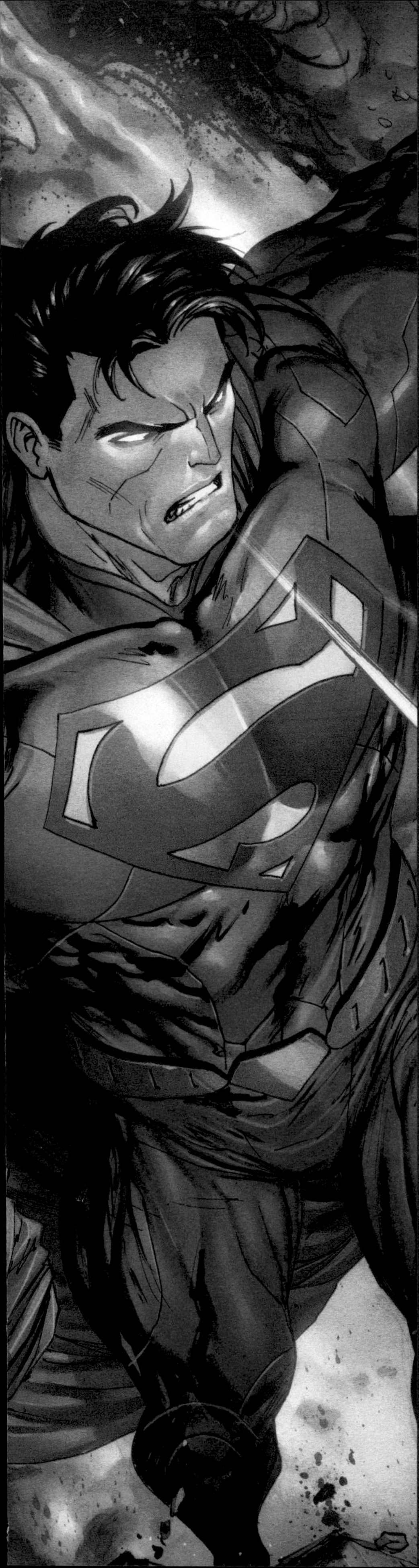

# VARIANT COVER GALLERY

**BATMAN #46**
*LOONEY TUNES* VARIANT BY
YANICK PAQUETTE WITH
NATHAN FAIRBAIRN & SPIKE BRANDT

**BATMAN #47**
HARLEY'S LITTLE BLACK BOOK VARIANT BY
ALEX ROSS

**BATMAN #48**
ADULT COLORING BOOK VARIANT BY
DAVE JOHNSON

**BATMAN #49**
VARIANT BY NEAL ADAMS,
WALTER SIMONSON
& LAURA MARTIN

**BATMAN #50**
*BATMAN V SUPERMAN* VARIANT BY
CHRIS DAUGHTRY,
JIM LEE & ALEX SINCLAIR

**BATMAN #50/SUPERMAN #50**
CONNECTING *BATMAN V SUPERMAN* VARIANTS
BY RAFAEL ALBUQUERQUE

**BATMAN #50/SUPERMAN #50**
CONNECTING *BATMAN V SUPERMAN* VARIANTS
BY TERRY DODSON & RACHEL DODSON

**BATMAN #50/SUPERMAN #50**
CONNECTING *BATMAN V SUPERMAN* VARIANTS
BY ED BENES & TOMEU MOREY

**BATMAN #50/SUPERMAN #50**
CONNECTING *BATMAN V SUPERMAN* VARIANTS
BY NEAL ADAMS & JEROMY COX

**BATMAN #50/SUPERMAN #50**
CONNECTING *BATMAN V SUPERMAN* VARIANTS
BY LEE BERMEJO

**BATMAN #50/SUPERMAN #50**
CONNECTING *BATMAN V SUPERMAN* VARIANTS
BY TYLER KIRKHAM & TOMEU MOREY

# VARIANT COVER GALLERY

**BATMAN #50/SUPERMAN #50**
CONNECTING *BATMAN V SUPERMAN* VARIANTS
BY GABRIELE DELL'OTTO

**BATMAN #50/SUPERMAN #50**
CONNECTING *BATMAN V SUPERMAN* VARIANTS
BY SEAN MURPHY & DAVE MCCAIG

**BATMAN #50/SUPERMAN #50**
CONNECTING *BATMAN V SUPERMAN* VARIANTS
BY JOSH MIDDLETON

**BATMAN #50**
*BATMAN V SUPERMAN* CONVENTION EXCLUSIVE
VARIANT BY DAVID FINCH,
MATT BANNING & JUNE CHUNG

**BATMAN #50/SUPERMAN #50**
CONNECTING *BATMAN V SUPERMAN* VARIANTS
BY GUILLEM MARCH

**BATMAN #50/SUPERMAN #50**
CONNECTING *BATMAN V SUPERMAN* VARIANTS
BY DAVE JOHNSON & DAVE MCCAIG

**BATMAN #50/SUPERMAN #50**
CONNECTING *BATMAN V SUPERMAN* VARIANTS
BY PATRICK GLEASON,
MICK GRAY & JOHN KALISZ

**BATMAN #50/SUPERMAN #50**
CONNECTING BATMAN V SUPERMAN VARIANTS
BY TIM SALE & BRENNAN WAGNER

**BATMAN #50/SUPERMAN #50**
CONNECTING *BATMAN V SUPERMAN* VARIANTS
BY AMANDA CONNER & PAUL MOUNTS

**BATMAN #50**
*BATMAN V SUPERMAN* VARIANT BY PAUL POPE

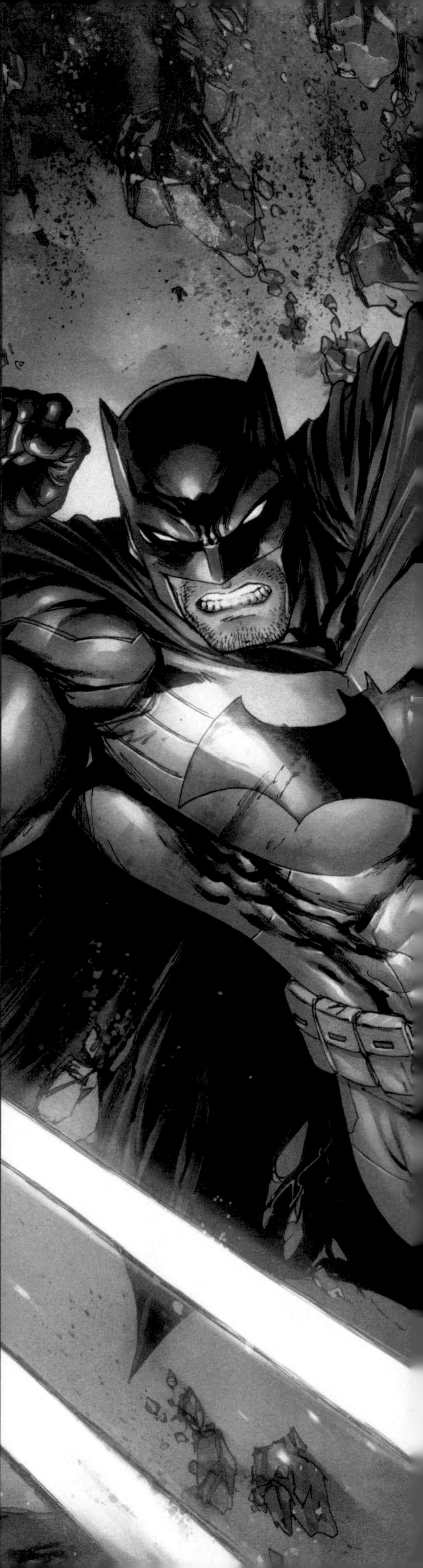

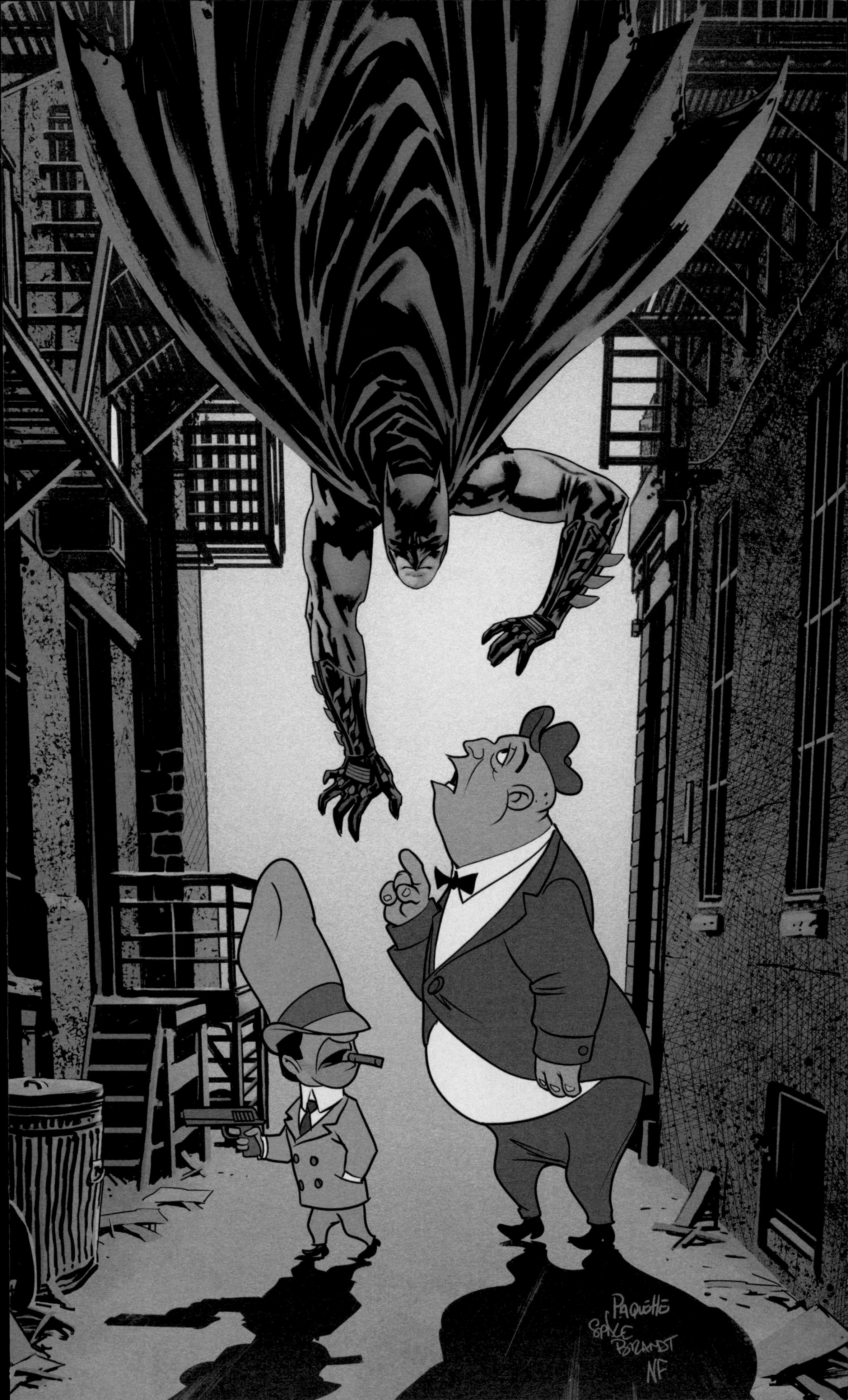

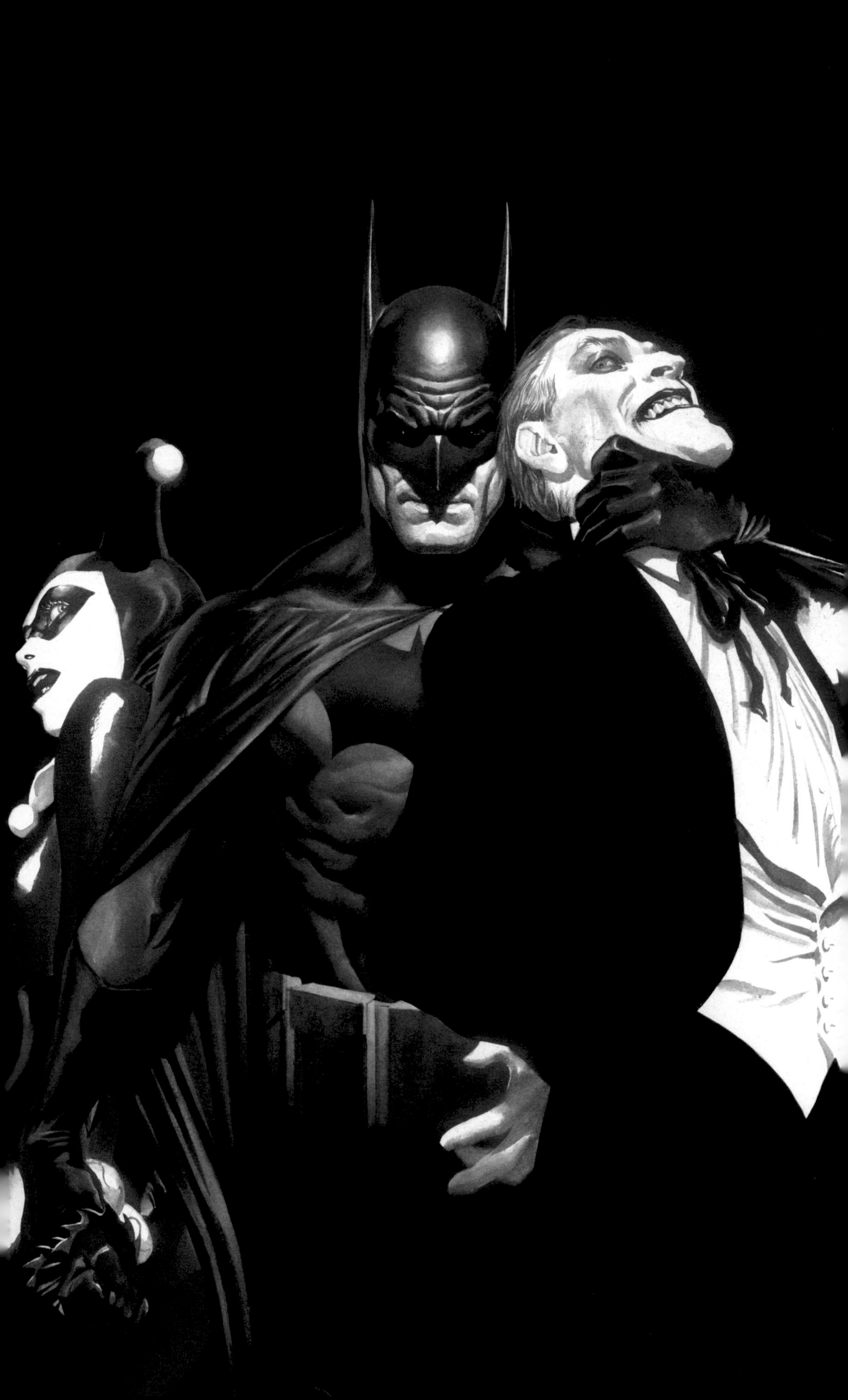

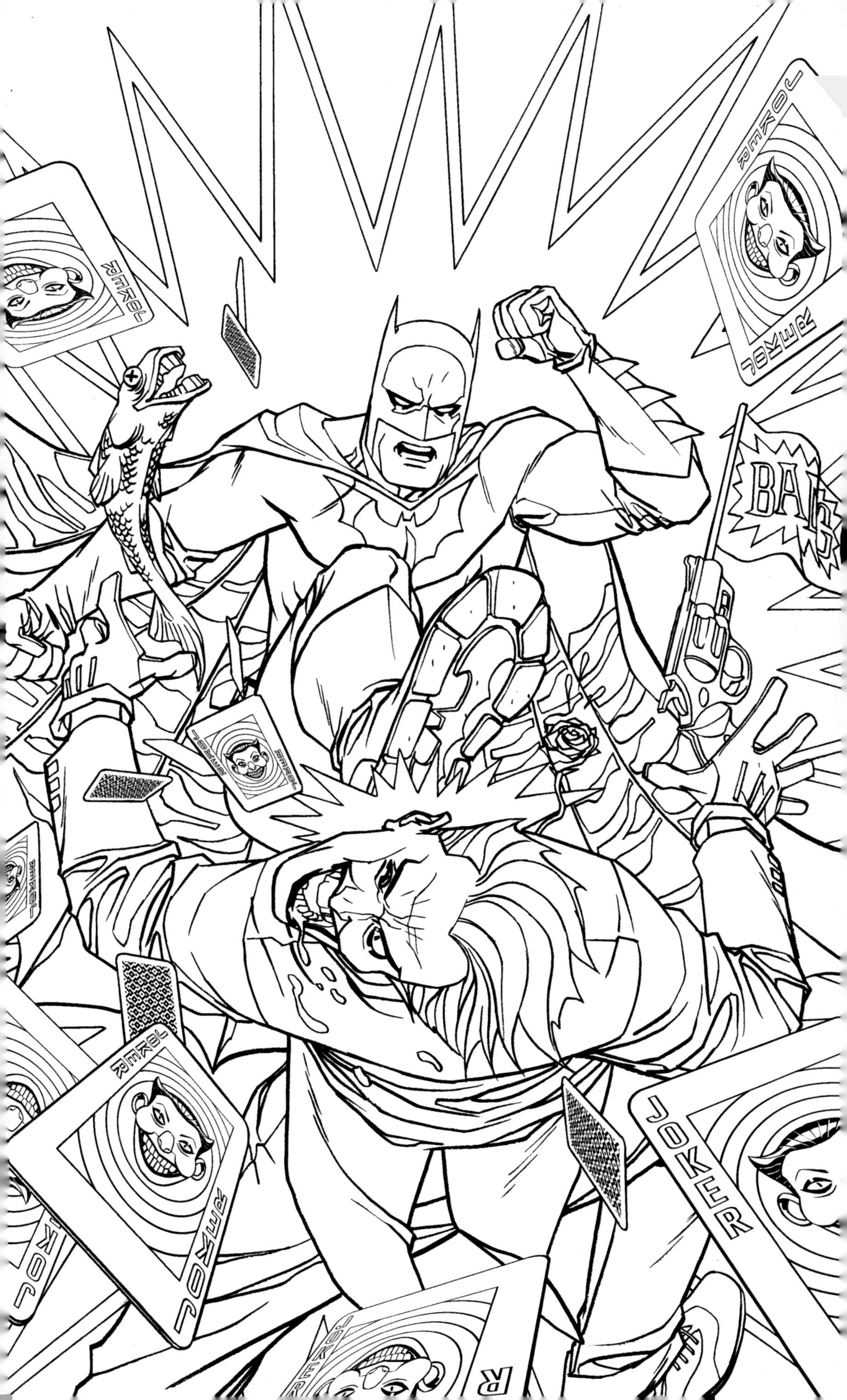
JOKER

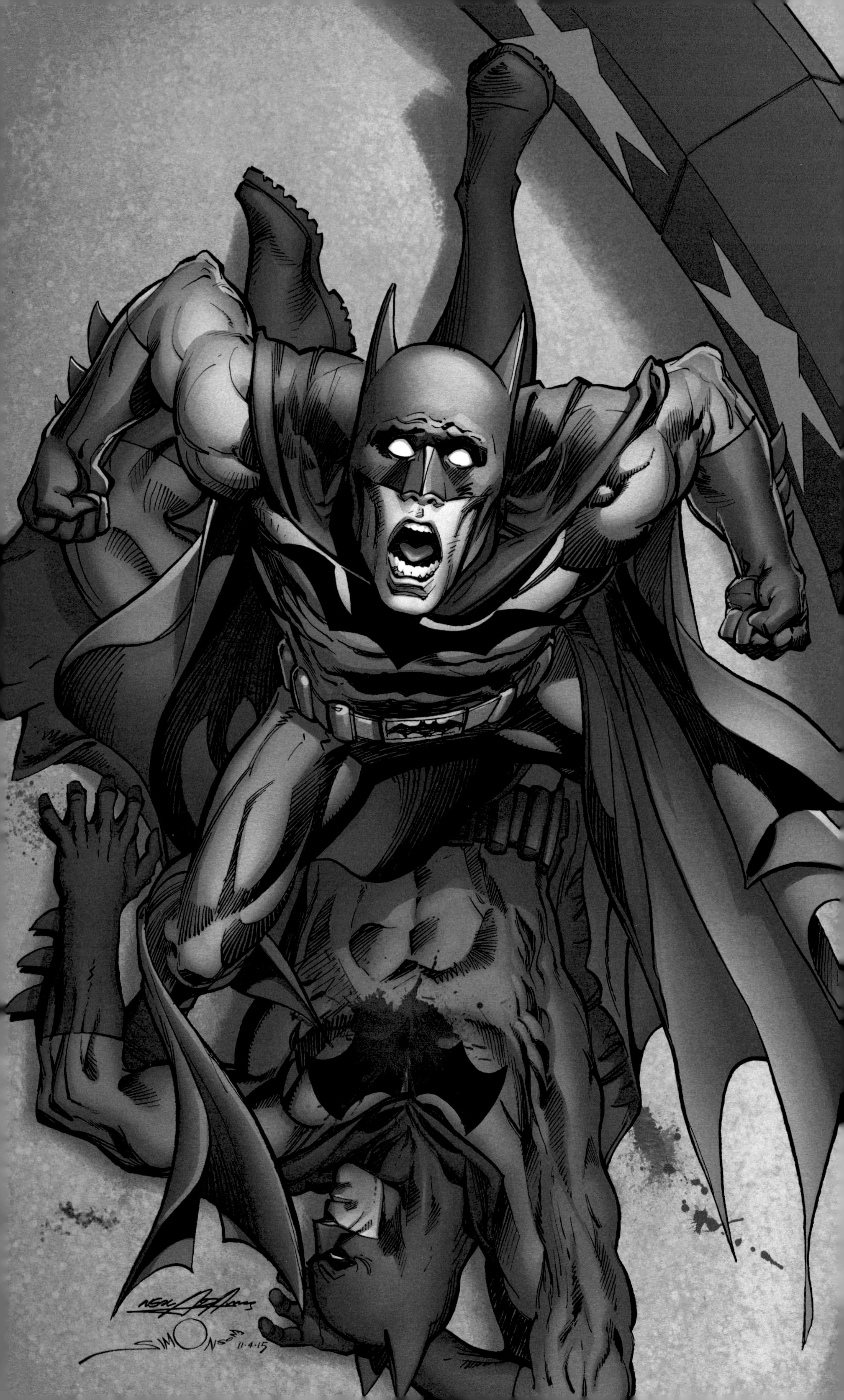

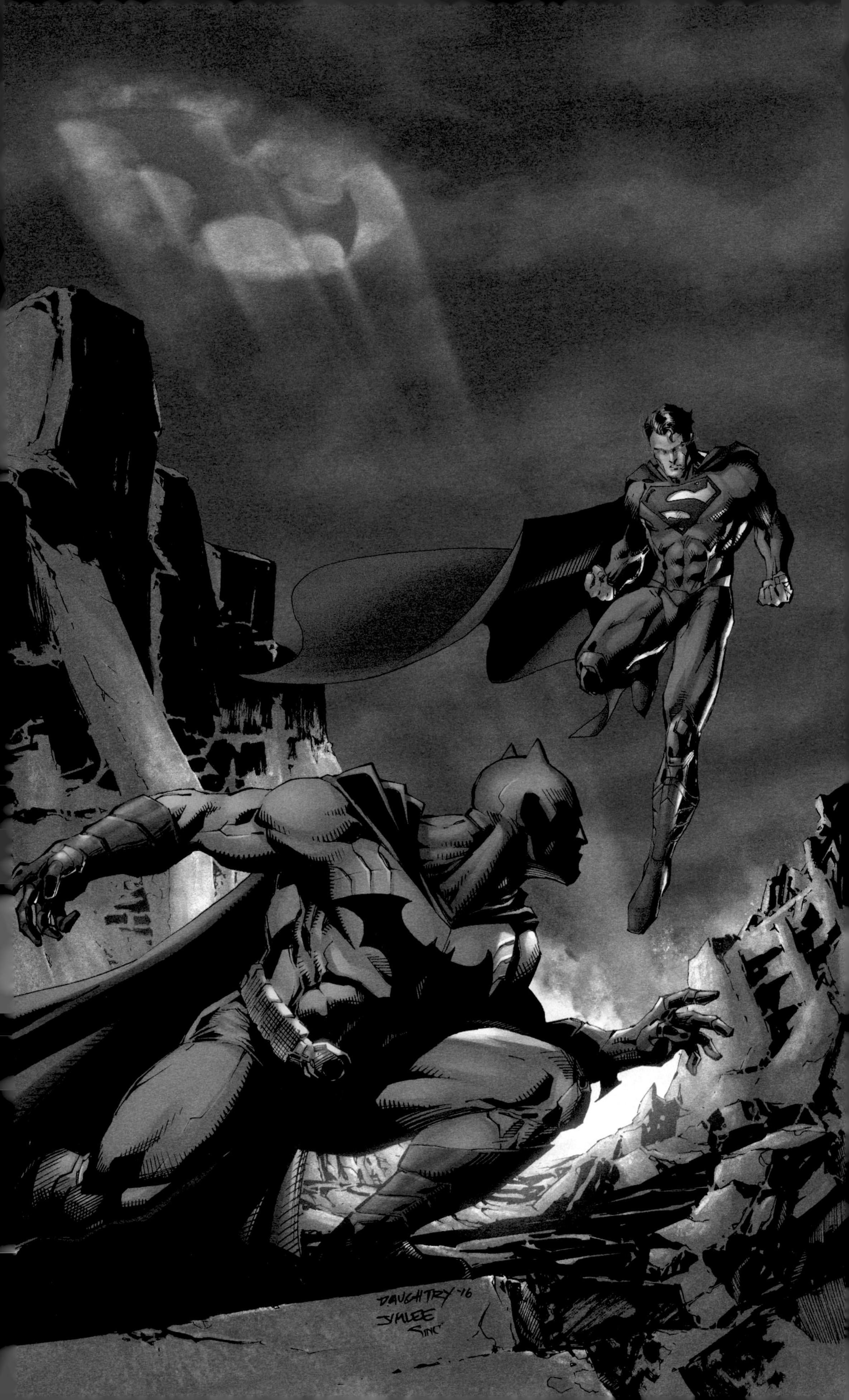
DAUGHTRY '16
JIMLEE

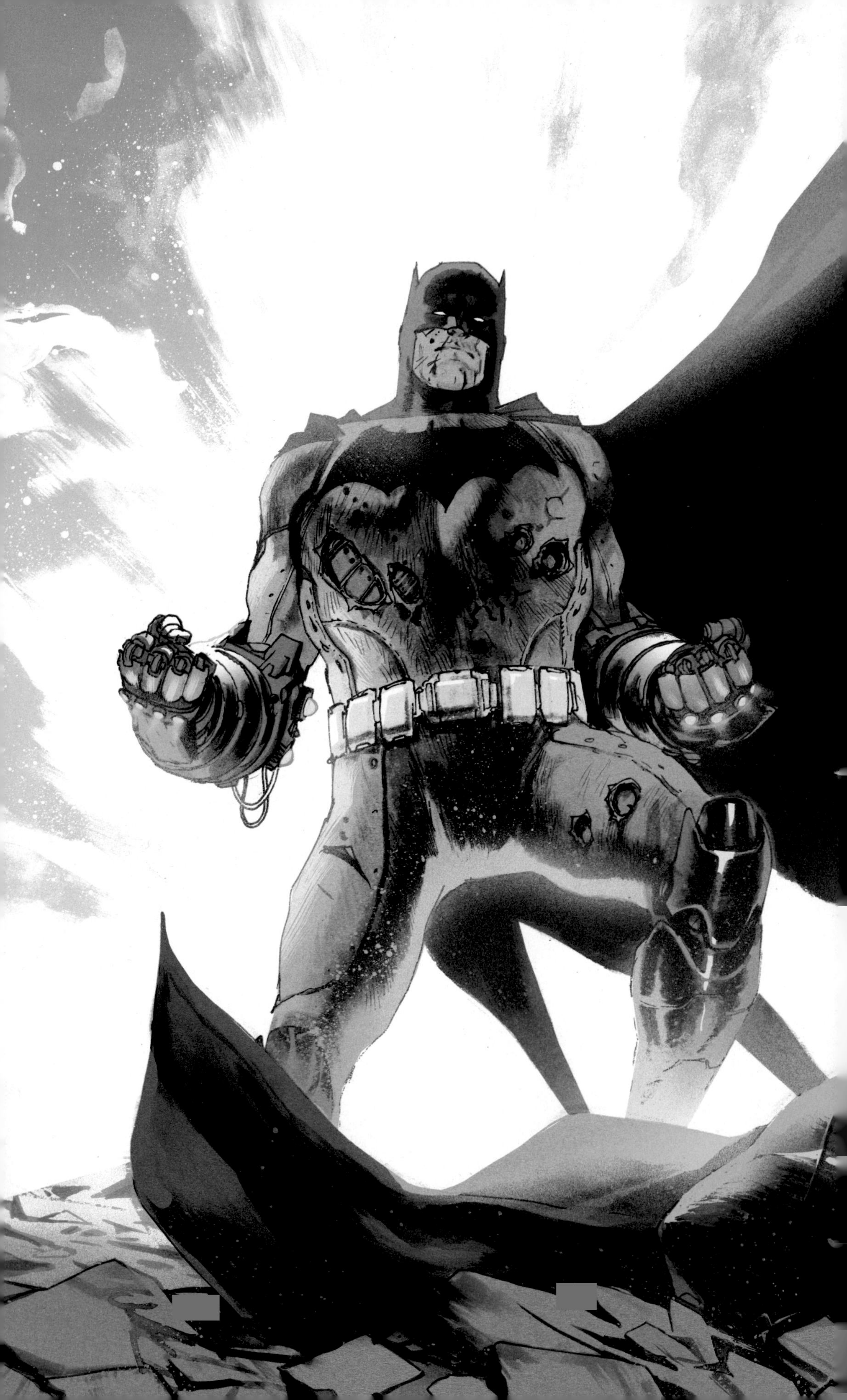

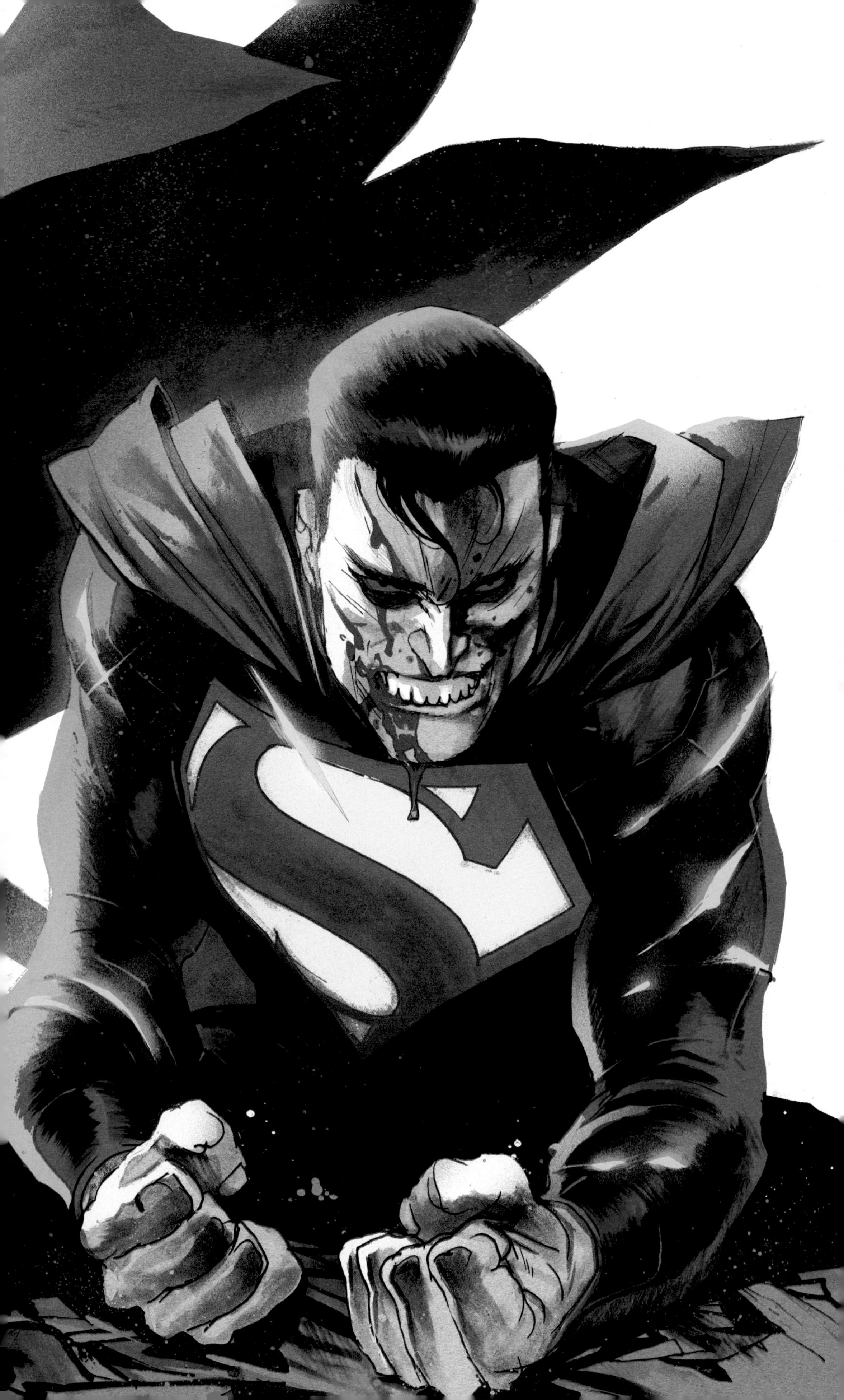

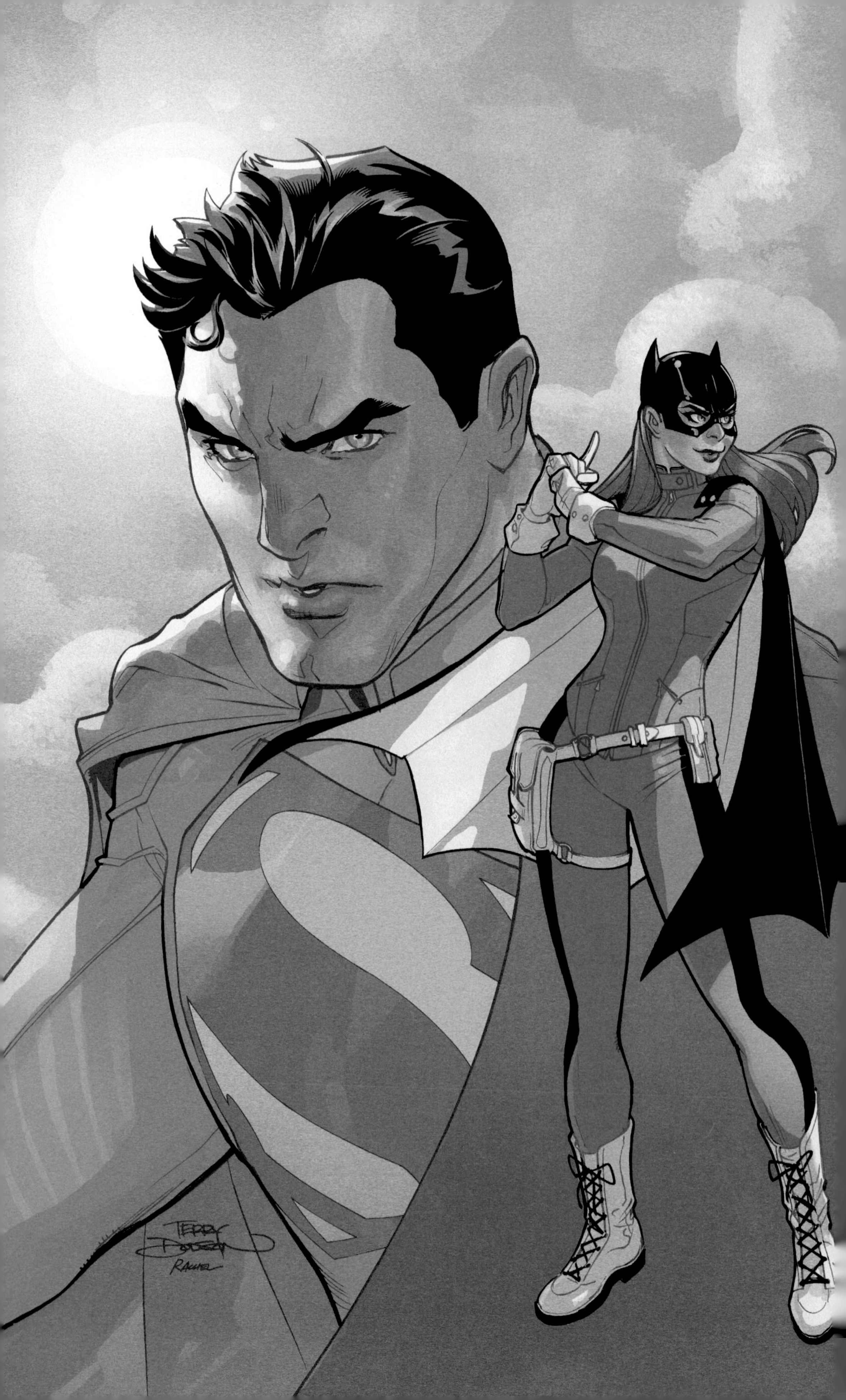

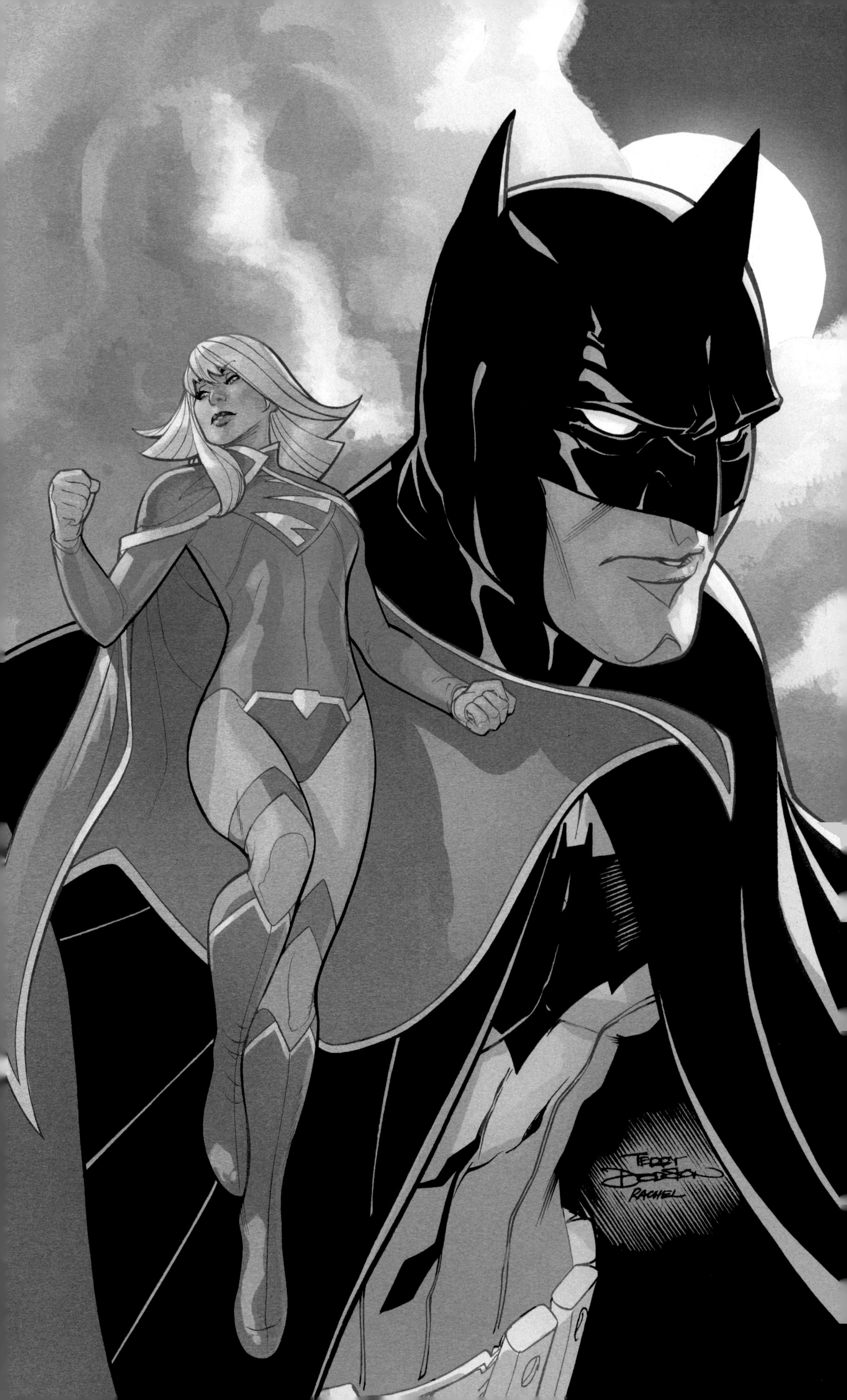
RACHEL

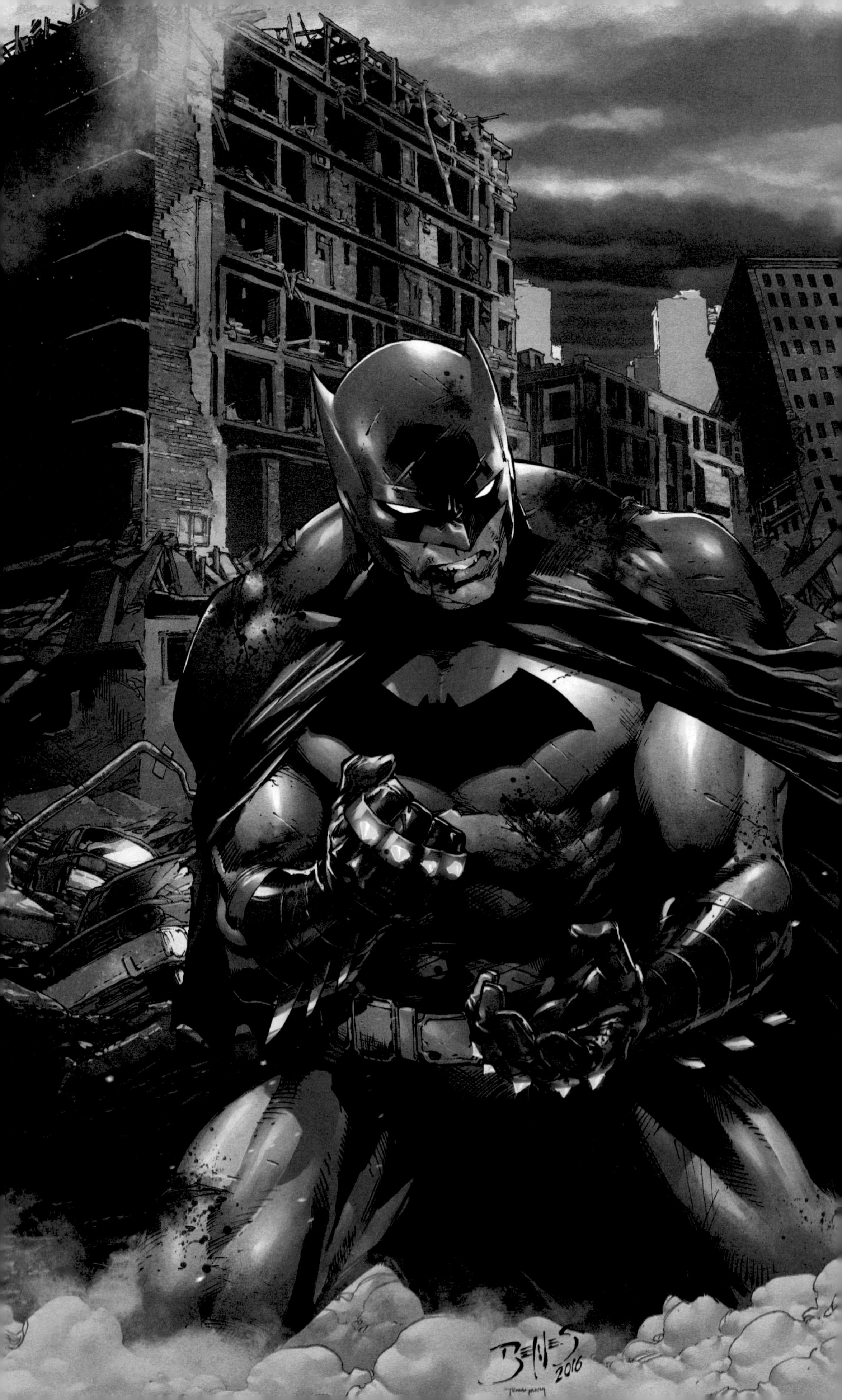

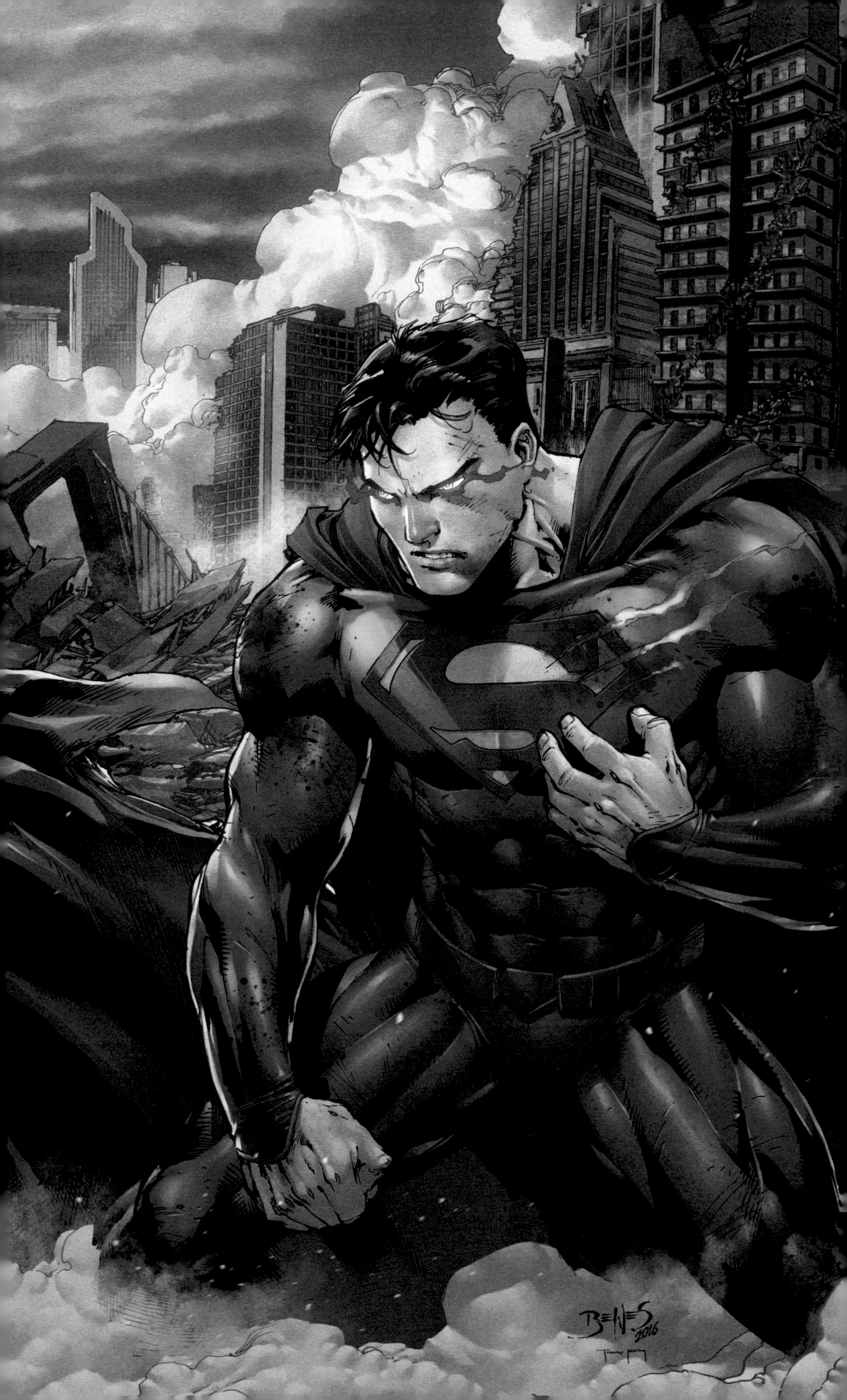
BENES
2016

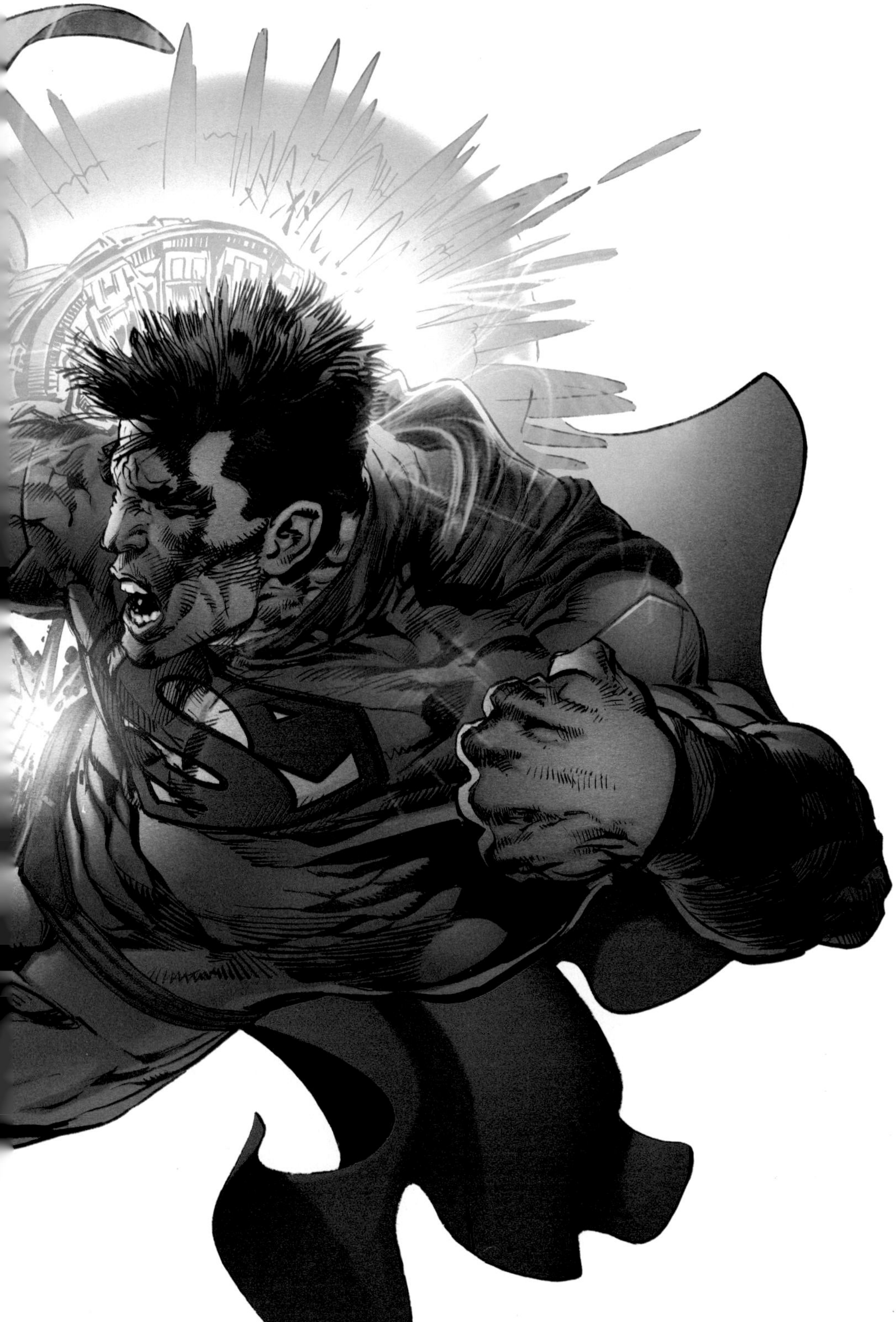

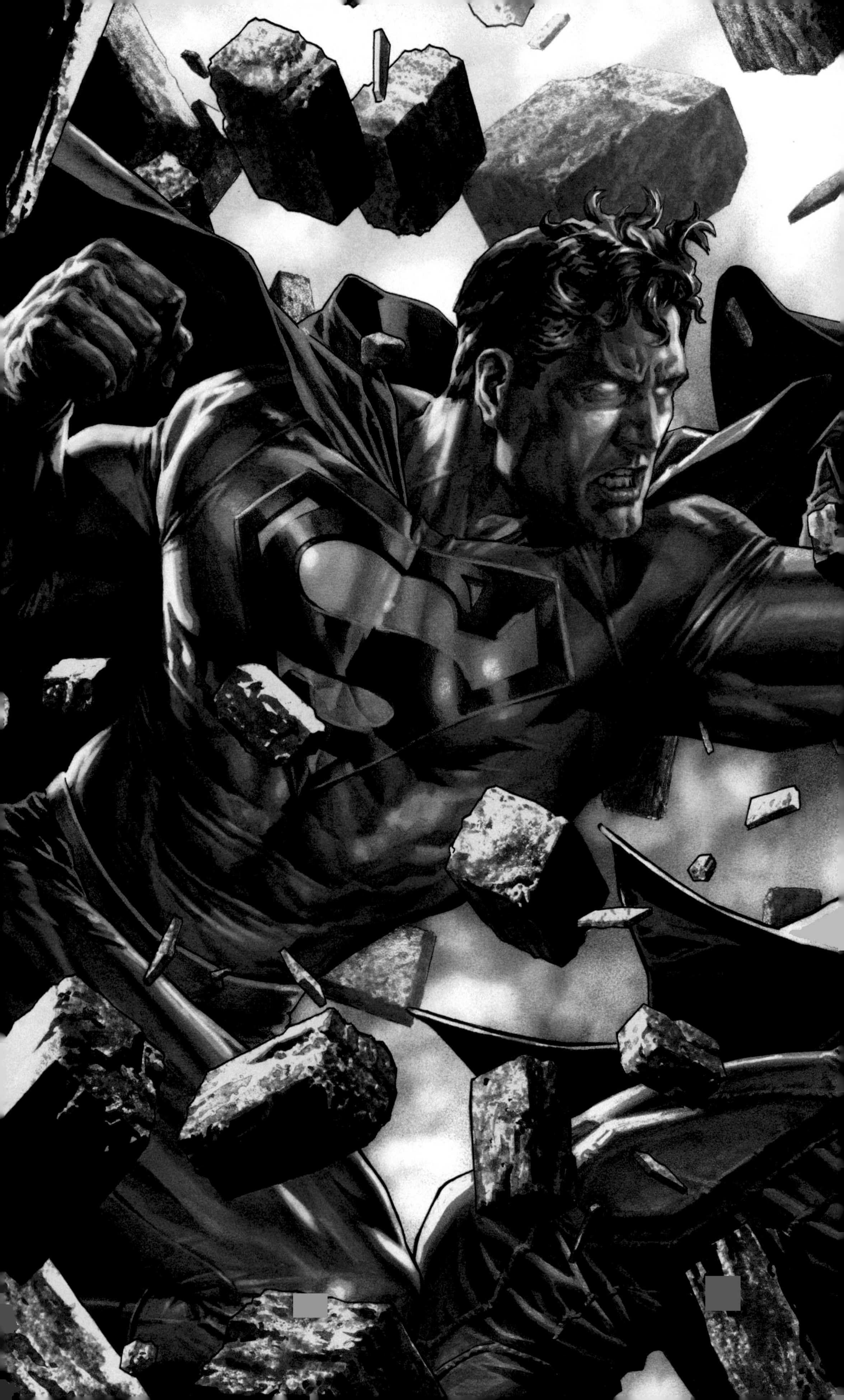

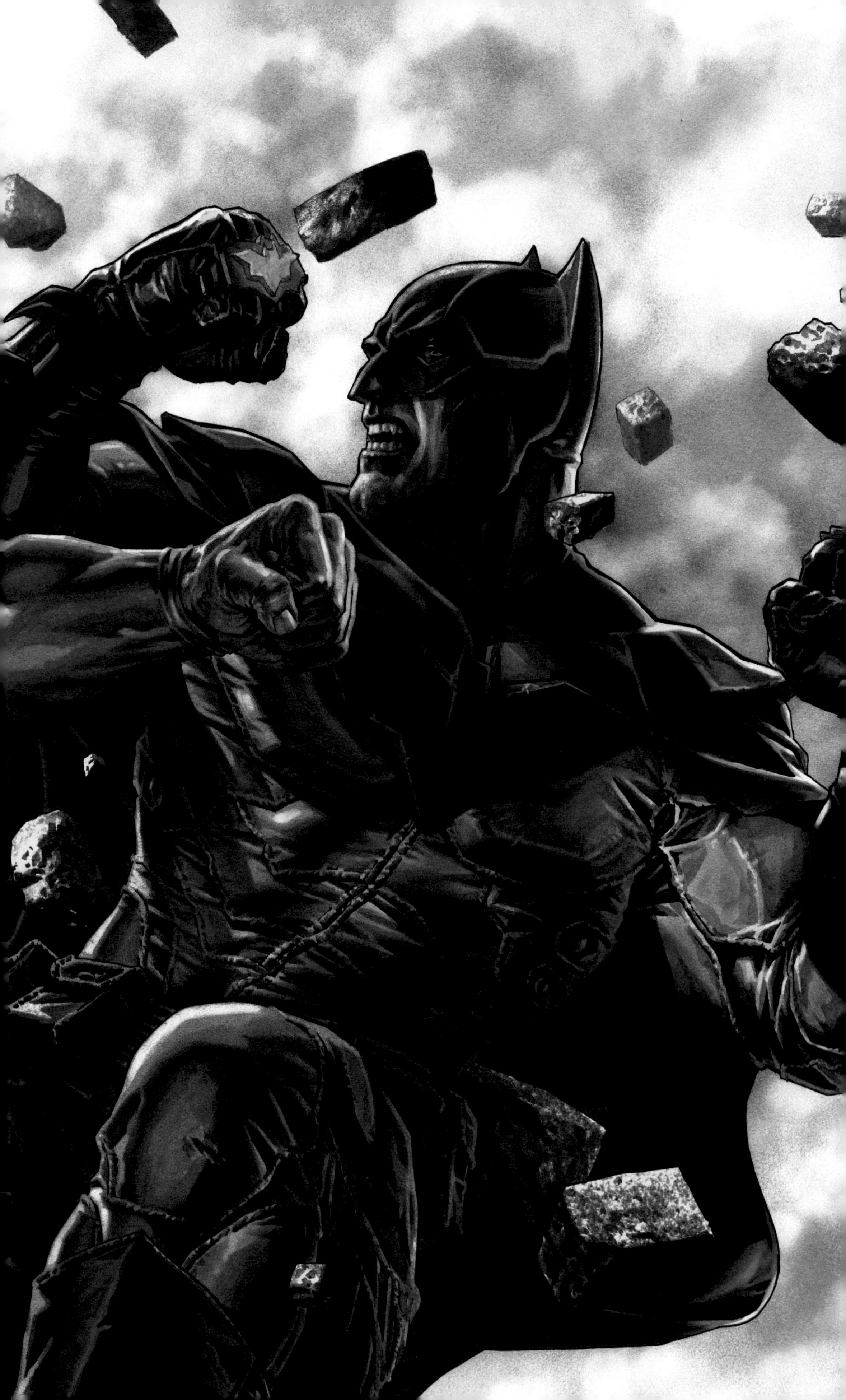

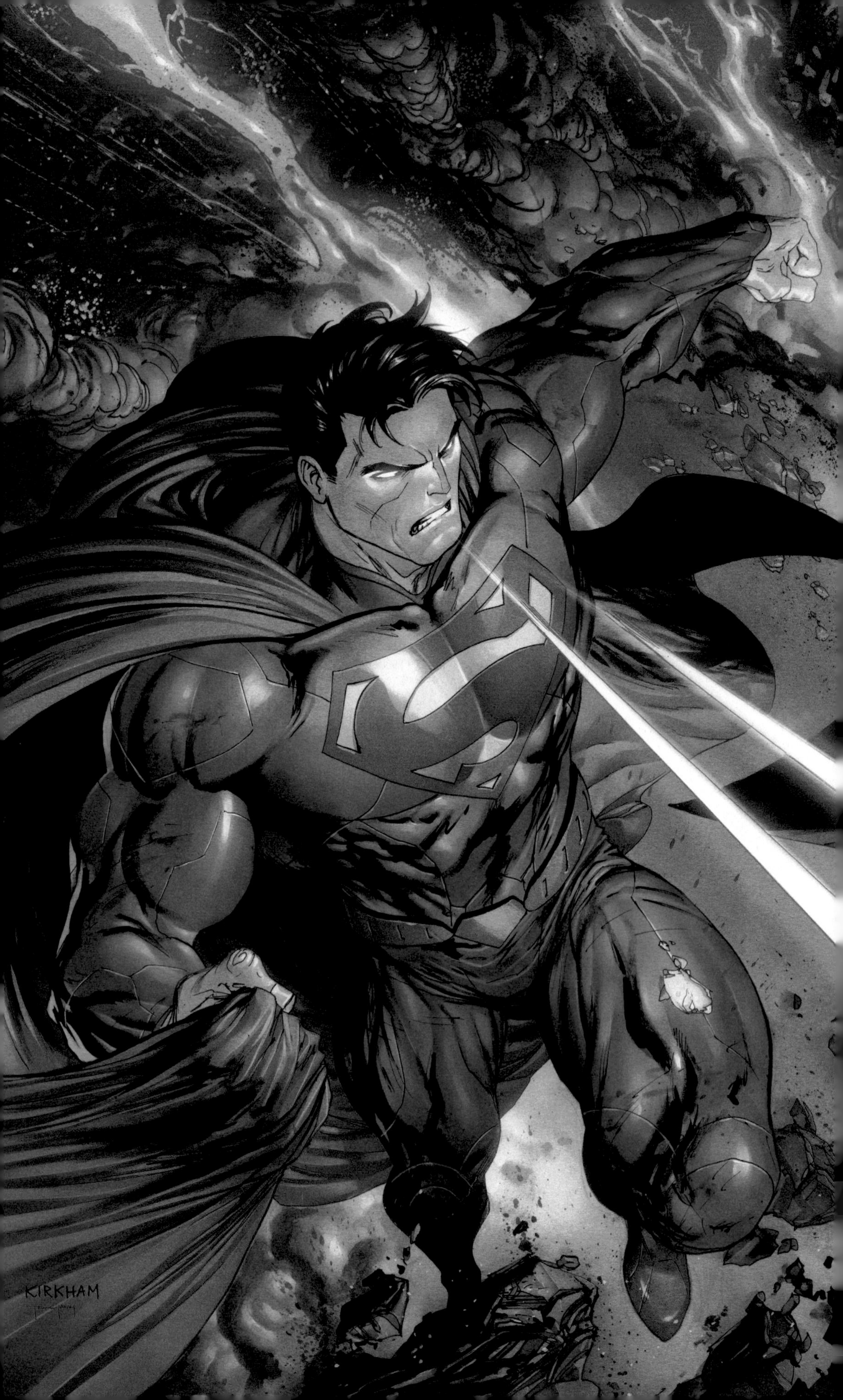
KIRKHAM

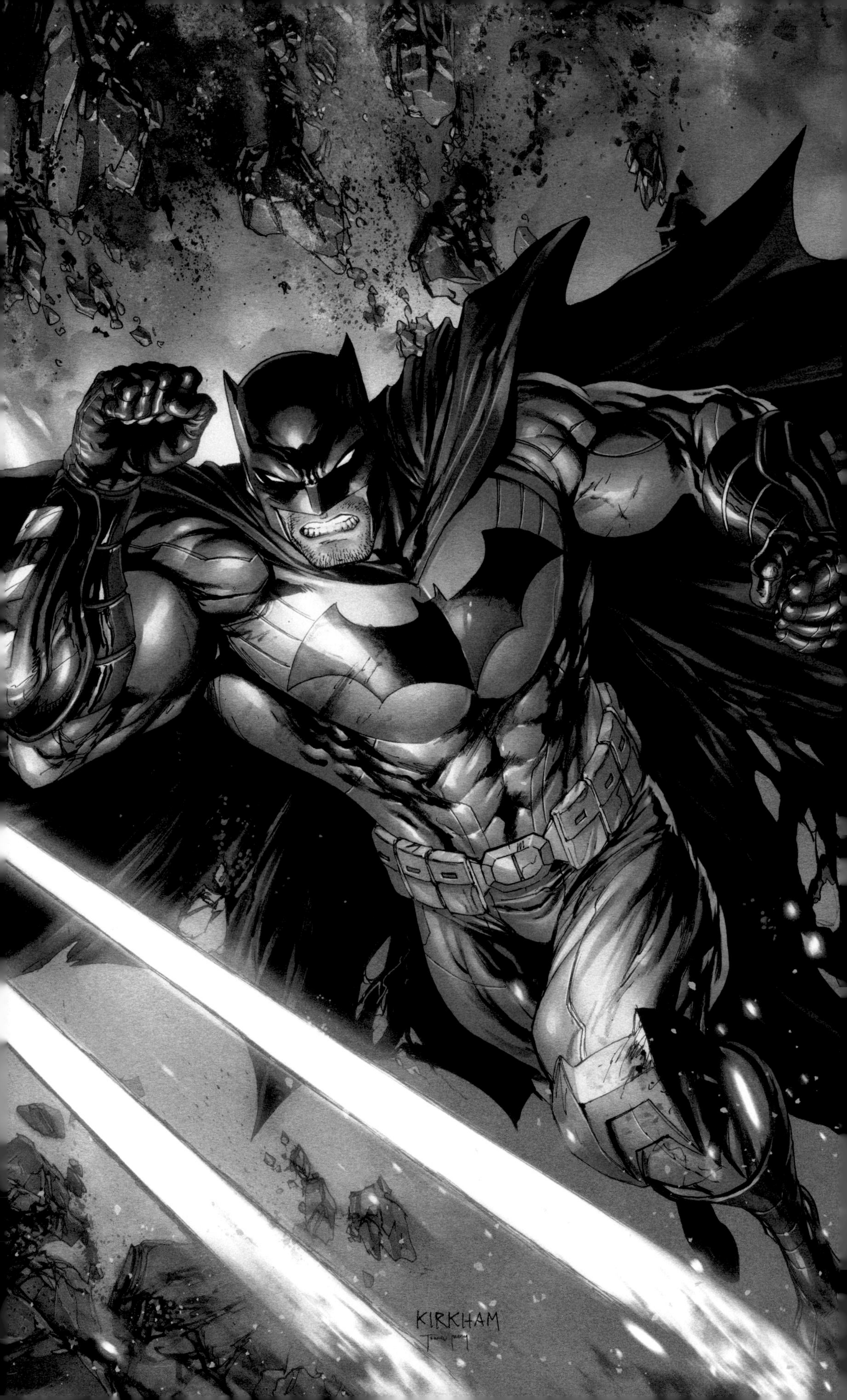
KIRKHAM

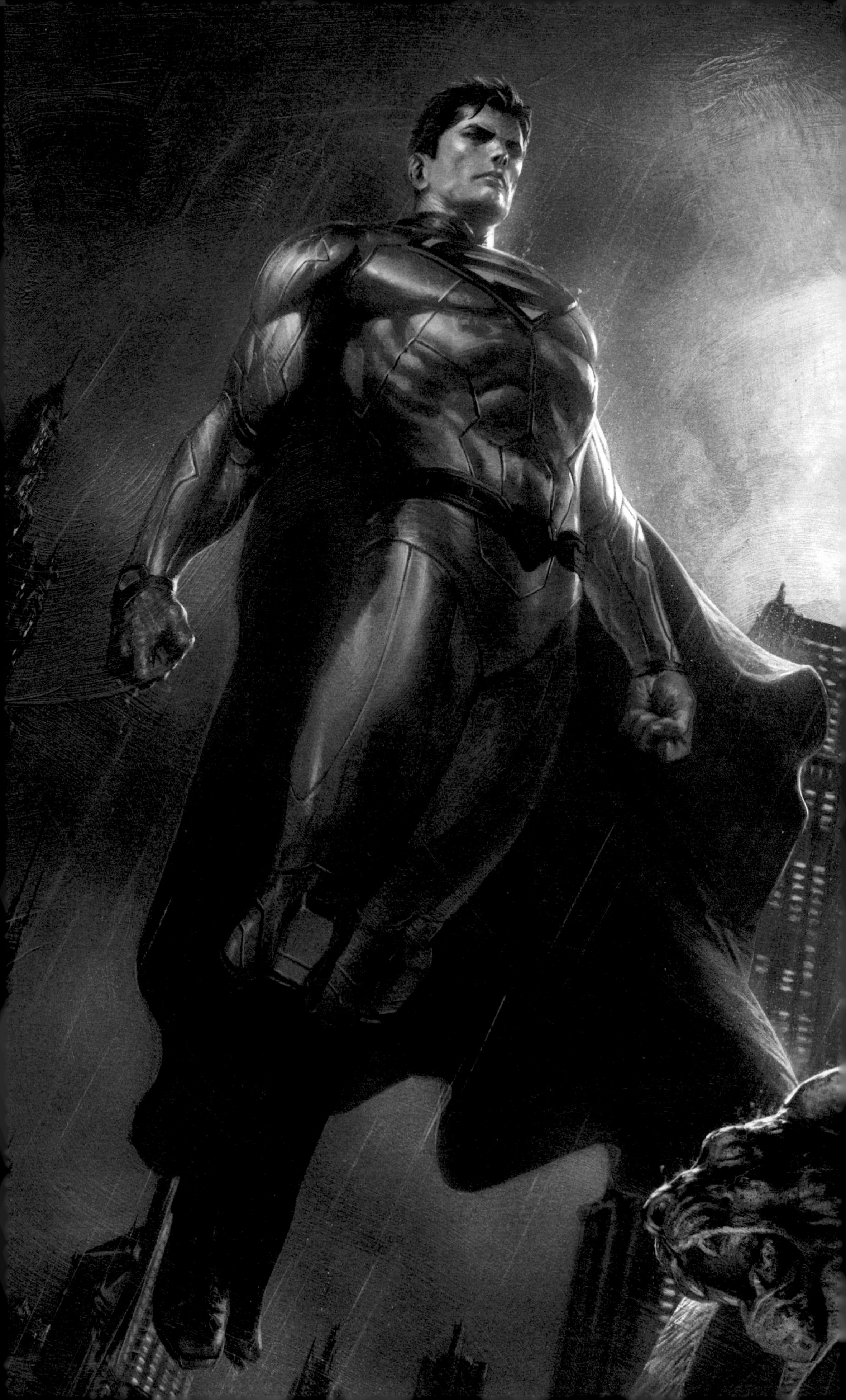

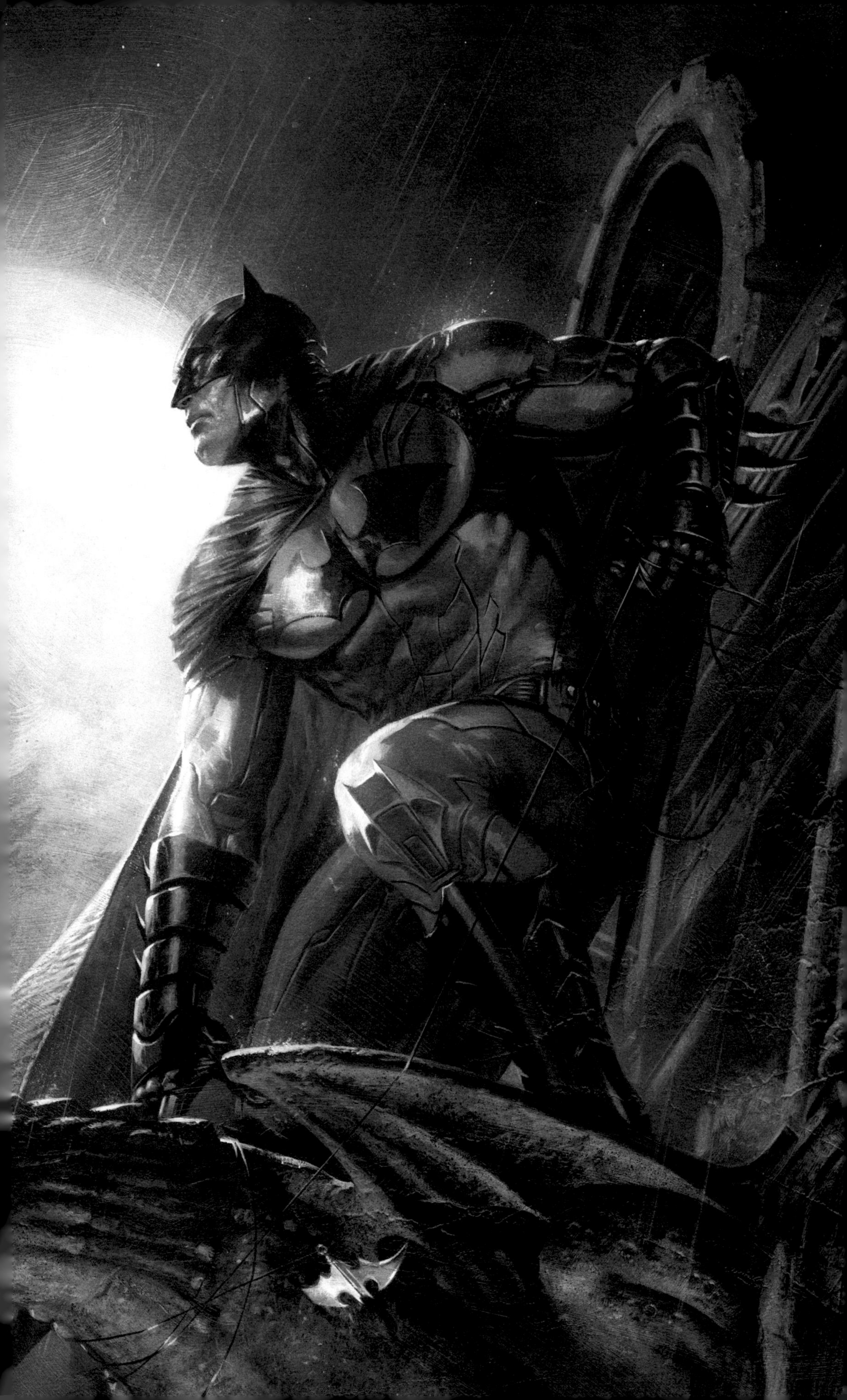

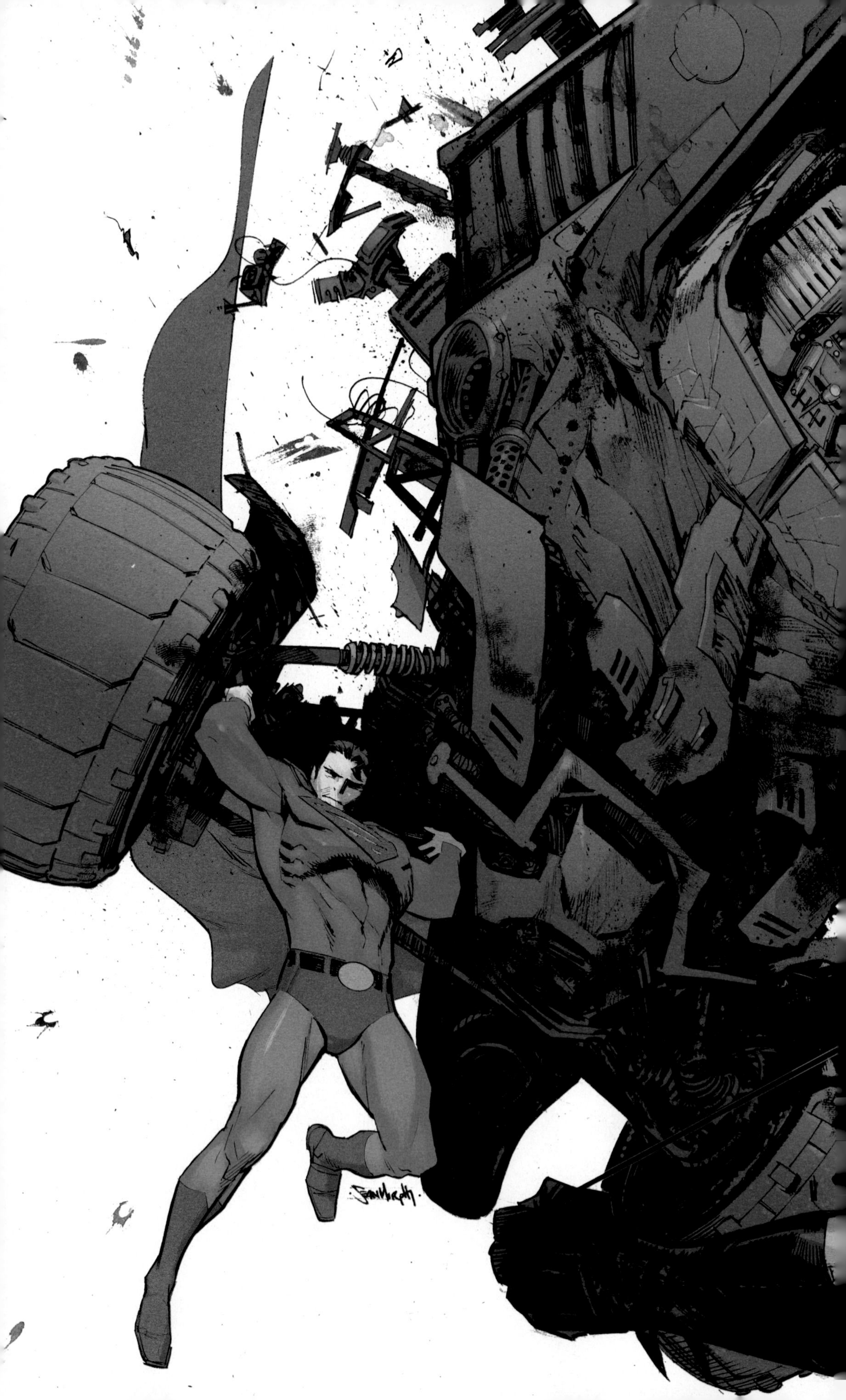

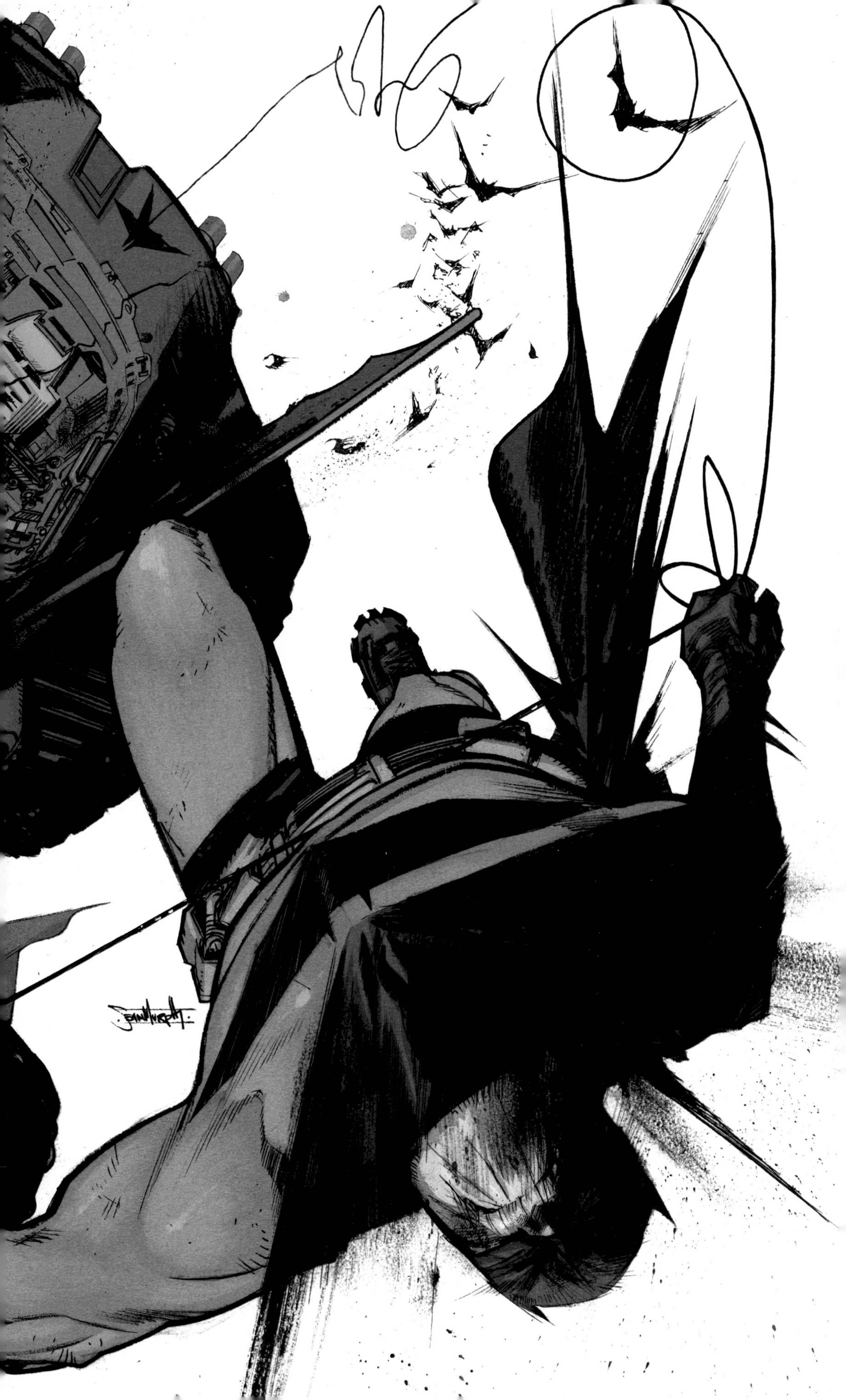

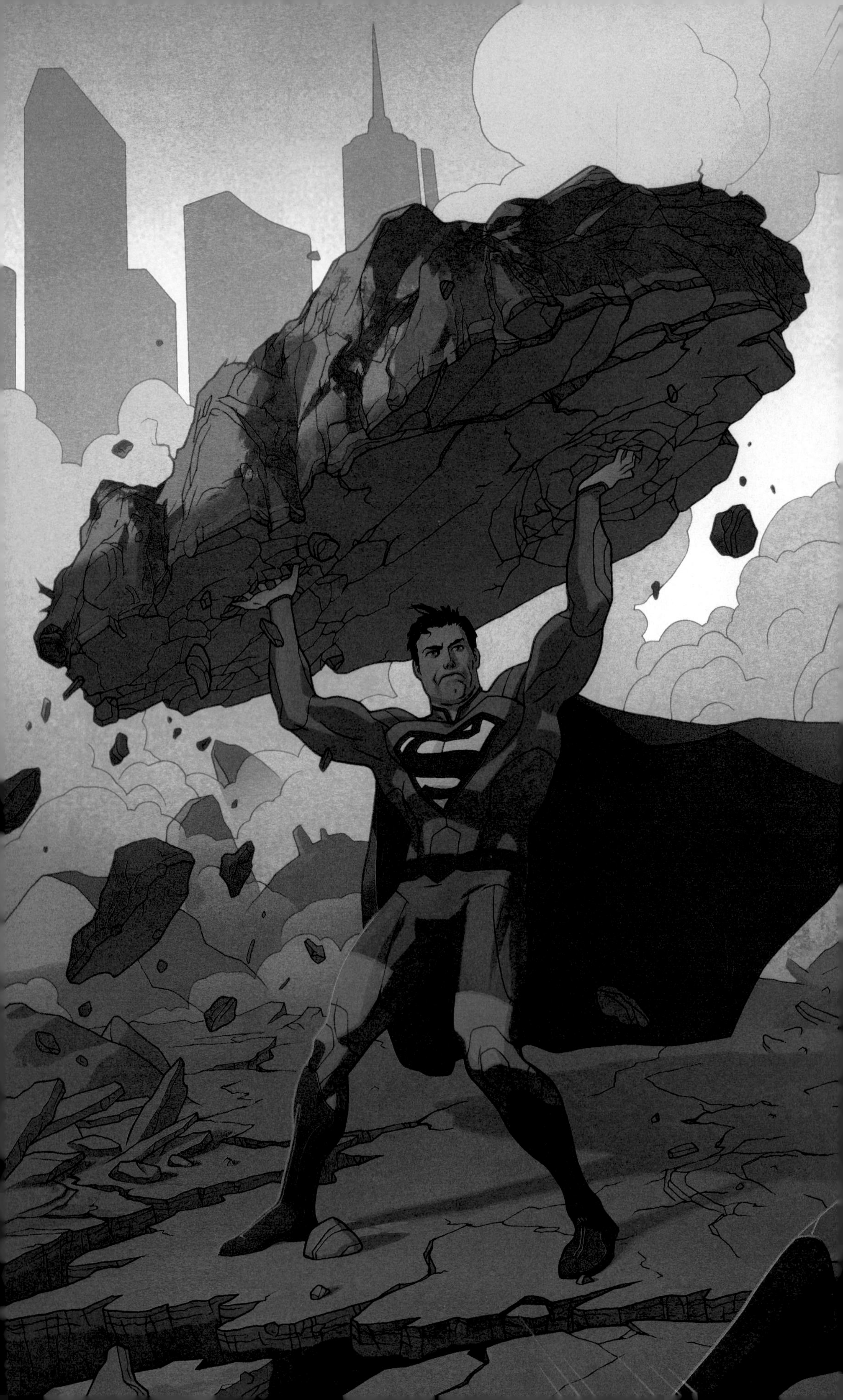

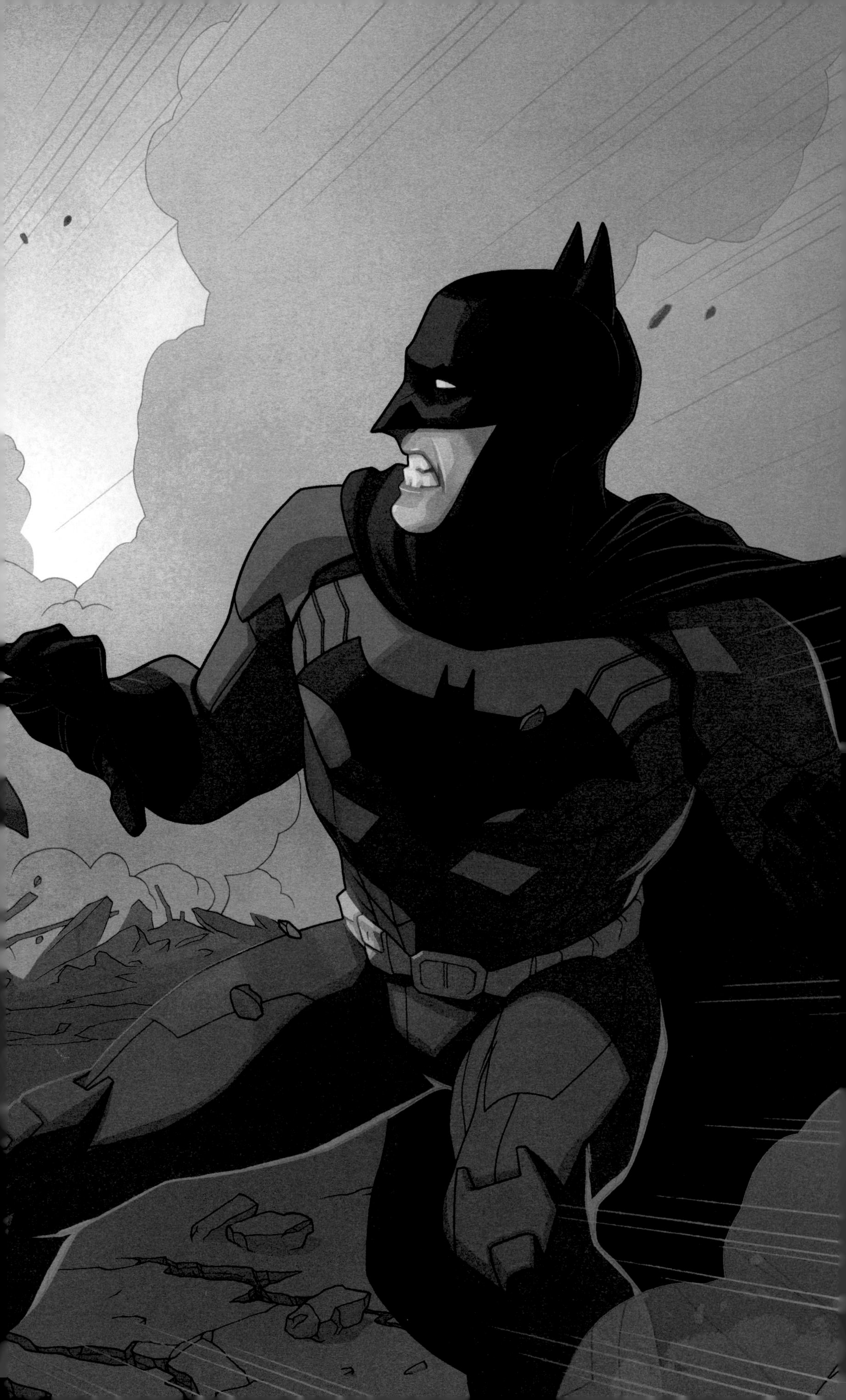

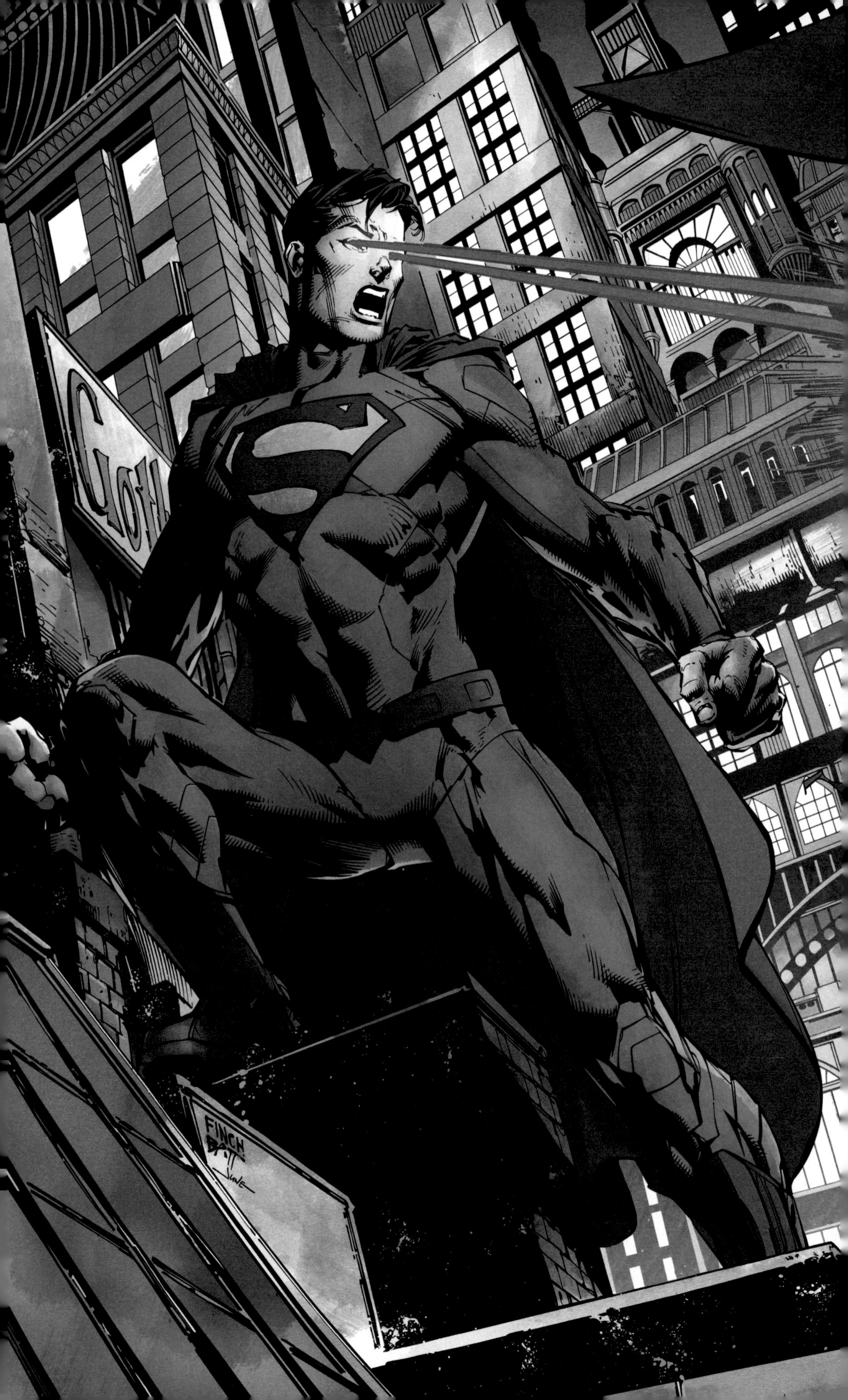

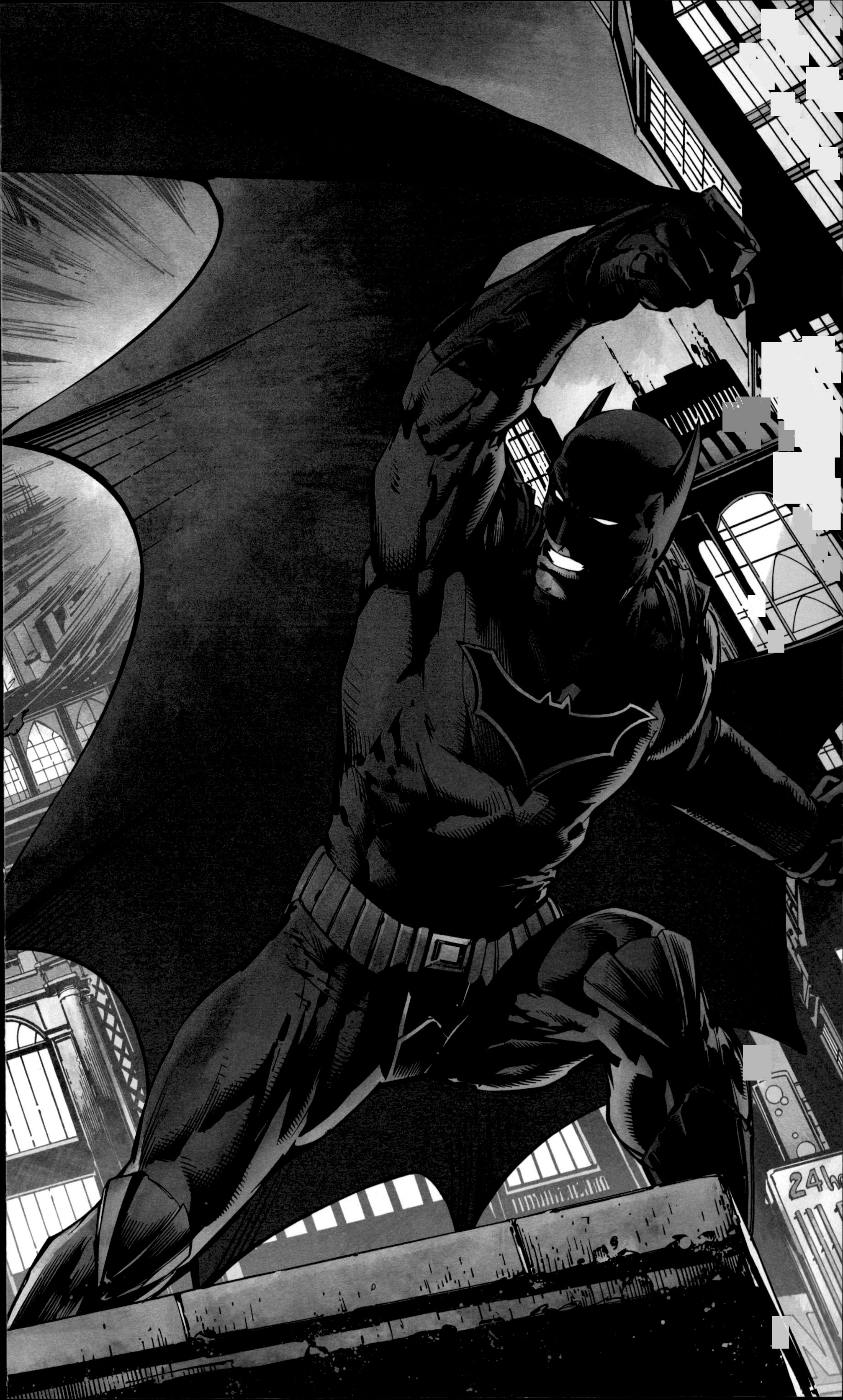

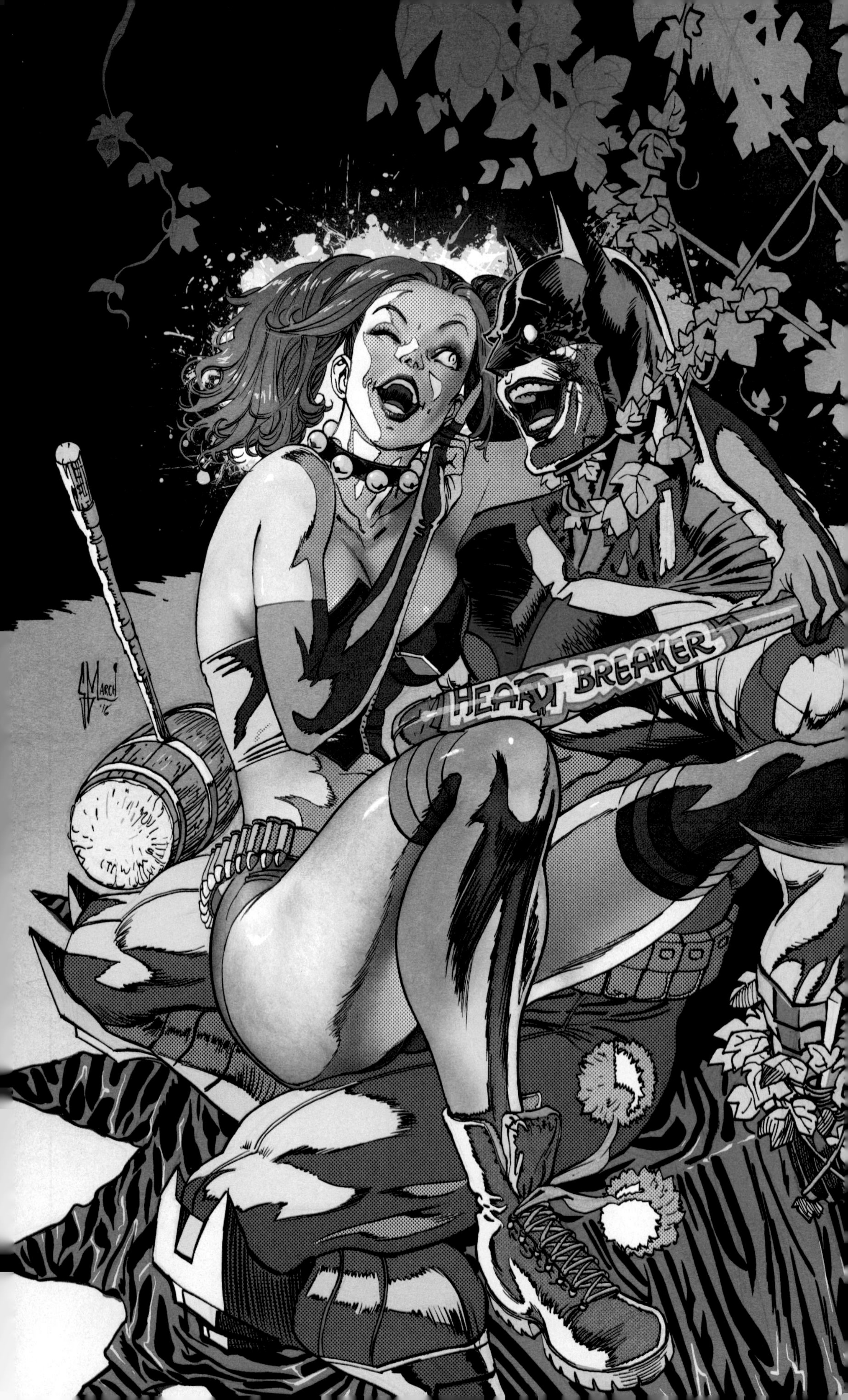
BREAKER

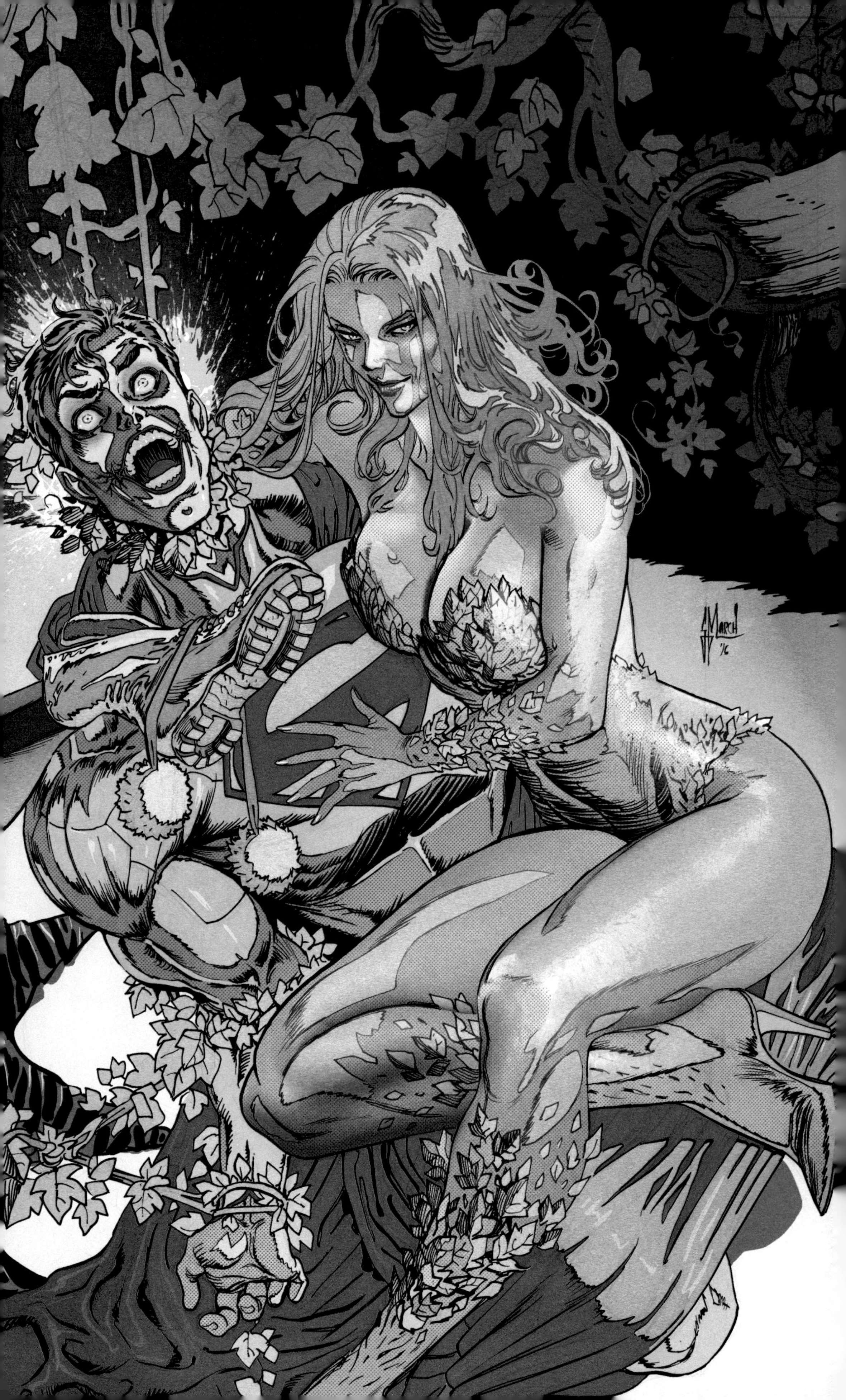

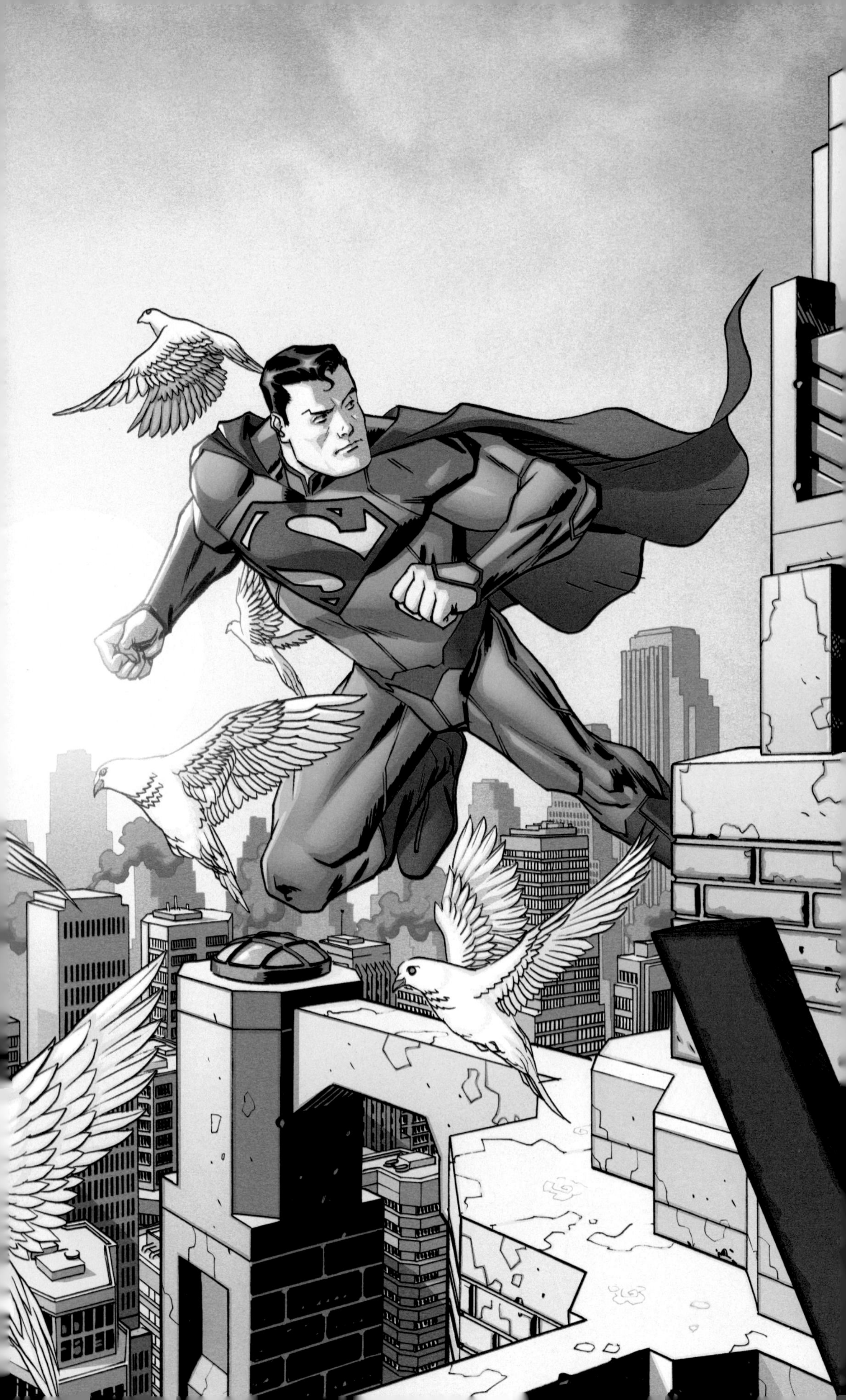

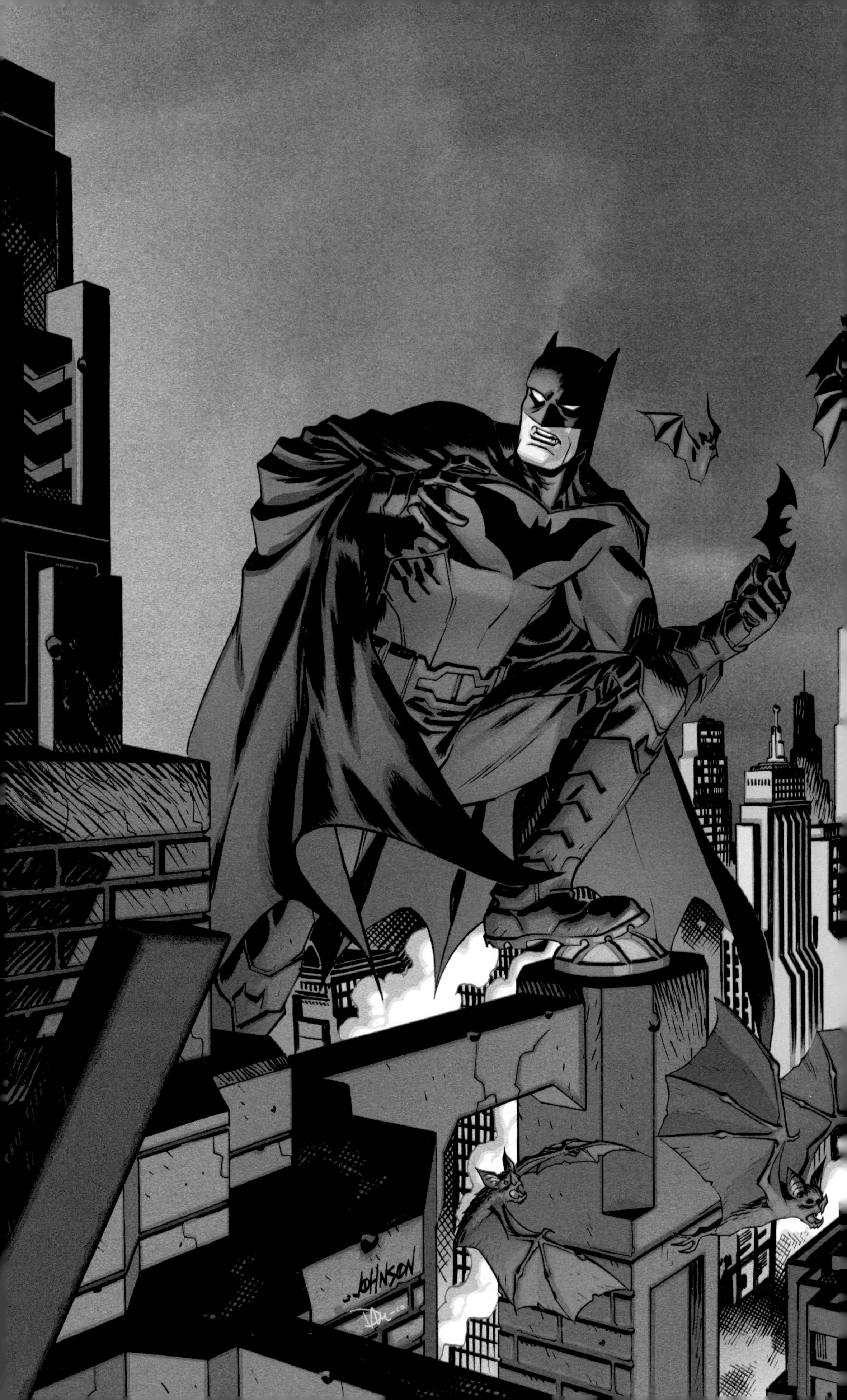
JOHNSON

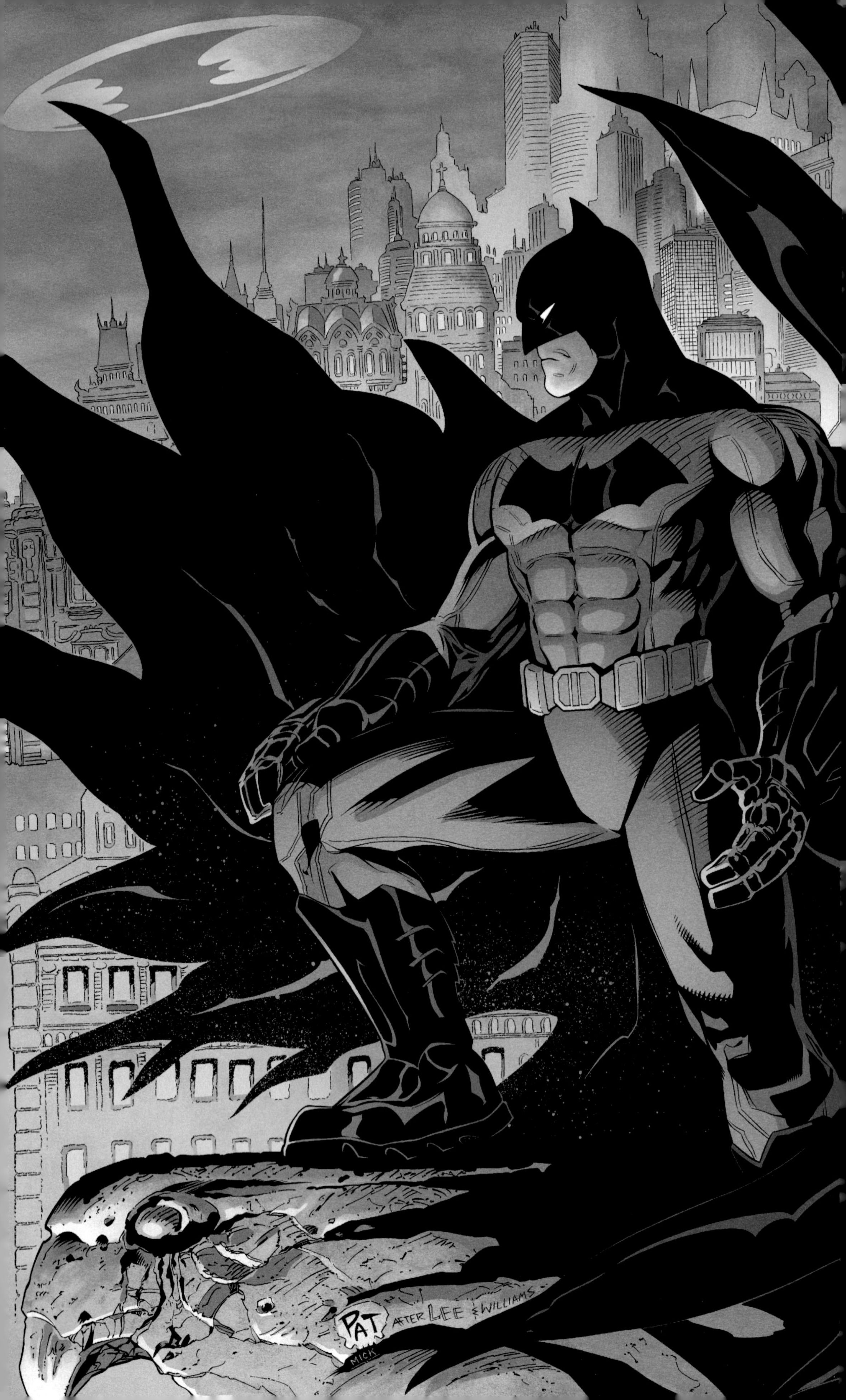

PAT
AFTER LEE & WILLIAMS
MICK

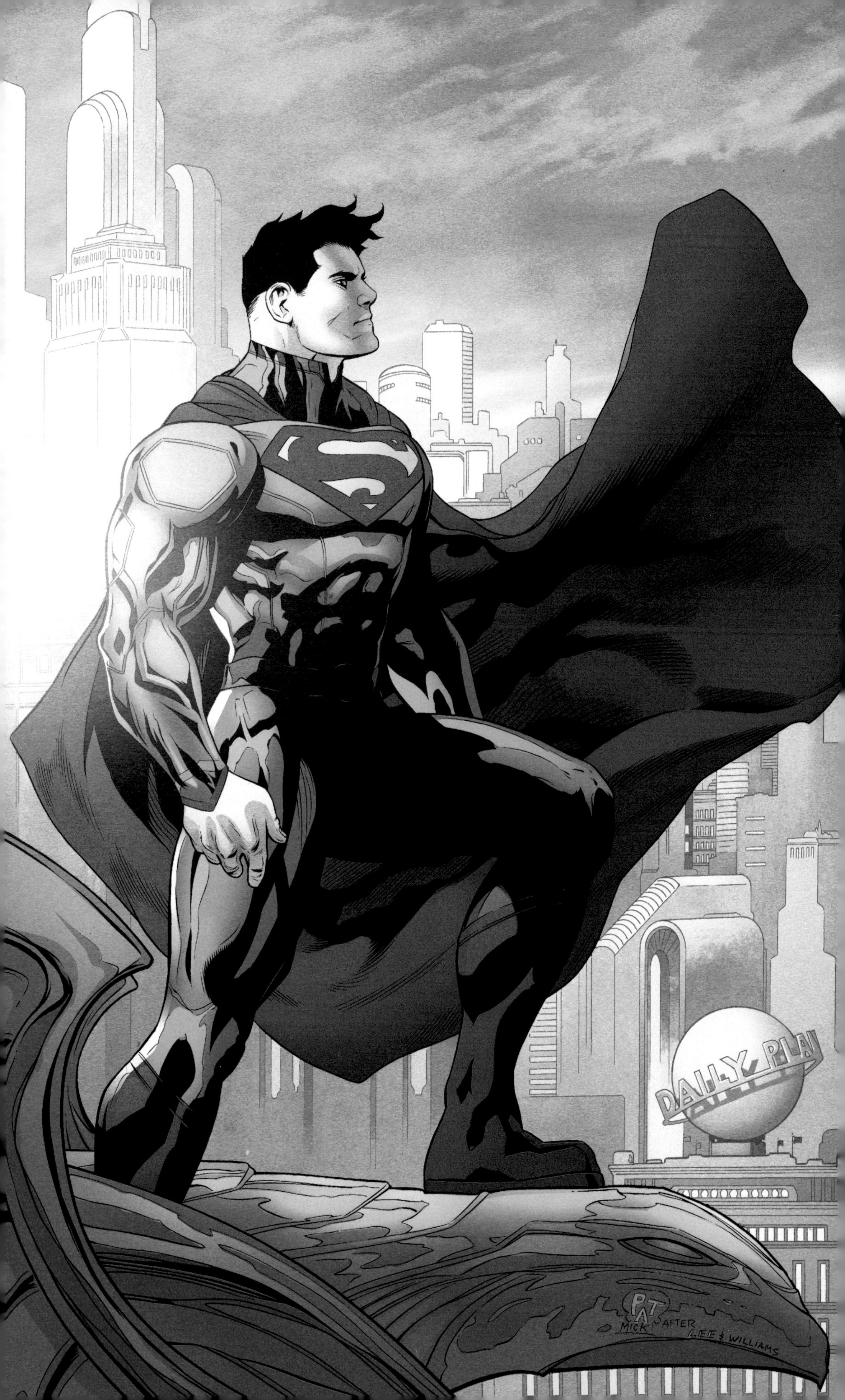
DAILY PLA
PAT MICK AFTER LEE & WILLIAMS

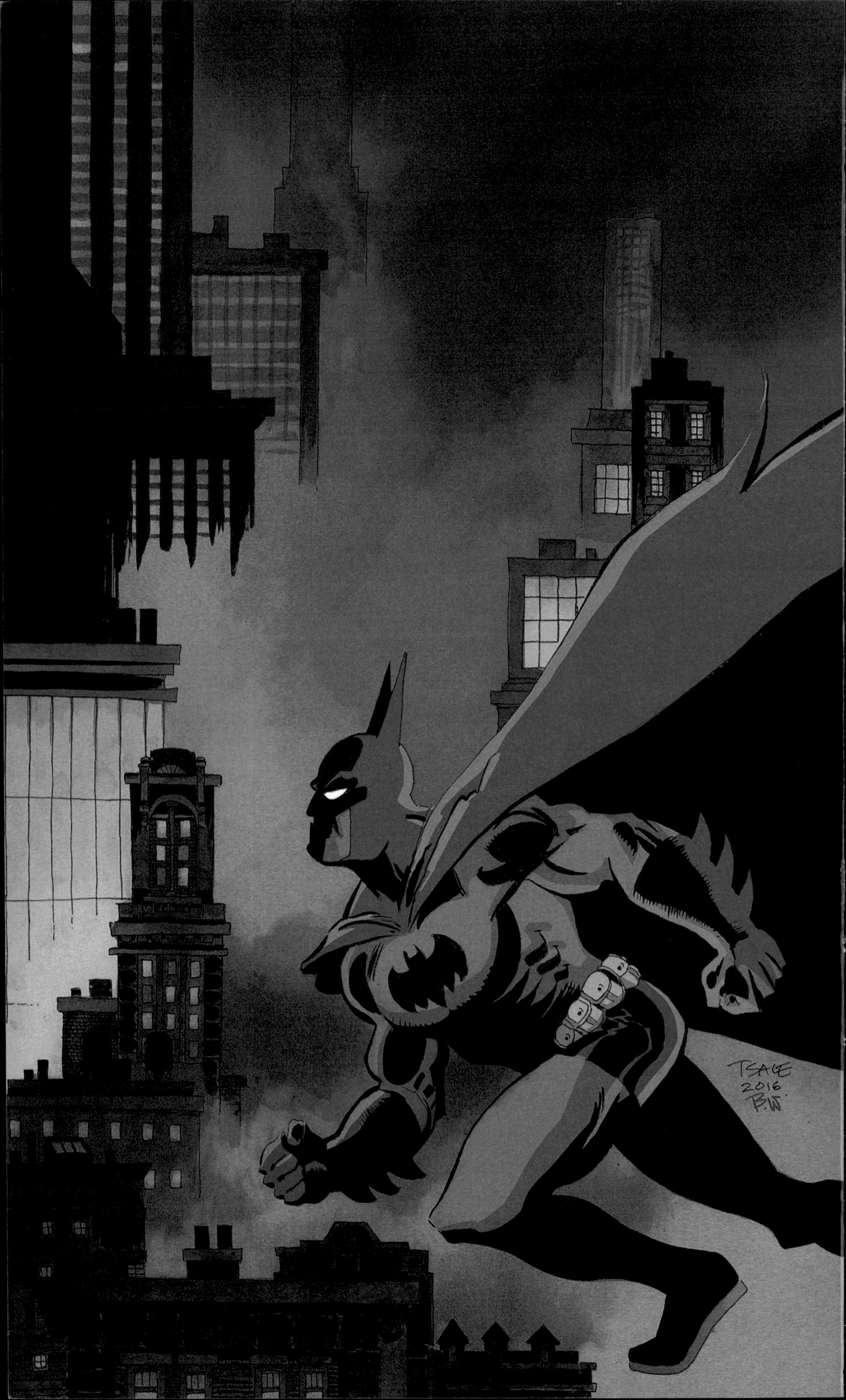
TSALE
2016
B.W.

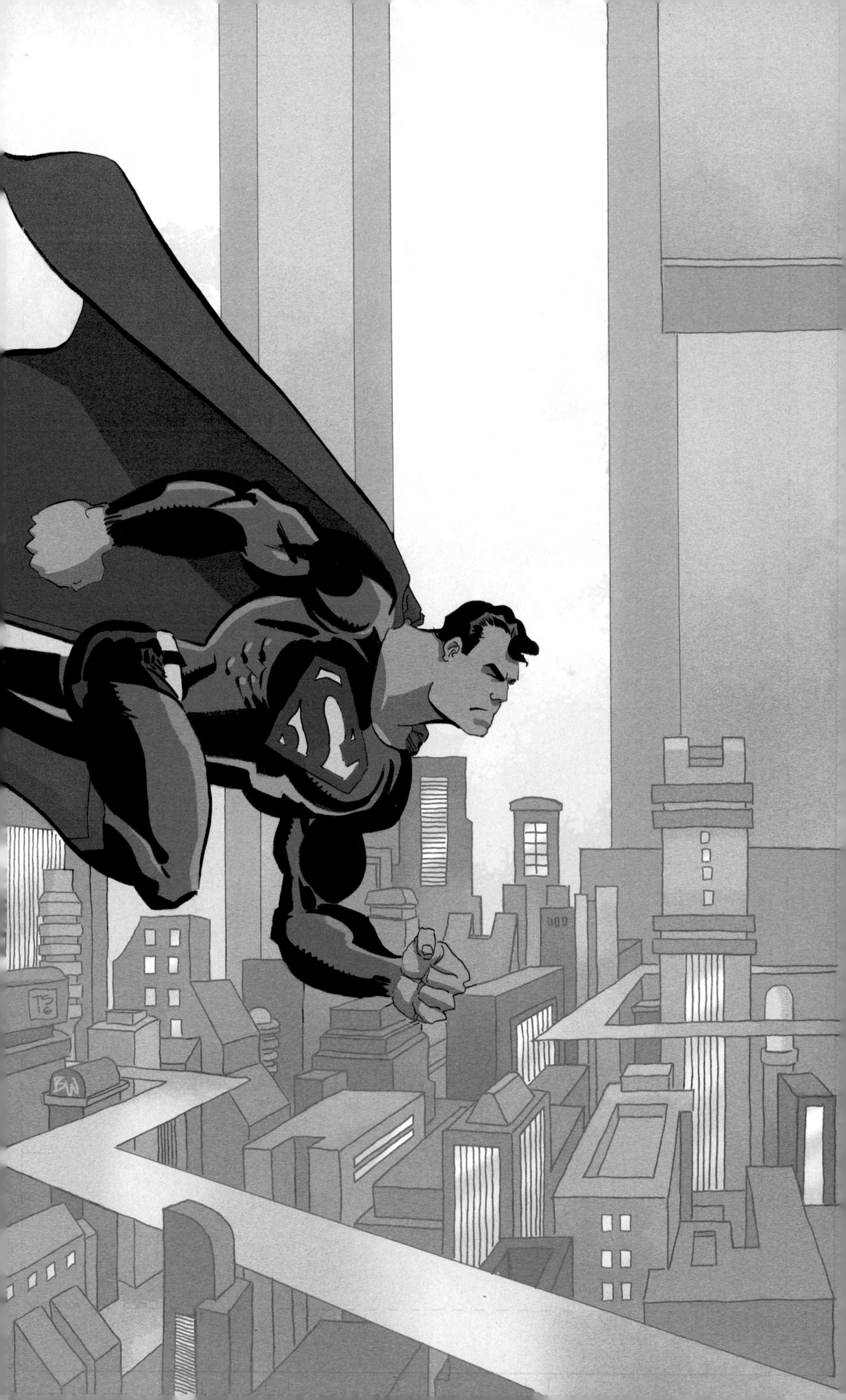

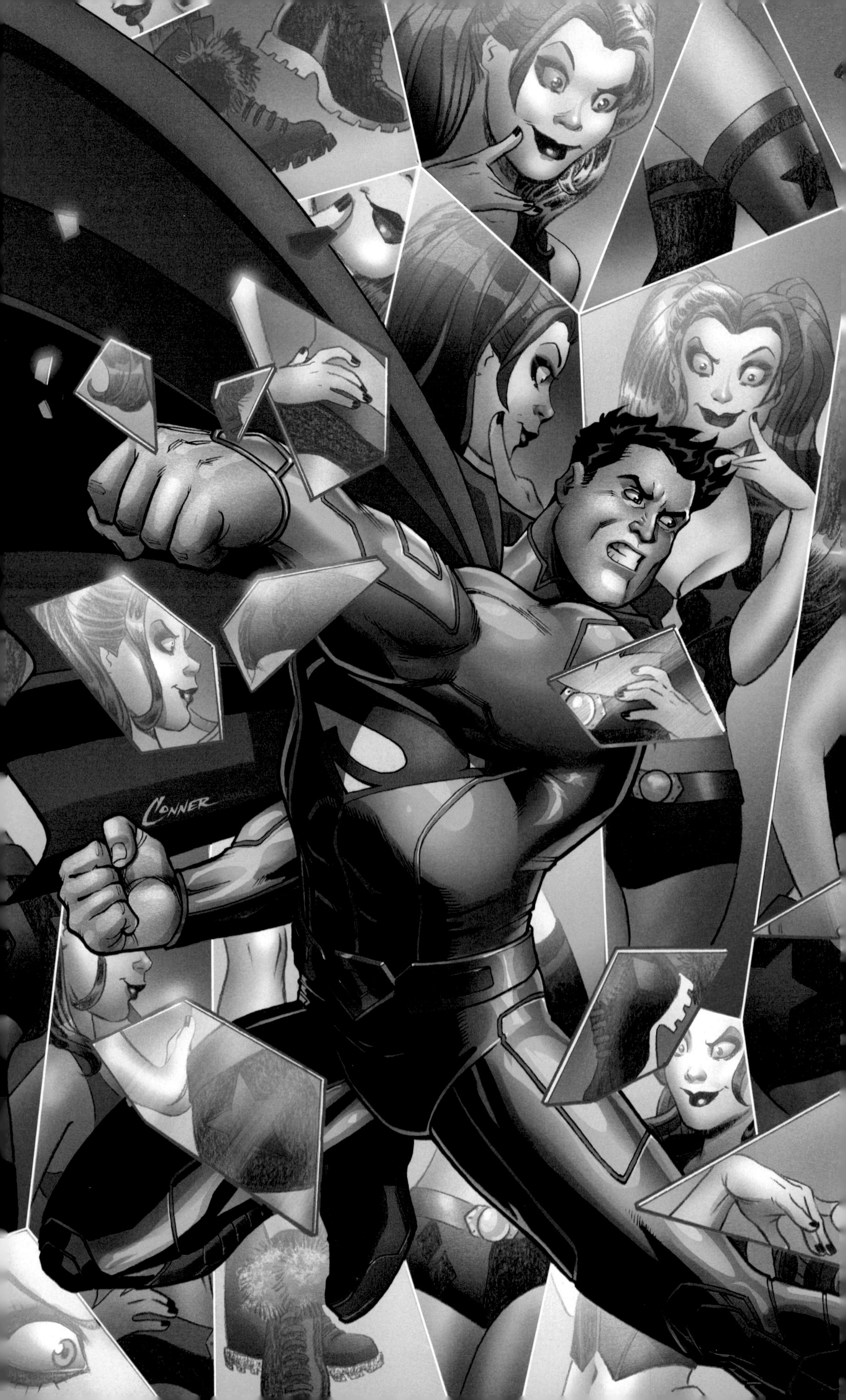
CONNER

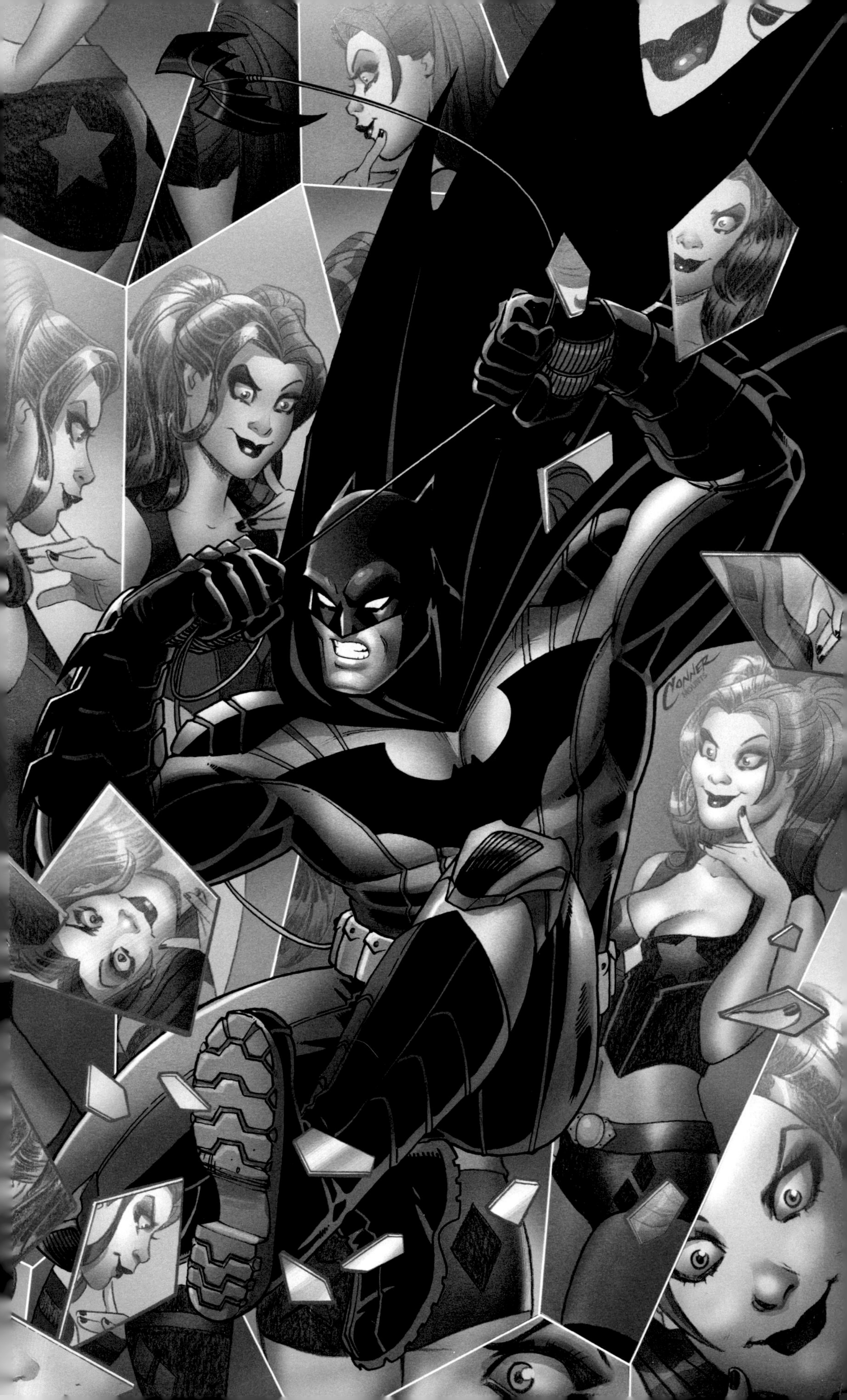
CONNER

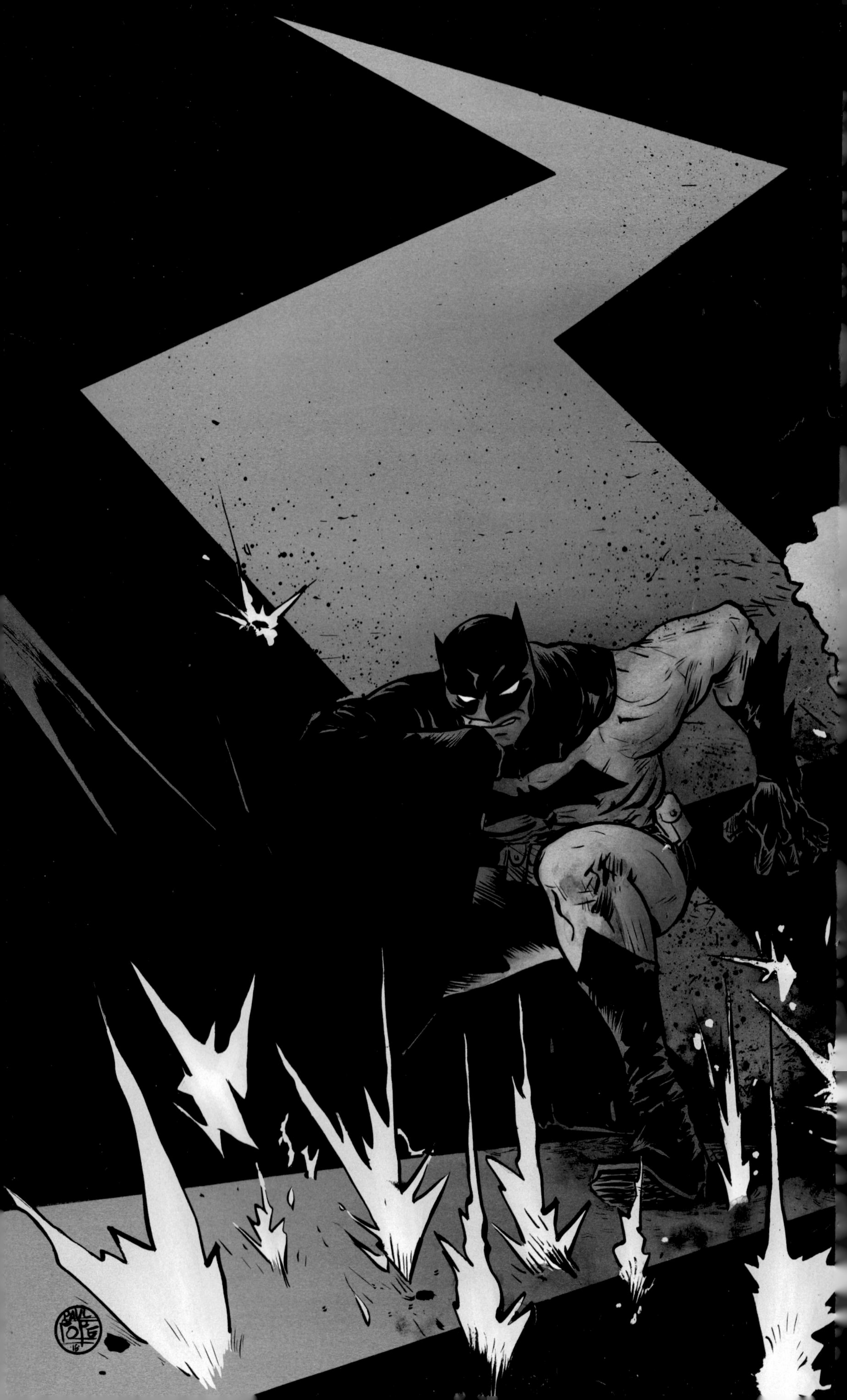